GEORGE TOWNSHEND

To

IRELAND

'May she do for mankind now such service
as her saints and scholars did for
Europe long ago.'

George Townshend

George Townshend, circa 1920. (There is good reason to believe that this is the photograph which he sent to the Guardian in response to his request. See page 82.)

GEORGE TOWNSHEND

Hand of the Cause of God
*(Sometime Canon of St Patrick's Cathedral,
Dublin, Archdeacon of Clonfert)*

by

DAVID HOFMAN

GEORGE RONALD
OXFORD

GEORGE RONALD, Publisher
46 High Street, Kidlington, Oxford, OX5 2DN

© David Hofman 1983
All Rights Reserved

ISBN 0-85398-126-4 (cased)
ISBN 0-85398-127-2 (paper)

12/91

Set by Sunrise Setting in Bembo 11 on 12 point
Printed in the United States of America

Gift

CONTENTS

ILLUSTRATIONS

Illustrations within the text

PREFACE

THIS is a book about a Bahá'í, for Bahá'ís, by a Bahá'í. Bahá'í terms and references abound and by far the greater part of the biography is set in the milieu of the emerging Bahá'í Faith. A glossary was considered, but it was felt to be unnecessary and that a few footnotes should suffice. As an aid, however, and, it is hoped, an encouragement, to the uninitiated, the opening words of Chapter 1 are now explained. Bahá'ís use the term 'Manifestation of God' to designate the Revealers of the holy books of mankind, the Founders of the great religions: Abraham, Moses, Jesus, Muḥammad, Zoroaster, Krishna, Buddha, and in our own day the Báb and Bahá'u'lláh. The term is not applied to the great Prophets of the Old Testament such as Isaiah, or to the Imams of Islám, but only to those few Appearances of the Divine Reality mentioned above. Their utterances, whether written or attributed, are, in this book, printed in italics.

The founding of the Bahá'í Faith, the lives of its Central Figures, its aims and principles, much of its history, the great range of its scripture and the rise of the world community bearing its name and promoting its purposes, are all disclosed in greater or lesser degree as the story of George Townshend and his life work unfolds.

Letters are a major source for this work; where their provenance is not given they were written by George Townshend to me.

The system of transliteration of oriental terms adopted for Bahá'í writings was not universally followed until the late 1920s, consequently quotations from sources before those days are not uniform in this respect.

ACKNOWLEDGEMENTS

Many people have helped me in the writing of this book, with information, encouragement and research. The three[1] Hands of the Cause now residing in the Holy Land have each provided information and been generous of encouragement, Amatu'l-Bahá Rúḥíyyih Khánum and Mr Furútan contributing items for the text, while Mr Haney very kindly read the entire typescript. Counsellor Adib Taherzadeh provided invaluable information, both documentary and by tape recording, about George Townshend's life in Dublin as a Bahá'í pioneer and later Hand of the Cause. Mr Townshend's Board members, Dorothy Ferraby and Marion Hofman, responded generously to requests for information and memories. The National Spiritual Assemblies of the Bahá'ís of Ireland and of the United Kingdom opened their files to me, while that of the United States of America kindly authorized its archivist, Mr Roger Dahl, to offer his fullest co-operation, a course which he has generously and fruitfully pursued. The National Spiritual Assembly of Australia went to great trouble to unearth the accounts of an old incident.

Mr Allan, the Registrar, and Mr Eager, the Librarian, of the Royal Dublin Society, have been most friendly and helpful, permitting me to photograph Orpen's portrait of George Townshend's father, to copy records of his services to the Society, and allowing me the hospitality of its magnificent Library. Mr Bryan Matthews, Assistant Headmaster and Archivist of Uppingham School, welcomed me twice to his Library, giving unstintingly of his time and knowledge in uncovering pertinent school records; on the first occasion my

[1] Written prior to the tragic death of the Hand of the Cause Paul Haney in an automobile accident on December 3, 1982.

daughter, May, rendered much appreciated secretarial assistance and on the second Mr Edward Cardell, with his expert technique, copied photographs from the school magazine. Mr Townshend's son, Brian, and his daughter, Una, patiently answered my importunate enquiries and contributed family lore and recondite information.

Very special thanks are gratefully expressed to Miss Katherine Powell of Tulsa, Oklahoma, whose diligent and enthusiastic researches in Utah and Tennessee discovered nearly all the material for Chapter 3. She received splendid co-operation from Mrs Arnold Mignery, Archives Supervisor of the Jessie Ball DuPont Library at the University of the South, Sewanee, to whom warm thanks are likewise extended. Miss Mary Watkins, of Nashville, Tennessee, kindly provided information about Nellie Roche and sent me invaluable documents, which are listed in Appendix 2.

Sir George Mahon, who appears in the narrative, has been wonderfully helpful in talking about the Townshends in Ahascragh, in devoting much time and effort to obtaining copies of essential historical documents, and liberally contributing to my collection of Townshend papers. His sister, the Hon. Mrs Crofton, added to her brother's memoirs and kindly allowed me to reproduce her personally illustrated copy of *The Fairies of Killupaun* to add to the collection. Miss Edith Satchwell of Ballinasloe lent me her photograph album for the same purpose. Mrs Trudi Scott sent me the letter from George Townshend to Bernard Leach cited on page 358. Professor Paul Reynolds, Dr Seasamh Watson, Mr Dominic Browne, Mrs Ursula Samandarí, Mr William Hellaby, Mrs Dorothy Frye, have all given invaluable help and the editorial staff at George Ronald, Publisher offered some splendid suggestions for revision of the first typescript. Through all the long period of composition, Roger White has been a continual mentor and support, unflaggingly transcribing my appalling handwriting into neat typescript; and Patricia Benton has given very generously of her spare time in repairing my depredations to Roger's script and producing a final copy.

To all the above I express my very warm thanks.

INTRODUCTION

THE primitive days of a world religion, being those of the Prophet Himself, are the most highly charged spiritually, and the most interesting to later generations. They acquire a rosy patina as the centuries roll on, completely fictitious as to the status of the new movement, its diffusion, its size, indeed its utter insignificance compared to the wonders of its later efflorescence. In the same way the great men and women of those early days, the first saints and heroes, are apt to be thought of by uninformed posterity as world-renowned figures in their own day, whereas they were generally as obscure and ignored as was the new Message from God for which they gave their lives. A biography of St Peter, written, say, about AD 100, portraying him as the first occupant of one of the most influential and longest enduring thrones in the whole world, would, in the unlikely event of its having received any attention at all, have been laughed to scorn. Yet no life of St Peter could ever have been or be written except with reference to Jesus Christ and the birth of Christianity.

Likewise with George Townshend, whose life is only relevant and explicable in its relationship to Bahá'u'lláh. He is one of the great figures in the early days of a new Dispensation destined to embrace the whole of mankind. He entered the new Faith at the end of its Heroic Age and served it for the first thirty-six years of its Formative Age. He received two Tablets from the Centre of its Covenant and more than 150 letters from its Guardian. He hoped and strove for recognition by the generality of Christians of the simple fact of Christ's return, but the wheel had come full circle and the Christians proved as dead to Christ's new call in the Person of Bahá'u'lláh as the Jews had been to that of Moses in the Person of Jesus. The Jews reaped their harvest of rejection, while Christendom, and all the world, are now reaping theirs.

It is no small matter in any age for a senior officer of the established religion, revered and honoured by his colleagues, to resign his high office in order to embrace and whole-heartedly promote the cause of a

new Messiah. Saul of Tarsus,[1] though of very different character from
George Townshend, did so, and for the same reason. As a result of his
dramatic experience on the road to Damascus, he understood that the
Christ he persecuted was none other than the promised Messiah
foretold by Moses. Paul immediately gave Him his love, his
allegiance, his life.

George records no such spectacular occasion in his experience, and
indeed he was not the sort of man to receive such a visitation.[2] But his
recognition of Bahá'u'lláh as Christ returned in the glory of the Father
was just as deep, just as overwhelming, just as compelling as was
Paul's recognition of Christ. Paul had no trouble over a divided
allegiance between Moses and Christ and reduced not one jot his love
for Moses. George was illumined by his perception of one Reality in
Moses, Christ and Bahá'u'lláh, and his love for that Reality blazed
forth as fiercely as had Paul's.

George Townshend entered the service of the Church of Ireland in
1916. Almost at once he became informed of the Revelation of
Bahá'u'lláh and embarked on a thorough study of its claims and
teachings with all the literature available in English at the time. He
became a dignitary of his church and his nomination for higher office
was urged more than once. But by that time he wanted only to be free
of the shackles of the 'old church' and enter entirely the New World
Order of Bahá'u'lláh. Three times he refused to let his name be
forwarded for a bishopric; he refused the Deanery of St Patrick's
Cathedral, Dublin. Had he become Primate we might never have
heard of him, unless as a literary figure. How many of the thousands of
archbishops and high priests are remembered? Becket for his political
stand and through glorification by Hollywood, Cranmer and Ridley
for their martyrdoms, Laud for his Prayer Book, Annas and Caiaphas
for their part in the crucifixion of Jesus Christ; a few others but a mere
handful over the milleniums. On the other hand the companions of the
Prophet and the outstanding early believers become household names:
Peter, James and John, Martha and Mary, Alí, Omar, Abu Bakr and
Khadijah, Aaron and Joshua. Paul abandoned the moribund forms
into which the living religion of Moses had crystallized, for the new
salvation, and lives eternally in human history. George Townshend
abandoned the self-satisfied and archaic church for the Christ-
promised Kingdom of God, and shines for ever in the new heaven of
the Promised One of all ages.

[1] He was not, strictly speaking, an officer, but was invested with authority from the
high priest; see Acts 8 and 9.

[2] It is an interesting coincidence that both men suffered from bouts of blindness. See p. 42.

Chapter 1

IN MEMORIAM

THE Manifestation of God, whenever He appears, selects a small group of people to form His closest and immediate confidants. These Apostles, Companions, Letters, receive the full import of His Message, are given both its inner and outer meanings and are sent forth to spread it abroad. They nearly all meet martyrdom and become the greatest figures of His Dispensation.

The Prophet's power, however, to raise up great souls to His service is not restricted to His earthly life. After His ascension He is able to illumine whomsoever He pleases and to invest those chosen with extraordinary powers to promote His Faith. A few become so great as to influence the course of history. Saul of Tarsus – to whom we have already referred – was such. George Townshend was another.

Unlike the humble apostles of Christ who, because of their relationship to Him, *'took precedence over the choicest of mankind,'*[1] George was a scholar, a distinguished author, a dignitary of his church, who laid all his great gifts and accomplishments at the feet of his Lord and by virtue of 'HIS STERLING QUALITIES HIS SCHOLARSHIP HIS CHALLENGING WRITINGS, HIS HIGH ECCLESIASTICAL POSITION UNRIVALLED ANY BAHÁ'Í WESTERN WORLD . . . HIS FEARLESS CHAMPIONSHIP CAUSE HE LOVED SO DEARLY SERVED SO VALIANTLY . . .' became 'ONE OF THREE LUMINARIES SHEDDING BRILLIANT LUSTRE ANNALS IRISH ENGLISH SCOTTISH BAHÁ'Í COMMUNITIES.'[2]

The morning after George's funeral, wandering round Dublin in the neighbourhood of St Stephen's Green and Trinity, thinking about

[1] 'Abdu'l-Bahá

[2] Shoghi Effendi, cablegram, March 27, 1957, to National Spiritual Assembly of the Bahá'ís of the British Isles. The other two were Esslemont and Breakwell.

him, I was impelled to jot down, in a convenient library, a tribute to
him from which the following extracts are taken:

> George Townshend was among the first to be named by the Guardian, in
> their lifetimes, as Hand of the Cause of God. He had already rendered
> distinguished services to the Guardian, such as writing the Introduction to
> God Passes By, and his resignation from the high offices which he held in
> the Church of Ireland was one of the great deeds of his sacrificial life.
>
> Among so many divine qualities which he displayed, it seems that the
> most constant motivation of his whole being was a deep and ever-
> consuming love for God. His early reflections and prayers disclose this,
> and his later poems to Bahá'u'lláh and 'Abdu'l-Bahá are ablaze with it. His
> last letters and the final years of his life bear added testimony. He identified
> God with Truth and his search for Him was passionate, unceasing,
> disciplined and relentless. And having found Him, his striving became
> only intensified, a dedicated effort to efface himself and live only by his
> 'Only Beloved'.
>
> Courage, humility, radiance, humour, gentleness, in addition to
> powerful intellectual qualities sustained by a profound scholarship are
> among the signs by which we seek to know him. But the man himself,
> selfless but inviolate, undemanding but powerful, temperate but direct,
> yielding but immaculate, belonged wholly to his Master and was not kept
> back from Him by anything which the world could do. He was an
> Irishman, a big man, and had won his Blue for running at Oxford. A high,
> domed forehead, sharp, high nose, blue eyes of the mildest temper and
> gentle mouth from which his speech emerged with the faintest Irish
> brogue, always in a moderate tone no matter how direct and forceful the
> thoughts expressed, were the visible temple of this great soul. He was 'a
> darlin' man', 'a wonderful man', a 'saint'. He gave of his inmost self,
> companionably, in true brotherhood, to his juniors and subordinates –
> which we all were – consulting us as equals or superiors.
>
> He corresponded with 'Abdu'l-Bahá in and about 1918–20, and the
> Tablets which he received became his terms of reference. The Master had
> written, 'It is my hope that thy Church will come under the Heavenly Jerusalem',
> and from then on he devoted all his energies to the attempt to bring to the
> clergy of the Church of Ireland, especially the senior ones who were his
> friends and associates, the same realization of Bahá'u'lláh as Christ
> returned in the glory of the Father, which he himself had. He
> corresponded with them, sent them his book The Promise of All Ages,
> talked with them, preached a sermon on the Bahá'í Faith in St Patrick's
> Cathedral, Dublin, of which he was a Canon. But all to no avail; the stone
> remained unmoved. He related that one of the bishops said to him, 'You
> know, Townshend, this is all nonsense'. By 1947 his Bahá'í activities had
> provoked an enquiry through the Archbishops of Canterbury and
> Armagh, and in consultation with the National Spiritual Assembly he
> resigned his clerical positions and moved with his family to a small
> bungalow in Dublin.

Let it be recorded that a man of seventy, with family responsibilities, holding high office in an honoured and well-rewarded calling, gave up all he had achieved, his beautiful country rectory – the scene of happy family life and long research – his position among the gentry, his future security in the form of pensions and other emoluments, to embrace poverty, indignity, the scorn and loss of friends, dependence on others, at the call of His Lord Whose authority he recognized in the Guardian. He and his family became founding members of the first Spiritual Assembly of the Bahá'ís of Dublin.

In 1951 he was named a Hand of the Cause of God and his relationship to the British community, as he himself said, underwent a change. He became the ray between the Guardianship and us; he loved us more dearly, encouraged us, prayed for us, spread his wings over us and was in truth our own dear Hand. Unable to attend our Conferences and Schools as his health declined, he was yet present at all of them, and exchanged messages with each and every one.

Towards the end of his life he began to plan the chief work of his mind, which had been developing and taking shape within him for years. He called it tentatively 'Christ and Bahá'u'lláh', and this finally became the title of the book which became a reality as he left this world.

George Townshend is known chiefly by his writings, which have been a source of enlightenment to many, and will lead many more to a realization of the Day of God. Through his major works and in innumerable articles in Bahá'í magazines, in the organs of various National Spiritual Assemblies, in teaching bulletins and pamphlets he has educated and illumined the Bahá'ís. His love poem to Bahá'u'lláh is a gem not dimmed by being set among the world's great mystical poems. 'Only Beloved! With a heart on fire' he cries, and discloses the whole tenor and keynote of his life in the last stanza:

> Make my whole life one flame
> Of sacrificial deeds that shall proclaim
> The new-born glory of Thy ancient name;
> And let my death lift higher yet the same
> Triumphal chant of praise!

The small band of British Bahá'ís, a few visitors, his fellow Hands of the Cause of God, will cherish the memory of one who never failed in his duty to *'diffuse the Divine Fragrances, to edify the souls of men, to promote learning, to improve the character of all men and to be, at all times and under all conditions, sanctified and detached from earthly things.'*[1]

Ireland has produced great generals and statesmen, poets and writers. At one time she was the teacher of Christianity to Europe and the mother of scholars and saints. But when the balance is set and the assayers of mankind do their work, who of his countrymen will surpass him?

This is the man it is hoped to present in the following pages.

[1] 'Abdu'l-Bahá, Will and Testament

Chapter 2

ANGLO-IRISH

THE Townshends of Castletownshend, County Cork, were a typical Anglo-Irish family. *Burke's Landed Gentry* and *Irish Family Records* show them as a vigorous, prolific, adventurous, talented and highly diversified set. The first to settle in Ireland was Richard Townshend (Townesende or Townsend), a colonel in Cromwell's Parliamentary Army. He is credited with personally handing the keys of Cork to Oliver himself on April 3, 1648. This was the time when a host of English and Scottish adventurers, chiefly from the aristocracy and landed gentry, sought their fortunes in Ireland and dispossessed the native Irish of their land.

Richard Townshend acquired Castletownshend,[1] Co. Cork, which became the seat of the family, and two other estates for which he was granted patents. He fathered nine children, whose progeny, together with those of other equally philoprogenitive Anglo-Irish families, took possession of the whole island, administered and developed it as their own land, using the native Irish as peasant labourers and workmen. Until 1921 they were British subjects, enjoying all the advantages of a master race and pervading the higher ranks of the British armed services, the Church, Parliament and the Civil Service, the Law, and later the professions and the arts. They were appointed to the judiciary, to viceroyalties and governorships throughout the Empire and, resting secure upon their Irish estates, filled an extraordinary proportion of the higher posts in the various estates of

[1] Jan (James) Morris, in the first volume of her brilliant trilogy on the British Empire, describes Castletownshend as 'perhaps the most striking enclave of all, where the Ascendancy seemed to be most neatly encapsulated', and after her visit there in 1970 she thought it remained 'the most telling single monument to the Anglo-Irish way of life'. *Heaven's Command* (Penguin Books, 1979, pp. 474–5).

the realm. They also served as pioneers and settlers in the great open spaces of the vast Commonwealth and contributed greatly to the advancement of knowledge, science and the arts. Not since the days of ancient Greece has there been so numerous and homogeneous a leisured class, freed from the necessity of daily toil, able to pursue unhampered the higher forms of human activity. The Townshends, in their many branches, permeated this Anglo-Irish gentry as pervasively as did the Anglo-Irish the whole of British life.

Irish history forms no part of our theme but some appreciation of the Irish scene in the latter half of the nineteenth century is essential to an appraisal of George Townshend's antecedents and upbringing and the formative influences affecting his character and development. A very succinct and objective account of the period is given by the American historian C. D. Hazen in his *Europe Since 1815*[1] and is printed as Appendix 1.

The onset of liberalism and the slow awakening of conscience in the late nineteenth century effectively changed the Irish – as every other – scene. And it was into this era of change and awakening that George Townshend was born. It was the period of that wonderful ferment in Irish life – the literary revival, Gladstone's Reform Bills, Parnell, the brilliant social life of Dublin – Fitzgeralds, Napiers, Wilde, Yeats – leading on to the time of Shaw, Lady Gregory and the immortal Abbey Theatre.

George's father, Charles Uniacke Townshend, was a considerable personage, an eminent figure in Dublin – and Irish – life. Philanthropist, highly successful business man and administrator, he owned and lived at Hatley, 10 Burlington Road, Dublin, a fine house adjacent to the extensive grounds of the Royal Dublin Society, of which remarkable institution he was Hon. Secretary for six years, 1887-93, and Vice-President from 1893 until his death in 1907. His portrait, painted by Orpen, hangs in the Society's Council Chamber at Ballsbridge.[2] He was a Justice of the Peace and initiated a hospital project for the poor in Dublin.

This was a time when, as George told his daughter Una, everything his father touched turned to gold. He founded a highly successful Land Agency, with offices at 15 Molesworth Street, a minute's walk from the present Dáil. It achieved immortality through being the first employer of a promising Dublin youth named George Bernard Shaw,

[1] G. Bell & Sons, London; Henry Holt & Co., New York

[2] A copy was made by the artist for Charles himself; it was inherited by George and his son Brian, who later gave it to Mr Stephen Powell of Birr, Co. Offaly, 'the grandson most interested in family heirlooms' and who very kindly supplied the photograph reproduced in Plate 2.

who later married a kinswoman of the Townshends, Charlotte Payne-Townshend. The history of Shaw's employment by Charles Uniacke is related extensively in St John Ervine's *Bernard Shaw*,[1] which states that 'G.B.S. was happier in Townshend's office than he had been for a large part of his childhood or was to be for a larger part of his early manhood'.

One incident related in Archibald Henderson's *George Bernard Shaw – His Life and Works*[2] is sufficiently pertinent to our theme to be repeated. In 1875 the American evangelists, Moody and Sankey, of the popular hymns, visited Dublin, and the newspapers were full of 'revival' and the 'wave of evangelism'. It seems that the *enfant terrible* wrote to a Dublin newspaper, *Public Opinion*, decrying in typically Shavian terms the efficacy of the revival on Dublin in general and declaring that the effect on individuals was to make them 'highly objectionable members of society and [induce] their unconverted friends to desire a speedy reaction'. This was taken as a declaration of atheism and set all Dublin by the ears. Charles Uniacke's liberal and tolerant attitude is seen in Henderson's comment that, 'Mr Uniacke Townshend, Shaw's employer, a pillar of the Church – and of the Royal Dublin Society – so far respected his freedom of conscience as to make no attempt to reason with him, only imposing the condition that the subject be not discussed in the office.' St John Ervine, describing the same episode, says that Shaw's action caused deep discussions among the apprentices in the office, and became 'so frequent and prolonged that Mr Uniacke Townshend, not unreasonably, reminded G.B.S. that his office was not a forum for acrimonious religious argument'.

Charles's first marriage, in 1854, terminated nineteen years later when his wife died at the early age of forty-three, leaving him with three sons and four daughters and an immensely busy life. This marriage is significant to our theme only for the influence of its large family on the first-born, George, of Charles's second marriage. It is an interesting coincidence that both wives bore the names Anna Maria, and both produced seven children.

The second marriage came about in this way.

Charles rendered distinguished services to the Royal Dublin Society, as the inscription below Orpen's portrait testifies (see Plate 1). When the Government in London proposed to take over the Society's Science and Art institutions, its library and most of its lands and collections (minerals, for example), to form the foundations of national institutions in Ireland, Charles was sent to London more

[1] Constable, London

[2] Hurst & Blackett, London 1911

than once as a member of delegations empowered to negotiate the best terms for the transfer.[1] He vigorously advocated and pursued a policy of expansion with a view to raising farming standards in Ireland, a course which required extensive grounds for the holding of livestock and agricultural shows and, above all, horse shows. Land was available and acquired in the Ballsbridge district of Dublin, but buildings had to be erected. A Galway architect, Samuel Ussher Roberts, of whom it was said that the best part of any house he designed was the stables, was introduced to Charles. The two men became firm friends and Roberts moved to Dublin to work on the very large commission for the Royal Dublin Society. He became a Vice-President of the Society and received a CB for his work. He purchased a house in Burlington Road almost next door to the Townshends, but later returned to Galway.

Charles and Sam were about the same age, and so were their daughters, of whom Charles had four and Sam three. When, at the age of forty-seven, Charles married Sam's eldest daughter Anna Maria, who was then twenty-four, he had been a widower for two years and three months. He took his young wife to Venice for the honeymoon. George was the eldest of the seven children (two sons and five daughters) of this second marriage and was born at Hatley on June 14, 1876.

The large house in Burlington Road, later to become a nursing home to which George, in old age, would be brought for care, and now the home of the School of Celtic Studies, was adequate for the two families, and Charles's income was sufficient to maintain them in lordly fashion. The girls went to finishing schools, and the boys to the usual preparatory and public schools of their class in England. The Townshend and Roberts families, however, in spite of the real friendship between Charles and Sam, did not get along too well together. George's daughter Una[2] relates:

> The Roberts girls, of whom Anna was the eldest, were tall and athletic, brought up to the outdoor life of Galway – horse riding, boat trips, picnics, practical jokes and a happy-go-lucky attitude to life. The petite Townshend sisters were brought up to be very correct, cultured Victorian ladies and were presented at the Viceregal court. They studied music on the continent and were taught to say 'prunes and prisms' before entering a room so that their mouths would be in the most attractive shape. Anna's eldest stepdaughter (hardly three years younger than herself) told her that *her* family were 'not quite gentry' and she left home to live with relatives in England.

[1] See Berry: *History of the Royal Dublin Society,* Longman, 1915
[2] Mrs Richard Dean, now living in Canada.

As soon as Sam was able to leave Dublin he sold up at Burlington Road and returned to Galway.

Anna brought up her own children in the way she herself had grown and inevitably George drew closer to his mother and his maternal grandfather than to his father. Anna was an artistic, informal, physically active woman. She took George and her other children to Galway for the summer months, to her father's house or sometimes a rented one. There they lived an idyllic life of picnics, bathing, riding and the carefree pursuits of the well-to-do. George became a good horseman, to the delight of his grandfather Roberts, himself a noted rider to hounds.

The records of George's boyhood and youth are scanty, and apart from the facts of his education are for the most part brief references in his letters, a few photographs, and the family lore generously contributed by his daughter.

At the age of ten he was sent to a 'prep' school in Watford, run by the Reverend R. Capron. Wynyards School, 99 Langley Road, has entirely disappeared, its premises having been taken over by the Hertfordshire County Council, and no trace of its records can be found. Neither can any of the four Caprons currently listed in *Crockford* claim any knowledge of a relationship to the Reverend R., though all were courteous enough to reply to enquiries.

After four years at Wynyards, George obtained a Foundation Scholarship to Uppingham, a famous public school set in the lovely 'shire' county of Rutland in the English southern midlands, to which his eldest stepbrother Thomas had preceded him by eleven years. George was assigned to Redgate, one of Uppingham's thirteen houses. By this time Charles Uniacke's Midas touch had slightly diminished, and he must have been more than pleased when George's entrance scholarship was converted to a 'House scholarship'.[1]

George's scholastic record at Uppingham was undistinguished, except in literature. In this subject he won two prizes during his five years (1890–95), in 1892 the English Prize and two years later the R. L. Nettleship Prize for English Essay, his subject being 'The Characteristic Features of Classical and Modern Poetry'. On leaving he was awarded a School Leaving Exhibition worth £25.

In sports he excelled. In his fourth year he came second in the mile (all ages) and second in the steeplechase (all ages), personally scoring 350 points out of the 2,290 which won Redgate first place; he was second in School Sports. In his last year he won both the mile and the steeplechase, and in School Sports he was again second. The

[1] Each housemaster agreed to take one boy free; i.e. one house scholarship per house. George was 'best in Redgate'.

1. Portrait of Charles Uniacke Townshend, painted by William Orpen, hanging in the Council Room of the Royal Dublin Society. The caption states: 'Presented to the Royal Dublin Society by some members, as a mark of their appreciation of the great services he has rendered to the Society, and to Ireland, November 1903.' (Reproduced by permission of the Royal Dublin Society)

2. *Charles Uniacke Townshend and his family: (standing, top row) George;*
Charlie; Charles Uniacke; Caroline; Bob; Loftus; Madeline; (standing,
middle row) Maud; Mildred; (sitting, middle row) Hildegarde; Beatrice
(Charlie's wife); Philip; George's mother (second wife); Dorothy; (sitting
front row) Kathleen; Geraldine. Of the fourteen children, only Jane is absent.

3. *Hatley, 10 Burlington Road, Dublin, where George was born. As*
seen in the photograph it is the School of Celtic Studies.

5. George Townshend in his last year at Uppingham, 1895

4. Office of Charles Uniacke's land agency, 15 Molesworth Street, Dublin

6. *Prefects at Uppingham*

7. *The Bridge of Sighs, Hertford College, Oxford*

Uppingham School Magazine records all the above and vol. XXXIII, 1895, adds the following:

> Among those remaining who are good at long distances Townshend and Cobby are conspicuous. The former without having much style runs very gamely and is sure to be thereabouts at the finish.
>
> In the Mile, Townshend was far from well, and before the final heat started we heard various conjectures as to the winner, as well as to the second and third. In our opinion Townshend has vastly improved since last year, and had he not been palpably over-trained would probably have done the distance in 4.50. [He came in first.]
>
> In the steeplechase Townshend seemed a little more himself and had no difficulty winning.

He won the confidence and respect of his masters and fellow students; he was made a prefect and elected to the Committee of Games and The Union Society. The school magazine records for the Easter Term, 1895, 'The Union Society, of which, by the bye, the president is now G. Townshend, has presented two entertainments this term.'

The photographs (see Plates 5 and 6) taken at Uppingham in 1895, when George was approaching his nineteenth birthday, reveal the wide drooping eyelids which so strongly marked Charles Uniacke's countenance. This feature, if one may judge from later photographs (see *frontispiece*) and an artist's impression (Plate 39) became more developed with age; when entering for the first time the Council Chamber of the Royal Dublin Society I was able immediately to identify Charles's portrait by this physical trait. It would be only too easy to imagine in these photographs the shy, introspective, good-natured youth we know him to have been, but in fact the same could be imagined for all in the groups. They are all so solemn and dressed up for the occasion.

In the Easter term of 1892 he was confirmed in the Anglican Church, a normal procedure at public schools for youths of Church of England families.

George's school life was happy and normal; he displayed no burning enthusiasm for any particular career, but his ability to deal with others was recognized in his appointment as a prefect and his bent for administration in his election to school committees. His literary talent was beginning to emerge and to receive training.

On leaving Uppingham, George became an exhibitioner at Hertford College, Oxford, which he attended from 1895 to 1899, reading classics and English. His academic record there was dismal. He received thirds in Mods (1897) and in Greats (1899). But, as at

Uppingham, he excelled in sports. He won a half-blue for cross-country running and represented his college at lawn tennis, on one splendid occasion pressing a seeded Wimbledon player to the verge of defeat. On graduating with a modest BA he had a good collection of cups for athletics but no scholastic distinction. The contrast between this mediocre standing at the age of twenty-three and his achievements and scholarly distinction in later years has provoked the suggestion that at Oxford he 'just didn't work' and Una relates that George himself confirmed this and acknowledged that his chief interest at that time was athletics.

He returned to Dublin with no plans for a career. The house in Burlington Road was fast becoming a hive of intellectual ferment, artistic activity, adventurous ambitions and political discussion. The children of the first marriage were members of the *avant garde*, associating with Yeats and the leaders of the literary revival while George's full sisters pursued emancipation and careers. With one exception they were all anti-Establishment, tending to become true blue Irish patriots, a development as disturbing to the conservative in John Bull's other island as the embryonic Bloomsbury set was to become in London.

Una relates: 'Charles Townshend had fourteen children, seven of whom were Anna's. There were five sons and nine daughters. The sons were lots of fun but conservative in their outlook, with the exception of George.' Loftus, the eldest of the first marriage, 'of a jovial disposition and liked by everyone', was in the family business. His wife and two daughters moved in the artistic and musical circles of Dublin. Charles 'played piano well and studied music in Germany where he married the wealthy daughter of the German Ambassador to Russia'. With her wealth he bought back into the family Castletownshend, where, according to Jan Morris, Townshends were still living in 1970. He had six sons. 'Robert was both practical and fun-loving, a great friend of Dad's. He became a civil engineer and spent most of his life in India. He died when staying with us in Ahascragh. Philip, Dad's full brother, chose a naval career but was axed after World War I. He married a wealthy Yorkshire woman and they used to go to horse races, cricket matches, Wimbledon, etc. He died two years after Dad.

'The girls were independent in their thinking (except for Jane, the eldest) and the half-sisters became friends of W.B. Yeats and joined his set. They were among those who founded the Abbey Theatre. One of them, Carrie, set herself the task of rediscovering the long since outlawed Irish harp, the emblem of Ireland. After much research and looking she found one in Wales. She then gave free lessons and many

copies of her harp were made. My grandfather was very proud of this accomplishment. Two of the elder half-sisters joined Sinn Fein, and all (except Jane) opposed the concept of Empire. The younger girls took up careers and engaged in athletic pursuits such as mountain-climbing and cycling.

'Two of the half-sisters, Caroline and Madeline, became concert pianists, Aunt Carrie studying with Liszt. My father's sisters, even the older ones, turned against the Establishment in various ways. The eldest sister of all, Aunt Janie, who was pretty well orthodox, stayed in the old ways, but Aunt Maude, the second one, was quite different. She became a Quaker for one thing. She was a great admirer of Mahatma Gandhi and she had lived on the Continent a good deal and she spoke a number of languages. She studied piano in Italy under Bonnemicci.

'Aunt Kathleen, my father's fourth full sister, qualified as a nurse and later decided to go to the States and join my father, so my grandfather gave her the fare and a little more money but when she arrived she had only a dime in her pocket. She stayed with my father for several years and then went to World War I with the American Nursing Service. After the war she stayed in Paris and worked with Coué[1] for a time and then became a writer and illustrator. She returned to the States.

'Aunt Geraldine, Daddo's third sister, was the most adventurous of the lot. She used to do a lot of trick bicycle riding when women were not supposed to ride bicycles and she was one of the first women mountaineers. She was also one of the first women at Cambridge, and there she met a budding poet, Wilfrid Gibson, and married him.'

Into this glamorous, extraverted, ebullient coterie, came George with no brilliant First or prestigious Fellowship, but only his meagre BA. Yet he possessed a quality which they lacked and which was of service to them all. Full of admiration for the activities of both families he was able to bridge the gap between them and act as peacemaker.

George's father was a formidable and rather remote figure whom

---

[1] 'Émile Coué, 1857–1926. French exponent of autosuggestion . . . developed and introduced system of psychotherapy known as Couéism.' (*Webster's Biographical Dictionary*). In the early twenties of this century there was a song about it very popular in the United States and Britain:

> I'm getting better every day.
> I'm getting better every day.
> Throw away your pills and potions,
> We've done with those old-fashioned notions.
> Hold tight and this is what you do,
> Throw your ears well back and say:
> Ah-ah-ah-ah-ah-ah-ah,
> I'm getting better and better every day.

George had done nothing to win by his scholastic record. Yet Charles Uniacke's good humour and sense of other people's rights, already shown in the case of the young Bernard Shaw, were extended to this rather unsatisfactory son. Anna wanted her first-born at home, so George was articled to a law firm in Dublin and lived at Hatley for four years, at the end of which time he took his degree in Law and was called to the Bar. At some point in this apprenticeship he became a leader writer for *The Irish Times* which indicates that his literary talent had not withered at Oxford despite the precedence of athletics. It has not been possible to trace any of his articles, for the records of that distinguished paper for the years in question were all destroyed by fire. The names of the leader writers were not printed so that the public libraries' collections of the daily issues are no help. Future biographers will find it difficult to trace any of these early essays.

George grew up very close to his mother. In his school holidays, especially the long summer ones, she would, as Una relates, take him off to the free and easy life of Galway where both could indulge their undoubted love of nature. In Dublin he would listen to the 'revolutionary', 'socialistic' talk of his brothers and sisters seated around 'a table full of good food spread out on a double damask table-cloth with a butler in attendance'.[1] But in Galway he saw at first hand the social injustices of the times and the appalling poverty of the peasantry – the true Irishmen of whose country he and his kind had taken possession. Often barefoot, undernourished, disenfranchised, ill-housed and ill-educated, Irishmen were exploited for their labour by the hated English, who in spite of their possession of the land were not regarded as other than intruders – the enemy (see Appendix 1).

We have no record of George's thoughts and probable troublings of conscience about these things. We only know that in later life he referred to them and conveyed to his children the sense of injustice felt by Irishmen against his own caste. Although the servant of the Establishment, he always identified himself with the Irish. In this his 'bridge-building' quality was again apparent for he received the love and respect of both sides.

George became a barrister by a 'Memorial of Admission as a Barrister' to the Honourable Society of the Kings Inns, in Dublin on October 7, 1903. He is listed in the Irish Law Directory as a practising barrister from 1903 to 1920 and is certified as having studied 'Civil and International Law and Feudal and English Law'. His listing in the Law Directory is no proof that he ever practised, but only that he paid his dues to the Society for the years listed. In fact he never argued a case but upon achieving his degree, expressed to his father his distaste and

[1] Una

No. 1.—LAW STUDENT'S MEMORIAL

FOR ADMISSION AS A BARRISTER.

TO THE RIGHT HONORABLE AND HONORABLE

THE BENCHERS

OF THE

HONORABLE SOCIETY OF THE KING'S INNS.

The Memorial of

Name in full.

_____ George Townshend B.A. Hertford Coll

Sheweth

That he is the _____ eldest _____ son of _____ Charles

Uniacke Townshend _____ of

10 Burlington Road, Dublin in the County of _____ Dublin _____

_____ and of Anna M. Townshend

otherwise _____ Anna. M. Roberts _____ his wife.

That he was specially admitted as a Student
into your Honorable Society, in _____ Michaelmas _____
Term 18 99, and into the Honorable Society of

_____

in Great Britain, in _____ Term, 18 _____, and
that he is not, nor, since he entered your Honorable
Society as a Student of Law therein as aforesaid,
has he been an Attorney or Solicitor, or Parliamentary
Agent, or the Partner, or in the employment of, or
acting as an Apprentice, or Clerk or Assistant for

lack of aptitude for such a career. Charles Uniacke's goodwill apparently knew no bounds, for he immediately sympathized with his son, now twenty-seven years old, and offered him two years' support and the fare to whichever part of the world George preferred. Una maintains that George was by now so disenchanted with the narrow life of Dublin, and the grave social problems of Ireland, that he jumped at the offer and immediately set out for the Rocky Mountains. He arrived in Salt Lake City, Utah, at the turn of the year, going through eastern Canada and entering the United States at Niagara. The choice of Utah has been the subject of some enquiry but no family associations are known. George's son Brian thinks its mention by a visitor caught his father's imagination.

Chapter 3

GO WEST, YOUNG MAN

THE next two years of George's life he often described as his happiest. Footloose and fancy-free he gave himself over entirely to a life of adventure and freedom, and in the wild grandeur of the Rocky Mountains indulged his love of solitude, introspection and contemplation of the ways of nature. He seems to have had no permanent address for some time, but spent his life in the saddle, camping out and wandering the still-unexplored recesses of that remote area. He worked occasionally as a logger when his funds ran out. This was between the beginning of 1904 and the end of 1905, before city-dwellers had learned to take all their disadvantages with them in their forays 'to get away from it all'. In later years he often recounted stories of his adventures to his children: fighting a forest fire; watching an eagle teach its chick to fly by pushing it off a ledge and diving down to rescue it; getting lost and trusting to his horse to find the way back to camp; a long visit to Yellowstone Park; Old Faithful, the great geyser famed and named for the regularity of its spoutings; the friendliness of bears; and always he spoke of the majesty and beauty and colour. This period concluded his preparation in the wilderness, and at the end of it he suddenly found the purpose of his life.

How he came to read the Bhagavadgita is not known, but there was found among his books, after his passing, a volume entitled *Sacred Books of the East*,[1] and it may well be that this long-treasured volume was the one which found its way to Salt Lake City and into his hands. Many people have speculated about why George became a priest. The enigma was compounded by the fact that within three years of

[1] A revised edition published in New York, 1900, by The Colonial Press.

ordination he abandoned the title and practice of priesthood, without,
however, renouncing his Orders, and 'taught school for a year in Salt
Lake City', before joining the English faculty of a university in
Tennessee. Further, when he took up once more the clerical life he
spent twenty-seven years straining to get away from it again.

The first enigma is resolved by George's own brief statement and
Una's elucidation; the second, questioning why he stayed so long in
the service of a church whose organization and spiritual authority he
firmly believed to have been superseded, resolves itself as his story
unfolds.

A brief account of the main events of his life, which he signed, and
which was drawn up for publicity purposes when he had achieved
such fame as to make necessary an authentic record, states: 'It was at
this time that he first read the sacred writings of the Hindus which
impressed him deeply, and from that time he has been a student of
comparative religion.'

Una relates:

> My father was never too much interested in religion until one day, when
> he was in the western States, he came across the Bhagavadgita and this
> really stirred him up and made him aware of a side of life that he had never
> given too much thought to. He became more and more enthused as he read
> it, and he felt he was unworthy to read this scripture. He just felt this is
> really tremendous, and then he was inspired to make up his mind that he
> was going to devote his life to finding out more about God, to the search
> for the knowledge of God and the Divine Truth.

George's diffidence is apparent in the contrasting nature of the
above descriptions by himself and Una. Given naturally to
understatement, and exceedingly so in everything relating to himself,
he yet was able, more than twenty-five years later, to convey to his
daughter something of the excitement, even the traumatic quality, of
the event, and we must accept Una's vivid account as in no way
contradicting his own modest version. Later still, fifty years after the
event, he sent the Guardian an account of it much closer to Una's than
his signed statement. His letter is quoted in Chapter 17.

There is no doubt that this was his awakening to the reality of
spiritual truth, and was the first major event of his life. He was born
again as Christ said we all must be.[1] The first effect upon him was to
transform him from an insouciant, unfocused, undirected being, to
one of passionate purpose. He had seen a vision of God and was
determined that henceforth all his energies of mind and heart would be
devoted to a deeper and deeper search for Him. Many have had such a
vision and been inspired in varying degrees, but the flame that was

[1] John 3:7

kindled in George's soul never declined, but drove him on throughout his life to acquire the knowledge he sought. When at last he recognized his 'Only Beloved', he served Him steadfastly through years of frustration and longing, acquiring the divine qualities which were to adorn the years of his greatness, until finally the fire within him became a conflagration into which he cast all he had and all he was, in the service of his Lord.

It would be only too easy to exaggerate this event, to the disservice of George's memory. Although a great change took place in his consciousness, it was no lightning stroke attended by unusual phenomena. Rather, the unaccustomed, blinding light of spiritual truth wrought a concentration of all his hitherto unfocused powers and gave direction to his will and his interest.

But this very change brought him face to face with a new problem. He was a new man with a purpose in life. How was he to set about accomplishing it? We turn once more to Una: 'He didn't know how he should go about this and what he should do with his life as regards work and way of living, but after some thought he finally decided to enter the Church.'

This seems a reasonable decision in view of his intention, his background and education. He became a deacon in 1905 and was ordained in 1906 by Bishop Spalding in St Mark's Cathedral, Salt Lake City, as priest in the Episcopal Church of America. This was the American counterpart of the Anglican Church in which he had been brought up. He commented in later life that he had been baptized in the Church of Ireland, confirmed in the Church of England (at Uppingham) and ordained to the priesthood in the Protestant Episcopalian Church in the United States of America.[1]

While still a deacon he was placed in charge of the Mission (to Mormons and Red Indians) at Provo, a town on the shores of Lake Utah some fifty miles south of the Great Salt Lake, where he remained for four years.

Still in the euphoria of his enlightenment, earning his living for the first time, assuming sole responsibility for work which would test his shyness and retiring nature, with what feelings of delight – and some

---

[1] The Church of Ireland, the Church of England, and the Protestant Episcopalian Church in the United States of America are legally separate autonomous bodies, though of the same Protestant persuasion and hierarchy. The Church of Ireland was the Anglican Church, established in Ireland until 1871 when Gladstone forced through Parliament its disestablishment. The issue was not only fiercely and hotly contested but provided the English language with its longest word – antidisestablishmentarianism. Even after 1871, the Church of Ireland remained the religion of the Anglo-Irish (see Appendix 1). The Church of England was established under Henry VIII and is still that estate of the realm; the United States of America has never had an established state church, being forbidden to do so by its Constitution.

pride – he must have welcomed this first step in his new life. With what feelings of gratitude and satisfaction he would have contemplated the magnificent physical surroundings of his post, at the foot of a great range of the Rocky Mountains, as far from civilization as it was possible to be. Here he could pursue amid the most rugged and splendid manifestations of that Nature whose Creator he had so lately come to adore, both the duties of his employment and the mystical path on which he had set his foot.

It was here that his sister Kathleen joined him. She shared to the full that love of natural beauty which Anna Maria had fostered in her children, and spoke in later years of a trip to Yellowstone Park, to which they travelled by buggy, camping out and enjoying the primitive life, the wild and magnificent grandeur of the great mountains, their waterfalls and forests and exhilarating air.

Our meagre knowledge of George's life in Provo is derived from five sources: the Canonical Church Register for 1905 to 1909, all in George's unmistakable handwriting; *History of Provo, Utah* by J. Marinus Jensen (published by the author in 1924 and found in Provo Public Library); *Utah – A Centennial History* by Sutton, also in the Library; a small booklet, *Parish History*, which is mostly copied from the Church Register and otherwise relies on parishioners' memories; and most valuable of all, the annual *Journals of Convocation of the Episcopal District of Utah, 1905–1918* in the possession of Dr W. H. Dalgleish, who has been kind enough to glean from them reliable and very pertinent information.

We learn from *History of Provo*, the chapter entitled *Episcopal Church*, that 'St Mary's, Provo's Episcopal Church was founded in 1892. From the first there have been able men in charge of the work. The Rev. George Townshend, a graduate of Oxford was the minister in charge from 1904[1] to 1909. A scholar of the first order he made a real impression on the life of Provo.'

It seems that he found, on arrival, a congregation of eleven adults, of whom three were church school teachers with eighteen pupils between them. Services were held in shop premises on Center Street. In addition to the pastoral care of this little flock, George held services once a month in Springville, a few miles south of Provo.

Dr Dalgleish's information confirms not only 1905 as the beginning of his tenure of office, but also the statement from *History of Provo* that 'he made a real impression on the life of Provo'.

---

[1] This is certainly an error. George did not become a deacon until 1905 when he was listed by Bishop Spalding in the *Journal of Convocation*. Also, the first entries by him in the Church Register are 1905.

He was present at the Convocation of 1907 (held at St Paul's, Salt Lake City) and was there appointed by the Bishop of Utah to the Finance Committee and the Committee on New Forms and Reports. His co-appointee to this latter committee became Bishop of Utah seven years later. Sometime in 1907 a plot of land was purchased in Provo on which to build St Mary's Church and at Convocation it was indicated that the consecration would shortly take place. Building was evidently quicker there and then than nowadays! He addressed Convocation on 'The Theological Situation'. The *Journal* of 1908 lists him as in charge of St Mary's (it was actually consecrated by Bishop Spalding in 1907), and records that at Convocation that year he was appointed to two more committees – Credentials, and Constitution and Rules. No wonder he was later to dislike 'administration'! He again addressed Convocation, this time on 'The Unoccupied Parts of Utah'. Of great interest is the *Journal's* notation that the congregation at Provo was steadily increasing and Bishop Spalding felt that George's influence was greater than ever before.

In the *Journal* of 1909 George is listed as 'non-parochial', that is he was no longer in charge of Provo and had no parish, though still a priest of the Protestant Episcopal Church. At Convocation Bishop Spalding's annual address included the following passage: 'We are to lose, I hope temporarily, the service of Mr Townshend, who is to teach next year in the Salt Lake High School, and I wish to express my appreciation of his work at Provo and Springville, where during his administration the Church and Rectory have been built. We owe also to Mr Townshend's able pen helpful contributions to the missionary literature of the Church.' These were no small services.

The Canonical Church Register for 1905 to 1909 names the eleven communicants, first of whom is Kathleen C. Townshend. Against her name, in the next column headed 'Removal' is the note, 'Removed to St Mark's Hospital, Salt Lake City'. There is no date and the hospital's records do not go back that far. We only know that she was a qualified nurse and accompanied George to Sewanee. In 1917 she went to Europe with the American Red Cross.

The Register records his first confirmation as April 17, 1906, his first marriage May 7, 1906 and his first baptism on January 1, 1906. The last entry in his hand is a marriage on January 20, 1909.

One more item about Provo of relevance to George's story is the appointment in 1914 of the Reverend William Bulkley to be vicar of St Mary's. We shall meet him again as the Venerable Archdeacon Bulkley replying to the Venerable Archdeacon Townshend on behalf of the Bishop of Salt Lake City, and recalling their days as fellow workers.

George's monograph *The Conversion of Mormonism*, which he
completed and published in 1911, relates of Provo: 'The District of
Salt Lake (as constituted in 1898) covered two hundred thousand
square miles and comprised Western Colorado, half of Nevada, and
the south-west corner of Wyoming, as well as Utah' – an area more
than twice the size of the British Isles, administered at that time by one
bishop, a handful of priests and four or five deaconesses. Provo is 'the
seat of the oldest and largest school and college of the Latterday
Saints', one of the first two places chosen by the Bishop of Utah for the
location of Missions and rejoicing in possession of 'a church and
rectory'; 'a priest and a deaconess are at work'. No mention of his own
great contribution to this happy situation.

Bishop Spalding, in a brief note, heartily commends this booklet to
'all who wish an accurate statement of the belief of the Latter Day
Saints, and also of the Church's Missionary Programme in Utah'. A
modest seventy-six pages, it is interesting to us for its content, but
more for its being the first literary work which we have from George's
pen.[1] It shows at once the mature, easy style of a highly skilled artist in
the English language, and is as pleasurable to read as it is to observe
any expert using his special tools. He writes with assurance and
fluency, and one wonders whether the years at Oxford were as
carefree as supposed. Somewhere he has learned to order his material.
He has done his homework, and cannot be faulted in his facts, which
are clearly and authoritatively, albeit interestingly, presented and
documented.

The book is most interesting for its revelations of two aspects of its
author's character. The first, a paragraph in his Introduction which
reveals his sense of justice and human rights (the shade of Charles
Uniacke hovers in the background):

> The ground covered in the following pages has always been the field of
> bitter contentions between Mormons and non-Mormons; and what I have
> written may be taken by some for controversial matter. But it is not
> inspired by the spirit of controversy. Not a line has been penned in
> animosity or unkindness. I have approached Mormonism not – like the
> Latterday Saint – as a celestial gift, nor – with the anti-Mormon – as a
> contemptible fraud, but as an object of dispassionate study like any other
> religious system. And I have written of the Mormon people with the
> respect due to fellow-men and fellow-citizens. Had I done otherwise, I
> should not have been loyal to the genius of our Church's efforts in Utah.
>
> But while I have sought to avoid causing offense, I have not hesitated to
> say frankly what I believe to be true. Mormonism is sketched here as the

[1] A short apologia, *Why I am not a Mormon*, published in Denver in 1907 has come to
light. It is dealt with briefly in Ch. 13, and is not considered as a literary work, being
more in the nature of a missionary tract.

facts – so far as I know them – show it to be. It appears to me a piece of mere justice to the Latterday Saint to offer him a positive view of Mormonism as those on the outside see it.

The second throws light on his predilection for peacemaking and the building of bridges between alienated people and communities, already observed in his attitude to the complex family life in Dublin. But there now appears a new dimension, that of the liberal, benevolent administrator. In his summing up of the Christian effort in Utah he makes a shrewd evaluation of the different methods pursued by the three missionary forces at work in the area.

There are in vogue at present three methods of dealing with the Mormon problem. The first is that of the Roman Church; the second, that of the evangelical denominations; the third, that of ourselves. The Romanists have contributed little or nothing to the solution of the difficulty, though by a studied display of their organization's great wealth and worldly power, aided by an unfailing courtesy of demeanor, they have fixed the sense of their Church's grandeur deep in the Mormon imagination. The Protestants have done splendid service to the State through their mission schools, and have shown admirable energy and devotion in the cause of their faith. But their preachers early adopted and are only slowly changing their militant and derisive attitude towards the Mormons and Mormonism. They tend to mingle politics with religion. Mormonism, as we all know, is a religion with a past, and they will not permit that past to be buried. As the Puritans of New England fastened the Scarlet Letter to the bosom of the adulteress's gown, so their descendants insist on keeping before the world's eyes those ancient follies and sins of the Mormon organization, which it would be more wise and charitable to forget . . .

Whether this attitude be right or wrong is the concern of those who adopt it. Everyone must note, however, that it has compromised the evangelical message which the ultra-Protestant missionaries have brought, and roused a spirit of hostility and suspicion. The number of converts made from Mormonism to a Christian Creed by their preachers is small indeed.

Our Church endeavors, as it has always endeavored in Utah, to confine itself to positive and constructive effort. It observes that the people are becoming more liberal, more independent, more intelligent, and that their faith is modified and developed to suit their growth. Its policy is to study the nature and causes of this growth; and then to work with it, direct it, and accelerate it. Not to win over stragglers from the Mormon hosts into its own fold, but radically to uplift the whole Mormon religion towards Christianity, not only to convert individual Mormons, but forthright to convert Mormonism; such is our Church's deliberate and consistent object.

Much has been done to this end; much more will be done. We believe that the preaching in Utah of the Historic Gospel, and of a more reasonable

and spiritual Faith, will put to shame the old Mormonism and compel
further eliminations and further substitutions. 'The Latterday Saints' have
an admiration for the good and the true as well as other men; and if the lives
of our Church people are more clean and kind than those of the Mormon
people, if our ministers are more courageous and intelligent than the
Mormon ministers, if our Church has in it more of the idealism and
heroism of Jesus than the Mormon system, if our religion gives purer light
to the soul in its aspirations after the Divine than does the Mormon
religion then there will be little need to decry Mormonism, for its eclipse
will be manifest to all seeing eyes and it will stand convicted and
condemned by the minds and consciences of its own votaries.

This attitude and this understanding of his mission at that time are
extraordinarily pertinent to the great effort of his life, described in later
chapters. Then he would undertake the immensely more formidable
task laid upon him by 'Abdu'l-Bahá: *It is my hope that thy Church will
come under the Heavenly Jerusalem.* His experience in Provo falls into
place – as do all the varied episodes of his life – as preparation for the
great work to come. Indeed, thirty-one years later (1941), the
Guardian of the Bahá'í Faith would instruct his secretary to write to
George that 'he is not surprised to learn that you are finding yourself in
this position, sometimes being upheld and sometimes being attacked.
It is a great bounty from God that you have had a training in this world
which so admirably suits you for a champion of His Faith and an
exponent of His Doctrines.'

George succeeded in his first assignment, pursuing faithfully the
objectives of his Church and pleasing his bishop. But – and again Una
is our guide – 'he said he realized that he had made a mistake, that this
was not really the ideal way to achieve what he wanted. He was in
something that was very static; it seemed to feel that it already had all
the truth and didn't want to look for any more anywhere. So he felt
that he hadn't really made the right move and it was many years before
he finally found what he had been searching for.'

George's own account of his reason for leaving the ministry is given
in his letter to 'Abdu'l-Bahá cited on page 45. There he states that after
working as a missionary in Utah, 'I became connected with an ethical
movement called The Great Work, abandoned the ministry for it,
believing it better and more sincere than the church . . .' and 'never for
an instant regretted what I had done.'

His first foray on the mystical path had proved abortive and he must
start again. Undeterred and unembittered by this initial setback,
detached from all he had built up in Provo and the obvious prospects
before him of advancement to high office, he set out on a new path
which he believed would bring him nearer to his goal. Throughout his

life he was to meet with disappointments and failures, but was never defeated by them. Frustration, mistakes, difficulties, not even defeat itself, could deflect him from his quest. His persistence, as great a feature of his character as his modesty, kept him, like the long-distance runner, in the field, and ensured that he would be thereabouts at the finish.

The Encyclopedia of American Religions lists the School of Natural Science under the general heading 'The Psychic Family'. John E. Richardson, an attorney from California, founded it in 1883 with the purpose of spreading the teachings of the School of the Masters, whose headquarters were in India. Richardson was taught without fee and instructed always to pass on the teachings as a gift. 'By an endless chain of Gifts shall the Great Work be established.' The Indo-American Book Company was established as the publishing arm of the 'Great Work' and issued the Harmonic Series as the basic teaching materials of the School of Natural Science.

The teachings of the school are given as:

> the Universal Intelligence is revealed through his immutable laws; nature is engaged in the evolvement of individual intelligences; nature impels individuals to higher levels of consciousness; the soul is immortal and passes successively into physical and spiritual bodies; man's free will works within a law of compensation (karma); willing conformity to the laws of nature leads to self-mastery, poise and happiness; by living the laws of nature, people come to know instinctively that spiritual reality exists and that life continues after death.

What was attractive in all this for George is, at this remove, not likely to be determined. It was certainly different from committees on New Forms and Reports or Constitution and Rules, and there is no doubt of his distaste for the general theology of Mormonism. We must remember too that it was the Bhagavadgita which had set him on his life's search and the oriental flavour of 'The Great Work' may have been inviting. More likely perhaps was the seeming repudiation of profit-making, and the positive attitude to attaining higher levels of consciousness. How or when or where he made contact with this movement is unknown. Neither do we know what he did to serve it. We only know – and again from his letter to 'Abdu'l-Bahá – that he continued to work for it until 1916, which is seven years after he gave up service to the church. During that time he earned his living by teaching.

Whether George ever confided his inmost thoughts to Kathleen is not known, but they were both in Salt Lake City during George's year of teaching High School – Kathleen at St Mark's Hospital – and they stayed together for the next six years. George gave up his rectorship of

St Mary's, Provo, early in 1909. His appointment at the Salt Lake City
High School would not require his presence until September. With the
summer before them and George with a job to return to, they made a
holiday trip home to Ireland. Charles Uniacke, that remarkable man,
had died in 1907, and Anna Maria welcomed her wanderers at a house
in Donegal which she had rented for the summer. Nothing more is
known of that visit, but they returned together to Salt Lake City,
George to the High School and Kathleen to the nursing staff at the
hospital.

The Reverend Norman Guthrie had founded in 1908, and had become
Director of the Extension Department of the University of the South,[1]
Sewanee, Tennessee. He was that rather flamboyant figure, who, as
Rector of St Marks in-the-Bouwerie, New York, 'kept religion on the
front page' by innovations not always acceptable to the hierarchy. The
obituaries of December 1944 recall some of his more publicized
actions, such as the installation of coloured lights, gongs and incense;
asking non-believers such as Isadora Duncan to speak at services;
tethering a black sheep in the churchyard. His *pièce de résistance* was the
presentation of eurythmic dances in the church by six young women
barefooted and clad in white draperies. This last persuaded his already
fuming bishop to remove St Mark's from his Episcopal visiting list.

In 1910 when George was teaching at Salt Lake City High School,
Guthrie was travelling through Colorado and on to California. There
is no doubt that he met George, although the circumstances are not
known, and engaged him for the Extension Department. George
himself records that he was 'engaged by Rev. W. N. Guthrie for
Extension Lecturing Work', and one of his letters to the university is
marked 'Thru Guthrie'. Further, Guthrie's official report as Director
of the University Extension Department, to the Vice-Chancellor for
the year 1909–10 states: 'During the year the Director has been able to
find a promising candidate for the kind of position granted Mr
Patterson during the past year, in Mr George Townshend, a graduate
of Oxford University, and highly recommended otherwise . . .'

George's status on entry to the university appears, to say the least, a
remarkable phenomenon. His engagement was as Assistant-Director

[1] This is a church college of the Protestant Episcopalian Church of the United States
of America. Its history is heroic. It was 'founded in 1857, it received its charter in 1858,
its cornerstone was laid in 1860 [with the help of a generous contribution from the
Church of England], it was reclaimed from an overgrown wilderness in 1866, and its
first nine students were admitted in 1868'. 'Although neither student nor teacher is
required to be Episcopalian, Sewanee is owned, governed, and supported by the
Episcopal Church.' (*Enduring Memorial*, published by the University Press)

of the University Extension Department, and he is so listed, as a member of Faculty. But he also entered as a student. His registration card, dated October 1, 1910, notes his BA (Oxon.) and is twice marked 'Grad. – Special Theology', and once more, '(Graduate)'. There was evidently to be no doubt about this unusual hybrid!

However, hindsight is a great clarifier and from its vantage point we may resolve the factors in this equation. We note first that after leaving Provo in 1909 George ceased to use his title of 'Reverend' and there is nothing in his record at Sewanee to indicate that his priesthood was ever known. He was always Mister or Professor Townshend. Dr Guthrie's report to the Vice-Chancellor spoke of George as 'a graduate of Oxford University, and highly recommended otherwise . . .' What can that 'otherwise' have been but George's considerable services to the Church at Provo, so highly praised by his bishop. But George was never one to claim honours or position for himself, and having abandoned the clerical practice he would certainly not maintain the use of its title, even though he remained an ordained priest. Nor did he use the uniform – the dog collar – until he once again entered church service. Guthrie would undoubtedly have known all George's qualifications and may have had to reveal them to the Vice-Chancellor, but if so the confidence was respected.

George's registration as a Special Theology student is entirely in keeping with the great aim of his life. Having recognized the limitations which service to an organized and self-satisfied church imposed on that aim, he yet considered that religious study, of which he had not yet had a great deal, would further it. He therefore entered for the divinity course at Sewanee. He was thirty-four on registration and may well have considered that the use of his title and the knowledge of his successful record would have prejudiced the opportunities open to him as a student.

His record at Sewanee is truly remarkable. He appears to have entered into his own and for the next six years pursued a vigorous, full and happy life. His powers of organization and execution were given full scope in the Extension Department and his personal study was pursued in the divinity course and in his service to 'The Great Work'. At Sewanee he seems to have shed the shyness and reclusive nature which had distinguished him hitherto, but which would reappear in later life. He was popular, cheerful, genial, respected for his great ability and knowledge, but not immune from the persiflage and ragging which is the common lot of faculty members at universities. In fact he joined in the spirit of fun with a number of articles in the student publication *The Sewanee Purple*. For instance when *The Purple* congratulated the Professor of Ethics, rather fulsomely, on election to honorary membership in the Luther Burbank Society, the next issue contained, under George's signature, this letter to the editor:

> The cause of humor is sacred. But I must protest against such jokes on professors as that which you published in the first column of the last page of your issue dated November 25th, concerning one of our professors and the Luther Burbank Society. We on the Mountain understand your fun. We know that the Luther Burbank Society is a commercial organization for advertising and selling a beautiful, sumptuous and costly edition of Mr Burbank's works; we know too that a large number of our professors have had repeated appeals made to them to join this society, and when they would not do so that they have been at last elected honorary members of it anyway. We in the University are aware of all this, and appreciate your sly and cryptic humor. But outsiders may not be able to do this. Misled by that courtly seriousness of yours, they may not see that you are joking. And they may suppose that our professors are indeed capable of swelling themselves with pride at such an honor as becoming a subscriber to *Scribner's Magazine*, an owner of an *Encyclopaedia Britannica*, or a member of the Burbank society (which you so wittily describe as 'this distinguished body').
>
> I therefore respectfully and earnestly urge upon you that when next you print such a paragraph as this, you put at the head of it a picture of Cap and Bells, or add a footnote, 'NB – This is a joke'.

Such light-hearted forays, however, did not exclude him from the columns of the University's more sedate organ *The Sewanee Review*; vol. XX, No. 1, of January 1912, contains his *England's Atonement for Old Wrongs* and vol. XXIII, 1915, his essay *Irish Mythology*.

We need not hesitate to ascribe this transformation to his spiritual awakening and subsequent experience of responsibility in Provo. And we should not underestimate his intellectual capacity. Allied with an ability to profit from solitary study and meditation, it would, in fact, be hard to overestimate it. The modest result at Oxford is no criterion for assessment of his brain power. He had won scholarships to school and university, and at Uppingham had taken two literary prizes; he had qualified in law and had been called to the Bar. He had followed the prescribed courses, had succeeded in his first employment, and now his training and talents were to be tested and fully deployed.

Guthrie put in appearances at Sewanee during the first year of George's Assistant Directorship, but after the Summer Extension School of 1911, removed to New York to take up his rectorship. He remained Director of the Department but, as we shall see, George did all the work.

George was not allowed to work exclusively for Guthrie's Department. His ability and knowledge were immediately recognized and he was co-opted into the English Faculty. A minute of the

8. *Views of Provo, Utah.* Top *1890; note steam trolley.* Below *1906;*

9. *The Church and Rectory at Provo, built by George*

COMMUNICANTS.

No.	NAME.		DATE ENTERED.	HOW AND WHENCE RECE
✓ 1.	Kathleen C. Townshend		Sept 26, '05	
✓ 2	Mary C. Winter (Mⁿ)		"	
3	V. L. Zoellner (Mⁿ)		"	
4	John Smith		"	
5	Mary Smith (Mʳˢ)	✓	"	
6	Jane Smith	✓	"	
7.	James Holmes		"	
8.	Josiah Beck.		"	
✓ 9.	Neil Winter		"	
10	Theresa Holmes (Mⁿˢ)	✓	"	
11	Bowen. (Mⁿˢ)		"	
12	Estelle R. Bersach.		April 17ᵗʰ '06.	Confirmed here.
13	D. H. Sigler (Mⁿˢ)		"	
14	Lloyd Sigler.		"	
15	Elizabeth Winter		"	

10. *First page of the Canonical Register of Provo, all in George's handwriting*

11. *Members of Sigma Upsilon at the University of the South, Sewanee, Tennessee. George is in the centre, back row.*

12. *Ruins of Parc na Silog, the house in Enniskerry to which George came home from America*

13. Nellie Jennings Roche, circa 1910

Committee on the Academic Department reads: 'That the recommendation of the Acting Dean of the Academic Department that assistance be secured for the Professor of English in the matter of teaching or correcting composition work be granted; and that Mr George Townshend be selected for the specified work, at a salary of $300 per annum.' This seems a modest enough beginning but was additional to George's appointment as Assistant-Director of the Extension Department, and a dollar, seventy years ago, was 'a dollar'. The prospectus for the University's Summer Extension Session in 1912 states: 'Board may be had from $6 to $10 a week', so an extra $6 a week was not to be sneezed at. And the Vice-Chancellor's report reads: 'I appointed Mr George Townshend, BA, as Assistant in English, and the Dean gives high commendation to his work and recommends an increase in salary.'

A later Vice-Chancellor's report states: 'Bishop Knight reported to the Board of Regents on the 22nd of May that a friend had made it possible to increase the salaries of the Professors for a period of five years, and the Board authorized the following salary list, beginning with the session of 1914–15: . . . Professor Townshend $1,000.'

And further: 'George Townshend, MA (Oxon.), who was appointed Instructor in English, has been acting as Assistant Professor in English for some time past. I believe that it was the intention of the Board to elect him to this position. I cannot find any record of such election: I therefore recommend that George Townshend, MA (Oxon.), be elected as Assistant Professor of English for the unexpired term beginning September 1, 1915.' Until the above confirmation of his actual position was made, he was listed as Instructor in English. Later that same year the record shows him Associate Professor of English and his Assistant Professorship was dated back, in the record, to 1913.

In his first few months George was inducted into the work of the Department by Guthrie himself, who included in his annual report for 1910–11, the following:

> During this past year the Director has had the constant advice and assistance of Mr George Townshend. He has acted as Secretary, and latterly as Assistant Director. He has prepared lectures during his stay at Sewanee and has acceptably delivered a number in the session of 1910. He has lectured in Southern University, Greensboro; Judson College, Marion; and before United Literary Clubs of Selma, Alabama; and in Chattanooga, Tennessee, before our own. It is hoped that Mr Townshend will continue his connection with the Department.

In addition to sending out capable lecturers to schools and colleges all through the South, the University Extension Department provided summer courses of eight weeks to all who cared to come, and the record shows that they proved popular. George played a part in this success. *The Sewanee Purple* for October 12, 1911, headlines:

RÉSUMÉ OF SUMMER EXTENSION SESSION
EMINENT CORPS OF LECTURERS
LARGEST ATTENDANCE AND GREATEST INTEREST SHOWN SINCE ITS INCEPTION

The University of the South, Sewanee, Tennessee, has just completed its third summer Extension Session. The success of the Session surpassed anticipation . . . Literature was treated by two lecturers, Mrs S. B. Elliott, who spoke on American Literature, and Mr George Townshend of the Extension Department, who delivered a course on the Celtic Revival, giving an insight into the spirit of contemporary Irish literature and Drama.

Every year George gave at least two lectures, generally on some aspect of Irish literature; one was 'Irish Wit and Humour', and another simply 'Irish Humour'. These may have been the basis of his later essay 'Irish Humour' dealt with in Chapter 13. In 1911 he gave papers on 'The Contemporary Drama of Ireland' and 'The Celtic Note in Irish Poetry'. In 1912 he presented a paper on 'The Boundaries of Prose and Poetry'. The *Sewanee Purple* for October 3, 1912, relates: 'The Extension Players were not able to present the dramas they had planned for, owing to the fewness of the available actors. The first play given was an original romantic drama in three acts, by Mr George Townshend, entitled "In Ireland's Cause".' None of these can, alas, be traced.

The Vice-Chancellor's report again:

'In the absence of a report from the Director I would state that last summer [1911] was the most successful effort the department has put forth, not only in the program but in the interest elicited, and from a financial standpoint. Rev. Mr Guthrie accepted the call to the rectorship of St Mark's-in-the-Bouwerie, New York City, and took charge early in the fall. He still retains the Directorship in the Extension Department with George Townshend, BA, as Assistant Director actually in charge. The program for the summer which is submitted gives promise of much interest and I anticipate as successful a course as last year.'

His hope was realized with George 'as Assistant Director actually in charge'. He was also 'Chairman, Prize Committee' and 'Editor, Departmental Publications'. The Prize Committee was formed in 1912 to adjudicate in a competition open to 'Southerners' by the Extension Department. A first prize of $500 and a second of $250 were offered for 'an epic poem of the Civil War'; the second prize to be awarded for the best 'plan and outline' of the projected poem and the first for the 'best book or canto' of it.

Reporting the 1915 course, *The Sewanee Purple* reads:

SUCCESSFUL SUMMER SESSION

The Public Lectures of the summer were given by Professor Thomas P. Bailey, Ph.D., and Professor George Townshend, MA, of the faculty of the University and they aroused great interest.

May 27, 1915 – Professor George Townshend made a tour of the prep schools in and around Lexington, Kentucky the latter part of last week, speaking in the interest of the University.

April 20, 1916 – Dr McBryde and Mr Townshend leave today for an extended visit among the preparatory schools of the state . . . Mr Townshend will speak at the following schools: The Brandan and Tate School of Shelbyville; the Hawkins School of Gallatin; and some of the Nashville schools.

Some idea of George's work in the English Department is gathered from the following excerpts taken from the University catalogue:

Curriculum
English 1c The Novel and the Drama. A study of selected types. (This course required of all Freshmen.)   Three hours – Mr Townshend

2c Essay-writing and Speech-making: a comparative study, with exercises in composition and delivery.   Three hours – Mr Townshend

1913–1914   Curriculum courses – Novel and Drama   Mr Townshend

Again, *The Sewanee Purple*:

May 13, 1915 – DR MCBRYDE RECUPERATING. [Dr McBryde was head of English Department]

Dr McBryde, who several weeks ago underwent a severe operation for appendicitis, is able to sit up again and hopes he will be out soon. He does not expect to meet any of his classes during the remainder of the year though. In the meanwhile, Mr Townshend is endeavoring to meet the combined English classes. [George might have worded this better!]

The following charming letter was written by one of George's ex-students in direct response to an appeal for memoirs of him; he is Theron Myers who matriculated at Sewanee in the same year that George took up his appointment, but was probably fifteen years (at least) younger. He wrote in 1977, sixty-seven years after:

I had the privilege of having Mr Townshend as instructor in Irish Poetry and in short stories. Being a native of Ireland he was uniquely capable of arousing an appreciation of his native poetry. He was also very proficient in his criticisms of short stories and went into minute detail regarding the structural form of a good short story.

Linked with his ability, his pleasing and impressive personality aroused affection and respect.

George's progress at Sewanee is summed up as follows:

1910–13, Assistant Director of the University Extension Department;
   Instructor in English; Special Theology student
1913–15, Assistant Professor of English
1915–16, Associate Professor of English

All through he remained Assistant Director of the Extension Department.

These appointments, while revealing his immensely vigorous and widespread activities, relate only to his academic duties. He played a full part in university life and until 1913, when he completed his course on Theology, he was a member of many student clubs and societies. After that he could no longer claim student status but retained his interest as honorary or faculty member. In that same year he applied for and received his MA from Oxford.[1]

He founded the Chess Club and was the local champion. He produced *Julius Caesar* (the full text), the first such undertaking at Sewanee. He acted in two Irish plays, Lady Gregory's *The Travelling Man* and *The Workhouse Ward*. He was a member of Phradian ('The Phradian Society furnished mature students with further opportunities for extemporaneous debate.' *The Sewanee Purple*); Pi Omega was a literary society to whose sessions he contributed talks about Oxford and showed 'stereoptican scenes' of that city. He advocated very strongly, both in the columns of *The Purple* and among faculty and students alike, the organization of 'a track team or field day' which 'the University has not had since 1907. . .' He topped his cogently argued case with a more emotional appeal: 'Who does not enjoy watching an Athletic Field Day? What can be prettier than a good hurdle race, or finer to watch than a quarter gamely run?' And he doesn't fail to involve his special qualifications for making such a proposal: '. . . because of my enthusiasm in track work engendered by seven years as a runner at school and college.' Later notices of field events indicate that his suggestion was taken up, although the 1974 Prospectus makes no mention of track events under Recreations.

There is no doubt that George thoroughly enjoyed America. He responded whole-heartedly to its optimism, its informality, its

---

[1] At that time Oxford University required no further examination or submission of thesis on the part of a graduate, but awarded its MA on proof of continuing interest and study over a number of years in the discipline for which the BA was awarded.

The University of the South, Sewanee, Tennessee

Shakspere's *Julius Cæsar*

presented in costume on an
Elizabethan Stage by

The Freshman English Class

under the direction of

Professor Townshend

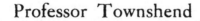

Forensic Hall, Saturday, June 12,'15
Under the Management of *Punch and Judy*

idealism. At some time during his twelve years' sojourn he became an American citizen.[1] Frequently in after life he contemplated returning and often regaled his children with stories of his life there. His love of nature found deep satisfaction in the grandeur and spaciousness of its incredibly vast wilderness, and in Sewanee, generally referred to as 'the Mountain' by the cognoscenti, he lived 'a thousand feet above the surrounding valleys', looking down upon 'the heavily forested slopes of the Cumberland Plateaus', and upwards to the stars. For in spite of the new personality – the genial, cheerful, companionable intellectual – his main purpose in life was ever the pursuit of that vision which had so enraptured him in Utah. Doubtless he did not advertise his all-consuming passion – for that is what it was – but preserved it inviolate in his inner private soul. The outward man was the manifestation of this inner purpose, and his ceaseless activity one means of accomplishing it.

Not every prospect was pleasing. Tennessee, in the deep south, was still, half a century after the Civil War, the scene of rigid racial division and prejudice. The relations between blacks and whites were almost identical with those between Irish and Anglo-Irish, which had played so large a part in George's desire to emigrate. While liberalism in this respect was advancing in Ireland, where the chief factors were national and religious prejudices, it had barely raised its head in Tennessee, where the great divide was colour. When President Taft visited Sewanee in November 1911 *The Sewanee Purple* recorded: 'Our colored brethren were not forgotten on Friday. Numbers of them shook hands with the President's cook.' George was well aware of all this and spoke of it, not always dispassionately, to his children. But America was vast, large-hearted and full of confidence and an unshakeable conviction that any and every problem could be solved. In spite of injustices it was, as yet, free of ancient hatreds and bitterness, and the American Dream was still of the brotherhood of man. The bounties of God were everywhere apparent and it was the perfect milieu for the seeker, the constant seeker of His Truth, uncluttered by the dust and débris of centuries.

At a later time George was to write of extreme difficulties which beset him in Provo. After he gave up the ministry and engaged in promoting 'The Great Work', he suffered severe neuritis which so affected his arms and eyes as to leave him unable to read or write for a period – an unbearable privation to one of his proclivities (see Chapter 4).

[1] By so doing he would not have forfeited his British citizenship, which was likewise unaffected by his becoming an Irish citizen at the establishment of the Free State in 1922, or the recognition of the Republic in 1949.

The photographs from Sewanee are something of a surprise to later generations. This is not the physical man we knew. The heavy eyelids are there and the geniality, but he seems smaller and lighter and the beard and moustache are incompatible with the gentle, deeply spiritual, almost ascetic countenance we remember.

One more event in his life in America, an experience common to most men, as important as birth or death, must be recorded. He fell in love and became engaged to be married. Nellie Roche of Nashville was nearly four years younger than George, and at the time of their meeting was a school teacher in that city. She was the great-great-granddaughter of General James Robertson, who founded the city of Nashville.

Nellie notes that they met in Sewanee in 1910, and records of their first meeting 'my impression of a definite spiritual destiny'. By 1913 they had agreed to get married. Nellie's parents had died before she met George, and Charles Uniacke had gone on in 1907. Anna Maria was now living in Enniskerry, a delightful village some few miles south of Dublin amid the lovely mountains of Wicklow. It was decided to hold the marriage from Anna Maria's house, spend the summer in Ireland and return to Sewanee in time for the autumn term. George would go first to make all arrangements, and Nellie would follow as soon as possible. The pleasant prospect opened before them of an academic life where George had every expectation of continued success and Nellie was 'native and to the manner born'.

He set out for Ireland after the summer term in July 1913 with all the hopes and expectations we may justifiably infer. He was about to enter a period of disaster, frustration and defeat.

Chapter 4

NELLIE

GEORGE took up residence with his mother at Parc na Silog,[1] a fine house in Enniskerry, and prepared for his fiancée's arrival. Instead, he received a telegram breaking off the engagement.

Until Nellie's autobiographical typescript, 'My Life Experience', and a number of letters she wrote to George in 1939, more than twenty years after their final parting in 1916, became available, the only explanation offered for this dramatic action tended rather to deepen than to resolve the mystery surrounding it. The story is that Nellie, waiting in New York to take ship, received there a message from her sister in California announcing a family disaster and appealing for help. She had to decide on the spot whether to ignore the plight of her sister and two small children or to stand by them and break her engagement to George. She sent him a cable saying she could not desert her family.

In view of George's clear intention to return to Sewanee to a well paid job with excellent prospects, this seems a highly inadequate reason for breaking a marriage engagement. Nevertheless, Nellie returned to Nashville and set about becoming a successful business woman, to such effect that by 1921 she became City Comptroller for that year. For thirty-five years she was a life underwriter for the Massachusetts Mutual Life Insurance Company and became known as the dean of the life insurance women of Nashville. Her obituary from *The Nashville Banner* of July 31, 1958, is printed in Appendix 2.

George returned to Sewanee and continued his successful career,

---

[1] On being informed that the house was now derelict, Una wrote: 'My grandmother lived there with Aunts Hill and Mill. The name means Willow Park and it was nicely kept in the old days. My aunts lived on there for a few years after her passing.'

already described. He and Nellie apparently remained friends, and George had no second thoughts about his intention to remain in America, which had been his motivation for acquiring its citizenship. What discussions took place between them, whether George attempted to repair the break, in what manner they continued their relationship, are unknown and likely to remain so. Our only sources for knowledge of this remarkable story in George's life are the personal memory of Miss M. R. Watkins of Nashville, Tennessee, Nellie's cousin, close friend and confidante, and a number of invaluable documents generously contributed by her. They are listed in Appendix 2. George's thirty-nine letters to Nellie are a treasure house of information and insight, but there are, alas, many gaps, and there is no trace of the fundamental item, Nellie's cable from New York. Fortunately George's letters disclose the extraordinarily high spiritual nature of their relationship and it is impossible to think that George would have asked her to share his life with him without disclosing to her his own great hopes and purpose. Neither is there any doubt that Nellie shared in and fully supported his aim. References in these letters to his life in Utah and to TK, founder of 'The Great Work', support this view.

The real reason for Nellie's sacrifice of her own happiness is discovered in the autobiographical notes of her life and her letters to George. Her impression at her first meeting with George of his 'definite spiritual destiny' became immensely reinforced as she quickly realized her very deep love for him and received the simultaneous conviction that it would 'not be fulfilled' and she would 'never live in Sewanee'. 'I broke your engagement', she wrote, 'to prevent my being a possible hindrance in your spiritual destiny and gave up my prospect of a family . . . and in a flash, in that crucible, the dross was consumed, and the pure gold of selfless love was born in all its beauty and freedom.' There is no doubt of her absolute belief that she and George were partners in a Divine plan to bring about his spiritual destiny which, when eventually fulfilled, would be seen, she was convinced, to be nothing less than the leading of the Anglican Churches and the British people into the promised Day of God. So precious to her was this conviction, which came to her after she had accepted George's proposal, that she willingly gave up her own deepest longings in favour of the guidance which she firmly believed to have been given her. Her acceptance of George was true and deep; she wrote:

> The love that God put in my heart for you is His gift to you and to me, but it is to be used for His purposes, not for ours. It has illumined all my life . . .

. . . It was all a part of this Divine plan that we were so rudely separated in 1913. We had such high hopes, but we were both so inexperienced and could so easily have lost the way, never to have found it again, as we have now, by God's good grace! And because God needed you for far greater service than I can ever give, he has permitted you an experience from which I have been spared, I could not have faced it. Now we can step out with a new life together – the Atlantic Ocean is a mere trifle! – and we *can and will solve your difficulties!* . . . Consciously and purposely working together we can move mountains! And it was for this very purpose that God was good enough to bring us together in 1910 and again in 1936. Now we can have an era of fulfillment, though we may never meet again on this plane. There is still eternity! This transcendent experience has completely outshone anything else I have ever even dreamed of in pure, unutterable joy! If I could only transmit it to you this very moment! And from this day my life and services belong to God and to the Bahá'í Faith and to you and yours.

It will be seen that Nellie faithfully fulfilled that intention. Her influence on and participation in George's life was to reach far greater proportions than could have been derived or imagined from an abortive love affair of three or four years. At the most frustrating, difficult and possibly critical period of his life, they were to renew their friendship as a result of their both having found, by separate paths and at different times, that Source of Truth in whose existence they so earnestly believed, and Nellie was to play a vital part, both practically and spiritually, in George's attainment to the 'definite spiritual destiny' which at their first meeting she had perceived to rest upon him.

The story is extraordinary and wonderful. It was played out on an exalted spiritual plane and could only have taken place at all between two highly developed, elevated souls. The facts may be related now although Nellie will not enter the story again for more than twenty years. It is best introduced in the recorded words of Mary Watkins:

Nellie told me of her friendship with Mr Townshend. As I recall, she said that she met him in Sewanee and that neither knew of the Faith at that time. When the engagement was ended, both thought their relationship was at an end.

Nellie, having a tremendous sense of responsibility, had to make a choice. She chose the breaking of her engagement, thereby electing to sacrifice her personal happiness for that of her family.

Nellie's own pencilled notes confirm her cousin's account and add to it. They read: 'Meeting at Sewanee – my impression of a definite spiritual destiny – attraction – foreseeing the leave-taking – sudden realization and no fulfillment – many intimations – conviction I'd

never live in Sewanee – plans Spring 1913 – discarded – parting 1916 –
note late 1916 enclosing leaflets – evident dismissal . . .'

Miss Watkins continues:

> In January of 1937 the National Spiritual Assembly met in Nashville. She
> met Dorothy Baker and Horace Holley[1] at this time. Winston Evans was
> also at the meeting. The following October, Nellie became a Bahá'í. She
> travelled with Dorothy Baker in the South in 1938. During these years she
> had no contact with George Townshend and did not know of his
> acceptance of the Faith. One day she read something that he had written
> about it. She wrote to him and thus began the correspondence between
> them. The strange part is that neither knew of the other's activities in
> becoming Bahá'ís. They had had no knowledge of one another for years.
>
> . . . she was an inspiration to him, a help in financial matters, and always
> ready to assist him and his family in any way she could. She inherited a
> small amount of money, all of which she sent to George Townshend. This
> money assisted him in breaking with the Anglican Church, so that he
> could pursue his destiny as a servant of Bahá'u'lláh.
>
> Nellie Roche gave her very life for the Faith. She was an inspiration to all
> who knew her, both Bahá'í and non-Bahá'í. Her work in the South, when
> to be a Bahá'í was almost to be a heretic, never wavered.
>
> I was with her at her death holding her hand, and as she died I whispered
> the Greatest Name into her ear. She responded briefly and said, 'God has
> made death a messenger of joy.'

The breaking of his engagement to Nellie was but the lifting of the
curtain on a period of trial and frustration. In spite of his success at
Sewanee, the failure of his marriage plans must have been a traumatic
experience, and Nellie's adamantine conviction that she was acting
under guidance in refusing to marry him of little comfort to him. Nor
is there any indication of real progress in the quest upon which he was
so whole-heartedly engaged. Indeed, he was about to receive a further
blow in this respect. 'The Great Work', the movement which he had
served so loyally for more than six years in the hopes of promoting his
spiritual progress and eventually attaining his quest, was in trouble.
Investigations at its headquarters in Chicago disclosed 'financial
mismanagement' and its founder retired. George was greatly upset.
He would later confide to 'Abdu'l-Bahá: 'In June 1916 I learned in one
moment the Movement for which I had done so much was based on
fraud.' While this could in no way affect the reality of his vision or
deter him in its pursuit, it was nevertheless a bludgeon stroke at the
centre of his life. This was the second false trail.

It is no great surprise, therefore, to find him preparing another visit
home, possibly reinforced by a sense of obligation to give Anna Maria

---

[1] Both became Hands of the Cause.

a better explanation of the breakdown of his proposed marriage plans than had been possible on the sole basis of Nellie's cable. The U-boats would have been no deterrent to his sixth crossing of the Atlantic, since he would travel in an American ship and the United States was not yet at war. He set out at the end of June, fully intending to return for the autumn term.

He arrived in Dublin in the aftermath of the Easter Rising of 1916. This tragic episode not only added fuel to the hatred of Irish for English, but the bitterness of failure was exacerbated by the severity of the punishments meted out to the insurgents. America would not reap the whirlwind of racial prejudice – its cities would not be burnt nor their streets run with blood – for another half-century. And in spite of the parting from Nellie, the prospect of an immediate return to the open, genial life of Sewanee must have seemed highly desirable.

But now a stronger compulsion than his own will directed him, through further calamity, to the path of his destiny. His old eye trouble returned with such severity that for some weeks he was entirely blind. He received treatment from several doctors and eventually one was found who cured him; but he was afflicted in this way and with his earlier trouble of neuritis more than once in later years.

Return to Sewanee was out of the question, and perhaps not so attractive as formerly. He offered his resignation by cable and followed it with a letter of explanation, citing his illness. The cabled reply read 'Released with regret' and a letter of sympathy followed deploring the circumstances, particularly when he had established himself so successfully in the work and life of the University.[1]

George's cup of adversity was now brim-full and overflowing. In one great wave of calamity he had lost his bride, his sight, his spiritual allegiance and his employment. How swift a transition! The way of the mystic is indeed hard.

Anna Maria must have been of the greatest comfort to him during this period, providing him with a home and loving care. After he had recovered his sight he had to consider starting life again, at the age of forty-one. Una says he 'tried one or two things' but eventually followed Anna Maria's advice. She pointed out to him that he was already ordained in the Episcopal Church and would doubtless be welcomed in the Church of Ireland (see page 21, footnote). *Crockford* lists him 'Curate of Booterstown [a suburb of Dublin] 1916–19'.

George's decision raises again the old enigma. Once already he had retired from church service and he stated in a letter to 'Abdu'l-Bahá, written in 1919, that he never regretted having done so. But

[1] Information from Una

circumstances were different now. He would not be a missionary and competing with others for souls. The Church of Ireland had in its gift the rectorships of a great many country parishes. Perhaps, if he could be given the incumbency of one in some remote part of the island, the duties of priest would not be too burdensome, but would allow him to continue his private and professional pursuits in one effort. After the full, adventurous life in America, now ended in disaster, he may well have looked again to the quiet retirement of the sweet Irish countryside and thought of pursuing his quest in peaceful meditation and study. Certainly no other profession required services so akin to his main purpose, nor would the pursuit of that purpose so benefit the duties of any other profession.

His rector at Booterstown was Arnold Harvey, later Canon and Dean of St Patrick's Cathedral, Dublin – the national cathedral of the Church of Ireland – and eventually Bishop of Cashel. He became a lifelong friend, and remained so, even after George renounced his Orders.

But now, severed from all he had built up, George was open to the bounty of God. And it came in full measure. He received from Louise Finley, the librarian at Sewanee, with whom he had boarded and who knew of his interest in religious movements, two or three pamphlets about the Bahá'í Faith. These arrived in the winter of 1916 as he was recovering from his blindness. He was 'at once interested' and wrote for books to the address given on the pamphlets.[1] He also sent one or two 'leaflets' to Nellie with his letter accepting the termination of their engagement, and that was the end of all contact between them for the next twenty years.

There was no reply to his application. He wrote again and in July 1917 received three volumes of *Tablets of 'Abdu'l-Bahá*, the sender supposing that the first parcel had been sunk by submarine action. It is likely that the compilation of 'Abdu'l-Bahá's public addresses in North America entitled *The Promulgation of Universal Peace* was also included in the parcel. On the same day that these books arrived he met his future wife, Anna Sarah Maxwell[2] (Nancy). The occasion was a picnic on the island of Howth, a beautiful resort in Dublin Bay, popular for rambles and family expeditions. Nancy was governess to the daughter of a General Stokes and was attending the picnic with her charge. She and George were married in 1918, and in March 1919

[1] It is a very reasonable inference that those pamphlets were the ones in use in the United States in 1916 which gave addresses in Washington and New York. One was a simple card and others were pocket-sized editions giving some general Bahá'í principles and a few facts about the Founders.
[2] The recurring 'Anna' is remarkable.

George was appointed to the incumbency of Ahascragh, near Ballinasloe, County Galway, and they settled into the rectory which was to be their home for the next twenty-eight years.

We have followed George's life sufficiently far to recognize two important factors affecting his development. One was undoubtedly the influence of a very few remarkable characters. Charles Uniacke, the great man, a true father-figure, honoured and respected, generous, tolerant, just; Anna Maria, young, gay, informal, lover of nature, creator of beauty; Nellie Roche, the confidante of his heart, high-principled and disciplined, seeking, like him, 'the beauty of the Friend'.

The other, far greater factor, was the guiding hand of his own destiny. At the beginning we stated that George, like Saul of Tarsus, was chosen by the Manifestation of God for a particular task. At all times he was sheltered, guided, protected; unconsciously for the first half of his life, more and more consciously in the second. Many men and women – perhaps most – try to escape the compulsion of their own talents. Those chosen for the service of God are not allowed to do so.

Shoghi Effendi wrote to him on December 1, 1933, shortly after he had been appointed Archdeacon of Clonfert, 'God is no doubt preparing the way for the spread of His Faith in a strange and mysterious manner. You are, it seems, His chosen instrument . . .'

We may see in the modest result at Oxford, which prevented his following an all-too-likely academic career had he obtained a first, the dissatisfaction with Law when he was qualified, the sudden vision of spiritual truth which ever after held him in thrall, the practice in administration and development of his literary ability at Sewanee, the disappointments and disasters which overtook him on his return to Ireland and which opened the way to a period of settled family life and a position of honour and influence – in all these we can see – none the less truly for the clarification of hindsight, the operation of Providence shaping him and his course for its own purpose and his immortal fame. The finger of God was upon him.

Chapter 5

THE TABLETS FROM
'ABDU'L-BAHÁ

ON June 10, 1919, two-and-a-half years after he had received the Bahá'í pamphlets from Louise Finley and three months after he had settled into Ahascragh, George wrote the following letter to 'Abdu'l-Bahá:

Dear Abdul Baha,

I am impelled to send you a letter, asking Mr Remey of America to forward it to you since I do not know your direction. I want to acknowledge the light and uplift and happiness and exhilaration which are coming to me through the knowledge of your teachings, the reports of your life and through the writings of Bahaollah; and to offer my thanks, deep heartfelt and ever-growing for this extraordinary benefit.

Recognizing that you are immersed in cares and important work, I should hardly have ventured to intrude upon you but that I read in Vol. ii of your Tablets the other day that it is necessary for every soul who believes in (his) Lord to send Abdul Baha a letter of acknowledgement in the Oneness of God.

Already I have tried to communicate with you sending out a spiritual message and trusting that through the operation of the universal consciousness the call of my heart would reach you across lands and seas. I wished to thank you and to ask you for help that I might make the better speed out of the Valley of Search into the Valley of Love. I am not impatient; not a bit! I am quite willing to travel for the hundred thousand years,[1] – but I am hungry and empty!

I lived in America for nearly 13 years, working at first as a missionary in Utah; then I became connected with an ethical movement called The Great

---

[1] *The steed of this Valley is patience; without patience the wayfarer on this journey will reach nowhere and attain no goal. Nor should he ever be downhearted; if he strive for a hundred thousand years and yet fail to behold the beauty of the Friend, he should not falter.* Bahá'u'lláh, The Valley of Search from *The Seven Valleys*.

Work, abandoned the ministry for it, believing it better and more sincere than the Church, and became at once involved in all sorts of hardships including neuritis which afflicted eyes and arms so that I could neither read nor write. But I never for an instant regretted what I had done, and in spite of my handicaps I held a professorship of English in the University of the South, Tennessee. In the spring of 1916 a remarkable spiritual intimation came to me, without sight or sound or any appeal to the senses, but overwhelming in its power, of a complete change at hand: something happy and wonderful but otherwise quite indefinite. In June 1916 I learned in one moment the Movement for which I had done so much was based on fraud. I came home to my people in Ireland, returned to the ministry of the Church I was born and bred in; and then in the winter of 1916 I was brought into touch with Bahaism by an American friend, Miss Louise Finley, of Sewanee, Tennessee, (herself not a believer – as yet).

From that hour to this I have read and studied the Bahai books and used the Bahai prayers, and found there a light and exaltation and spirit of triumph which fill me with joy and enthral me and carry me on to seek and seek. Every morning now I rise early to give the first hour of the day, the most precious of all, to prayer and meditation. The consciousness of the Great Presence has already begun to dawn on me and I live now in a new world, awestruck, wondering, humble and uplifted, and wishing eternally for more light in my darkness and more strength in my weakness. I have recently married and my wife by her example is the best as well as the dearest of my near-by teachers. I never was so happy – I never was happy at all, but I will be happier yet! I want so much to win out of the thraldom of self and error and this blindness and ignorance. I am able to read and write again, and I read nothing but the work of regenerate souls, Bahai writings and the Bible and Tagore: I could learn little from others as ignorant as I! Help me a little if you have time to remember the least of all strugglers. And let my last word be – from my heart and soul all *thanks* and *blessing!*

Yours
George Townshend

It is at once apparent that at this time he had no idea of the station of 'Abdu'l-Bahá. Although enthralled by the Bahá'í message he is still the seeker, and his letter is written in companionable terms to one whom he recognizes as a great spiritual leader and far along on the Path. The address and signature are the normal ones between friends. Perhaps the inexpressible hope, the excitement that must be subdued lest he be disappointed a third time, may be sensed in his appeal for help. But he must be wary. His instant, heart-in-mouth intimation on receiving the pamphlets had not been disappointed by deep and persistent study, meditation and prayer. Could this be, really be, attainment at last? He *must* be wary. But he must know. At all costs he must know!

The semi-humorous reference to his willingness 'to travel for the hundred thousand years', followed by '. . . I am hungry and empty', would not have concealed from 'Abdu'l-Bahá his passionate longing for truth.

He received his answer six weeks later, with a translation made by 'Shoghi Rabbani, Bahjeh, Acca, Palestine. July 24th, 1919', the future Guardian of the Bahá'í Faith.

> To his honor Mr. George Townshend, Galway, Ireland:
> Upon him be greeting and praise.
>
> ### He is God.
>
> O Thou who art thirsty for the Fountain of Truth!
> Thy letter was received and the account of thy life has been known. Praise be to God thou hast ever, like unto the nightingale, sought the Divine rose-garden and like unto the verdure of the Meadow yearned for the out-pourings of the cloud of guidance. That is why thou hast been transferred from one condition to another until ultimately thou hast attained unto the fountain of Truth, hast illumined thy sight, hast revived and animated thy heart, hast chanted the verses of guidance and hast turned thy face toward the enkindled fire on the Mount of Sinai.
> At present, I pray on thy behalf that the fire of love be set aglow in thy heart and spiritual sensations may stir and move thy soul, so that thou mayest be quickened, mayest fly and soar toward the Ideal Friend, mayest sacrifice thy soul to the Beloved of the World and consecrate thy life to the diffusion of the Divine Fragrances. If thou attainest unto such a bounty thou shalt become the sign of guidance, shalt become an enkindled candle in the gathering of men, shalt be baptized with the spirit of life and the fire of the Love of God, shalt be born again from the world of nature and shalt attain unto everlasting life.
> Upon thee be Baha'il Abha.
> (Sgd.) abdul Baha abbas

Such a reply, to such an appeal, is beyond comment. Our best course, as so often when faced with the ineffable, is to be as matter-of-fact as possible. Let us then first consider the address: it is significant for future developments. 'O Thou who art thirsty for the Fountain of Truth!'

George had not yet confessed his faith in Bahá'u'lláh. In his early forties, he had just emerged from a long-extended period of restlessness, adventure and persistent search. That period ended when he began his determined examination of the Bahá'í Faith, married and settled down in a remote part of the British Isles, ideal for his middle years of contemplation, study, literary work and preparation for the final heroism.

Note what the Master[1] says about his early life: *That is why thou hast*

---

[1] 'Abdu'l-Bahá. This title, in Persian, Áqá, was conferred on Him by Bahá'u'lláh.

been transferred from one condition to another until ultimately thou hast attained unto the fountain of Truth, hast illumined thy sight, hast revived and animated thy heart, hast chanted the verses of guidance and hast turned thy face toward the enkindled fire on the Mount of Sinai.

The call to the Bar, the journalism, the repair to the wide open spaces, ordination, missionary work, the teaching of English literature, none could satisfy the heart's perpetual hunger for Truth, until once more in the Ireland of the turn of the century – that same Ireland which had been too narrow a field for his wide-ranging search – at a moment of frustration and disaster he *attained unto the fountain of Truth.*

The transferring from one condition to another was the means of ultimate attainment. The reason for that attainment was that *Praise be to God thou hast ever, like unto the nightingale, sought the Divine rose-garden and like unto the verdure of the meadow yearned for the out-pourings of the cloud of guidance. That is why thou hast been transferred* . . .

Thus the Master's exposition of George Townshend's progress! Now, perhaps the most weighty, significant and crucial portion of the Tablet. Here is an illumined soul, of great spiritual quality, who has traversed the Valley of Search. The Master wants him to continue the journey, to enter the Valley of Love and complete the course:[1] *At present,* (note the decision has not yet been made) *I pray on thy behalf that the fire of love be set aglow in thy heart and spiritual sensations may stir and move thy soul, so that thou mayest be quickened, mayest fly and soar toward the Ideal Friend, mayest sacrifice thy soul to the Beloved of the World and consecrate thy life to the diffusion of the Divine Fragrances.*

This was 'Abdu'l-Bahá's hope for him, and He opened before his eyes a vision of such glory, should he attain, as would satisfy to overflowing this passionate seeker's longing.

If thou attainest unto such a bounty thou shalt become the sign of guidance, shalt become an enkindled candle in the gathering of men, shalt be baptized with the spirit of life and the fire of the Love of God, shalt be born again from the world of nature and shalt attain unto everlasting life.

The promised rewards of sacrifice and consecration are described in terms which would have the utmost significance for George. No wonder that later, in the time of his attainment, he was to cry out 'Now the very gates of heaven are flung open and its treasures poured forth.'

In such a 'jewelled utterance' as this Tablet there are lessons for us

---

[1] In *The Seven Valleys* Bahá'u'lláh describes the traveller who completes the Valley of Search and '*shall straightway step into the Valley of Love and be dissolved in the fire of love. In this city the heaven of ecstasy is upraised and the world-illuming sun of yearning shineth, and the fire of love is ablaze . . .*'

THE TWO TABLETS FROM
'ABDU'L-BAHÁ

14. The first Tablet, translated by Shoghi Effendi, Bahjí, July 24, 1919. See page 47.

هوالله

ای شخص منور لاهوتی وذات محترم ملکوتی نامه شما رسید جمیع کلمات دلالت بر ترقی روحانی و انبعاثات وجدانی بود این احساسات ملکوتی شما قوه جاذبه ایست که جاذب تأییدات ملکوت از راست وابواب حقائق و معانی بر شما باز خواهد نمود و تأییدات ملکوت از خواهر سیه قلب انسان مانند آشیانه ایست و تعالیم حضرت بهاءالله مانند مرغ خوش الحان البته از این لانه آهنگ ملکوت بکوشها میرسد و نفوس را احساسات ملکوتی می بخشد و ارواح را زنده میکند امید وارم که کلیسای شما در ظل اورشلیم آسمانی درآید سستی اعضا جسمانی مضری ندارد اگرچه روح بر قوت است چنانچه حضرت مسیح میفرماید که تن ناتوان و محزون ولکن روح در بشارت کبری است پس بدان بهین روح جسم نیز تقویت گردد مطمئن باش که در ظل الطاف حضرت بهاءالله پی به خبر عزیز حرم محترمه و سایر خاندان از قبل من نهایت تحیت و احترام برسانید و علیک البهاء الابهی

دسمبر ۱۹۲۰

abdul baha abbas

حضرت قبیس جورج نوزلند قیس کلیسای ابرلندا علیها بهاءالله الابهی

15. *The second Tablet, translated by Lutfu'lláh
Ḥakím, Haifa, December 19, 1920. See page 50*

ایرلاند

جناب جورج تاونشند علیه البهآء والثنآء

Mr.   George   Townshend.

The Rectory, Ahaseragh, Co.

Galway, Ireland.

۹

حضرت قبس جورج نوزبلد قسیس کلیسای ایرلندا علیه بهآء اللـه الأبهی

His honour Rev. George Townshend,   Ireland.

Unto him be Baha'Ullah-el Abha!

16. Envelopes in which the two Tablets were enclosed; the first one is at the top

all. Note the emphasis on 'search' and 'yearning'. Attainment is mentioned three times: once in respect of what he has done, . . . *ultimately thou hast attained,* and twice in respect of the future; conditionally, *If thou attainest unto such a bounty* . . . and resultantly . . . *shalt attain unto everlasting life.* The seeker must make the first move. Bahá'u'lláh, in *Hidden Words,* confirms this teaching of Christ's: *O Son of Being! Love Me, that I may love thee. If thou lovest Me not, My love can in no wise reach thee.*[1] We must seek to find, and knock to have it opened to us.[2]

A few months after receipt of this Tablet, George sent his declaration of faith to 'Abdu'l-Bahá in the form of a poem, which he later published under the title *Recognition*:

Hail to Thee, Scion of Glory, Whose utterance poureth abroad
The joy of the heavenly knowledge and the light of the greatest of days!
Poet of mysteries chanting in rapture the beauty of God,
    Unto Thee be thanksgiving and praise!

Child of the darkness that wandered in gloom but dreamed of the light,
Lo! I have seen Thy splendour ablaze in the heavens afar
Showering gladness and glory and shattering the shadows of night,
    And see no other star.

Thy words are to me as fragrances borne from the garden of heaven,
Beams of a lamp that is hid in the height of a holier world,
Arrows of fire that pierce and destroy with the might of the levin
    Into our midnight hurled.

Sword of the Father! None other can rend the dark veil from my eyes,
None other can beat from my limbs with the shearing blade of God's
    might
The sins I am fettered withal and give me the power to rise
    And come forth to the fullness of light.

Lo! Thou hast breathed on my sorrow the sweetness of faith and of
    hope,
Thou hast chanted high paeans of joy that my heart's echoes ever repeat
And the path to the knowledge of God begins to glimmer and ope
    Before my faltering feet.

Weak and unworthy my praise. Yet, as from its throbbing throat
Some lone bird pours its song to the flaming infinite sky,
So unto Thee in the zenith I lift from a depth remote
    This broken human cry.

[1] Bahá'u'lláh, *Hidden Words*, No. 5 (Arabic)
[2] cf. Matt. 7:7; Luke 11:9

'Abdu'l-Bahá's reply was written on December 19, 1920, and translated by Luṭfu'lláh Ḥakím:

> *His honour Rev. George Townshend, Ireland:*
>
> *Unto him be Baha'u'llah-el Abha!*
>
> *He is God!*
>
> *O Thou illumined heavenly soul and revered personage in the Kingdom!*
> *Thy letter*[1] *has been received. Every word indicated the progress and upliftment of thy spirit and conscience. These heavenly susceptibilities of thine form a magnet which attracts the confirmation of the Kingdom of God; and so the doors of realities and meanings will be open unto thee, and the confirmations of the Kingdom of God will envelop thee.*
>
> *The heart of man is like unto a nest, and the Teachings of His Holiness Baha'u'llah like unto a sweet singing bird. Unquestionably from this nest the melody of the Kingdom will be transmitted to the ears, bestowing heavenly susceptibilities upon the souls and quickening upon the spirits.*
>
> *It is my hope that thy church will come under the Heavenly Jerusalem.*
>
> *Do not mind the weakness of thy physical limbs! Praise be to God thy spirit is full of vigour. His Holiness Christ says that the body is weak and grieved, but the spirit is in the greatest joy. Then know thou that through this very spirit thy body will be strengthened! Be assured thou art under the favours of His Holiness Baha'u'llah!*
>
> *Convey on my behalf greeting and respect to my dear daughter thy revered wife, and other members of thy family.*[2]
> *Unto thee be the Glory of Abha!*
> *(Sgd.) abdul Baha abbas*

How are we, who are we, to comment on such an outpouring of divine love and praise? Its contemplation overwhelms us, as it must have done George! Yet, to our own advantage and certainly to our greater understanding of his life, we may, like him, approach it – as

---

[1] There is a point here not quite clear. 'Abdu'l-Bahá's reply mentions '*Thy letter . . .*' The brief curriculum vitae which George signed after his appointment in 1951 as a Hand of the Cause of God, reads '. . . 'Abdu'l-Bahá wrote him a second letter acknowledging a declaration of faith written in verse which had been sent to Him a little earlier.' No accompanying letter can be traced, either in the Bahá'í Archives at the World Centre or in those of the National Spiritual Assemblies of Ireland or the United Kingdom. Yet the poem makes no mention of his wife or of physical disability, both of which are commented upon in the Master's second Tablet. However, George mentioned both in his letter of June 10, 1919.

[2] A nice anecdote arose from this translation. Luṭfu'lláh Ḥakím rendered the last paragraph, '*Convey on my behalf greeting and respect to dear daughter, thy revered wife, and other members of thy family.*' Una would not be born for another four months (April 1921), and George was delighted with what he saw as the Master's prescience. When relating the story he would add, 'And she is very spiritual'. The correction was not made until now (for this book) and George was never disillusioned of his happy thought.

dispassionately as may be – for an indication of 'Abdu'l-Bahá's estimation of him, His promises to him, His hopes for him and His gifts to him.

Compare the Master's address in this Tablet, to that in the first one where the seeker is addressed, *O Thou who art thirsty for the Fountain of Truth!* Now to the declared disciple He writes, *O Thou illumined heavenly soul and revered personage in the Kingdom!* Can we not hear in this the Master's joy that His prayer for George was answered, a note of His pride in George himself as well as the loving statement of his exalted station in the Abhá Kingdom. Already the heavenly quality was there, perceived by the Master, though not yet fully proven by the years.

'Abdu'l-Bahá twice refers to his *heavenly susceptibilities* and clearly states that they *form a magnet which attracts the confirmation of the Kingdom of God*. And so he is promised, as an inevitable result of his own striving, *(the progress and upliftment of thy spirit and conscience – These heavenly susceptibilities)* that *the doors of realities and meanings will be open unto thee, and the confirmations of the Kingdom of God will envelop thee*. A single perusal of any of his works will disclose the fulfilment of the first promise, and his life testifies to that of the second. As the years went by, believers from all over the world wrote to him asking questions about the meaning of scripture; National Spiritual Assemblies asked him for articles which they could publish to enlighten the understanding of the friends in their care, and the Guardian of the Faith sought his help and advice and recommended his writings to the constant study of Bahá'ís. A few weeks before his passing, George said that the last few years had been the most difficult but the most wonderful, for confirmations had surrounded him.

The second paragraph of 'Abdu'l-Bahá's letter is both a gift and a promise. The gift is knowledge, conveyed as by a loving father to a favourite son, and the implied promise is that use of this knowledge would enable him to bestow *heavenly susceptibilities* (note the phrase again) *upon the souls and quickening upon the spirits*.

It is my hope that thy church will come under the Heavenly Jerusalem. This central, single sentence of the third paragraph, at the heart of the Tablet, immediately became George's charter of action, which he followed relentlessly for twenty-five years. This long chapter in his life is dealt with later.

Now comes the loving cheer and advice about his physical weakness. *Praise be to God thy spirit is full of vigour . . . through this very spirit thy body will be strengthened!* And then – how the Master loved him! – *Be assured thou art under the favours of . . . Baha'u'llah!* This assurance, as we shall see, was to be a solace and comfort to George in the darkest and most perplexing days of his life, and a bulwark against frustration and defeat.

George copied out both Tablets in his own hand and doubtless committed them to memory, for although he seldom referred to his receipt of them he could, in speech or writing, quote from them immediately. We have no record of his immediate reaction to the second Tablet, and can only surmise the overflowing joy, humility and gratitude which must have suffused his soul.

On November 16, 1921, he wrote his 'Surrender, the cry for Deliverance' and noted that it was 'posted next day', which the envelope confirms.

> To 'Abdu'l-Bahá,
>   Haifa, Palestine.
>
> O Holy One who dwellest in the remote heaven and heaven of heavens!
> Master of the will of the world, Director of Destiny,
> The One Hope of all Humanity,
> My Desired One, the Conqueror of my Heart, Teacher and Guide!
> As the dark earth moves into the light of the sun,
> as Error turns to Truth, Ignorance to Knowledge, weakness to strength,
> so do I now address myself to thee.
>
> The Truth which thou hast spoken has enveloped and consumed me. I have no thought nor hope nor longing other than this.
> It illumines the Past, makes clear the Present, bestows hope for the Future. Where the rays of this Sun fall, there is Beauty and Love, Wisdom and Gladness; beyond lies a wilderness, a desert, the haunt of despair, horrible, detestable.
>
> To the Truth which thou dost reveal, to the divine Love which thou dost dispense, to the Hidden Mystery which is in thy keeping, I offer and resign myself wholly and utterly, to be its witness, its soldier, its thrall, seeking nothing else, knowing nothing else, though deserving nothing here or hereafter.
>
> Freely, willingly, with a song of exultation in my heart and blessings on my lips, I make this surrender. I cannot live nor exist and do otherwise than thus yield myself. That from which I flee is no longer tolerable. That to which I turn is the reality, the inborn Truth of all men and of the world as of me.
>
> My submission has to be. It is part of the nature of things, of the order of the Universe. Aught less would be misery and death.
>
> Of earthly perplexities I say nothing. I cannot tell what may be my field of labour or the manner of my witness – whether I am to remain as I now am seeking to find and to proclaim the veritable Christ or to chant in fuller tones the Day of God from some unfaded Tree.
>
> This one thing I ask: that I may have the wisdom to understand and the firmness to obey implicitly the command of God.
>
> A creature of Time, a child of Error, helpless and impotent, I bow

before thee and the Eternal Truth which shines through thee and here commit myself utterly and for ever to the good pleasure of God.

That mercy which I crave for myself I crave for those too whom the bounty of God has given me, my wife, my little son, my little daughter.

Praise and thanksgiving be unto thee, O mighty glorious inscrutable Lord of Forgiveness and Love, Who hast guided the feet of this wanderer to the highway of the Kingdom.

Thy Servant and Suppliant
George Townshend

It was sent by registered post, addressed to Sir 'Abdu'l-Bahá 'Abbás. The Haifa Post Office stamp reads '8 Dec 21'. 'Abdu'l-Bahá ascended on November 28, 1921.

Chapter 6

RELATIONSHIP WITH
THE GUARDIAN

OBSERVERS of the growth of the Bahá'í Faith in the early years of its
Formative Age have commented, wondering at the ways of God, on
the hardships with which this infant organism had to struggle. The
Heroic Age over, the Revelation delivered, the martyrs offered up in
their thousands, the Covenant established, it would seem that growth
should have been rapid and irresistible, like new verdure in spring. But
the fertilizer of man's spiritual progress has ever been sacrifice and the
foundations of God's Kingdom on earth must go deep into rock. The
young, heroic Guardian, who presided over the opening and the
evolutionary development of the Formative Age, had first to maintain
the unity of the Faith against those members of Bahá'u'lláh's family
who thought that 'Abdu'l-Bahá should have placed the reins of
authority in *their* hands, then to explain to the scattered community of
Bahá'ís what the Revelation meant, then to train it in Bahá'í theology,
principles and administrative procedures. He succeeded in all these
and every other task and finally launched a unified, organized,
spiritually elevated world community on a triumphant world crusade.
He died as the tide of his success was beginning to flow, exhausted by
the never-ending herculean labours of his office, a sacrifice to the
development of the Cause of God.

Throughout his ministry he was grossly short of staff, unable to lay
the burdens of the growing Cause on the slender shoulders of newly-
formed and undeveloped administrative bodies, deprived of expert
help in many fields where he could have put it to the service of the
Faith. And yet whenever a need was absolutely essential, it was met.
Thus, when he needed a lawyer of distinction to present the Bahá'í
claims to Bahá'u''lláh's house in Ba<u>gh</u>dád to the League of Nations

Commission, he could send Mountfort Mills. When he needed a spiritually refined and dedicated architect to undertake the supreme task of designing and raising the exterior of the Shrine of the Báb, his father-in-law, Sutherland Maxwell, sometime President of the Royal Architectural Institute of Canada and Vice-President of the Royal Canadian Academy, was available. His need for a professional literary authority with the spiritual perception to understand his own work, was filled by George Townshend.

George's first contact with Shoghi Effendi was in 'Abdu'l-Bahá's lifetime, when the Master's Tablet beginning '*O Thou who art thirsty for the Fountain of Truth*' was translated by the future Guardian. It is dated July 24, 1919. After that the first letter we have is from George to Shoghi Effendi, dated October 16, 1925, but it refers to a letter from the Guardian of March 1923 'written on your behalf by M. Dreyfus-Barney'. It is inconceivable that George would not have written to the Guardian immediately after the ascension of 'Abdu'l-Bahá in November 1921 and the reading of the Will and Testament proclaiming Shoghi Effendi Guardian of the Cause of God, but alas there is no trace of the correspondence before George's letter of October 16, 1925, except a reference in his letter of November 22, 1944 to 'the loyalty I offered long ago as soon as ever I heard of your being the Guardian of the Cause'.

The whole correspondence is a study in itself. The folio contains 147 letters from Shoghi Effendi to George and four to the Townshend family, more than two hundred from George to Shoghi Effendi, and a few cables. They cover the years 1925 to 1957. Thirty-five of them are simply recording dispatch, or acknowledgement, of typescripts. In addition a number are referred to but not yet discovered.

Four outstanding features dominate this remarkable exchange. First the enormous amount of work which George did for the Guardian; second the very high regard in which the Guardian held not only George's literary ability, general judgement and scholarship, but George himself; third the development of the relationship between the two men; and fourth the revelation of George's character and spiritual progress.

George's literary services to the Guardian began with his letter of February 27, 1926, which reads:

> I have been told that you invited Miss Rosenberg[1] to Haifa to help in translating work, though (as I believe) she knows little or no Persian. I am

[1] One of the first English believers. She became a Bahá'í in 1899 and made extended visits to both 'Abdu'l-Bahá and the Guardian, assisting in the transcribing of the Scriptures into English. (See *The Bahá'í World* vol. IV, p. 263; also *A Compendium of Volumes I–XII of the Bahá'í World*, p. 466, compiled by Roger White.)

encouraged by this to offer now my services, such as they are, in this kind
of work. Having myself no knowledge of Persian and being a clergyman
resident in Ireland, my help can not be anything better than advice as to
English idiom and grammatical structure.

It is a shame that we English people should leave the translating into our
language to one whose native tongue is not ours. And I want to
acknowledge my deep gratitude to those orientals who have made
intelligible to us these priceless divine writings. I offer all I have to offer in
this way, slight as it is.

My thought is that the proposed English rendering of certain passages,
when not judged quite satisfactory, might be sent to me for suggestions as
to usage, etc.

There should really be a committee for this revision, for one man's
judgment is not enough.

I believe some such work as I speak of – by whomsoever it is done – is of
great importance, chiefly for clearness and correctness in the rendering but
also for the dignity of the Cause. Great developments and (I fear) fierce
denunciations are doubtless not far away and good translations will help in
every way.

I will give a few illustrations to show my reasons for thinking this work
of value.

Throughout all the published translations there recurs the difficulty of
our English possessive (the subjective and the objective). For instance in
the Prayer of Healing (*Hidden Words*, p. 90)[1] 'Thy remembrance' – this has
a strange sound in any case; its natural meaning is 'the remembrance Thou
hast of me'; by a rare and forced use it may mean 'my remembrance of
Thee'. Personally I used it in the first sense for two years, and thereafter for
seven years in the last sense.

The reader can only judge by the context as to the meaning, in such
cases. This confusion can only be avoided by some literary device; it is due
to an inherent fault in our language. It recurs in such phrases as 'Thy
nearness' which means 'Your nearness to me' rather than 'mine to you',
'Thy love', 'the love of God', and so on . . .

You will think me a crank on these details! So I am! I like language and
have had some experience as a journalist and a professor, but I am not a
grammarian at all.

Shoghi Effendi's immediate reaction, expressed in his letter of
March 28, was a warm welcome 'as a dear fellow worker' and the
sending of the first part of his translation of *Hidden Words* for editing.
The Guardian's own note reads:

I wish to add personally a few words and assure you of my deep and

---

[1] An early publication (1923) of the Bahai Assembly, London, was entitled *Hidden
Words, Words of Wisdom and Communes*. In addition to the *Hidden Words* of Bahá'u'lláh
it contained a number of 'Supplications' and 'Communes'. This is certainly the book
referred to by George, and contains on its page 90 the 'Prayer of Healing', which is
reproduced, next to the Guardian's translation, on page 58.

heartfelt admiration of your valuable help and suggestion. I am hoping
that the enclosed rendering will meet with your approval. Please alter and
revise it with all freedom, for I have a great appreciation of your literary
taste and attainments. I wish to assure you also of my prayers for you and
your dear family that the blessings of the Almighty may ever surround
you.

George returned the translations with his comments on April 21 and
received the Guardian's reply of May 1 with this personal note:

> I deeply appreciate your most valuable suggestions and am glad to learn
> that you will continue in the days to come to collaborate with me in such
> an important, arduous and delicate task. I am taking the liberty of
> forwarding to you some of my recent translations and if you feel that you
> would like to reshape and reconstruct the whole sentence or bring about a
> fundamental change in the expression of the thought in some passages,
> please do not hesitate. I would greatly value your opinion as to the
> standard of English represented by these recent renderings and would
> appreciate your detailed comment, criticism and suggestion.

There followed what must surely be extremely rare, if not unique,
in Bahá'í history, a personal letter from the Guardian, written entirely
by his own hand on a simple sheet of plain paper, informally and
without mediumship of secretary. The letter is dated July 28, 1926.

> My dear fellow-worker:
> I am deeply grateful to you for the very valuable, detailed and careful
> suggestions you have given me in connection with my recent translations
> of Bahá'í writings. As I have already intimated your excellent judgement,
> your literary ability and your keen sympathy and devoted care in revising
> and altering various passages which I have rendered into English are
> deeply appreciated by me and I shall make use of your suggestions in any
> future publication of these translations.
> I hope to send you some more in future and I trust that their
> consideration will not add unduly to your occupation nor prove
> inconvenient and burdensome.
> I am considering ways and means for a better method of collaboration
> and consultation in this important field of work, and I trust that if my plans
> will materialize you will be enabled to lend close and effective assistance.
> With kind regards and best wishes,
> I am your grateful brother,
> Shoghi

The work on *Hidden Words* went ahead, and finally, on March 7,
1927 George returned the last pages to Haifa, with

> . . . my suggested rewording and M. Dreyfus-Barney's correction of my
> Ms. together with a very few notes on questions raised by him.
> I have done my utmost.

I hope fervently that the result of all this combined effort may be as little unworthy as possible of the great opportunity and that the British public will now note and acclaim this exalting and unparalleled monument of religious and literary genius.

The acknowledgement was dated March 18 and was written by Miss Ethel Rosenberg, who had explained in a previous letter 'what we have been doing – comparing your suggestions word by word with the original text – and whenever possible accepting your emendations'. She is to take the revised text back to London for publication by the National Spiritual Assembly and states that 'He has also put on the title page (after his name) "and revised with the Assistance of G. Townshend and E. J. Rosenberg."' The Guardian's appended personal note was:

My dear and valued co-worker:
    I am glad to inform you that at last I have managed to devote the necessary time to the consideration of your splendid suggestions in connexion with the revision of the Hidden Words. Miss Rosenberg and myself (I wish you were with us also!) have carefully altered the text in the light of your suggestions and I trust that it will soon be published in London. The assistance you and Miss Rosenberg have rendered will be acknowledged and I wish to thank you from the bottom of my heart for your unique and invaluable collaboration.

The reason why George's and Miss Rosenberg's names do not, after all, appear on the title page is dealt with in Chapter 8.

Bahá'ís must for ever be grateful to George for his submission to the Guardian of the inadequacy of the English possessive case and its particular illustrations in the prayer cited below. The new translation which the Guardian shortly produced has made this prayer, revealed by Bahá'u'lláh, one of the best loved, most memorized and widely used in the vast treasury of Bahá'í prayers. The reality of George's collaboration with the Guardian is seen by placing an earlier version side by side with Shoghi Effendi's simple and clear rendition:

1923 version	Shoghi Effendi's translation
O my God! Thy name is my healing, Thy remembrance is my remedy, Thy nearness is my hope, Thy love is my joyous companion, and Thy mercy is my healer in this world and in all the world. Thou art the Giver, the Knower, the Wise!	Thy name is my healing, O my God, and remembrance of Thee is my remedy. Nearness to Thee is my hope, and love for Thee is my companion. Thy mercy to me is my healing and my succour in both this world and the world to come. Thou, verily, art the All-Bountiful, the All-Knowing, the All-Wise.

This 'unique and invaluable collaboration', so auspiciously begun with *Hidden Words*, would continue for the next eighteen years and apply to the vast majority of the Guardian's prodigious output in English. The record shows that every translation made by Shoghi Effendi from the original Persian or Arabic which is known to us was sent to George for review and editing. In addition, the Guardian's monumental history of the first hundred years of the Bahá'í Faith,[1] and his challenging essay on the disruption of the old order and the advent of the World Order of Bahá'u'lláh[2] were both sent in typescript for the same purpose. These huge and delicate tasks were by no means George's only contribution. He wrote the Introductions to *The Dawn-Breakers* and to *God Passes By*, for both of which he chose the titles at the Guardian's behest. He wrote the essay presented to the World Congress of Faiths in 1936 on behalf of the Guardian (see page 125); he wrote, at the Guardian's specific request, essays for separate volumes of *The Bahá'í World*; he made selections of poetry for it; he gave his advice, on request, as to the wisdom, timeliness of publication and literary standard of the Guardian's compilation of *Prayers and Meditations by Bahá'u'lláh*. Most touching, and perhaps most revealing, was Shoghi Effendi's request to George to suggest the epitaph for inscription on the monument of Bahíyyih Khánum, the Greatest Holy Leaf, Bahá'u'lláh's daughter and the greatest woman of the Bahá'í dispensation. The Guardian's memorial to her is a paean of love and gratitude, praise and admiration. His secretary's letter to George of August 25, 1932, indicates that a copy of that tribute had been sent to George and describes plans

> for the erection of a befitting monument above her grave which is situated on an eminence, in the vicinity of the Holy Shrine on Mount Carmel, facing Bahjí and overlooking the beautiful bay of 'Akká. The monument will be all in marble and will be surrounded by lawns and gardens the arrangement of which Shoghi Effendi will personally supervise.
>
> The selection of a proper epitaph is such an important matter that he feels urged to turn to you for assistance, realizing full well your peculiar gift of suggesting a few befitting statements that would be at once original, forceful and dignified.
>
> . . . The Guardian would wish you to send him as many specimens as you can, each of about ten or fifteen words or less. He will then choose what he believes to be the most appropriate.

It seems that George's part in this project was not implemented, for the inscription, in gold letters, on the beautiful monument above the grave of Bahíyyih Khánum is in Persian, the first verse of a Tablet

[1] *God Passes By*
[2] *The Unfoldment of World Civilization*

revealed by Bahá'u'lláh to His daughter. George would not have known of this Tablet and it would seem that the Guardian himself discovered it in the course of research on her life. The point for us is that Shoghi Effendi turned to George for assistance in so delicate and subjective a task.

The sum total of these specific tasks is astonishing and all was done in the midst of his professional duties and while he was writing his own major works.[1] He reviewed and edited the Guardian's translations of *Hidden Words* (1926–7); *Kitáb-i-Íqán* (January–May 1930); *The Dawn-Breakers* (1930–31); *Gleanings from the Writings of Bahá'u'lláh* (December 1934–May 1935); *Prayers and Meditations by Bahá'u'lláh* (1937); *Epistle to the Son of the Wolf* (April 1940); and the monumental original work *God Passes By* (February 1943–April 1944).

For those who have never made the attempt it must be hard to visualize the difficulties of putting into idiomatic English, translations from languages so alien to it as Arabic and Persian. And when the original Persian or Arabic is that of Bahá'u'lláh the difficulties become almost insuperable. The Hand of the Cause 'Alí-Akbar Furútan, who for twenty-four years was secretary of the National Spiritual Assembly of the Bahá'ís of Írán , kindly contributed the following to this subject:

> Bahá'u'lláh employed both Persian and Arabic; He referred to the former as the luminous and the latter as the eloquent tongue. In both, His Revelation was clothed in words and concepts of such exalted spirituality that even the greatest scholars, native to both languages and steeped in the literary forms and conventions of their immense literatures, were confounded by Bahá'u'lláh's literary invention, exaltation and style. In Shoghi Effendi's translations we have not only good literary English but the authorized interpretation of the Guardian of the Faith.[2]

George himself had written in 1926: 'The Anglicisation of any language but more especially of an oriental language is a delicate and subtle business.'

English-speaking people are for ever fortunate that the Guardian of the Bahá'í Faith grew up with Persian and Arabic as his natural languages. From an early age he studied English in order to be of service to 'Abdu'l-Bahá,[3] Who in His wisdom sent the future Guardian

---

[1] See Ch. 13, 'The Writer'.

[2] A unique feature of the Bahá'í Faith is the protection of its Scripture from unauthorized interpretation – the source of schism. According to the sacred text only 'Abdu'l-Bahá and the Guardian were allowed to 'interpret' the revealed Word – in the sense of saying what it intends.

[3] See *The Priceless Pearl* by Rúḥíyyih Rabbani, pp. 30, 37; Bahá'í Publishing Trust, London 1969.

to Balliol College, Oxford, where he immersed himself in the great works of the language and began the shaping of his own mastery of it which was to blossom with such vigour and splendour during the years of his ministry. Like the Guardian,[1] George's love was English, but it was his native tongue, which he used with superb artistry.

We have already seen the Guardian's instant response to George's modestly phrased offer of February 27, 1926. That Shoghi Effendi appreciated the inadequacy of existing translations (which ranged from bizarre to banal) and the need for a board to undertake the work is clear from the secretary's part of his letter:

> It must have been very distasteful to you to read some of the offhand and ungrammatical translations that more out of necessity than choice won circulation and were even published. Furthermore, it was always the expressed wish and desire of 'Abdu'l-Bahá to have proper and adequate translations that would not only convey the true spirit of the original but also possess some literary merit. And for this he emphasized the necessity of a board of translators. Such a board it has unfortunately been impossible to form as yet.

George continued the discussion in a letter of April 21, 1926:

> I write to thank you warmly for your note and your message through Soheil Afnan and also for your great kindness in granting me the great privilege of working over your rendering of some [of] the sacred texts.
>
> This small work I have now done to the best of my ability and with the greatest delight. As regards English idiom and usage, structure and vocabulary, I have used – as you said – the greatest freedom; but I regard the changes suggested as conservative though dependent on personal judgment. That emendations might not seem arbitrary I have often appended an explanation of my reasons.

The Guardian's secretary assured him 'of Shoghi Effendi's earnest prayers for your success and of his sanguine hopes that you will in future render great and valuable services to our dear Cause. The translations that have been published in the past, in some cases especially, lamentably lack the final touches of capable students both in Persian and English, and it is along this line that Shoghi Effendi trusts you will be able to help the promotion and progress of the Bahá'í Movement.'

Towards the end of 1929 George made definite proposals about the organization of translations, acknowledged by the Guardian's secretary on December 12 of that year:

> The conception itself is so timely and important that it could not be improved upon, but its execution is bound to meet with certain

[1] ibid. p. 37

difficulties, especially when you remember that those who could attempt such a difficult and delicate task as translation, whether in the East or the West, are not only very few but are separated from one another by miles and miles. The Guardian will still make an attempt to get some sort of a body get to work as soon as possible.

The Guardian quickly realized that he had found in George a loyal servant, not only of great capacity, but one whose mind and heart responded with his own to Bahá'u'lláh's Writings. When returning the last pages of typescript of *Hidden Words* George had written: 'There is a note, a music, a voice in the Writings of Bahá'u'lláh, even in translations, which never was heard in English literature before and which has such power that it seems to shake the air as one reads. If other proof were lacking, this Mighty Voice would be proof enough. Literary people all must feel it.'

He strikes the same note much later in a letter to Nellie Roche:

> The vibrations of Bahá'u'lláh's writings are so intense they shiver me with an exaltation and a power I can hardly stand: like standing out in a great storm with the winds roaring and the waves raging and the trees shrieking and crashing and the whole scene uplifting one with its tremendous power and energy and beauty till one is transported and feels part of the titanic drama. I think men will have to develop a lot before they can react rhythmically to Bahá'u'lláh's writings: perhaps we are not meant to – the Infinite has come among us nearer than ever before and we are stunned by its Presence.

The writing of the Introductions to Shoghi Effendi's translation of Nabíl's Narrative, *The Dawn-Breakers*, and to *God Passes By*, entailed the closest detailed collaboration between the Guardian and George. The literary value of these two essays is dealt with in Chapter 13, but the consultation and marvellous, swift, effective co-operation, revealed in the correspondence, is highly pertinent to our present theme.

The first mention to George of Nabíl is in a letter of April 17, 1930 from Shoghi Effendi's secretary, while George was completing his review of the final pages of *Kitáb-i-Íqán*:

> As to the 'Íghan', Shoghi Effendi is very grateful for your kind assistance. He is now working on the translation into English of Nabil's history. This is the most extensive, detailed and interesting history of the Cause still in M.S. form and as the author, a Bahá'í poet translated by E. G. Browne, was in close association with Mirza Musa, Bahá'u'lláh's only true brother, it carries a good deal of authority also. Shoghi Effendi would be grateful if you would go over his translation of Nabil and make suggestions and alterations like the 'Íghan'. Of course in this case you need not be as literal as with sacred writings. Shoghi Effendi wishes me also to suggest to you

that with your desire to write Bahá'í plays and tableaus you had better wait for this translation, for in it you will find an embarrassing wealth of material for what you have in mind. I am sure you will find his history quite interesting, as the author was a man of great imagination.

Throughout May, June, July, August and September the Guardian sent 'consignments of the typescript', a hundred or more pages at a time. The covering note of September 20, 1930 says:

Though the history goes down until the passing away of Bahá'u'lláh yet His expulsion from Persia is the best and most logical place to stop for the present.

Shoghi Effendi hopes that this work has not been a too heavy tax upon your time and energy, and wishes me to thank you for all the help you have rendered him.

George's first comment on the whole book is found in his letters of September 27 and November 5, 1930 to the secretary:

The account of the early martyrdoms in the last manuscript you sent is the most terrible, pitiful, rousing thing. I knew little, almost nothing of it, and I find it stimulating to think this Faith has such antecedents, such splendid glorious heroes to keep on the tradition of. It all quickens in one a new desire, a new courage, a more grim determination.

At the same time I was struck by the purely physical character of it all. In the West so far all has been utterly different. We have not the persons of the Great Ones of God to inspire us to be rallying centres. We are trained in loneliness and our efforts are within rather than without. When the hour of combat comes the struggle will be, I doubt not, fully as bitter and merciless, but it will be with intellectual weapons that we shall be assailed. To face these and conquer will need I think as indomitable a courage as that of the early martyrs – I do not mean to compare any westerner with those exalted souls, but to be mocked and cast out as a fool and have one's faith distorted and misrepresented by the most astute and crafty critics will be a keen test of one's sincerity and firmness and as hard to withstand as blows of steel or biting fire. I trust and pray God is strengthening us to play the man, during these times of preparation.

. . . The whole thing is the most thrilling, pitiful, glorious and powerful picture. The action of the Cause, like its writings and the *aura* that is about it all, is lofty and majestic beyond anything one could imagine or reach to in mind, let alone in deed. Like the teachings themselves this courage and resolution seem to call one to a devotion such as one never knew. Its effect on me is immeasurable; the world here around me seems less real.

Now the serious consideration of publication arose. The Guardian consulted George, who advised delay. The exchanged telegrams referred to are, unfortunately, not available, but their loss is well compensated by the ensuing correspondence. Shoghi Effendi's secretary to George, October 14, 1930, written from Oxford:

After completing the translation of the history to the exile of Bahá'u'lláh to Baghdad, Shoghi Effendi began to think whether it could be published in its present form. Last week he sent you a cable and has received the answer. Naturally, in such a short cable you could not explain your reasons for delaying the publication. There are quite a number of questions to consider before we can give this book to the public. The first is its division into chapters with proper indexes, maps, footnotes, etc. that make such a book comprehensible to the public at large. This part of the work Shoghi Effendi has already done and he is in the process of completing. Another consideration is the subject matter itself. Would the account of these three battles which the Babis fought, even though purely defensive in character, cause misunderstandings? Immediately Bahá'u'lláh proclaimed His mission He forbade even defensive war and declared that it is preferable to be killed than to kill, hence we have no such wars during His dispensation. But still a critical public may not understand such things nor desire to make such discriminations.

October 22, 1930:

This afternoon I received your letter of Sept 27th. In the light of the great appreciation you express in this letter for the narrative, your advice as to the postponement of the publication seems still puzzling to me. If those heroic deeds have made such an impression upon you, would not the reading of the narrative arouse the friends to greater sacrifices and stimulate them to more intensive service? It was not mere physical torture that the friends in Persia had to endure but also moral persecution for they were cursed and vilified by all the people especially when they ceased to defend themselves. Anyhow the Master used to say sometimes that the Western friends will be severely persecuted but theirs will be primarily moral.

November 4, 1930 from Haifa:

This afternoon I received your letter dated October 23rd 1930 which elucidates your point of view more than your previous ones. I always maintained that such a book could not be published without a detailed introduction which would give the reader the proper outlook on the subject.

Some of the early writers considered the different encounters insurrections against the existing dynasties or a desire to establish the Empire that the Qá'im was to create. Lord Curzon in his book on Persia categorically denies the contention that the early followers of the Bab had any political motive and Bahá'u'lláh who was a prime mover of the activities of the friends in those days wrote in the Íqán – a book He revealed only a few years after – that the Sovereignty the prophets establish is *spiritual*.

Anyhow Shoghi Effendi believes that as you are well informed of the western outlook and already have the whole book of Nabil – that is the part to be published at present – you are more fitted to write that introduction. If there is any special material you desire to have, or any passage in any Tablet you desire to quote and which you would like to be retranslated, you could write me or directly to Shoghi Effendi . . .

Shoghi Effendi feels that the introduction should stress the fact that the followers of the Bab were only seeking to protect themselves from the repeated and fierce attacks of the enemy. In fact as soon as they were told that no further attacks would be attempted against them they were willing to leave their stronghold and depart to their homes. Nabil shows how they were treacherously deceived. Furthermore the Bab has not in His writings given any hint whatever to any aggressive warfare even for religious purposes, to His followers.

Shoghi Effendi would have himself attempted to write the introduction if he did not feel that you are infinitely more competent in handling a theme in a manner that would suit the western mind. Your excellent essay on the Hidden Words prompts him to make this request and he feels sure that whatever you write on that subject would considerably enhance the value of the narrative and will constitute a distinct service to the Cause.

The Guardian wishes me to thank you most heartily for the assistance you have rendered him and assures you of his prayers for the success of your endeavours to serve the Cause.

George wrote 'on the same day as my wire, explaining my reasons for advising against publication now.' This letter is unfortunately missing but on October 17 and October 23 he stated his view clearly:

Briefly, I see no reason to think the general public will be interested in the book. Perhaps many of the Bahá'ís will not either. The history has no direct bearing of any kind on the present Bahá'í situation in England or (I think) the West.

Further, it will *not* give a favourable view of the Bábí or Bahá'í Cause, unless it is seen *in its proper perspective*. To the cold and uninstructed public to whom it would be presented it would seem an unedifying story of cruelties and local fanaticism, and would be a misleading introduction to the revelation of Bahá'u'lláh.

I hate to offer an opinion against action in the Cause which now needs activity over here so much. But though ready to hope I am, in this matter, blind, my present opinion is very distinct . . .

As regards the publication the telegraphed question was in short whether the history as it stands 'would appeal to western people' and would I advise publication. In my opinion such as it is and for what it is worth the answer is a negative; for I can't think it would at all appeal to westerners nor does it seem appropriate as propaganda to the situation today in England. The violence would pain and shock people; and the traditional criticism of Mohammedanism is that it's an aggressive military religion. The history – as it stands – would tend to give an unfavourable view of both Babism and Bahaism. But – I am so glad there is a 'but' to this most unwilling counsel for *not* doing something! – if there is to be an *introduction* as your letter says, with notes, and if the contrast between Babism as shown in the history and Bahaism could be stressed and the highly pacific character of the Bahá'í Revelation be emphasized, the publication now might be made safe. Bahá'í students and other readers of oriental history and literature would welcome the book. Personally, I'd be more than delighted to see it and have it. But I see no reason to hope that the general public in the West would take any interest in it; and of course the expense of producing so large a book, even the part only (as your covering letter says) as far as the Passing of Bahá'u'lláh, would be heavy. . .

Again on November 5, having received the secretary's letters of October 14 and 22, he sent further clarification:

I am sorry that my opinion of the probable effect of the publication of this History upon the general public of the west, at this time, is puzzling. I fear it must seem to imply a much lower opinion of the western public and their receptiveness than I really hold. I regret my expression in the telegram was so brusque, but this judgment on the question asked is settled and clear. Please heaven I am mistaken.

But when (as in your last letter) you introduce the question how it will impress the *Bahá'í community*, that is quite another matter. I am afraid (as I've said) that the effect of publication as propaganda, as a *first* line of attack, will be disappointing. But the history will be of the utmost interest and value to all reading and thoughtful Bahá'ís and to very many will be a source of strength and inspiration giving them a desire for fellowship in such heroic consecration. It will show them in action such an ardour of worship and devotion as is unknown and alas undreamed of in this western world of ours.

But I am glad there is to be an introduction and notes. The work is so highly oriental, and presupposes so much knowledge of Persian history, life and customs, that an occidental, however sympathetic, is sometimes at a loss . . . It is wonderful, wonderful: precious. But it will take something different from that to shake England now. She *will* be shaken up however, and thoroughly, and soon. I hope Shoghi Effendi will give us the History in book form as soon as may suit.

George went immediately to work and on November 18 sent the draft 'of an outline of the proposed introduction' with the following comment: 'I was struck at once by a sense of my incompetence to write the introduction; but being asked I will do it, with your kind help. I can see that my ignorance may perhaps fit me to write for those as ignorant of eastern history and customs as I and much less interested in them.'

Shoghi Effendi's instant response (November 30) was to express his 'extreme satisfaction at your readiness to write the introduction', to acknowledge with deep gratitude receipt of 'the entire manuscript with your valued emendations' and to send a mass of material which would give George the facts he needed and a great deal of general information to enable him to write an informed, relevant essay 'in a manner that would encourage the general reader to read the book', parts of which it was recognized were 'uninteresting to the general public'. 'You will know exactly how to present and introduce this sort of work to the intelligent public in the West.' The material sent comprised, Extracts from Lord Curzon's *Persia and the Persian Question*; 'Abdu'l-Bahá's résumé of the circumstances which led to the defensive actions taken by the Bábís in Mázindarán, Nayríz and Zanján; an account of the doctrines of Shí'ih Islám and an explanation of the Báb's claim to be the Qá'im; a brief biography of Nabíl; explanations of the unity of the Bahá'í Revelation as one whole, embracing the Faith of the Báb and that of Bahá'u'lláh, and of Bahá'u'lláh's forbidding self-defence, which should not be taken to mean that a Bahá'í could not defend his life against any irresponsible assailant, religious or not; an account by Dr Cormick, 'an English physician long resident in Tabríz', of his meetings with the Báb. All these items were given full comment.

This action was so typical of the Guardian of the Faith that it is related in the above detail. He backed his lieutenants to the hilt and once having given his confidence did his utmost to enable them to render their services. In this case the Guardian stated what he wanted and sent all the material necessary. George wrote, ordering his material in the manner most likely to engage the interest of the Western reader.

He seized upon the episode of Dr Cormick, which is undoubtedly of prime interest and importance to western minds, since he is the sole Westerner known to have met and talked with the Báb. Cormick described Him as 'a very mild and delicate-looking man, rather small in stature and very fair for a Persian, with a melodious soft voice, which struck me much . . . In fact his whole look and deportment went far to dispose one in his favour.' George further stressed Western interest by referring to Professor E. G. Browne's *Materials For the Study of the Bábí Religion* and mentioning that Dr Cormick's letter was addressed to 'a fellow practitioner in an American mission in Persia'. He further laid great stress on the similarities between the Revelations of the Báb and Jesus Christ:

> The cause of the rejection and persecution of the Báb was in its essence the same as that of the rejection and persecution of the Christ. If Jesus had not brought a New Book, if He had not only reiterated the spiritual principles taught by Moses but had continued Moses' rules and regulations too, He

might as a merely moral reformer have escaped the vengeance of the Scribes and Pharisees. But to claim that any part of the Mosaic law, even such material ordinances as those that dealt with divorce and the keeping of the Sabbath, could be altered – and altered by an unordained preacher from the village of Nazareth – this was to threaten the interests of the Scribes and Pharisees themselves, and since they were the representatives of Moses and of God, it was blasphemy against the Most High. As soon as the position of Jesus was understood, His persecution began. As He refused to desist, He was put to death.

For reasons exactly parallel, the Báb was from the beginning opposed by the vested interests of the dominant Church as an uprooter of the Faith. Yet, even in that dark and fanatical country, the mullás (like the Scribes in Palestine eighteen centuries before) did not find it very easy to put forward a plausible pretext for destroying Him whom they thought their enemy.

Even a cursory reading of his Introduction reveals the masterly way in which he incorporated all the Guardian's ideas and material into an essay and a series of notes which, together, strike a chord attuning the occidental mind to the 'tales of magnificent heroism'[1], which adorn Nabíl's bizarre and tragic epic. In all this we see once again George's bridge-building qualities at work.

One further, entirely circumstantial parallel in the stories of Jesus and the Báb may be noted. Dr Cormick achieved eternal fame by being called in to attend the Báb; Zacchaeus achieved it by climbing a tree to see Jesus pass by. The Manifestation of God is the Source of all honour and glory.

Shoghi Effendi asked George to suggest a title for the work. He himself had thought of 'Idylls of the Immortals', subtitled 'Nabíl's Narrative of the Early Days of the Bahá'í Revelation'. He wanted George's alternative or modification. George's first response did not seem 'arresting enough'; he wrestled with it and eventually produced 'The Dawn-Breakers' with the addition of the Guardian's subtitle. The Guardian thought it 'very appropriate' and used it, thereby ensuring its immortality. Not only has the great work been reprinted in a number of editions, some abridged, but four decades later groups of Bahá'í youth in many countries of the world, fired, as was George, by the heroic story of their spiritual forebears, and calling themselves The Dawn-Breakers, have formed groups for presenting the Bahá'í teachings in various art forms, drama, song, mime and ballet and combinations of them, not unlike the morality plays of old. 'The Dawn-Breakers' is a name to conjure with in the ever-growing Bahá'í society.[2]

[1] Lord Curzon

[2] See *The Bahá'í World*, vol. XV, p. 345: 'The Dawn-Breakers of Europe'. Also Australia formed a Dawn-Breakers youth singing group. In the Nine Year Plan Mr and Mrs Russ Garcia of Los Angeles in their trimaran named *The Dawn-Breaker* sailed through the islands of the South Pacific ocean to bring the Faith to small island groups.

The reason for George's name not appearing as the writer of the Introduction is given in Chapter 8. Perhaps this can be repaired in future, particularly in view of the letter written on the Guardian's behalf acknowledging receipt of the typescript: 'Shoghi Effendi sincerely hopes that you will reconsider your decision and if possible permit him to mention your name,' and George's own specific request made in his letter of April 16, 1931, cited on page 110.[1]

The writing of the Introduction to *God Passes By*, twelve years later, was a task admirably suited to George's training, predilection and literary attainments. He was on home ground now. The huge success of *The Dawn-Breakers*, which the entire Bahá'í world absorbed into its heart and mind, the progressive unfoldment by the Guardian in his World Order letters of the supernal vision of the Bahá'í era, revealing Bahá'u'lláh as its presiding Genius and His Dispensation the opening chapter of that vast thearchy,[2] profoundly affected George's spiritual development and his understanding of the great theme of the unity of world history, the theme which he so cogently argued in his major works.[3] The history of the Primitive Age of the Faith was now familiar to him; he had written of its saints and heroes. His ties with the Christian hierarchy no longer inhibited his open and unrestricted proclamation of Christ's return – he was indeed but four years away from his complete freedom – and this magnificent story of the unfoldment during a hundred years of a modern religion, at least two of whose Central Figures were known to living men and from One of Whom he had received two letters, was his daily meat and drink. George never faltered. Having read every line of the Guardian's monumental work, having gloried in it, wept over it, lived with it from February 1943 to February 1944, offered his editorial 'suggestions, criticisms or corrections' as he deemed necessary, he wrote with full heart and flowing pen. His essay is a masterpiece.[4]

The choosing of the title for this 'survey', as all the Guardian's correspondence called it, taxed George's imaginative invention. Only after letters and two cables urging the point had been received did inspiration come to him. He cabled 'God Passes By' and received the instant reply 'DELIGHTED TITLE EAGERLY AWAITING LETTER'.

The collaboration between the Guardian and George on this great work followed the normal pattern already established between them,

[1] In 1980 the Universal House of Justice notified those National Spiritual Assemblies with publishing agencies that George had written the Introduction to *The Dawn-Breakers* and future editions should indicate it.

[2] See Shoghi Effendi, *The Dispensation of Bahá'u'lláh*.

[3] See Chs. 13–16.

[4] See Ch. 13.

and yet it seemed to draw them closer together than had previous projects of similar nature. It was undertaken during difficult times – the darkest days of the Second World War – when communications were far from regular, normal help was unobtainable and both men were under great strain. Their *modus operandi* was for the Guardian to send the first typewritten pages of the work in hand, with a description of it and his request for George's services. Thus the first intimation to George of Shoghi Effendi's centennial history of the Faith was contained in a letter dated February 27, 1943 from the Guardian's secretary, which, as we shall see, did not reach Ahascragh for some months:

> The Guardian has instructed me to write you on his behalf and to forward to you the enclosed pages for your perusal.
>
> He has been working for quite some time on a book to be published in conjunction with the Centenary Celebrations of our Religion in May 1944, and which would give, in relatively brief form, an outline of the most important phases and events in the evolution of our beloved Faith during its first hundred years.
>
> He is, as you know, under ordinary circumstances over-worked and pressed for time, and the addition of this literary effort is weighing on him very heavily. He feels he is so rushed and engrossed in the tremendous amount of labour involved in it that he lacks perspective on it, and cannot judge of its merits. He would, therefore, very deeply appreciate your opinion as to whether you consider it in a sufficiently advanced state to be published, both in regards to style and treatment of subject matter. He would also like to have your corrections, comments and general suggestions.
>
> The part enclosed is a section dealing with Bahá'u'lláh's life and works in 'Akká. It is chosen at random as representative of his treatment of the subject and style in general. Naturally it is preceded by the chapters on the ministry of the Báb and the earlier years of Bahá'u'lláh's life in Baghdád, Constantinople, Adrianople, etc.

Sheaves of typescript were not always sent in chronological order, but as they became available from the typist of the day. In the case of *God Passes By*, the Guardian of the Faith typed the whole tremendous work himself, and generally sent his instalments without correction of typing mistakes. His secretary's letter of December 29, 1943 explained the position:

> Had he had more time at his disposal he could have, naturally, devoted more of it to putting the finishing touches on his manuscript; unfortunately, however, the work of the Cause is so great and so pressing that he lacks the advantages enjoyed by most authors of being able to devote themselves whole-heartedly and single-mindedly to their task. As it is, this survey has taxed his strength greatly and at times seemed too

much of a burden to carry it through to completion! As he lacks anyone here qualified to do the typing and the tremendous amount of transliteration of oriental words, he is forced to do that too.

Altogether there were twenty letters – consecutive from February 27 to August 11, 1943 – containing the batches of typescript, and on October 14, 1943 'a duplicate copy of the chapter on the Martyrdom of the Báb' was sent as the first had failed to arrive. The war-time mails were appalling, and as packet followed packet with no acknowledgement from George the Guardian became anxious and on May 11 cabled 'KINDLY CABLE WHETHER SEVERAL INSTALMENTS SURVEY FIRST BAHÁ'Í CENTENARY MAILED FOR YOUR COMMENTS REACHED YOU LOVING GREETINGS APPRECIATION.' George's cabled reply was received on May 15 and apparently denied any knowledge of the project. Shoghi Effendi's secretary wrote on May 16, sending a further instalment (the ninth): 'Yesterday your reply to his cable was received, and he trusts that the manuscript will by now have begun to reach you. It is about ten weeks since he sent the first instalment.' From then on communication was conducted by cable with sheaves of typescript going every few days until all had been sent. In these cables the Guardian reiterated his request for George's comments, advice, amendments. 'OWING LENGTH DELAY COMMUNICATIONS ANXIOUS KNOW YOUR REACTION VIEWS REGARDING GENERAL TREATMENT PRESENTATION SUBJECT AND STYLE CENTENARY MANUSCRIPT.' (May 29) 'WOULD APPRECIATE ANY AMENDMENT CORRECTIONS DEEMED ADVISABLE LOVING GRATITUDE.' (June 1) 'FIRST INSTALMENT GRATE-FULLY RECEIVED STOP KINDLY CABLE NUMBER INSTALMENTS REACHED YOU TO DATE ALSO YOUR IMPRESSION REGARDING STYLE AND SUBJECT MATTER AS COMPARED PREVIOUS INSTALMENTS LOVING ABIDING APPREC-IATION.' (August 3)

The cables were clear enough but the brief letters by his secretaries accompanying the instalments confirmed what the Guardian wanted and his deep gratitude for George's work.

> He would very much like to receive your criticisms, suggestions, corrections, and general views concerning the treatment of the subject matter and the whole presentation of this historic review. (April 11, 1943).

> He hopes these pages reach you safely. It is a great hardship for him that just at such a time, when he is engaged on such an important historic review, communications are so uncertain and take so long! In the past you were always of great help to him in these matters, and he trusts that, in spite of the difficulties involved, you will be able to help him this time too with your valued criticisms. Assuring you of his loving prayers. (April 17, 1943)

What a pity the war has so slowed up communications that he feels hurried in this major work; he has to get it to the friends in America for publication, if possible, before May 1944. (June 2, 1943)

Due to the inordinate delay in delivery of the letter of February 27, this appears to have been the first intimation to George that the Guardian hoped it would be published in time for the centenary celebrations in April/May 1944.

He trusts that the former instalments have been reaching you safely and that this work of his is not taxing your strength too much? I need not tell you how deeply he appreciates and values your assistance. (June 16, 1943)

He is most anxious to know whether you consider that this work is really in a suitable condition for publication. He has been engaged on it for so long, and is himself so overburdened with work and cares, that at times he doubts the advisability of publishing it, feeling that the style may be poor as compared with his previous writings. (August 2, 1943)

George's comments as he returned the different bundles of typescript revealed his appreciation of the great work.

I enclose the 7th instalment of the Survey. The work impresses me immensely and I foresee it will arouse great public interest and will be of the highest value in strengthening the faithful and stimulating their teaching work. (June 26, 1943)

Herewith the last of the eight instalments of your Survey which have reached me. I have done my best, such as it is, to comply with your directions. While, having got the instalments out of order and been intent chiefly on small details, I cannot say much on the larger questions you mention, my belief is that the work is worthy of the occasion and will fulfil the purpose for which it is designed. It will be an invaluable and indispensable handbook, with a unique place in Bahá'í literature. I am thrilled and possessed by it. I have made all speed and trust the whole manuscript will be published in USA at the date desired. (June 29, 1943)

I received this last evening and have gone through it as promptly as possible. My chief trouble was to prevent my tears spoiling your manuscript as I read your account of 'Abdu'l-Bahá's activities in the west. (August 25, 1943)

I return the last instalment of the Survey that has reached me, and am sorry to think it must be nearly the very last, and that my work on these is almost over. I shall miss it, and the thrill and the illumination and the detachment of it. How I wish I could in however small a way do some work that would lighten your burden of toil and care. (October 11, 1943)

It is all infinitely interesting and precious and will, I feel sure, be of the utmost value in strengthening and establishing the Faith in the west. Hitherto our information on the history of the Faith has been piece-meal, and uncertain on many points. Now an even light covers it all. (undated)

The first pages of the *Kitáb-i-Íqán* were sent on January 13, 1930 and the remainder in three instalments on January 19, February 9 and March 12.

> He leaves it to your discretion to suggest such terms as will render it more idiomatic, just as you have already done with the *Hidden Words*.
>
> I must also express his profound gratitude for the alterations which you have found the time to make in Shoghi Effendi's rendering of the Íqán . . . wherever there is a parenthesis it means that Shoghi Effendi offers you an alternative word, term or expression from which he would wish you to choose the most suitable.
>
> He wishes me to express his deep appreciation of the trouble you are taking and the painstaking efforts you are lavishing upon his rendering. Of course the book is so important that the most minute detail is worthy of consideration. This is why he is anxious that you should unhesitatingly point out and alter what should or should not be capitalized. In the same way he would appreciate your suggestions regarding paragraphing and what alterations you deem advisable in this respect.

A request in the letter of January 19, 1930 is of great interest, both for its subject matter and for its evidence of the meticulous care with which the Guardian translated the sacred text:

> He would like to draw your attention to the word 'tribulation' on page 9. Bahá'u'lláh is quoting the famous words of Jesus recorded in Matthew 24:29–31, 'Immediately after the tribulation of those days shall the sun be darkened . . . ' etc. The Authorized Version reads 'tribulation' whereas the Arabic, from which Bahá'u'lláh is quoting, gives 'narrowness'. As there is a difference, Shoghi Effendi would like you please to find out what the original in Greek or Hebrew is. If you think proper he would welcome such alterations from you which would make the language of the rendering more Biblical as he thinks it preferable.

George advised that both Matthew and Mark used the Greek word 'Thlipsis' which 'has two meanings (1) pressure (2) oppression or affliction (a derived meaning), if you say 'oppression' you might possibly be true to both Arabic and Greek. I take it the Arabic is a translation from the Greek in which, so far as scholars now know, the Gospel was first written.'

Shoghi Effendi rendered Bahá'u'lláh's text 'Immediately after the oppression of those days . . .', and gave a footnote which reads: 'The Greek word used (Thlipsis) has two meanings: pressure and oppression.'[1]

The page facing the first page of text of Shoghi Effendi's superb translation of *Kitáb-i-Íqán* bears the following note: 'This is one more

---

[1] See *Kitáb-i-Íqán*, p. 16 (UK), p. 24 (US).

attempt to introduce to the West, in language however inadequate, this book of unsurpassed pre-eminence among the writings of the Author of the Bahá'í Revelation. The hope is that it may assist others in their efforts to approach what must always be regarded as the unattainable goal – a befitting rendering of Bahá'u'lláh's matchless utterance.'

Gleanings from the Writings of Bahá'u'lláh was sent in four instalments, from December 1934 to April 1935. The Guardian's careful selection was made, according to his secretary's letter of January 10, 1935, for the purpose of presenting 'to the believers a befitting and authoritative rendering of the fundamental teachings of the Cause regarding God, soul, creation, the nature of Divine Manifestations and similar subjects. In addition he is very keen to make of this work a means through which the non-Bahá'í public may be given the opportunity of acquiring an exact knowledge of, and a genuine interest in, the Message.' George had been asked, in a letter of December 16, 1934, 'as to whether their publication together with further translations which he will later send you is suitable at present. Also he specifically requests you to go carefully over the manuscript with the view of improving its style and of making it as idiomatic as possible.' The Guardian chose the title but asked George if he could think of 'a more suitable one', which apparently he could not. When returning the final pages, on May 8, George wrote 'I did the work as quickly as I could though I am worried I can't get more idiomatic English for it: the material seems to call for special force and beauty.' The Guardian instructed his secretary to write '. . . how deeply grateful Shoghi Effendi is for the helpful and unfailing assistance you have so kindly extended to him in the accomplishment of this important work . . . Your invaluable cooperation is, indeed, beyond all praise, realizing what a great sacrifice of time and energy it has called for on your part. But you should feel confident that your efforts will be fully rewarded, and will be gratefully and eternally appreciated by the Guardian.'

One of George's most outstanding characteristics, his unassuming modesty, is clearly revealed in this correspondence about *Gleanings from the Writings of Bahá'u'lláh*. The Guardian's secretary had written on May 13, 1935, 'Your two envelopes containing the Guardian's translations have been duly received, and your suggestions and comments have been carefully noted and much appreciated by him. These passages you have just returned are the last instalment of his translations from Bahá'u'lláh's writings. So you will be receiving no further translations in the future.' Poor George took this to mean, and really thought, that his work had been unsatisfactory, and that his help in this particular field would no more be needed. The Guardian's personal note, in his own hand, to the letter of May 22, 1935, 'I cannot refrain from expressing in person my deepfelt gratitude for the suggestions you have given me in connection with my translation of the writings of Bahá'u'lláh . . . ' did not entirely remove this feeling. In September he sent the Guardian the clipping from the *Church of Ireland Gazette* of his essay on 'Abdu'l-Bahá and received his delighted reply (see Chapter 8 p. 122), but that was nothing to do with his work on the Guardian's translations. Then on December 20 he received the letter containing the Guardian's request to write and read a paper on the Bahá'í Faith at the forthcoming World Congress of Faiths and the feelings of gratitude which overwhelmed him ('I see happiness beginning!'; see p. 125) may well have been the greater because of the above misunderstanding. But all was not over yet. On January 1, 1936, he received the Guardian's 'generous and highly appreciated gift of "Gleanings" just arrived. I am reading it with intense interest and much profit. The volume is very well produced and a delight to the eye. What a boon it is to have one's own publishing company! I never was sure why my work on the text of the Gleanings was unsatisfactory or why you suddenly said you would never send me any more manuscript. I never worked harder on any translation nor under so severe a handicap. I had, or thought I had, an intuitive idea something of the kind might happen and for that reason I kept saying I was working my best.' He continues with an assurance that he was working on his paper for the Congress and then concluded 'I *always* give the best of the day to Bahá'í things and my leisure to my professional work. This does not conduce to professional success!'

The reply to this was a full explanation from the secretary of the 'absolute misunderstanding' and many assurances of the Guardian's deepest appreciation and boundless gratitude for George's services 'on several occasions in connection with his translation work'. The Guardian added his personal note 'Wishing you the fullest success in your work for the preparation of the paper, and thanking you again from the depths of my heart for your past and present services . . . '

This would have been the storm in a teacup which it appears to be, were it not for the pure quality of George's humility and his obvious gratitude that this field of service was not to be closed to him. At this time he was meeting frustration on all fronts. *The Promise of All Ages*, although a *succès d'estime*, had not done what he had hoped it would; there were no signs that his longing to free himself from the Church in order to serve Bahá'u'lláh fully and completely would ever be realized; Nancy was in direct opposition; he was depleted physically, suffering from headaches so severe that he could only continue with medical aid. And when the new task was given him by the Guardian and the gift of the published copy of *Gleanings* reached him, the tension broke, hope revived and he poured out his heart in gratitude.

During the last days of 1936, after the excitement of the World Congress of Faiths in July and the disappointment of his hopes that it would bring about a change in his personal circumstances, and while he was discussing with the National Spiritual Assembly of the British Isles his new plan for his future services to the Faith, the first pages of the Guardian's translations of *Prayers and Meditations by Bahá'u'lláh* were received. He was asked to perform his usual review and editing and to say whether he thought publication of the compilation in its present form advisable. The entire typescript was sent in four instalments, the last being returned by George on April 6, 1937.

His covering note returning the first consignment read, 'It is very wonderful. Nothing like it in the world. So many, many thanks. Yours loyally in the Cause.' When pressed for his view about publication he wrote, 'It seems to me the West is ready for these prayers of Bahá'u'lláh but that a clear and full biographical account explaining the conditions under which those prayers were uttered will be necessary. (Very little information about the life of the Manifestation is available in the West). Some quotations from Nabíl's Narrative vol. 2 might, for instance help to set these prayers in due perspective; but something more than Nabíl would be needed.' Six days later: 'I return with a number of proposed amendments the translations which reached me a few days ago. It is wonderfully uplifting.' On March 17: 'My letter answering your query about its publication probably crossed your last letter. In view of the large amount of material now on hand, my idea, for what it is worth, is that the only necessary and the best introduction to these Meditations, for a western reader, would be a summary narrative in 200–300 words of the main points in Bahá'u'lláh's life and works, with a reference to His companions in misfortune. This will provide a background, connect the prayers with actual earth and help to explain references and allusions in the text.'

The Guardian's appreciation of George's assistance with this compilation was deep and loving, although he did not act upon his recommendation for a brief note of introduction. 'I truly and deeply appreciate the assistance you have extended to me in my work in connection with these translations and, I assure you, I will continue to pray for the removal of every obstacle from your path, and for the complete realization of your highest hopes and dearest wishes.'

On April 6, 1940 the Guardian's secretary sent George 'about half' the manuscript of a new translation by the Guardian of Bahá'u'lláh's last written work, *Tablet to the Son of the Wolf*. It had already been inadequately translated by Julie Chanler and published in 1928 by the Bahá'ís of the United States. George was again asked to perform his 'usual review and editing', and after that there is a gap of fourteen months in the correspondence. All we know at present is that the Guardian's superb translation was published in 1941 under the title *Epistle to the Son of the Wolf*.

This splendid literary collaboration took place over a period of eighteen years (1926–44). At certain times there could have been observed the interesting spectacle of mails from Haifa carrying the Guardian's typescript for 'englishing' by George, while the crossing mails from Ireland conveyed to Haifa instalments of George's *The Promise of All Ages* or drafts of his Introductions or specially commissioned essays, for correcting and comment by the Guardian. What a great lesson in objectivity!

Throughout these eighteen years the Guardian did not hesitate to draw upon George's talent for contributions to the major publishing project launched during his ministry. Horace Holley, Secretary of the National Spiritual Assembly of the United States and Canada,[1] proposed to the Guardian in 1924 'that the time seemed opportune for the organization of a committee of Bahá'í editors, chosen from the Orient, Europe and America, to gather together the necessary data, facts and other information for an annual reference book on the Bahá'í Cause'. The Guardian warmly welcomed the idea and the National Spiritual Assembly of the United States and Canada was requested to launch the project. The first volume was published in 1926 under the title *Bahá'í Year Book* and covered the period from April 1925 to April 1926. Thereafter the Guardian himself assumed responsibility for the editorship, with a staff of editors drawn from several countries to gather the material for him, and the volume became biennial;[2] volume XVII was published in 1981. The Guardian placed great importance upon its development, not only for its recording the rise and establishment of the Bahá'í Faith in the world, its value as a reference book of current Bahá'í thought and activity, but for his use of it to introduce the Faith to leaders of human affairs in all departments of life, including heads of state.

George was asked on December 12, 1929, to contribute to the forthcoming volume (III) and thereafter to every volume which appeared during his lifetime. All volumes from II to XIII inclusive

---

[1] The Canadian Bahá'í community established its own National Spiritual Assembly in 1948 and was incorporated by Act of Parliament in April 1949. See *The Bahá'í World*, vol. XI, p. 309.

[2] See Preface to *The Bahá'í World*, vols. XIV *et seq.* for its publishing history.

contain essays from his pen, and volumes VI, X and XII each contain two, while volume VIII has three. The Guardian would ask him to write on any theme he liked, or would offer him a wide choice, as for volume III: 'The article he feels could be on any aspect of the Bahá'í Cause; but he would suggest some such subject as "Bahá'í Literature" or "The Writings of Bahá'u'lláh" or preferably, what he thinks might appeal to you most, namely "The Hidden Words" as a piece of religious literature. The article could be written in a way as to arouse interest in the work especially among mystics.' Or again he would ask for an essay on a specific subject such as *'Queen Marie of Rumania and the Bahá'í Faith'* which was published in volume VIII as part of Section XI of Part One. As in the case of the Introduction to Nabíl's Narrative the Guardian overwhelmed George with information and materials and, three weeks later, sent him an account of the memorial service held in Washington at the time of the Queen's death 'and of the floral tribute arranged by the American believers' with the request that he use the material in this article.

It is interesting that in volume VI (1934–1936), *The Epic of Humanity* (Chapter 1 of *The Promise of All Ages*) is signed Christophil whereas 'Bahá'u'lláh's Ground Plan of World Fellowship' is by Archdeacon George Townshend.

George rendered further service to volumes of *The Bahá'í World* by selecting for inclusion a specified number of poems from among the many which the editorial staff had gathered.

His article on *Hidden Words* so pleased the Guardian that he instructed his secretary to write (February 9, 1930) '. . . he wants your consent to have it published as a separate pamphlet to accompany copies of the *Hidden Words* which he might wish to present to interested and sympathetic persons. It forms a splendid introduction to it. In that case also, would you wish to have your name appended to the article, or rather any objections for not doing so? If you think it is more publicity than you care or find it convenient to have, it could be cancelled.'

George agreed, and on April 11 the Guardian sent him one hundred copies of the essay, bearing his name 'published here in Haifa' and informed him that he had sent leather-bound copies of the *Hidden Words* together with 'copies of your *Reflection*' to a dozen very distinguished people who had some friendly connection with the Faith.

George was delighted: '. . . please thank the Guardian cordially for his thoughtfulness and kindness in sending me these copies of my little essay. I much appreciate the gift and am charmed to see my work so beautifully set off.' Having just had a proposal for some publicity 'turned down flat' in London he added the wry comment 'It is a pity that propaganda in England should have to be conducted from Palestine! Rather like Geneva which is set in the midst of Europe but is run and supported wholly by Asia and America.'

Any attempt to trace the relationship between two individuals will inevitably reveal something of both of them. This story of George Townshend must have already conveyed intimations of the character of Shoghi Effendi, Guardian of the Bahá'í Faith, and since there is no doubt that after 'Abdu'l-Bahá the person who exercised the greatest influence upon George was Shoghi Effendi, it is highly relevant to our theme to appreciate, in some degree, his station and character.

One outstanding characteristic, his kindness, so often displayed in his thoughtfulness for others, came prominently into play as a result of the collaboration over *God Passes By*. The Guardian had originally intended his survey to be published in time for the centenary celebrations of the inauguration of the Bahá'í era (May 1944), but as the pressing needs of his office, as Head of the Faith, impinged more and more upon his colossal task, and as wartime conditions only exacerbated the difficulties, he accepted that it would not be possible to make the book available by that time. Nevertheless he continued to press for its publication as soon as possible, and that meant that George was under pressure to get his Introduction to the printer before the composition and proof-reading of the main body of the work was completed.

Immediately upon receipt of George's manuscript, Shoghi Effendi cabled, on March 18, 1944, 'INTRODUCTION RECEIVED AND AIR MAILED HOPE REACHES TIME LOVE', and on April 24 he cabled again, 'INTRODUCTION REACHED STATES IN TIME'. George's instant responses to both cables were revealing of himself and of the Guardian. On March 22 he wrote (using for the first time one of the microfilmed air letters[1]) acknowledging a letter and cables, 'It seems rather dreadful for you to be thanking me when really it is so much the other way round'. To the second cable he replied, 'How good of you to cable that glad tidings that my Introduction was in time. My heart has been singing ever since; and the vision opening.' The Guardian gave him further information in a letter of July 28 in which the secretary wrote,

Owing to pressure of priority work in the States *God Passes By* will not be

---

[1] One of the economies effected by the British Post Office, and adopted by the Irish, when all mail going abroad was censored, was to provide forms of uniform size on which letters could be written and left unfolded. Hundreds going to the same area could be microfilmed onto one roll, reprinted the other end and delivered in the usual way.

delivered by the printer until after the end of August. The Guardian was sorry the book could not be gotten out in time for the Centenary; but such things cannot be avoided in wartime, and the real miracle is that the manuscript should have gone to you and been returned and gone out again to the USA and been safely received! Proofs have been given, however, for use in special courses of the Bahá'í Summer Schools. He thought you would like to know these things, after all the pains you took with the manuscript.

Later, in 1945, when George had reported a serious and prolonged attack of neuritis so severe that it prevented his writing (except with his left hand), the Guardian's letter of August 12, written by his wife, who had been for some years acting as his secretary, read

He was *extremely* sorry to hear you are suffering so much with neuritis, and that it is preventing you from writing – when you have so much rich thought to share with others and your heart longs to alleviate the misery of many seeking souls. You may be sure he will most ardently pray for your healing and that you may resume your important work for the Cause.

It will make you happy to hear that the Australian National Spiritual Assembly has presented copies of *God Passes By* to all Archbishops and Bishops of the Anglican Church in Australia and New Zealand; so you see your hope that it would reach the clergy, and your special appeal to them in the introduction you wrote, are bearing fruits in distant lands!

The Guardian assures you and your dear wife that he will often pray for you both and for the solution of your problems, With loving greetings from him.

And a postscript was added: 'A second edition of *God Passes By* has already been printed in the United States.'

On March 16, 1945, George wrote:

This is to thank you warmly for your generous gift of *God Passes By* and for the treasured inscription you have been kind enough to put in it.[1]

The sight of my name on the title page of such a record humbled me to the dust, but then thrilled me.

This brief survey of George's literary services to the Guardian records the practical interchange, on the surface as it were, of an underlying, deep and evolving relationship between two men of greatly differing temperaments, backgrounds and ages (George was twenty years older than Shoghi Effendi), brought together by Providential dispensations of time, history and purpose for the service of the Lord of Hosts. One, His hereditary successor, Guardian of His Cause, recognized the other as 'His chosen instrument'. George, a senior officer of the Christian

[1] 'To George Townshend with loving appreciation Shoghi.'

hierarchy, well understood the nature of spiritual authority and gloried in the knowledge that his loyalty and service were given to one whose appointment, in direct line from the Prophet Himself, was incontestably clearer, more authentic and definite than anything in the entire field of religious history.

Shoghi Effendi was invested with full authority by 'Abdu'l-Bahá's Will and Testament, in which he was named as His successor, sole interpreter of the Word of God, permanent head of the Universal House of Justice, the one to whom all must turn, under the shelter and guidance of Bahá'u'lláh and the Báb. Such authority was incontestable and, reinforced by the Master's loving tender language in describing him, by His injunction to 'take the greatest care of Shoghi Effendi', and further by the Guardian's own natural endowments, which were those of genius, rapidly won for him the love and dedicated service of the entire Bahá'í world. And however much he consulted experts or those he later appointed to the highest office in the Faith, however graciously he referred to his 'co-workers', however much he encouraged the developing institutions of the Administrative Order to assume the responsibilities laid upon them in the sacred text or signed himself to all believers and Bahá'í institutions 'your true brother', there was never any question of *primus inter pares*. He was the Sign of God, Bahá'u'lláh's spokesman, the Head of the Bahá'í Faith.

This point is of particular importance in relation to the work which George performed for the Guardian. No one should ever imagine for a moment that the translations into English which the Guardian made of the sacred text were ever anything but his own. However much he turned to George for advice on syntax, 'englishing', polishing and refining of style, idiomatic usage and the like, he was the final arbiter who decided whether to adopt, reject or amend any or all of George's editorial suggestions. Bahá'ís will never forget that the Guardian's translations are different from all others, whether already made or to be made in future. The Guardian was, after 'Abdu'l-Bahá, the sole interpreter, the expounder of the Word, named as such in the Master's Will and Testament. His translations of the scripture therefore are imbued with this authority and are the only ones which may be so regarded. The House of Justice has authorized others since his passing, but these and all future ones can only be translations, with no element of interpretation in them.

In such an exalted and lonely position as the Guardian occupied, close personal friendships were inevitably very few indeed, but the correspondence between Shoghi Effendi and George clearly indicates such a relationship. On the Guardian's side it was compounded of admiration, gratitude, confidence, and a growing affection often expressed in personal notes of informal geniality. More than once, when George had written about some new work on which he was engaged, Shoghi Effendi replied encouragingly and added, 'More power to your elbow'. As early as 1929 he asked George for a photograph of himself. George, somewhat diffidently, made no reference to this request for two years and three months, when he wrote 'Some months ago you were good enough to ask me for a photograph and I have been waiting till I got one suitable to send. But without more delay I am sending by this or next post one taken some twelve or thirteen years ago: the best I have.' This was the time when the anomaly of his clerical position was beginning to harass him and the remainder of his letter, cited on p. 110, was an emptying of his heart and a cry for spiritual support. It contained a typical 'Townshendism' akin to the Guardian's 'more power to your elbow' – 'The shrinking does not go as deep as the ardour!' The Guardian's personal note, appended to his letter of reply (April 30, 1931) which assured him that Divine guidance and confirmation 'will never fail you', read:

> My dear and valued co-worker: I am delighted by the tone of your letter, which I trust and pray will be but a prelude to great and memorable services to the Cause. I was so pleased to receive your photograph which I have placed in my study, a constant reminder of an invaluable fellow-worker and friend. I will fervently pray that your highest aspirations may be speedily and fully realized. I urge you to make a special effort to initiate a vigorous campaign of publicity in the Press and arouse the National Assembly to further such activities which I feel are essential for the spread of the Faith. With my love and best wishes, Shoghi.

Note the absence of the usual 'your true brother' in favour of the more personal ending. In fact the Guardian infrequently used that phrase in closing his personal notes to George; occasionally it was 'your true and grateful brother', but more often simply 'Shoghi'.

Five times the Guardian invited George to Haifa, not as a pilgrim (though he would doubtless have seen all that pilgrims did) but 'as my guest' or 'at our home'. On April 21, 1926, in answer to the first invitation, George explained that although he nursed 'an irrepressible and rising hope' to be able to accept, it would, humanly speaking, be more than twenty years 'when I retire and can get more than ten days leave at a time'. (Air travel was still in the future, even Lindbergh's solo flight across the Atlantic more than a year away.) George's reply clearly indicates that he had no thought, at that time, of renouncing his Orders; he was busy developing his 'attack from the rear' by which he hoped to win, in fulfilment of 'Abdu'l-Bahá's hope, the whole-hearted and joyful entry of his church into the 'Heavenly Jerusalem'.

His reply to the second invitation (March 1927) offered 'a thousand thanks for your kind invitation . . . How I wish I could! Some happier day, some happier day!'

In May 1941 George expressed to the Guardian his need 'as soon as the war is over and circumstances permit', to accept his kind invitation if it were still open. Shoghi Effendi's reply, written on August 1, was immediate (George's letter took two months in transit) and characteristic; 'Dear and prized co-worker: I wish to assure you in person of a most hearty welcome, and reaffirm my keen sense of abiding appreciation of all that you have achieved for our beloved Faith. The record of your many and unforgettable services is surely outstanding and in many respects unique and exemplary. My prayer is that you will be enabled in the days to come to render still more distinguished services. Your true and grateful brother, Shoghi.' This was the Guardian's evaluation of twenty years of George's service, and his loving regard only increased as the years went by and his prayer was answered.

George replied from a full heart: 'Thank you so much for permission to visit you in the Holy Land and for saying I will there be your guest. The thought of this has ever since been before me: I need to go there *so* much. First I want to ask pardon of Bahá'u'lláh and of you; and then to absorb all the inspiration I possibly can. I want to gain strength for a big task that lies ahead of me; and I am getting old and not many years of work remain to me.'

On July 15, 1949, two years after his resignation from the Church, George wrote:

I cannot resist the urge to write to you and say that the first and most earnest desire and need of my life is now to accept that generous invitation you once gave me to go to Haifa and see and talk with you and walk and worship in those sacred spots and there be touched by the divine fire and be burned up by it. If my wife were with me it would be better still. This is only a need and a desire; I have no means. But I pray 'Abdu'l-Bahá will before long grant fulfilment. Without meeting you there is no centre to one's efforts, no foundation, no heart's vitality.

Shoghi Effendi replied:

The progress of your work, which I watch with ever-deepening interest and genuine gratitude and pride, is truly an evidence of Divine guidance and protection ever since your historic decision to dissociate yourself from the Church and proclaim the Gospel of the New Day. The Beloved will, no doubt, continue to guide your steps and bless your high and meritorious endeavours. I am particularly pleased to learn of the hearty and valued collaboration of the members of your dear family, for whose welfare and success I will pray from the depths of my heart. I will be so glad to welcome you at our home as soon as the present obstacles are removed.[1] Persevere in your labours and rest assured that the Concourse on high will reinforce your efforts. Your true and grateful brother, Shoghi. (August 8, 1949)

George never visited Haifa and never met the Guardian; these two longings of his heart were among the many which were frustrated, dispensations of Providence by which his patience and fortitude were tested and developed to the point of utter submission and complete freedom. But irony, present on more than one occasion in George's life, was not absent from his efforts and yearning to meet the Guardian. Some of the correspondence about his Introduction to *The Dawn-Breakers* was sent by Shoghi Effendi's cousin and secretary of that time, from Oxford (see page 64). George had taken Nancy to England for medical treatment and had returned to his rectory at Ahascragh where he was by himself 'with one servant' for several weeks. The secretary had explained his presence in Oxford to do some reading which he hoped would provide notes for Nabíl's history. George wired him an invitation to visit him for two or three nights and sent explicit directions about trains and boats, but received a reply that 'I am leaving tomorrow morning for home. Shoghi Effendi has finished all his work for the book and quite a number of pilgrims are awaiting him in Haifa. I hope we will be there in a week or so.'

George realized the situation at once and wrote, on November 5, 1930,

If I had had the *nous* to guess in time as I guess too late that Shoghi Effendi was surely with you in Oxford (since you would probably not have gone to Oxford alone on such a task) I would have flung all aside and gone over there at once to express personally my loyalty to the Cause and its Guardian. It might not have been in order but I would have taken a chance on that! Too late now, and it can't be helped. But I'm not dead yet and much will happen before long. Many, many in England have been brought by God to the very threshold of this Revelation: I have sought and found and seen it! But of that another time. Only, be sure of *changes* in these parts and have golden hopes of us!

The irony is only apparent in hindsight and its sourness utterly dissipated by George's cheerful gratitude for, and indeed wonder at the ineffable bounty of recognizing the Lord of Hosts in His Day and being allowed to serve Him. Resilience was one of George's greatest characteristics. He never ceased to hope and to believe in good outcomes.

---

[1] The new state of Israel was in the unsettled aftermath of its War of Independence, and pilgrimage to the World Centre of the Faith was severely restricted.

Another facet of this fascinating relationship is the Guardian's delegation to George, long before he appointed him a Hand of the Cause, of duties which would normally be undertaken by so high-ranking an officer. As early as 1928, when George's service at Geneva was under discussion (see page 103) the Guardian had intimated, through his secretary, that 'he looks forward to the day when you will be to him a general at the Front', and more than once he authorized him to give advice to the National Spiritual Assembly of the British Isles,[1] or to 'arouse the National Assembly', as already quoted. In 1925 George's letters to the Guardian were full of plans and ideas for action showing his zeal and care for the welfare of the Faith. The Guardian encouraged him in such projects as getting Miss Rosenberg to

> put together the numerous notes she has in her possession, recording teachings of Abdul Baha given early in 1901 in Haifa by Him in person to her. These deal chiefly with Bible subjects. And further that she should with her own hand state when where and how she received these teachings from Him, with all possible detail of time and circumstance. What I feel and seek to impress on her is that she alone can bear personal testimony to these words being His. They are secondhand to all the world save her, and always will be. If she does as she proposed to do, and leaves the notes as they stand for others to deal with, when she has left us no one ever will be able to say all that *she* can say now.

George offered to raise the money to cover the cost of printing from the Irish Bahá'ís (himself) 'if only *she* would do the real work'. In August of that year he urged the National Spiritual Assembly to at once collect and prepare for publication all the letters written by 'Abdu'l-Bahá to people in those islands, and he sent photographic copies of his own two, with the translations. Neither of these projects was ever brought to fruition.

The Guardian's confidence in George has, perhaps, no clearer evidence than arose from George's proposal to compile a book of prayers revealed by Bahá'u'lláh, the typescript for which he sent to the Guardian in May 1931. Shoghi Effendi fully approved the arrangement, urged him to submit it to the British National Assembly for its sanction and publish it in England. 'The idea is surely splendid, especially if you revise the language and make it truly readable and appealing to the English-speaking friends.' (May 16, 1931) On another occasion the Guardian urged him to revise the gauche translation of a passage George wished to quote in one of his works,

---

[1] For example, the British National Spiritual Assembly as late as 1929 styled itself 'National Spiritual Assembly of the Bahá'ís of Great Britain and Northern Ireland'. George represented to the Guardian that it should be ' . . . of the British Isles'. The Guardian authorized him to bring this to the notice of the Assembly, and himself sent his 'corroboration of the correction you had proposed, in fact he is grateful for it'.

since his essay would be ruined if he did not do so. The great value which the Guardian placed on George's revision and editing of his own translations and original works is already apparent, and was continually confirmed by requests to 'take more liberties' or to 'be more merciless' with the Guardian's own text.

When, in 1937, the announcement was made of the Guardian's marriage to Mary Maxwell, of Canada, (thenceforth known as Rúḥíyyih Khánum), George offered his congratulations on the personal event 'and on this most significant and hopeful sign of the great marriage between East and West'. He received a reply to which Shoghi Effendi added 'May the Beloved bless and reward you a thousand-fold for your incessant, noble and superb services to His Faith.'

Encouragement, constant encouragement, with increasing signs of admiration and affection flowed from the Guardian. As George met frustration after frustration, disappointment of his hopes, ill health and loneliness, with spiritual resilience, fortitude and optimism, the Guardian's love became increasingly apparent and George's devotion to him the sustaining power of his life. The progress of this uplifting, heavenly inspired relationship may be seen in many smaller facets as well as in the main bulk of the correspondence, where it shines forth in brilliance. For instance, George was never sure, for some years, how to address the Guardian. He knew of no Bahá'í protocol akin to the prescribed formality with which he would address his bishop or archbishop. Indeed, there was none, and his sense of the Guardian was more akin to fealty to his spiritual liege than any conventional respect for a senior officer. Thus his letters began variously 'Dear Guardian', 'Dear Guardian of the Cause', 'Dear Guardian of God's Cause', infrequently 'Dear Shoghi Effendi' which was the general way encouraged by the Guardian himself, occasionally 'Dear Shoghi Rabbani'. After he was appointed a Hand of the Cause, at the end of 1951, he used 'Dear Shoghi Effendi' regularly, until, as his health declined and Una wrote his letters for him to sign, he became closer and closer to the final Reality and wrote only 'My dearly beloved Guardian'.

His letter of July 25, 1945, already referred to on page 80, is perhaps the most revealing of all the two hundred or so which he wrote to Shoghi Effendi. Anxiety for the Guardian's disappointment over the long delay in writing the book which he so much wanted George to complete, courage, humility, spirituality, cheerfulness, all are apparent in this outpouring of his heart's confidences:

> As regards my projected book on 'Christ and Bahá'u'lláh' I think I ought now to tell you that I have not been able to write a word of it nor make

notes for it because of increasing neuritis in my arms. This has bothered me for nearly three years and lately has become so bad that I now can only write a few lines a day with my left hand.

There is no one to help me in this lonely place; and as we have no maid Mrs Townshend is overworked.

I have had to abandon all literary work and practically all my precious correspondence for a long time.

Last autumn when I prayed for relief the answer was not to write, to pray and to learn the greatness of God.

I realise a wisdom in this; my scribbling was a form of escapism. The theme of Christ and Bahá'u'lláh is ever in my mind and the book will be much better for the delay and the full preparation.

But the frustration has been severe; and it has not been very easy to do my daily work.

On the other hand since I sent you that Introduction to "God Passes By" 'the doors of realities and meanings have been opened'[1] to me, my vision has cleared, my mind sharpened; instead of death, there is life. I go forward, but I cannot see one foot ahead of me. I recognise you are and have been my best friend, and I am filled with longing to be with you.

The trouble I have to tell you of is physical and I trust temporary: my other news is of hope and happiness like that I knew when first I heard the voice of 'Abdu'l-Bahá long ago . . .

P.S. That is not too bad for one's left hand, is it? And all written in a single day.

George's deep sensitivity to the overwhelming burden shouldered by the Guardian was expressed in his letter of September 2, 1950, written after reading news of a descendant of Bahá'u'lláh's turning against the Faith:

I cannot refrain (and I hope it is not presumptuous) from sending you this line to express my deep loving sympathy with you in your terrible sorrows and suffering, so many and constant and various; this must be the cruellest kind of all. I feel always so much too of the burden cast on you by the timidities and negligences of us all (or of most of us) everywhere and at all times in not doing our full duty and so leaving failures and gaps which bring unnecessary difficulties and troubles and sorrows to others and especially to you.

The Guardian's personal reply was:

Assuring you of my deepest loving appreciation of your high endeavours, of the sentiments of sympathy you have expressed, and of my ardent and continued prayers for your protection, welfare, and success in your truly outstanding and historic services to the Cause of Bahá'u'lláh. (October 6, 1950)

---

[1] See second Tablet from 'Abdu'l-Bahá, Ch. 5.

Shoghi Effendi, ever thoughtful for George, would send him interesting information about the Faith or news of its activities. In July 1944 he told him about a number of celebrations which the Bahá'ís had organized in various countries to mark the centenary of the birth of the Faith in May 1844, particularly the one in Wilmette, the headquarters of the Bahá'í community of the United States and Canada 'where 1,600 believers were present in the Temple auditorium to view the portrait of the Báb, unveiled for the first time in the Western world'. When Shoghi Effendi was correcting and editing the typescript of *The Promise of All Ages*, George had asked about dates of publication of Bahá'u'lláh's works, and received the following fascinating information, written by the secretary:

> The earliest published writings of Bahá'u'lláh date from the nineties of the last century. Over forty years ago the Aqdas, a volume of general tablets including Tarazat, Ishraqat, and others were published in Ishkabad (Russia) and Bombay respectively and copies of these though rare are still procurable. Simultaneously with these if not earlier some of the writings of Bahá'u'lláh were published by the Oriental Dept of the Imperial Russian University at St Petersburgh under the supervision of its director Baron Rosen (more particulars about these could be found in the books of E. G. Browne) and these of course are not undated like some of those published in Bombay.
>
> The main bulk of the writings of Bahá'u'lláh however are to be found in manuscript form written by noted scribes after the fashion of orientals. These scribes did not leave all their manuscripts undated and Jinabi Zain a very noted Bahá'í scribe always dated his copies of the writings of Bahá'u'lláh at the end of the volume in what E. G. Browne calls 'colophones' and the description of some of these colophones could be found in the works of the Cambridge Professor.
>
> The son of the above-mentioned scribe is still living in Haifa and does very much the same work as his father. He claims that as early as 1868 his father used to write copies of the Iqan for the Bahá'ís in Persia as a source of livelihood, and that after 1885 when he went to Akká to join Bahá'u'lláh's party his entire work and time was devoted to copying the sacred writings for sale among Bahá'ís. These copies are to be found all throughout the East and are almost invariably dated.

The Guardian encouraged Bahá'ís who were travelling to visit George in his remote Galway post, on one occasion giving a letter of introduction to Siegfried Schopflocher of Canada, whom he later appointed a Hand of the Cause. Among the American believers whom Una remembers either visiting Ahascragh or meeting in Dublin, were Willard Hatch, Mr and Mrs Mottahedeh, Mason Remey, Marion Little. It was Mrs Little who explained to Nancy the breakdown of the Geneva project.[1]

[1] See pp. 103–4.

The Guardian arranged that reams of typescript sent for his editing be double spaced, to save George's eyes; he constantly expressed concern for his health; understood his covert references to Nancy's opposition and showed warm sympathy with his predicament, on one occasion[1] writing, by his secretary, 'He hopes that your dear children will find their happiness in life in service to the Cause, and with partners who share their devotion and their ideals. It is indeed difficult and sad for a dedicated believer to be married to someone who is not equally on fire with the Faith.' By then the Guardian was well aware of George's family situation, not only from such statements as 'I am sure my wife will be with me', or 'she will be a tower of strength when the time comes', or 'I think I shall have the strong and invaluable co-operation of my whole family', but as early as 1935, when George was preparing the paper he was to read at the World Congress of Faiths, he had added a postscript to his letter of December 20, 'In correspondence on this or other matters please don't refer to the possibility of material dangers for me. I like to show letters to my wife, to keep her with me, and there is no need to alarm her. I am quite ready to put my trust in God.'[2] And in June 1942 he had written, 'I think the family will all come out with me harmoniously when I depart; and I am anxious the resignation should be managed wisely and constructively, as part of a plan. Things take a little time to shape, and 'tho' there is no opportunity for this action visible now, I send this to tell you what is in my mind and what is taking shape.'

All through the long years of Nancy's vagaries, opposition, threats, and bouts of helpfulness, the Guardian would take any opportunity to express delight at 'Mrs Townshend's splendid co-operation' or to express his thanks for her assistance, giving every encouragement to her to continue helping George in his invaluable service. About six months after they had left Ahascragh and moved to Dublin he wrote, personally: 'That the members of your dear family are extending you their assistance in these historic and meritorious labours is an added source of joy and satisfaction. You are all often in my thoughts and prayers, and I will continue to supplicate for all of you the Master's richest blessings.' Towards the end, when Una was pioneering in Malta and a plan had been organized for George and Nancy to join her (in the hope that the climate would benefit George's failing health) Nancy wrote to the Guardian, giving a pitiful picture of George's physical condition and explaining why it was not possible for them to go. She enclosed her letter with George's own of November 26, 1953, which read (George was a Hand of the Cause now):

[1] June 2, 1953
[2] See p. 125.

My dearly beloved Guardian,

On getting back from Stockholm I reconceived and largely rewrote with joy and confidence my book "Christ and Bahá'u'lláh" during August and September. Since then I have not felt so well. But I shall be able to complete the book as a song of triumph and praise to God, celebrating His love through the ages and His victory now.

I hope I shall get strong enough again to show in deeds my deep loving gratitude to you and the great Cause. I do not feel in myself at all as sick as I did a year ago; but I am physically weak and everything is falling on my brave wife's shoulders. She is a *Maxwell*; they must be a great clan! She does not like writing or talking about her troubles or difficulties, but thought it her duty to write to you now.

This is just a postscript to her letter.

Ever with submission and humility . . .

P.S. Of course we are both longing to go to Malta – but I'm not worth sending anywhere in my present condition!

The reply on December 10, was addressed to them both, 'Dear Bahá'í Friends,' and revealed yet again the Guardian's kindness and thoughtfulness for George: 'He advises Mr Townshend not to worry too much about his book, and to work on it only as his strength permits. Undoubtedly when finished it will be a great asset to the Faith.

'You are both in his thoughts and prayers, and your dear children as well.'

When the Malta project had to be abandoned and Una recalled to help at home, the Guardian's reply of August 28, 1954 to the news (conveyed in George's letter of July 24 which unfortunately is missing) was:

He said it was not an imperative instruction that you should go to Malta, but a hope; and to tell you you must not grieve anymore. You must not feel upset or distressed about anything, including the fact that you asked your daughter to come home.

None of us are infallible. It is the purity of our intention that counts; and you may be sure the Guardian is well aware of your single-hearted devotion. You must put away the dark thoughts, and be happy and grateful for the many great bounties God has given you.

The Guardian will pray that your health may improve.

The Guardian's personal note reads:

May the Spirit of Bahá'u'lláh continue to sustain you in your truly historic services, to aid you to enrich the fine and imperishable record of your manifold services to His Faith and its nascent institutions. Your true and grateful brother, Shoghi.

His last letter, typed by Una on July 24, 1956, eight months before he died, began, 'O my beloved Guardian', and reported completion of the book which Shoghi Effendi so eagerly anticipated. His letter reads:

> My immediate job is to get well and play my part in following up the publication but at present I have not made any improvement in health, either as regards my balance or my strength.
>
> I have been almost nine years thinking about the book. Is it not possible that the moral and intellectual effort expended on it have put a strain on my nervous system which should soon disappear now that the strain is lifted? What I want with all my heart is to get well enough to work for the Cause, not simply to continue to live. I have had for many years in the depths of my being a hope and conviction I should succeed in this. I could not have described what the work would be (nor can I now). This hope corroborates 'Abdu'l-Bahá's promises in his letter of 1919. I am on tenterhooks. Is there anything I can do to help the fulfilment of my longing to work thus for the Cause? The doctors can do nothing and do not understand the situation. I know you will help me all you can and I appeal to you for aid as I seem to have got to the end of my tether. It is all very exciting!
>
> With deepest love and thanks for your long patience with me,
>
> Ever your servant . . .

and he managed to sign it shakily but recognizably. Una added her own postscript:

> My father is breaking his heart with the thought that he is disappointing 'Abdu'l-Bahá by not achieving all that he should have achieved. Last winter I asked him why it was he was so keen to get well instead of longing for the 'Abhá Kingdom. He said, ' 'Abdu'l-Bahá wants me to bring my Church under the Heavenly Jerusalem and to do lots of other things I haven't done and if I don't get better I'll die a failure.'
>
> I didn't write about this before as I thought the completion of his book would be followed by an improvement in his health but this doesn't seem to be happening. He gives the impression of petering out through the frustration of his longing.

The Guardian's reply to Mr George Townshend and Miss Una Townshend marvellously closed the correspondence, though not the relationship. It was dated August 26, 1956.

> He feels Mr Townshend should rejoice, as indeed he himself does, that his book has now been finished. It is a great triumph, and no doubt will be a real help in the teaching work.
>
> He should feel very happy that he has done so much for the Cause in a field where no one else had the ability to serve it in this manner. He has in truth pleased the beloved Master by his outstanding services.
>
> The Guardian assures you both of his constant and loving prayers.

The last word was the Guardian's personal note:

May the Almighty guide, sustain and bless you in these days of stress and trial, remove every obstacle from your path, cheer your hearts, and fulfil every desire you cherish for the promotion of His glorious Faith. Your true brother, Shoghi.

To the last, George was upheld, sustained and reinforced by his commander-in-chief, who instantly supplied his utmost need, assured him, encouraged him, voiced his fame abroad, prayed for him and loved him, and at his death ensured his everlasting fame and influence by setting him, together with Breakwell and Esslemont, in the constellation which would for ever shed lustre upon the Bahá'í communities of the British Isles.

March 21 is a festival in the Bahá'í Faith. It is New Year's day, according to the calendar inaugurated by the Báb and confirmed by Bahá'u'lláh. On the morning of that day in 1957 Brian entered his father's room in the Baggot Street Hospital and gently spoke of a cable from the Guardian. George raised himself in his bed, forcibly seized Brian's coat with both hands, and begged to know what was in it. So strongly did his father hold him that Brian had difficulty retrieving the cable from his pocket. He read, 'LOVING THOUGHTS FERVENT PRAYERS SURROUND YOU BE HAPPY CONFIDENT.' George relaxed on his pillow and in greatest joy lifted his right hand above his head and waved it in a characteristic and triumphant gesture. He died four days later.

The Guardian died within eight months. Posterity must be eternally grateful that George preceded him, so that we know on the testimony of the Sign of God himself, whom we have had among us.

Chapter 7

THE OLD CHURCH –
THE CHOSEN INSTRUMENT

WE MUST now return to 1919 and the installation of the Reverend George Townshend, MA (Oxon.) to the incumbency of Ahascragh in the diocese of Killaloe, Kilfenora, Clonfert and Kilmacduagh, County Galway.

George was about to enter what must appear from any outward point of view the happiest and most satisfying period of his life. After the adventurous years, he was settled into a fine house in the Irish countryside, remote enough to satisfy his love of solitude; his children would be born and grow up there; his major literary works, with the exception of his final 'crowning achievement' and a number of essays, would be produced; he would rapidly achieve an honoured position in his profession and win the love and respect of his colleagues; 'the Archdeacon' would become an important figure in the countryside and he would have the leisure to indulge his love of poetry.

And yet the next twenty-eight years, during which he pursued the task which he believed to have been laid upon him by 'Abdu'l-Bahá, were to be the most frustrating, the most educative, the most demanding of fortitude, patience and persistence. His own understanding of Bahá'u'lláh's Revelation, constantly developing and deepening as he meditated upon and studied it, brought him early to the realization that just as the new world order of Bahá'u'lláh could not be overlaid on an obsolescent and lamentably defective system of national relationships, neither could the ecclesiastical systems of Christianity in all or any of their various divisions be repaired or modified to the requirements of the Kingdom of God on earth, whose establishment was the purpose of Bahá'u'lláh.

We must now trace this growing awareness and his long protracted struggle to escape from the strait-jacket in which his determination to realize 'Abdu'l-Bahá's hope, his concern for the welfare of the infant Bahá'í Faith, and his family responsibilities confined him. His longing to be free had many ups and downs as various schemes seemed feasible or desirable, but proved impracticable or abortive, and the long frustration was part of the hard and stony path which great spirits must seemingly traverse. If the way of the transgressor is hard, the way of the mystic is harder; but though the former may flourish like the green bay tree the latter may enter the Kingdom of Heaven.

In George's life there was no dichotomy between spiritual and secular matters; in fact he did not recognize 'secular' as having any validity whatsoever. The most practical, mundane realities were but the necessities of spiritual training and only spiritual growth would enable men to meet and conquer the problems of the world. He knew that difficulties must be solved by himself, with the help of God. 'I rely on Bahá'u'lláh to give me courage and serenity in dealing with the difficulties that will arise.' 'I pray with all my heart Bahá'u'lláh will . . . forgive me for my shortcomings and help me to travel straight and hard on the path on which my foot is set.' 'I wish I could become just an instrument for 'Abdu'l-Bahá to employ as He pleased.' As the greatest crisis of his life approached, he would ask the Guardian 'to pray that I may be swiftly so changed as to be fully and abundantly adequate to any emergency and any opportunities.' He was ever ready to seek in himself weaknesses or immaturities which had kept or might keep him from victory. 'When I am fit to bear the burden Thou wilt lay it on my shoulders.'[1]

Scarcely had he established himself in his rectory, in time-honoured and approved fashion, as family man and parish priest than he wrote his first letter to 'Abdu'l-Bahá, clearly revealing that his search for Truth had not ceased with his settling down. Eighteen months later he was accepted as a Bahá'í by 'Abdu'l-Bahá. No immediate dilemma arose from his professional commitment to a church which had taken not the slightest notice of Bahá'u'lláh. In spite of the Tablets to the Pope, to Christian kings, to priests in general and of 'Abdu'l-Bahá's widely reported Western tour, the Christian clergy of all denominations were generally not aware of the new Revelation. George conceived it his duty to inform those of his own ministry. '*It is my hope that thy church will come under the Heavenly Jerusalem*' became his mandate and he set himself to its achievement. Without in the least neglecting his parochial duties, or those of higher office as they were laid upon him, he began a deliberately planned campaign to bring not just a few fellow priests but the whole Church of Ireland with all its

---

[1] *The Altar on the Hearth*, p. 126.

hierarchy of priests, bishops and archbishops, with the entire foundation of a Christian community, to recognition of the fulfilment in Bahá'u'lláh of the central promise of Christ's Message, His return in the glory of the Father.

In those early days of the Faith of Bahá'u'lláh the believers had not yet realized the unique feature of His Revelation. Overwhelmed and beatified by their knowledge of Him as God's new Messenger, the very Promised One of all ages, they were content to leave it to Him to establish His Kingdom on earth, not realizing that He had made provision for that very consummation in His revealed Word. 'Abdu'l-Bahá's Will and Testament would not be disclosed until the end of 1921 and even then its implications tended to be overshadowed by the all-important, soul-appeasing appointment of a successor, endowed with authority to interpret the Scriptures and direct the unfoldment of the new Dispensation. It became the task of Shoghi Effendi, Guardian of the Bahá'í Faith, to point out to the believers that enshrined within the sacred text of the new Revelation was an Order whose underlying principles, basic institutions and *modus operandi* were divinely revealed and were indeed the actual embryonic structure of the long-awaited, Christ-promised Kingdom of God on earth. Theirs was the task to build that Order, whose charter was 'Abdu'l-Bahá's Will and Testament.

Prior to the Guardian's awe-inspiring and galvanizing revelation of Bahá'u'lláh's fuller purpose,[1] and before the rolling up[2] of the old order of the world had gone beyond hope of repair, the Bahá'ís saw no need to come out of their old organizations and confessions, believing that reform and a general recognition of the unity of purpose of all religions would achieve the desired aim. Bahá'u'lláh's injunction to *'consort with the followers of all religions in a spirit of friendliness and fellowship'*[3] was taken as approval of membership in all or any existing religious organizations and again it was the Guardian who explained the difference between association and affiliation. The friends gradually came to realize that the former would promote harmony and friendship whereas the latter would add chaos to confusion and utterly defeat the development of 'one fold, and one shepherd'.[4]

George was no exception to this, since the World Order of Bahá'u'lláh was as yet undisclosed by the Guardian. Perhaps in one

[1] See *The Goal of a New World Order; The Unfoldment of World Civilization*, by Shoghi Effendi.

[2] One of Bahá'u'lláh's prophetic utterances: *Soon will the present day Order be rolled up, and a new one spread out in its stead.* Cited by Shoghi Effendi in *The Unfoldment of World Civilization; The World Order of Bahá'u'lláh*, p. 161.

[3] Ṭarázát, second Ṭaráz

[4] John 10:16

passage of George's impassioned 'Surrender' may be discerned some intimation of a change: 'I cannot tell what may be my field of labour or the manner of my witness – whether I am to remain as I now am seeking to find and to proclaim the veritable Christ or to chant in fuller tones the Day of God from some unfaded Tree.' That 'unfaded tree' may be more significant than poetic. We cannot know. Certain it is that he strove with all his might to bring his Church into the new order, and equally certain is it that the possibility of difficulties arising from his position as an officer of that Church had already occurred to him. His letter of October 16, 1925 to the Guardian contains the following statement: 'I feel assured my work is now to be done as a Christian clergyman and my opportunity as such grows clear.' So he had thought about it. As long as he was able to maintain this view of membership in the Bahá'í community, he could tell the Guardian 'We have seven Irish Bahá'ís – the two Ffordes,[1] my wife, my sister,[2] my two children (aged four and five) and myself!' The time would come when he would be the only Bahá'í in the whole of Ireland.

George wrestled with this problem of his service to Bahá'u'lláh. How could he best fulfil 'Abdu'l-Bahá's hope, that his Church would enter the New Jerusalem? By working from within that Church and accepting all the limitations and restraints it would impose upon him, or by resigning and proclaiming the great news as vociferously and vigorously as he could? Interest in religion had been receding for years and there were few signs of a general spiritual awakening. Bahá'u'lláh Himself had written half a century before, *The vitality of men's belief in God is dying out in every land . . . The corrosion of ungodliness is eating into the vitals of human society.*[3] Were George to abandon his Church he might lose all influence with it and become a solitary voice crying in the wilderness. His contact with the handful of Bahá'ís in London[4] had not encouraged him to think of them as providing any strong base from which he could launch a campaign. Indeed the Bahá'í community of the British Isles was still in its stage of germination and would not begin to 'put forth leaves and blossoms' for another full decade.[5]

---

[1] A couple from Donegal whom Una remembers staying with them at the rectory.

[2] Maude; see p. 15.

[3] See *Gleanings from the Writings of Bahá'u'lláh*, XCIX.

[4] He visited London in August 1925 and again late in 1927, and returned disappointed from both visits.

[5] This community, at its Convention in 1944, asked the Guardian to set them the goals for a Six Year Plan. After a slow start, they swept to unbelievable victory, winning for themselves the love and admiration of the Guardian of the Faith, the 'palm of victory' in pioneering (leaving one's home to reside in another place at home or abroad to establish the Faith), becoming the envy and cynosure of the Bahá'í world

George was no iconoclast or revolutionary, but the mildest and most moderate of men. He had a good inkling, though probably at that time no true conception, of what he was up against. Naturally optimistic and cheerful, he set out with high hopes on a task which he believed could be accomplished.

He knew from his study of the Bible the strength of old establishments. No outspoken proclamation of the great news would be of any avail, except to classify him with the cranks. The basic principles enunciated by Bahá'u'lláh were not whole-heartedly, or in their entirety shared by his fellows; some would be utterly rejected. The idea of a succession of Manifestations of God of Whom Christ was one, was blasphemy to them.

What then was he to do?

There were two good starting points. He was already an officer of that Church which he was to lead to the light, and his own belief in Christ and Christian values was unquestioned. In addition, his knowledge of the new Revelation gave him an insight, not shared by his hierarchy, into the transformations which were required in the whole body of current Christian doctrine and attitude to enable an entire community to enter the New Jerusalem.

Let him therefore first win a hearing by presenting the message of Christ from the Bahá'í point of view, in a modern, vigorous, attractive way, such as 'Abdu'l-Bahá had done in His public addresses in the West. Further, he could, in this same context, dwell upon the marvellous signs and wonders of the time which, although of daily occurrence, were not related in the general mind to Christ's prophecies, and represent them as those very portents described by Christ Himself to occur at the time of His return.[1] No Christian could object to such a reading of the Gospel and, could he make it attractive and urgent enough, the dying spark of true love for Christ might yet be fanned into a flame of zeal and dedication such as had not been seen in Ireland since the early centuries.

His letter of October 18, 1925 explains his view to the Guardian:

> In these highly conservative communities, an approach to Bahaism through the Christian Churches may be appropriate and helpful. Christianity may be toned up by conscious and informed effort from within. Thus prejudice and tradition will be taken from the rear. You will

---

and earning for their descendants a 'glorious destiny', the first indication of which was the leadership of the first international plan of the Faith – the opening of Africa – involving the co-operation of five national communities, the British being the co-ordinator. The Guardian wrote to George on October 6, 1950, by his secretary, 'The victory of the Plan in the British Isles seemed almost miraculous, and has been a great stimulus to other countries.'

[1] Matt. 24

see, and doubtless you knew long ago, the strategic importance of this. In
the British Isles, perhaps a tremendous attack may be developed from the
rear, which over here is the point of vantage.[1] What this means to me is
that my first task is to make Christians (myself to begin with, then others).
When people have become really Christian, they will find themselves
Bahá'ís.

Dr John E. Esslemont,[2] a Scottish physician who became a Bahá'í in
1914, and who shares with George and Thomas Breakwell the
distinction of being one of the 'three luminaries shedding brilliant
lustre annals Irish English Scottish Bahá'í communities',[3] writing
from Haifa on October 28, 1925 on behalf of Shoghi Effendi, appears
to convey in the following passage the Guardian's approval of
George's plan. 'Shoghi Effendi is much interested to hear of your
literary work.[4] He fully agrees with you that different people must be
approached in different ways and that valuable work for the Bahá'í
Cause can be done within the Christian Churches by promoting the
"Christianity of Christ". 'Abdu'l-Bahá said that when people become
true Christians, they will find themselves Bahá'ís.'

In pursuit of his plan he composed a small book of prayers and
meditations 'for use in the home (and in the study)', to which his
Bishop wrote a Foreword. He wrote to the Guardian, 'Any Christian
who accepts *The Altar on the Hearth*[5] will be a long way on his road for
all the fundamentals of Bahá'ísm are in it – open and plain and
vigorous, and based on the Bible!'

The opening *Prelude*[6] is a poem which amply justifies this claim, the
last verse being an excellent example of George's proposal to infiltrate
from the rear:

Be of good cheer!
What kings desired in vain God gives to you
And in this wondrous day before our eyes
Unseals His ancient book of mysteries[7]
Making all things in earth and heaven new.[8]

[1] Similar apparently unconscious (or were they?) expressions of humour will be met
as our story proceeds.

[2] Author of *Bahá'u'lláh and the New Era*, for many years the only general account of
the Bahá'í Faith published in the West. Referred to by the Guardian as 'Esslemont's
immortal book'.

[3] Cable from Shogi Effendi, March 27, 1957; see p. 365.

[4] *The Altar on the Hearth*; see below.

[5] The Talbot Press, Dublin and Cork 1927. See Ch. 12.

[6] Sending it to the Guardian on April 30, 1936 he noted '. . . better called *The Day of
God*'. Shoghi Effendi printed it, under that title, in *The Bahá'í World*, vol. VII.

[7] Dan. 12:4,9

[8] Rev. 21:5

Truth hath come down from some far flaming sphere;
Lo, in our midst her sacred fires burn!
And see – trace back these countless rays of light
To the One Point wherein they all unite,
And bow your forehead in the dust to know
That God Himself is here![1]

The essay which follows, *Of Religion, of Happiness, and of the Modern Home* plunges at once *in medias res*:

'The purpose of this book is to bear witness to the truth that the power of God is now abroad among men in its fulness, and that happiness in the home (and elsewhere) is to be attained only through conscious communion with that power.'

The initial acclaim which this little gem of a book received in the Irish press seemed to portend success for George's plan of campaign. It rapidly sold out and established him in the affections of the Church of Ireland, the citadel which he must win over to Bahá'u'lláh.

The Archbishop of Dublin sent him the following letter:

Dear Canon Townshend,

I have received your little book The Altar on The Hearth and thank you much for it. I have been reading it in various parts and am much touched by its thought and diction. In your preface you indicate the difficulties which beset those who live in the modern home and I think that your spirituality and refinement of outlook should be a real help to readers of your book.

I would suggest your sending a copy to Lady Arnott, the President of the Mothers Union in Ireland; if your book commended itself to the Committee it might thereby secure a considerable circulation.

I like the one or two poems which you have introduced here or there.

Hoping that you will find an entry through The Altar on the Hearth into many homes.

I am
Yours very faithfully
John Dublin

The five essays comprising his book *The Genius of Ireland*[2] were written during this period and followed the same plan of announcing the 'Glad Tidings' but without ever specifying the facts. The leaflet announcing it states, 'The purpose of this book is to suggest the character of the contribution which Ireland may make to the coming civilization.' In it he attains the peak of his literary style and proclaims throughout that a new day of God has at last dawned. Every essay dwells on this theme.

[1] ibid. 21:3
[2] The Talbot Press, Dublin and Cork 1930. See Ch. 13.

Ideas for books and essays flooded his mind, springing from his eagerness to serve the Cause and bring the light of the new day to Christendom.

> I have in my head and heart two other books. One is to be on the Divinity of Art, the text being *'Art is Worship' 'Abdu'l-Bahá'*. This is partly done. The second is to be on the divinity of History, dealing with the Bible as it in truth is. The working out of 'Abdu'l-Bahá's teaching is the sole intent of each and all of them. The third is still very vague in my mind.[1]

But this slow preparatory approach to announcing the great message, although producing literary jewels and avoiding confrontation, would never proclaim Bahá'u'lláh as Christ returned in the glory of the Father.

The impossibility of his position soon began to worry him. The longing for *the Fountain of Truth* which had driven him on for so many years was growing into a desire, rapidly to become a consuming passion, to be free of all restraint in his service to Bahá'u'lláh. He is champing at the bit for action.

We must reflect again on that guiding hand which had led him *from one condition to another* and had brought him, just as he was about to attain *the Fountain of Truth* to a settled pattern of life in his native land. Had the knowledge of Bahá'u'lláh come to him even a few months earlier he might never have settled down at all. Family life, regular duties, the peaceful countryside, were the best background for his own development and prodigious services to Bahá'u'lláh. The work he did for the Guardian, his literary output, his exposition of the relationship between the Revelations of Christ and Bahá'u'lláh, the foundation he laid in Ireland for the future upbuilding of the Kingdom of God in that blessed and tragic island, were all accomplished against the background of an honoured and stable position. His struggle for freedom was not from the pattern of stability but from the shackles of an archaic and superseded system to which he had committed himself before knowledge of the New Jerusalem was given him. All through the long difficult years he never lost faith that when he was ready, God would act. 'When I am prepared to take the field Thou wilt assign me a place in Thy army of Light.'[2]

But the circumstances of his life conspired to make him the most harassed and tormented of men, while to outward appearances his lot seemed happy and enviable. The long, dry, disciplining years,

---

[1] Letter to Shoghi Effendi, October 16, 1925. The first book mentioned was never completed although he filled two exercise books with his notes. The second eventually became *The Promise of All Ages*; the third could be any one of several which he planned and worked on.

[2] *The Altar on the Hearth*, p. 126

although full of activity, of service to and advancement in his profession, of family life, of work for the Guardian, of writing, of growing fame in the Bahá'í world, were none the less years of constant defeat and frustration of the inmost desire of his heart.

On February 27, 1926 he wrote to Shoghi Effendi offering to help with English translations of the Persian and Arabic of the sacred text, a move which involved him for the rest of his life in close collaboration with the Guardian. This is fully related in Chapter 6, 'Relationship with the Guardian'. It is pertinent to us now for its revelation of George's full appreciation of his anomalous position; 'This tiny help in a small field is all I can now – it appears – offer to the Cause. So long as I have to provide for my family as I am doing at present I cannot do anything openly. I hope and pray God will raise me to a spiritual station where I shall be fit to be by some means released to serve Him in every way all the time. To have to stay as I am seems an appalling and impossible fate.' Note again the belief that spiritual growth in one's self is the way to overcome difficulties.

Note, too, that the confidence expressed in his letter of October 16, 1925 (see page 96), that his work would be performed as a Christian clergyman, has gone and he now knows, though does not yet fully understand, or even grasp, the compulsions that would force him to renounce his Orders. At present the prospect of 'an appalling and impossible fate' is personal, constricting his services to Bahá'u'lláh, separating him from his fellow believers, leaving him out of the main current of Bahá'í development. He has no inkling of his own great station or spiritual destiny or of the demand which the rapidly growing Order of Bahá'u'lláh would make of him. George wrestled with this problem for nearly a quarter of a century, bearing the appalling and impossible fate with fortitude and cheerfulness and gradually coming to realize that he must either resign or be unfrocked. Lest anyone should think he chose the wrong course in remaining in the Church and attempting to realize 'Abdu'l-Bahá's hope for it, the following excerpt from a letter written on October 5, 1946, a year before his resignation, on behalf of the Guardian to the National Spiritual Assembly of the Bahá'ís of the United States and Canada, whose members, like the rest of the Bahá'í world, knew nothing of George's prodigious work for the Guardian, is pertinent: 'He considers that our dear Bahá'í brother, George Townshend, can best serve the Faith at the present time where he is; he is now contacting many high ecclesiastics in his church, and also is engaged on a new book. Perhaps in the future the way will open for him to travel and teach, but at present his literary work is unique and very important.'

But now arose an opportunity which seemed to offer the ideal resolution of George's problems. In 1925, at the behest of the Guardian, the International Bahá'í Bureau had been opened in Geneva. Its purpose was to act as an auxiliary to the World Centre in Haifa in the dissemination of news to Bahá'ís, as an intermediary between Haifa and other Bahá'í centres, and to foster relationships with international movements centred in Geneva.[1] The work proceeded with the voluntary help available, but on September 9, 1928 a number of eminent Bahá'ís gathered at the Bureau to discuss ways of organizing its work on a more satisfactory basis. The minutes of the meeting record a suggestion to appeal to four people as 'workers', the fourth being 'Canon Townshend, England'.

The details of George's part in this episode are unfortunately not available, due to the very poor secretarial service which the Guardian received from his cousins and brother, a situation not relieved until some time after the Guardian's marriage in 1937, when his wife took over the secretarial duties. His own relatives had far too often written his letters, not as though on his behalf but as if they themselves were the correspondents; neither were they careful of the incoming letters and many are missing, knowledge of them deriving from their acknowledgement. Four such letters from George at this period are among the missing. The first two are not strictly related to the Geneva project but are indicative of what may be contained in the other two. His letter of March 2, 1928 is acknowledged by the secretary of the time, assuring George of the 'pleasure it is both to our Guardian and to us all, to hear from you and of your boundless enthusiasm to come out openly and join in devoted service to our Cause'. There is no personal note from the Guardian and the secretary takes it upon himself to say 'I do hope you will insure the future from the material point of view, before you take the step that all those who have had the pleasure of knowing you, eagerly await and expect.' George's second letter was dated May 22 and apparently set out his 'inmost thoughts in connection with the Bahá'í Faith', and the obstacles which he would have to overcome in order to serve it fully.

On November 23, 1928, two letters from George dated September 16 and October 7 were acknowledged; neither can be found. The first contained 'earnest assurances' and the second 'an actual and courageous offer', together apparently with the news that George had paid a lightning visit to the Bureau for one day,[2] accompanied by his wife, and was now prepared to move to Geneva to assume its

---

[1] See *The Bahá'í World*, vol. IV, pp. 257–61.

[2] This is confirmed by a report in *Bahá'í News*, April 1929 (No. 31). The date of George's visit has been put, by others, as 1929 but the evidence is conclusive for September 1928.

directorship. Mrs Julie Chanler, a wealthy American Bahá'í, had offered to finance the project, and Mountfort Mills, who had already rendered historic services to the Guardian,[1] was working on the practical arrangements. The secretary's letter reads as though all is decided and then continues:

> However, your letter made us expect a communication from our precious Mountfort, describing the possibilities of such a step on your part and elucidating the situation from its financial point of view. You will, I trust, realize that no matter how eager Shoghi Effendi might be to enlist your more active cooperation in common service to the progress of the Faith, he is most reluctant to advise any step unless all necessary provisions have been made for the adequate support of your family and the education of your children. While he looks constantly to the day when you will be to him a general at the Front, he is sorry to realize the necessity of such material considerations.
>
> However, he is still hopeful that all these difficulties will be surmounted and we can at last have you at Geneva. This is why he is still awaiting eagerly news from Mountfort . . .
>
> This short and hastily written letter is sent only to assure you that Shoghi Effendi is still thinking of you and Geneva, and that he is eagerly awaiting Mountfort's on the subject.

Both Mrs Chanler and Mountfort Mills were at the meeting in Geneva on September 9, and George may well have received a letter as a result of the 'suggestion' recorded above. But it is utterly impossible to conceive that he acted with such lightning decision as would have been necessary for his visit to have been made in response to such a letter. By 1928 George was known to many leading Bahá'ís and was in touch with them; some had even visited him in Ahascragh. There can be no doubt that the project for him to become Director of the Bureau had been under consideration by Mrs Chanler, Mountfort, George himself and perhaps others for some time before the meeting of September 9.

Una's record is now pertinent:

> An International Bahá'í Bureau had been established in Geneva and there was a proposal for my father to go over and take charge of it. I think it was in the fall or winter of 1928 that my father and mother went to Paris and met Mountfort Mills who took them on to Geneva. They just loved and were thrilled by Geneva, and when my father was asked how much he would need he mentioned that he would have to educate his two children, and they said, oh yes, they understood that. Then my father and mother came back home again full of high hopes that this was going to go

[1] He presented the Bahá'í case for possession of Bahá'u'lláh's house in Baghdád to the Permanent Mandates Commission of the League of Nations. See *The Bahá'í World*, vol. IV, pp. 198–209 and vol. IV pp. 237-47.

through, but a long time went by without anything happening, and then eventually they heard that it wasn't going through. Daddo always blamed himself for this as he thought perhaps he had asked for too much money and he was very unhappy about it; he felt he must have made some mistake. Some time later Mrs Little, an American pioneer to Europe, came to visit us and she explained that the project for Daddo was to have been financed by a Mrs Chanler but that she turned against the Cause and so the money never came through. I think this relieved Daddo's mind quite a bit, for he had blamed himself for the failure.

The episode appeared to close with a letter from the Guardian's secretary written on January 20, 1929, in which he acknowledges one from George of January 8 (also missing) and states: 'Although we all regret that final arrangements for Geneva are beset with various difficulties, Shoghi Effendi is highly pleased with your kind assurances. He writes on your envelope: "assure him my affection, admiration, appreciation".' One further comment in a letter (March 14, 1929) from Maude Townshend, George's sister who was living in Dublin at the time, to Emogene Hoagg[1] is of interest:

> I don't know if there is any chance of my brother going out to Geneva, I wish there were, he would (I think) be much more in his element, and his present post is one of stagnation, he has not a single individual with whom he can discuss subjects or thoughts – he is bringing out a volume of essays shortly. His wife is just the practical helpful companion that he needs, for he gets very much in the clouds at times.

The large number of missing documents in this chain of events is remarkable and leads to the supposition that a great deal was not put on paper. This would accord with George's anxiety – well documented on other occasions – not to jeopardize in the slightest degree his commanding position *vis-à-vis* the Church of Ireland, which he had to win over to Bahá'u'lláh and did not wish to antagonize. In addition to the four letters already mentioned, the extremely scanty records of the Geneva Bureau which are available contain nothing about the subject. Mountfort Mills and Mrs Chanler certainly knew about it when they attended the meeting of September 9, 1928; in fact Mountfort had met the Townshends in Paris and accompanied them to Geneva on his way to that meeting. The whole project was kept in confidence, doubtless in order not to embarrass George should it not be successfully concluded.

However, in spite of the absence of records, it is possible to suggest

[1] Mrs H. E. M. Hoagg, an outstanding Bahá'í worker and pioneer from 1898 until her death in 1945. She went to Geneva in 1928 to assist Mrs Stannard in the work of the Bureau and was later called to Haifa by the Guardian to type the script of *The Dawn-Breakers*. See *The Bahá'í World*, vol. X, pp. 520–26.

that early in 1928 the proposal was put to George that his talents and full-time service to the Faith of Bahá'u'lláh could be secured by his moving to Geneva and assuming directorship of the International Bahá'í Bureau. Financial support could be arranged and there would be no need to renounce his ecclesiastical titles and Orders. Many clergymen, both Protestant and Roman Catholic, took up work outside the Church, and no great wonder would be aroused were George to do the same. This reading of the known facts would account for George's (missing) letters of March 2, May 22 and September 16 containing assurances of his determination to 'come out openly and join in devoted service to our Cause' and outlining the problems to be solved. His visit to the Bureau in September enabled him, on returning to Ireland, to make his 'actual and courageous offer' of October 7.

The Geneva project, seen against the unfolding pattern of George's life and destiny, was bound to prove abortive. It nowhere fitted his character or offered the tests and discipline which his chosen course at Ahascragh imposed upon him. Nor would it have challenged his creative capacities. He would have exchanged the 'red and mystic way' *under the favour of Bahá'u'lláh*, for a life of comparative ease and social activity, and no foundation of sacrifice would have been laid in Ireland for the establishment of the future Bahá'í community there. It is not possible to visualize his elevation to the rank of Hand of the Cause while still in Orders. One overriding factor which tends to confirm this evaluation is the absence of any direct approval from the Guardian. According to the correspondence the first intimation Shoghi Effendi received of the proposal was a clear offer from George with only Mountfort Mills's report lacking to make it a *fait accompli*. The secretary's letter of November 23, 1928 clearly indicates the Guardian's doubts about the feasibility of the project while stating at the same time that 'he looks constantly to the day when you will be to him a general at the Front', that is, in the future.

This entire incident was typical of at least five other occasions during George's struggle to escape from his clerical life. Some event, action, centrepiece, in this instance directorship of the Geneva Bureau, would become the lodestar of his highest hopes and he would pursue with full energy and confidence whatever course the circumstances required. Every project, while bringing benefit to the Faith in general, proved abortive as far as George's personal hopes were concerned. He was frustrated at every turn.

But the Geneva episode, though typical, differs in two respects from others which we shall meet as we follow this period of his life. It was his first attempt to leave the Church, and established the fact in his own mind, while giving notice to others, specifically his family, that even in middle age – he was now fifty-four – he would take any opportunity which might arise or which he could promote, to change his profession. Secondly, it was not initiated by himself, but engineered by others, whose perception of George's spiritual destiny was not enlightened by the hindsight which we enjoy. In comparison with the stress and anxiety of later attempts, Geneva was a casual affair, neither engaging so hotly his eager pursuit nor bringing such deeply felt disappointment as would attend the failure of future efforts.

George's visit to Geneva, though brief, was a great refreshment to his spirit, both for the holiday and the association with the group of eager and stalwart Bahá'ís whom he met there. His continuing interest in the Bureau is disclosed in letters during the next three years to Emogene and Miss Culver,[1] letters which are fortunately preserved. They are the only record we have of his exchange of ideas at that time with fellow believers, and provide wonderful insight into his emotional attitudes to the Cause of Bahá'u'lláh and comments highly pertinent to our theme of his developing understanding of the new Revelation. His letter to Miss Culver of October 12, 1929 is particularly illuminating:

> For a long time past we have owed you a letter in reply to your very welcome letters and picture card. One reason why I did not write sooner was the very fulness of my heart. My hurried trip to the Bahá'ís in Paris and in Geneva gave me spiritually and intellectually a vision of God's Cause on earth in its beauty and its sweetness and in its apparent obscurity and weakness that has filled me with so many emotions I cannot dare to express myself about it. Geneva is to me a haven of spiritual beauty: God keep it unspoiled. Paris the very opposite, a cockpit of worldliness. I hope no Parisian will misunderstand me! The pity of having that serene and majestic power, so manifest in Geneva, lying in the midst of a roaring world quite unrecognized, undreamed of, and unworshipped, is so awful and heart-breaking that the contemplation of it bewilders and stuns me. Years ago when I first came into the Cause I prayed that some day I might visit Haifa and spend a night in prayer at the Holy Shrine. This would be the highest earthly privilege. And I thought someone answered me every time I uttered this prayer – 'When your heart goes there, your body will follow it.' Ever since, while I have been living in this remote and unimportant spot, my heart has been travelling; and I don't feel so far away as I once was.
>
> One of the most interesting proofs of the truth of this Revelation is its continuously growing influence on a soul which admits and welcomes it. The light increases, understanding deepens, difficulties solve themselves, one's mental surroundings change and change and change, one's inward

[1] See *The Bahá'í World*, vol. XI, pp. 507–9.

happiness becomes sturdier, and one's sense of utter dependence on the one side and of exaltation on the other becomes more vivid and intense – more a part of one's very self. Well, to me Geneva is an echo of Haifa. I have seen Geneva and felt there a spiritual power I had not felt elsewhere . . . How great a privilege is yours and Mrs Hoagg's to be so bravely and successfully upholding there this great Cause through these difficult times. I have no doubt difficulties will *increase*; but they will be different difficulties from those that you are conquering and in many ways less hard to battle against. A new phase is – I feel sure – at hand, and the present ignorance and apathy of the world will pass away. A period of conflict and opposition and persecution and every kind of controversy is approaching. The whole condition of the Bahá'í Cause will be completely transformed. Whatever we then have to complain of, it won't be men's indifference!

His devotion to 'Abdu'l-Bahá and his determination to gather and preserve all records of Him are revealed again in his letter to Emogene of the same date as above; it urges her to obtain 'any facts still ascertainable about 'Abdu'l-Bahá and Switzerland, especially Geneva. Such details of a personal character about Him are *real history*, and if not recorded immediately will die out of all human remembrance and knowledge . . . If you can get these facts, or cause them to be got, it will be a work of vital value. Geneva seemed to me so spiritual a place, and I long to picture more clearly Him in the midst of it.'

George often commented on what he considered the anomaly of the Bureau and did so in this letter to Emogene of October 12, 1929:

How strange and incongruous it is, though, to see this Bureau in the heart of Europe supported, directed and wholly run by Asia and America. I often smile when I think of this; and how I wish Europe could be wakened up to a knowledge of the Truth. But there is a good time coming – coming *very* near too, and Europe will take her proper place with her sister continents.

In April 1930 he sounded the same note:

. . . it is a constant hope of mine that we Europeans will support a bureau which geographically is chiefly ours and not lean much longer on the generous aid of two remote continents. It's all wrong! But Europe is in a bad case.

Julia Culver, who rendered devoted service to the Bureau, had to go away to a mountain resort for some time to recover health, and George corresponded with her between October 1929 and March 1931. His cheer and encouragement and sympathy were warm:

Health is so vital for one's best work that I hope *so* much you are really better; and I hate to think of you being laid up and suffering and having sleepless nights.

The Cause is now coming out of the trough of the wave and mounting hour by hour toward the crest. Everything goes in waves. This uplift will touch and vitalise you and the good news from every side will bring you cheer. 'Rejoice in the gladness of your heart!' Did you ever count how many times in *Hidden Words* Bahá'u'lláh counsels joyfulness? And see the only kind of sorrow He permits![2]

Have an easy mind and do not let anything harass you. The bugles of heaven are blowing strains of thankfulness for your faithful, staunch and determined efforts to obey the Centre of the Covenant and keep the Geneva Bureau going. Listen to the bugles and do not mind the yappings of mortals.

He sounds again the note of working out his own salvation:

Yes, I too wish my hands were freer and I were financially independent. But it will all come in God's good time. What belongs to us always will come to us, and I don't let myself be impatient for release as I once did. When I am ready and equipped for my work, I shall be taken up and transferred to where I ought to be.

Later he wrote:

How this Revelation grows on you. My interest and understanding and appreciation deepen continually; and I long for the day when I shall be qualified to leave this life and serve the Cause only all the time. It would be a very high privilege and perhaps I shall never be fit for it.

This state of grace was his best preparation for the difficult years now opening before him, years which would test to the utmost his patience, his submissiveness, his fortitude and resilience. Twenty years later he would write, 'How bitterly I regret that I did not come in twenty years ago – as I might have done. This delay has seared and scorched me to my inmost heart.'

[1] *O Son of Man! Sorrow not save that thou art far from Us. Rejoice not save that thou art drawing near and returning unto Us. Hidden Words,* No. 35 (Arabic).

Chapter 8

THE STRUGGLE WITHIN

GEORGE's editorial recommendations to the Guardian for the translation of *Hidden Words* resulted in Shoghi Effendi expressing his intention of acknowledging George's 'unique and invaluable collaboration' by placing his name, together with that of Ethel Rosenberg, on the title page. George's request to the Guardian not to do this[1] was acknowledged by the Guardian's secretary, who assured him of the Guardian's understanding and compliance. To this day the booklet bears on the title page: 'Translated by Shoghi Effendi with the assistance of some English friends.' George felt that so intimate an association with Bahá'í Scripture would identify him too openly with the new Revelation and would jeopardize his plan of approach 'from the rear'. The same consideration impelled him, three years later, to beseech the Guardian to allow the Introduction to *The Dawn-Breakers*, which he had written under the direction of the Guardian, to go unsigned. His own great work *The Promise of All Ages* was first published in 1934 under the pseudonym 'Christophil', although there were other considerations, in this case, as we shall see. He wrote a series of articles for *World Order* magazine under the initials A.G.B.[2] and C.P.L.,[3] all of which were later published as pamphlets under his own name. No connection to these initials can be traced and it has been suggested, somewhat waggishly perhaps, that they represented 'A Good Bahá'í' and 'Christophil'.[4]

[1] In a letter of May 22, 1928

[2] *The Approach to Religion; Religion and the New Age; The Well of Happiness; Constructive Religion*

[3] *The Wonder of It*

[4] Not so waggish after all. A belated enquiry to Una evoked the reply, 'When I asked Dad what the initials stood for he told me "A Galway Bahá'í". C.P.L. I have never seen.'

However, on April 16, 1931 George wrote one of his most significant letters to the Guardian:

I want to take this opportunity of saying something new about my personal relation to the Cause. I have begun to realise lately that unless some of us over here make some sort of a breakaway nothing will ever happen. We all shall perish. I am now impelled, for my part, to take this step. With a retiring disposition, and my professional connexion, I am little fitted for doing this. But I have come at last to this point. Though what I do is my own choice, and not an easy one, it is not all due to my own volition. I have heard a call which I cannot disobey. I will not say anything about the psychology of it which to me is impressive and startling. But in my heart I have torn away from much that held me; and I am conscious of a new concentration on Bahá'u'lláh and His service. From now on I shall find opportunities of expressing this new attitude by speaking and writing of the teachings, and showing my own interest and enthusiasm. I do not wish to appear to violate my ordination vows; but I shall have plenty of room to say much without doing that. I wish I had accepted your invitation to put my name to my Nabíl essay . . . If through any cause an opportunity of doing this arises I hope you'll let me make the change or that you will make it for me,[1] saying 'G. Townshend' too instead of an English correspondent.

I shrink from the publicity and the lifelong struggle which this line of action will entail. My disposition is, or has been, for privacy and poetry. But I cannot resist the pressure that is within me. The shrinking does not go as deep as the ardour! A growing love for Bahá'u'lláh moves me and what I am really doing is committing myself and my life wholly and unreservedly to Him. Power to face anything and to do everything will come out of that; and He will increase continually my faith and my courage. I hope I shall have the support of your prayers.

I can't be very definite about what I'll do. I am just starting out and I don't know where I am going. I will meet things as they come; and it won't be long before opportunities and changes of all sorts make their appearance.

The passage *'Though what I do is my own choice, and not an easy one, it is not all due to my own volition. I have heard a call which I cannot disobey'* is highly pertinent to our proposition that George was raised up by Bahá'u'lláh for His particular service.

In November of the year (1931) in which George was writing the above, one of the Guardian's most significant expositions of the Bahá'í Faith appeared in a general letter to the Bahá'ís of the West and was published under the title *The Goal of a New World Order*.[2] It opened to

[1] See p. 69, n.1.

[2] Copies of the typescript of this and other of his *World Order* letters were sent to George by the Guardian. See Ch. 6.

the understanding of the Bahá'ís a new and wonderful vision of their Faith:

The call of Bahá'u'lláh is primarily directed against all forms of provincialism, all insularities and prejudices. If long-cherished ideals and time-honoured institutions, if certain social assumptions and religious formulae have ceased to promote the welfare of the generality of mankind, if they no longer minister to the needs of a continually evolving humanity, let them be swept away and relegated to the limbo of obsolescent and forgotten doctrines. Why should these, in a world subject to the immutable law of change and decay, be exempt from the deterioration that must needs overtake every human institution? For legal standards, political and economic theories are solely designed to safeguard the interests of humanity as a whole, and not humanity to be crucified for the preservation of the integrity of any particular law or doctrine.

Let there be no mistake. The principle of the Oneness of Mankind – the pivot round which all the teachings of Bahá'u'lláh revolve – is no mere outburst of ignorant emotionalism or an expression of vague and pious hope. Its appeal is not to be merely identified with a reawakening of the spirit of brotherhood and good-will among men, nor does it aim solely at the fostering of harmonious co-operation among individual peoples and nations. Its implications are deeper, its claims greater than any which the Prophets of old were allowed to advance. Its message is applicable not only to the individual, but concerns itself primarily with the nature of those essential relationships that must bind all the states and nations as members of one human family. It does not constitute merely the enunciation of an ideal, but stands inseparably associated with an institution adequate to embody its truth, demonstrate its validity, and perpetuate its influence. It implies an organic change in the structure of present-day society, a change such as the world has not yet experienced. It constitutes a challenge, at once bold and universal, to outworn shibboleths of national creeds – creeds that have had their day and which must, in the ordinary course of events as shaped and controlled by Providence, give way to a new gospel, fundamentally different from, and infinitely superior to, what the world has already conceived. It calls for no less than the reconstruction and the demilitarization of the whole civilized world – a world organically unified in all the essential aspects of its life, its political machinery, its spiritual aspiration, its trade and finance, its script and language, and yet infinite in the diversity of the national characteristics of its federated units.

It represents the consummation of human evolution – an evolution that has had its earliest beginnings in the birth of family life, its subsequent development in the achievement of tribal solidarity, leading in turn to the constitution of the city-state, and expanding later into the institution of independent and sovereign nations.

The principle of the Oneness of Mankind, as proclaimed by Bahá'u'lláh, carries with it no more and no less than a solemn assertion that attainment to this final stage in this stupendous evolution is not only necessary but inevitable, that its realization is fast approaching, and that nothing short of a power that is born of God can succeed in establishing it.

George experienced to the full the profound effect which this letter produced on the entire Bahá'í world community. It must indeed have been a powerful impetus to his developing understanding of the independent character and world-embracing role of Bahá'u'lláh's Revelation.

Two years later, after further revising and editing of the Guardian's translations, and writing essays at his request for inclusion in *The Bahá'í World*, as well as for *World Order*[1] magazine, he wrote again, on April 23, 1933:

> I trust and pray that very soon God will release me from my clerical position and permit me to serve His Cause openly, and do nothing else. I am ready now to go anywhere and do anything for Bahá'u'lláh. I have somehow to earn my livelihood; I myself can live on a pittance, but I have two children to educate and a very sick wife, who may not live but a few months more, to provide for. There is no other difficulty now. I don't see anything to do at the moment; but I am determined to get free somehow unless God refuses me, and something may materialise before long. I merely mention my position to you at the moment.

He was now working on his great book *The Promise of All Ages* and asking the Guardian's permission to send it to him for comment, a request which Shoghi Effendi welcomed, and in a personal note to George, he assured him of his eagerness to receive and read it. George wrote in reply: 'I have felt it presumptuous to ask you to read this script. But I am anxious to avoid error; and the waters I am sailing on are deep.' He explained his thoughts about it *vis-à-vis* the Church.

> The publication is not planned as that of an official Bahá'í statement of any kind, but on the contrary a tribute from a working clergyman and an appeal to his brother Christians . . . The book will, under God, cause great commotion among the orthodox and advertise the Cause. Developments cannot be forecast; but the author will have to follow it up and will very soon lose both his reputation and his livelihood. This I have faced on my own initiative and my own responsibility and simply through faith in Bahá'u'lláh and desire to 'magnify His Cause' as He has said.
>
> The publicity and the controversy which will ensue, and to which in my lifetime there will be no end, are highly distasteful to me. So much the better. I rely on Bahá to give me courage and serenity in dealing with the difficulties that will arise. What I offer now are outward things: my profession, my living, my good name. Through this offering I hope to learn to offer more so that I may see with His eyes and hear with His ears and live with His love.

[1] Published quarterly, at that time, by the National Spiritual Assembly of the Bahá'ís of the United States and Canada.

While contributing a further article for *The Bahá'í World*[1] he wrote to the Guardian on September 24, 1933:

I am engaged in preparing the introduction and conclusion to *The Promise*. These oblige me to consider what it is the will of 'Abdu'l-Bahá that I should propose to the church readers of the book that they should do. The whole question of the attitude of the Christian churches is involved and the first step must be made as natural for them as possible. This book is of course one shot in a big battle and must be related rightly to the general effort of the western or European Bahá'ís.

I may mention that Mrs Slade and Mr and Mrs Romer alone know definitely about *The Promise*. Mrs Slade thinks it better at present not to show it to others: this is her idea and I am sure she is right. Mountfort Mills, and one other English Bahá'í (a man), are to be shown it as soon as possible.

It is difficult, now, to realize the nervousness felt, as late as the last decade before the Second World War, about the reaction of the Establishment to any deviation from orthodoxy. The fears and caution seem exaggerated, even astonishing, to the present-day observer. But those fears were very real and not entirely unjustified.

Ecumenism was an unknown word and Islám, as everyone knew, a false religion filled with unmentionable things![2] Even after the war, in 1947, Bishop Barnes's book,[3] which examines the origins of Christian doctrines without assuming them all to be Absolute Truth, caused a furore of outraged propriety; 'He should be unfrocked' was heard from more than one quarter. The scandal, and worse, which would attach to a senior priest resigning his office in order to join another religion cannot be imagined. Change from one form of Christianity to another was tolerated, though even that could cause a nine-days' wonder.[4] But to abandon the Establishment for some unknown oriental cult with a queer name (Christianity, of course, arose in England and the Bible was English!) smacked of heresy and madness.[5]

---

[1] *The Descent of the New Jerusalem*, see *The Bahá'í World*, vol. V; and footnote p. 240.

[2] The interesting study of why Buddhism and Hinduism were socially acceptable whilst Islám was the repository of all evil (Judaism of course was for Jews) has yet to be made.

[3] *The Rise of Christianity*, Longmans Green and Co

[4] Newman's transition, though more than half a century old, was still of lively interest.

[5] As late as May 12, 1981, *The Kerryman*, reporting the welcome given, in Tralee, to the new Bishop of Ardfert and Aghadoe, the Right Reverend Walton Empey, stated: 'Emphasising the value of belonging to a Christian faith Bishop Empey warned of alternative beliefs and diversions such as alcohol, drugs, sex, humanism, and Communism. He also named the Bahá'í faith and other "weird oriental types of religion".'

The Bahá'ís in the West at that time were extraordinarily oblique in their methods of communicating the great news. This was called indirect teaching and derived from 'Abdu'l-Bahá's warning not to lift the veil too suddenly. Although Christian influence had undoubtedly declined there was still deep devotion to the Person of Jesus, and not only among the diminishing number of church-goers. Any sudden presentation of Bahá'u'lláh as the Christ Spirit in a new human form would meet the same shocked opposition as had greeted Jesus' claim to be Messiah.[1] George's carefully-thought-out approach to Christians, based on 'Abdu'l-Bahá's example, seemed the safest way and suited the general temperament of the believers of the time. But they carried caution too far. It is true that blasphemy, since eviscerated of any meaning by the permissive society, was (and still is) a crime at common law in Britain,[2] but the possibility of being taxed with it was viewed with greater horror than the improbability of being prosecuted, and would certainly have contributed to the fantastic fear of open proclamation which prevailed among the early believers. To be labelled blasphemous or eccentric would be socially disastrous, and pre-emptive of any chance of winning sensible people to the Faith.

While it is true that there were movements,[3] under the most respectable auspices, to bring about dialogue between the world religions, there was no thought of unity in hierarchical or theological terms. It was a very good thing to know about other Faiths but, of course, Christ was the 'only begotten' and Christians alone had full access to Truth and Salvation. Bahá'u'lláh's teaching on the oneness of religion was unknown; tolerance and a gentlemanly agreement to differ were the objectives.

The obscurantism of the first decades of the twentieth century, in relation to the Bahá'í Faith, is the more remarkable when one considers the calibre and renown of those late-nineteenth-century historians, scholars, diplomats, philosophers and savants who made of the 'Episode of the Báb' a leading item in the intellectual discussions of Europe. Some even gave their allegiance to that 'Charmer of hearts' while others acknowledged the new Revelation.[4] But the First World War dealt a shattering blow to religious faith and the twentieth century pursued its rake's progress while the foundations of its house were disintegrating. The 'Higher Criticism' of the Bible had enabled the

[1] John 5:45-6

[2] The last prosecution took place in July 1977, when the editor of *Gay News* was convicted for publishing a poem which suggested that Jesus Christ was homosexual; he was given a suspended sentence of nine months imprisonment and fined £500.

[3] e.g.: the World Fellowship of Faiths; the Society for Friendship Between Christians and Jews.

[4] Tolstoy, Forel, Vámbéry, Nicolas, Cheyne *et al.*

ordinary man – that elusive creature – to make fun of Biblical metaphors but did nothing to repair his crumbling faith. The Church, still useful for christenings, marriages and funerals, while otherwise losing its hold on men's outlook, yet retained some faint echo of that massive authority which it had exercised in the Middle Ages when the great cathedrals were built, monuments to its former might and power in the same way that the ruins of medieval castles, as Lord Briggs maintained in his brilliant broadcasts, proclaimed the erstwhile ascendancy of the barons.

At any rate, the old respect for the Church, compounded of awe and fear and recognition of the moral standing of the clergy, was still a potent factor in social stability. George and the leading British Bahá'ís of that time did not question the need for caution. The Establishment was powerful and the 'nothing sacred' permissive society still thirty years away, unimagined and unimaginable. George anticipated that publication of his book would result in his trial for heresy (he mentioned this in several letters) or at the very least in obliging him to give up his position in the Church. He was ready to face all and anything, and to defend his position as a true Christian. On November 21, 1933 he wrote to the Guardian: 'I expect to insist strongly that my acceptance of Bahá'u'lláh does not oblige me to renounce my membership in the Christian church. I have no doubt, of course, I must very soon give up my place as an officer of the church.' The irony of his statement is only appreciated after knowing that he would struggle for another fourteen years to obtain his freedom and then would accomplish it only by a willing renunciation of far greater proportions than he now foresaw.

We have already noted George's caution in not allowing his name to be associated with Bahá'í publications, and his subsequent realization that he must come out openly and declare his allegiance to Bahá'u'lláh. His intention to publish *The Promise of All Ages* under his own name is disclosed in his letter already cited: 'The appearance of the author's name will also be likely to arouse other Bahá'ís to propagate the message and will startle many non-Bahá'ís; for people will see that the author (unless he were mad) would not do this unless he were sure that what he wrote was true.' But now another factor entered the equation: family opposition.

What part Anna Maria played in George's marriage is not known but George was her first-born and at that time was leaning heavily upon her. He had already followed her advice in the matter of his profession, and it would doubtless please her to see him settled and married to a sensible, practical woman who would care for him.

Anne Sarah (Nancy) Maxwell was of Scottish ancestry, shrewd and conservative. She was a cheerful, practical Christian, loyal to her upbringing and tradition. She is entitled to our full sympathy and appreciation. She married George when he was forty-two, starting again at the bottom of the professional ladder, and understood his need for a settled home life. She had little appreciation of the motivating passion of his life and never completely accepted the new Revelation to which he was becoming more and more in thrall. His desire to give up his lovely country rectory, his respected position and great prospects outraged her and she ascribed this aberration to 'Townshend family restlessness'. She was loyal to him and stood by him when he was attacked, but would not support him when he contemplated simply abandoning everything and moving to some small house in Dublin, hoping to support them all on what he could earn as a writer. From all sensible, balanced points of view she was right. But God's captive knows no such viewpoint, and George strained and struggled, determined to secure his freedom, maintain the unity of his family and 'get out' in a dignified way. Nancy went to great lengths to accommodate to his longing to spread the news of Bahá'u'lláh's Revelation, even though she did not recognize Him as Christ returned. She argued reasonably that for George to give up his position of influence, whence he had the attentive ear of the whole Church of Ireland and could slowly, slowly, win their interest and eventual co-operation was self-defeating. She agreed to entertain the local gentry, and all who would come, to meetings in the Rectory at which George would speak of 'Abdu'l-Bahá, and a number of such 'fireside meetings' were held. Here once again, irony – fantastic irony – entered the picture. George was so circumspect in his desire to observe 'Abdu'l-Bahá's counsel not to lift the veil too suddenly, that Nancy felt he was too cautious and did not make the most of his opportunities!

Fortunately we have two letters from Nancy's own hand in which she sets out her point of view and her evaluation of George's character, invaluable documents which will be presented as the story unfolds. For the moment we must be content with the thought that in one of them she uttered, as a *cri de coeur*, one of the great aphorisms of all time, 'Living with saints is not a bed of roses!!!' She obviously knew her R.L.S.

One more powerful ingredient in this mixture of hopes and fears, straining at the leash, family opposition and constant frustration was George's exaggerated hope of setting the Thames on fire. He always expected far greater results than ever happened – immediately. They *would* come – later – in full measure; even now the tide is flowing. For the rise of the Bahá'í Faith in Ireland since his passing is built on the foundation of sacrifice which he laid and which inspires the Irish believers to do for Bahá'u'lláh with brilliant zeal and dedication what their distant ancestors did for Jesus.[1]

Nor can we ever discount the restless artistic temperament with which he was blessed – or afflicted – certainly beset, always struggling for perfection, satisfied with his work at one moment, finding it utterly inadequate the next. And over and beyond this compulsion for creative expression was the consuming fire of the mystic within him, which drove him on, as more and ever more wondrous worlds of God opened before him, to serve his 'Only Beloved', Him and Him alone. He *must* tell afflicted humanity of its danger and its opportunity – its glorious opportunity.

Examples of his over-optimism have already been seen in his expectations of results from the publication of *The Promise of All Ages*.[2] In other letters to the Guardian, written between December 1933 and September 1934, we read:

> Later, I hope to go over to London to try to arrange for a concerted policy and concerted action in the activity that will arise; for the Bahá'ís will at once become the centre for all sorts of scrutiny and questions, and the strain will be very great.

> There is in my heart no doubt a great extension of the Cause in the West is at hand. How we are going to face up to the emergency is the problem! In my own little way and in my own little sphere I am doing all I can to get ready.

> I nourish the strongest hopes that in 1935 I shall become financially independent and be able to follow up the Promise, as it is really incumbent on me to do so. I am not going to fail, whatever happens.

> I sent fifty copies of the Promise for review. Five reviews so far have appeared – one vituperative, two contemptuous, two laudatory. It seems very possible a ferment may be starting.

He was encouraged in his optimism by the Guardian, who greatly admired *The Promise* and entertained the highest hopes for it. Shoghi Effendi's secretary wrote on his behalf:

> Your much-appreciated essay on the Cause is, indeed, in many ways unique, and when published will stimulate the interest of a vast number of intelligent people in the Message. By the controversy which it will probably create it will, it is hoped, give a tremendous and unprecedented publicity to the Faith and in this way attract many people to the Cause.

> . . . he considers the circulation of this valuable book as an essential, nay

[1] See Townshend, *The Genius of Ireland*, The Talbot Press, Dublin and Cork 1930; *The Mission of Bahá'u'lláh*, George Ronald, 1952. See also Ch. 13.
[2] See p. 112.

indispensable, preliminary step for the growth and progress of the Movement in England.

Shoghi Effendi's impression is that the book if properly read and pondered is bound to create a sensation in many religious and educational circles, and may awaken the interest of many enlightened persons in the principles and teachings of the Faith. As to the friends, they will be undoubtedly much stimulated and refreshed from its reading, and their knowledge of certain fundamental aspects of the Cause which have been hitherto either misunderstood or underemphasized will be further deepened and clarified.

As soon as it is ready for distribution will you kindly send him the 150 copies which he has already ordered through Mrs Slade.

The Guardian himself wrote:

I have read the manuscript with great care and am deeply impressed. I thank you from the depths of my heart. I can never forget so magnificent a service at so critical a time.

I deeply appreciate these evidences of your attachment and devotion to the Cause of God and its steadily expanding institutions. I trust and pray that the publication of your epoch-making book will lend a mighty impetus to the spread of the Faith in your land, and arouse genuine and widespread interest beyond its confines. May the Almighty bless your high, your exemplary and persistent endeavours.

I am fervently praying for your complete recovery and the speedy publication of your book. However and wherever it may be published, whether your name be associated with it or not, it will, I feel confident, arouse tremendous and sustained interest among Bahá'ís and non-Bahá'ís alike. It will indeed constitute a monument of the spirit animating you in His service.

I will, for my part, disseminate it as widely as I can and trust that the hopes I cherish for its share in lending an impetus to the world-wide spread of the Cause will be completely fulfilled.

The Guardian's encouragement of George's optimism in no way lessened George's – and other Bahá'ís' – fear of the Establishment. The extraordinary difficulties in finding a publisher, even with the offer of complete financial backing, the refusal of distinguished people – old admirers of 'Abdu'l-Bahá – to write a Foreword, repeated procrastination of the publisher in bringing the book out, necessitating two visits to London by George to force them to fulfil their contract, all served to dash George's hopes and sour his pleasure at completion of this, his first Bahá'í book. He summed it all up to the Guardian:

The whole business since last Christmas of vainly trying to get someone to write a Foreword, some literary agent to take charge of the manuscript, some publisher to produce it, and the refusal of everybody to help or touch the manuscript in any way till well on in the summer we found S.M. Ltd – it's all been tragic. I set my heart on having it out not later than May 23.

But looking back I do not regret anything we did nor think that any other course would have produced a better result. I do not understand yet this boycott of the Bahá'í Cause. I am told the Cause is regarded by Church authorities and others supposed to be informed as definitely a dead issue in England. We'll see. This blind opposition seems part of that dreadful infatuation by which those who disbelieve are led to incriminate and destroy themselves. Our situation over here is pitiful beyond any words . . .

The following passage from his letter to the Guardian of May 24, 1934, expands the above summary. Mrs Slade, one of the early believers in England, and her husband Marcus Slade, KC, had been trying to help him with the publication:

. . . but we have found so far no publisher, large or small, prepared to take the manuscript on any terms whatever, not even with the author's undertaking to bear all expenses. What is still more surprising, no agent will handle the book. I have already told you, I think, that not one of the men of note we approached for a foreword will even read the manuscript; and when the manuscript was sent to . . . some weeks ago he, too, though expressing a favourable opinion of the work, declined to commit himself in any way.

Simpkin Marshall have the manuscript now and have kept it a long time. I have written to the Slades to say that we must somehow get the thing out soon and that if need be I will print it privately. There are some drawbacks to such a course, for it is expensive, lessens the chances of a good circulation and makes rather a hole-and-corner business of the whole matter. The public has not learned to expect much of a privately printed work.

The Slades tell me that the cause of the publishers being all afraid of the Promise is that in it the Bahá'í Movement is presented so as to seem more threatening and dangerous to existing institutions than it has been made to seem hitherto. It is shewn not as any exterior or parallel movement, but as in that central position direct from Christ which the churches have always claimed as their special and sole monopoly.

Because of future developments I want, if I may, to explain to you the author's personal position. The publication of the Promise must involve my giving up all the church offices I hold (which are many)[1] either by expulsion or by resignation. The reason is that the agreement under which I hold office is that I am to teach and promote the doctrine of the Church of Ireland and to 'banish' all else. By publishing the Promise I break this agreement, and have no legal defence against sentence of dismissal.

[1] See Ch. 12.

I have not however been able to make any provision for my family, or for myself. Therefore I intend to withhold my name as the author till such time as the sales supply me with a means of subsistence. As soon as ever I have, or see before me enough to keep going, I shall resign (if I have not been already expelled!) and if the All-Merciful permit me serve the Cause openly and undividedly.

I believe it will be to the advantage of the Cause, the book and the author, if the Promise is produced *not* as an official Bahá'í work but as a tribute coming out of the Churches. My personal position as a practising clergyman may be to me highly embarrassing but it is also a special and particular opportunity. A tribute from a man who has everything to lose by making it is obviously worth more than an easier tribute; and to have it come from a loyal Christian and Churchman makes it the most direct and express challenge to the Churches that one can well imagine, and ought to help to cause the maximum confusion and to promote reform movements that will all lead people on into the Bahá'í Fellowship.

He commented further on his change of intention to publish under his own name, in a letter to the Guardian on August 10, 1934: 'For the protection of my family I am using the pseudonym "Christophil" till I can afford to give up my present post. It will not be a very effective cloak as too many know my secret.' The decision to publish it in this way was made as a peace-offering to Nancy, who foresaw disaster should the promotion of 'another religion' be charged to him. Financially the book was a failure and he was left with more than half the edition on his hands. Nearly all the copies sold were bought by the Bahá'í community of the United States, to whom the Guardian had recommended it. The entire press of the British Isles produced nine reviews. No bookseller would stock it and it made no impression on the public. But that was not the end of it.

It was republished in 1940 by Lindsay Drummond Ltd., published again in 1948 by George Ronald in a revised edition; reprinted in 1957; issued in paperback in 1961, again revised and re-set in 1972, and is still in world-wide demand and being translated into an increasing number of languages.

The title page of Lindsay Drummond's edition ascribes the authorship to

George Townshend, M.A. (Oxon.)
Canon of St Patrick's Cathedral, Dublin
Archdeacon of Clonfert

The editions published since his death bear the word *Sometime* before his ecclesiastical titles.

When the original publishers asked George to remove the remaining copies or permit them to destroy them, the Bahá'ís in

London gave them accommodation, and George revealed once more his persistence and courage. He wrote to the Guardian (April 6, 1937): 'This means the book goes off the market. Exit Christophil! I will find some better way of getting the book again before the public later. I am keeping busy on literary work of a Bahá'í nature.'

Together with all things Bahá'í, the world has rejected George's work, only to find that it does not disappear. It is ever thus with the Cause of God. Rejected, it lays its foundation; ignored, it builds its structure; persecuted, the blood of the martyrs nourishes its growth; hated and contemned, it offers peace and fellowship. The only successful way to deal with it, in the past, present or future is to wholeheartedly embrace it, work for it, seek its mysteries and hope to receive its bounties.

George began to feel the loneliness of his position. His love of solitude, introspection and quiet study gave way, in face of the need for action, to a longing for discussion with other Bahá'ís and participation in their activities. He finished his letter to the Guardian describing his visit to London in August 1934 to enforce his contract with Simpkin Marshall: 'I had a glorious visit to London, saw Mrs Slade and a blind . . . friend of hers, and put up for the night with Lady Blomfield. How I long to associate and work with my real companions!'

The depth of his loneliness and the intensity of his desire to see Bahá'ís are only too apparent from his correspondence with Mrs Stuart French, on the occasion of her visit, with her husband, to Europe in 1934. Mrs French served for many years as secretary or chairman of the Editorial Committee of *The Bahá'í World*, and she and George were known to each other through correspondence. While in London she wrote to him in glowing terms about *The Promise of All Ages*, just published, and asked him for an essay or poem for the next volume of *The Bahá'í World*. George's reply, August 17, 1934, was:

Thank you so much for your letter about *The Promise of All Ages*, which has just reached me and which I answer at once. It is a busy day but the sooner I get off my request to you, the more likely you are to be able to accept it. I had hoped to meet you when I was in London (I only go there about once in three years!) and was greatly disappointed at not doing so. I do wish I could go again to see you but I fear I cannot just now; and yet I very badly want to take this opportunity of meeting you when you are near – of course I remember our correspondence and I know your name so well. Could you and Mr French possibly run over here and let us have the pleasure of having you in our home for a visit however brief? My difficulty is that our house is full of guests and is likely to be so for a few weeks; but if you would be our guests in Ballinasloe which is close by and where there is a very comfortable hotel (Hayden's) I could run in for you after breakfast and you could spend the whole day with us here till the late evening. This seems the best I can do and I so eagerly hope you may be able to accept such hospitality as I can offer. Two American Bahá'ís have come to Ireland to visit us, Fred Schopflocher stayed here years ago, and Willard Hatch got as far as Dublin where we had a day with him. How I treasure the memory of those visits! I seldom, very, very seldom, see a Bahá'í: once in three years, and then only for an instant . . . What a pleasure it will be if you come. Euston 8:30 p.m. via Holyhead and Broadstone to Ballinasloe 10:20 a.m. is the programme.

   . . . I fear I am asking a great deal; but I so much hope you will come, and my wife of course joins me in promising you a very warm welcome . . . P.S. You might manage a couple of nights, *any*time except August 23, 24, and preferably not the 25th.

The Frenches couldn't change their plans and George expressed his disappointment in further correspondence.

The next appearance of his 'literary work of a Bahá'í nature' was his beautiful essay *'Abdu'l-Bahá: A Study of a Christlike Character'*. In somewhat casual manner, after the main part of his letter (hiding his delight and pride in its success), he wrote to the Guardian on September 5, 1935:

I enclose a paper on 'Abdu'l-Bahá in *Church of Ireland Gazette*. It has this much interest that it is probably the first article of its kind to be printed in a clerical paper over a clergyman's name. An old clergyman named Palmer wrote me such a touching letter about the article and begged me to reprint it.

This was really progress and evoked from the Guardian the following reply in his own hand at the end of his secretary's letter of September 28:

Dear and prized co-worker: I am truly grateful to you for your recent and most notable service to the Cause of God. I would certainly urge you to present a copy of the paper to the Editor of the *World Order* magazine, Horace Holley, who will I am certain be very glad to include it in the magazine, and thus enrich the material which he is collecting for publication. The friends in America and elsewhere would greatly and gratefully welcome such a noteworthy contribution on your part.

It had, and still enjoys, a huge success. Horace Holley welcomed it, and printed it immediately in *World Order*[1] as the first essay in a Symposium entitled 'Seven Candles of Unity', a title taken from 'Abdu'l-Bahá's cogent statement on the progress of world unity. It was republished in pamphlet form together with George's earlier

[1] October 1936, vol. II, No. 7.

reflection on the *Hidden Words*[1] of Bahá'u'lláh, and the cover carried a note '(Reprinted from the *Church of Ireland Gazette* by request)'. It has been published many times since, in organs of national Bahá'í communities, in other pamphlet forms (Australia), in a compilation of George's essays,[2] and has been used for study classes and at summer schools. The essay develops a thought of Canon Cheyne's cited by George, 'No one, so far as my observation reaches, has lived the perfect life like Abdul-Baha.'[3]

This was the first tangible result, after the publishing fiasco of *The Promise of All Ages*, of the resolve stated in his letter of April 16, 1931 to proclaim Bahá'u'lláh by 'speaking and writing of the teachings' openly and under his own name. We shall hear no more of pseudonyms or 'English correspondents' but more and more of effusions from his pen and actions on behalf of the Bahá'í Faith, which would eventually provoke outrage and complaint to the highest authority.

Now an opportunity of service opened before him which filled his longing heart with gratitude and enabled him to devote all his energies to a single task, laid upon him by the Guardian.

Sir Francis Younghusband, the famous explorer, mystic and lover of the Báb,[4] had organized, with a few kindred spirits from various religious backgrounds, a society to encourage fellowship and understanding between the followers of the great world religions, based on mutual knowledge of each other's Faiths. It was called The World Fellowship of Faiths and was launching its second international congress under the title 'World Congress of Faiths', in Queen's Hall, London, from July 3 to 16, 1936. The chairman of the congress was Sir Herbert Samuel, first High Commissioner in Palestine (1920–25) and later Viscount Samuel of Carmel, while Sir Francis Younghusband, the founder, was British National Chairman of the World Fellowship. The Guardian, as head of the Bahá'í Faith, was asked in a personal letter from Sir Francis to contribute a paper, and this task he delegated to George. His secretary wrote to George on December 9, 1935:

[1] See *The Bahá'í World*, vol. III.
[2] *The Mission of Bahá'u'lláh*, George Ronald, London 1952
[3] T. K. Cheyne, *The Reconciliation of Races and Religions*, contains a persuasive presentation of the Bahá'í Faith and a statement of Dr Cheyne's acceptance of it. When in Oxford in 1912, 'Abdu'l-Bahá visited this distinguished 'higher critic' and embraced him warmly. Among George's papers is the photostatic copy of a letter written by Professor Cheyne to John Craven, one of the very first believers in Britain and among the group which welcomed 'Abdu'l-Bahá at Liverpool Dock on His return from North America to visit the United Kingdom for the second time. In this letter Cheyne states 'Why I am a Bahá'í is a large question, but the perfection of the characters of Bahá'u'lláh and 'Abdu'l-Bahá is perhaps the chief reason.'
[4] See Younghusband, *The Gleam*, John Murray, London 1923; also *Modern Mystics*.

The enclosed program is self-explanatory. It was sent to the Guardian in letters that Sir Herbert Samuel and Sir Francis Younghusband have recently written, inviting him to take part in the activities and deliberations of the projected conference of the World Fellowship through Religion to be held in London next July. The subject which Shoghi Effendi, as well as the leaders and representatives of other religious organizations have been asked to present in the form of a paper is the following: How to promote the Spirit of World Fellowship through religion.

As the Guardian does not have the time to either write such a paper or to be present himself in that meeting he has asked the British N.S.A. to act as his representatives, and to appoint somebody to deliver the address. The task of preparing this address, which is going to be officially published, is one which he has unhesitatingly decided to entrust to you, as you are undoubtedly the best qualified English believer to undertake a work of this nature. It would be in many ways splendid if you could also read it yourself before the audience. But for various reasons that are quite obvious you may find it impossible to do so. He has thought best, therefore, to leave to the N.S.A. the matter of choosing a proper one to read the paper which should be ready by *the end of January*, when it has to be handed over by the British N.S.A. to the committee in charge of the meeting.

George's reply of December 20, 1935 and its two postscripts contain all the elements of his life; his longing to serve Bahá'u'lláh by service to the Guardian, his relationship to his Church, his family situation, his over-optimism, and the overriding aim of his existence:

An hour ago your letter reached me regarding my writing and reading a paper on the Cause as contributing to 'world fellowship through religion'. My heart is charged with gratitude to God for thus giving me the opportunity which recently I have been planning to make in some way for myself. I will write that paper and will go to London and read it myself; and the power of the All Merciful will be with me to convince and to move. My heart's thanks to you.

I must be free to present the case, however, in such a way that I shall not seem guilty of a definite breach of my ordination vows. I swore that I would protect the church . . . and it will not benefit the Cause nor my appeal if I stand up as a forsworn clergyman. This does not mean any lack of force, definiteness or conviction in my words: by no means. In my heart and in my head I know what line I'll take, and it will be the battle-cry of the Kingdom, a fighting speech, a call to action, and a promise to be with those who contend for the Truth of the New Age. But it will not be proclaimed as 'official' nor will it contain an invitation to join an 'anti-Christ' organisation. It would be no more effective or appealing if it did – in fact, much less.

The fact that a clergyman (and worse still an archdeacon) presents this argument will itself cause immense comment and criticism. That is what the emergency needs. My position in the Church will quickly become untenable, of course, but you will understand this will cause me no spiritual sorrow.

Getting the work done within a month is my difficulty. I am a slow worker, and for two years have been in an acute spiritual stress, and depression, and ill health. I am recovering now and will do my utmost to speed up.

P.S. In correspondence on this or other matters please don't refer to the possibility of material dangers for me. I like to show letters to my wife, to keep her with me, and there is no need to alarm her. I am quite ready to put my trust in God.

P.S. I see I have said very little of my thanks to you for giving me this opening. I see happiness beginning! I pray God will be with me continually: tell me how I can draw nearer to Him.

The first postscript is noteworthy. It is his second intimation to the Guardian of the absence of whole-hearted support from Nancy for his own complete dedication to Bahá'u'lláh and intention to leave the service of the Church as soon as he could. In one of his letters about *The Promise of All Ages* (December 7, 1933) he had written: 'Very many thanks for your interest and your prayers for Mrs Townshend. Her enthusiasm over this book and its publication seems to me almost miraculous; and this adventure instead of causing disunion in the home as I feared has promoted and deepened union.'

George's reply within the hour, although posted on December 20, did not reach Haifa until January 4. The Guardian, knowing his man and recognizing the shortness of time, instructed his secretary on December 27 to write to George emphasizing the Congress Committee's requirement to have the paper by the end of January. The following day the Guardian

received a most encouraging letter from Sir Francis Younghusband regarding the representation of the Cause at the projected World Congress of Faiths. As Shoghi Effendi feels that Sir Younghusband's letter will greatly interest you and further stimulate you in your task of preparing the address, he has directed me to send you enclosed a copy of it.

By January 4 George's letter had arrived and evoked a reply in which the secretary was instructed to write:

He is the more pleased to learn that you have decided to read the paper yourself at the meeting which, of course, constitutes a most remarkable and irrefutable proof of your unwavering loyalty to the Cause, and of your intense desire to help, by every means in your power, in furthering its interests throughout England.

God may be using you as an instrument for the vindication of His Truth, and the moment may perhaps be near when you will have to make full use of the opportunities He has given you for the propagation of His message.

May Bahá'u'lláh guide you in every step you are taking for the spread of His Faith, and may He also assist your wife to help you in discharging your ever-increasing and weighty duties and responsibilities towards the Cause.

Shoghi Effendi himself wrote:

I truly admire, and am deeply touched by, the tone of your response to my request. Your courage and determination in the face of the developments that may ensue as a result of your resolve to read the paper are worthy of the highest praise. Bahá'u'lláh will no doubt be watching over you, will sustain and inspire you and make you victorious. For you and your dear wife, who will share with you the glory which such an action must some day bring you, I shall pray from the bottom of my heart. Rest assured and persevere.

This is but one example of the constant support with which the Guardian responded to George's needs, however indirectly or modestly expressed, and is dealt with in Chapter 6.

On January 1 George wrote again (dating his letter 1935 instead of 1936):

I feel the importance of getting some rough copy of my proposed paper for the Congress to you, and so am doing my utmost to get some shape on my material. I will enquire about airmail which may save some days. If my health were better there would be little difficulty. Next week, please goodness, I will be able to post something.

On January 10 (he got the date right this time, but added a note to it 'due to leave England airmail 13') he wrote:

I am sending off today a rough copy of the paper 'A Ground-Plan of World Fellowship: by 'Abdu'l-Bahá', to submit it to you with a view to my reading it at the Religious Congress in July.

It appears to me to suit the occasion, giving the audience such a broad view of the significance of the world situation and of the Bahá'í approach to it as they have never had and giving too quite as much of the Bahá'í message as they can be expected to assimilate at one time. The fact that this Ground-Plan is presented by a clergyman will, in a way, draw attention to it.

This subject has possessed me for many months. I was planning to write it in a 10,000-word pamphlet and to go myself to London to see Sir Francis Younghusband and try to interest him in it when your invitation arrived. Possibly this is what 'Abdu'l-Bahá referred to when he wrote to me: *if thou attainest unto such a bounty thou shalt be made the sign of guidance, an enkindled candle in the gathering of men* . . . I hope I shall have His full support in this supreme trial. I need not say this whole enterprise needs all the courage and all the faith that is in me.

Sending you today this rough draft represents an intense effort on my part, in spite of health conditions which made the work very difficult. By airmail it should get to you in time to be examined and returned before the end of the month. I shall meantime tune it up a little without introducing anything you could possibly object to . . .

I have the hardihood to hope and believe this adventure will really start Bahá'í things in England. The Ground-Plan is so exactly apposite to our need that such an Assembly as that in July *must* be stirred to its depths by it. The first problem is to be sure the author, full of his subject, can read it himself. I am anxious to avoid any technical irregularity which would enable the Church to block my action. *Afterwards*, let the commotion rise and spread. I enclose the title and description I propose; and trust this will meet with your approval. The fact that the invitation to me comes from the Bahá'í Assembly constitutes a definite connexion with the Movement and is as much as that Congress will stomach.

In haste, and with a heartfelt request for your intercessions on my behalf with Bahá'u'lláh, which I so sorely need, I am Yours in the Great Cause . . .

This letter, in addition to the expression of George's usual great expectations is significant for its indication of his constant watchfulness for opportunities to serve the Faith and to challenge the 'old churches', whose inferred and crystallized doctrines he would later identify with the 'false prophets' warned of by Christ.[1] What joy must have flooded his heart when after 'many months' of planning how to get Bahá'u'lláh's Revelation presented at the Congress, he received an open invitation to do so. And from what a source; no one else than the Guardian of the Faith himself! The influence upon him of 'Abdu'l-Bahá's letters, now seventeen years old, and his ever-deepening humility which seemed to increase as his powers and insight grew, are apparent in this letter. There is also, alas, the notation of ill health, which afflicted him frequently from now on, due in large degree, we may well infer, to the restless striving and continual frustration of his deepest desire.

On January 22 the Guardian sent the draft back with a few amendments, chiefly directed to showing the 'Ground Plan' as originating with Bahá'u'lláh, and 'Abdu'l-Bahá its Expounder. George replied on January 28 'in headlong haste': 'I have rewritten all the part I sent prematurely to you, and have tried to give it point, directness, force, and to centre it more definitely around Bahá'u'lláh and 'Abdu'l-Bahá.' This was followed two days later by a less hasty letter:

Your letter with the rough draft of my Ground-Plan arrived this morning.

[1] Matt. 24:4, 11, 24; Mark 13:22

You will have seen from the finished manuscript which is due to reach you some days before this that though your letter came too late I had already carried out your main instructions very fully. At the beginning of the paper, and at the end, and again in the title, the Ground-Plan is attributed to Bahá'u'lláh. I completely rewrote all the sections sent to you – but you will have seen this.

At the moment my manuscript is being typed in England and ought to start to Haifa by airmail on 31st.

Well, it's gone to the printers now over my name and the other matter is settled and I'm in the lists now for a definite battle with the enemies of the Cause.

The next thing is to arrange that I can read it. This is in men's eyes over here an utterly outrageous proposal; but though anxious I'm not apprehensive. I believe it is to happen. Unless indeed the Bahá'í National Spiritual Assembly plays into the enemy's hands by lack of caution. I heard today they had appointed me their official representative – it's a matter of words but (as I said at first) I can't be that. I am writing to them about it, for I had asked them especially *not* to do this. What I proposed from the beginning was to read this as a clergyman submitting the Plan to the audience. Even this is unheard of indiscipline on my part. To do more would make me liable at once to legal action and be a breach of the promise I gave on ordination. I do not propose to do this when I can read the paper without it. At the same time I'll have to keep all the National Spiritual Assembly cheered up for I've a clearer picture of victory than they have at the moment!

Of course that paper, already sent, is the gage of battle. But I'm determined to read it in person if it's in any way humanly possible, for this will add enormously to the effect. And I look forward now to facing all these angry puzzled bishops, and by the help of the all-merciful Bahá'u'lláh spreading this Truth at the top of my voice in spite of them.

Though not apprehensive about his own fate, he displays anxiety lest something go wrong and prevent him from reading his paper. (It very nearly did at the last moment.) The long postscript to his letter clearly shows the strain and nervousness from which he was suffering, increased by his uneasiness about his relationship to the Church, and the inability of 'the London Bahá'ís' to mount any effective campaign. In spite of his protestations to 'Abdu'l-Bahá and to himself he *was* impatient, 'possessed', as he put it.

As the point now is important for the Cause in England I had better submit to you more clearly my proposed effort and its limits and nature. I am taking the money of the Church and I can't in common decency try to destroy or subvert it. (Back in 1923 I asked the London Bahá'ís to help me get a secular job – in vain. My wife and I are now more than willing to get another job that I might be free to work for Bahá'u'lláh – she sees I am now possessed by it.) What I propose is to say 'Wake up all you Church people and Christians; reform yourselves and your Churches according to this Plan of Bahá'u'lláh's, for it is the only way of deliverance.' I appreciate this is not enough, is not the whole message; but (1) it is the *best* way to starting the fire now (2) if a clergyman is to hold the match it is the only way of starting it. Other methods, whatever they be, tried in England have so far failed. (1) The Bahá'ís all tell me so with one voice, and have done so for years. (2) Some three years ago or so the Church of England after examination reported 'in England the Movement has practically ceased to exist.' If only the fire once *catches*, who will confine the conflagration? 'Abdu'l-Bahá wrote to me, 'It is my hope thy Church will come under the heavenly Jerusalem'; and therefore I do not wish to create an open breach.

After July, if I can do that reading, a wholly new situation will open up (so I feel constantly) and the power of God will be poured forth on us over here in fuller measure. The difficulties lie between now and July. For my part – such as it is – I must now keep Bahá'u'lláh ever in my heart; then I shall be a new man.

Now that desperate sense of failure, the private torment of so many artists, assailed him, and on April 3 he wrote to the Guardian:

I have now realised for the first time how utterly inadequate to the occasion is my essay on Bahá'u'lláh's 'Ground-Plan' and heartstricken I write to offer first of all to you the deepest and (I may say) the most unhappy apology for this failing to give the required service, and to make such explanation as there is. The cause was not lack of work or of will; it was sickness. I had not been well for some time and as I mentioned to you anticipated possible difficulty in finishing before the date given. Early in January my headaches were so continuous I feared I could not go on, but I did so with medical help. I ignorantly thought in the end the essay so painfully written was fairly adequate though far from what I had hoped.

The National Spiritual Assembly procured me from the Congress some extension of time and I amended my manuscript putting in all your corrections and including two quotations from *Gleanings*. This affected only the first few pages. As a whole, I have grievously failed to bring out the wonderful startling Truth I had seen with a new clearness and certainty, and had felt was just the fact to strike and challenge the British public now: I mean the exclusive and exact fitness of that many-sided Plan of Bahá'u'lláh's for this ordained stage of our evolution. This is *in* the essay but not dominant.

Early in February I was laid up with a fever and am now getting strong. The first result is I'm able to recognise the failure of my essay, and I send this to say how humiliated and ashamed I feel to have used this splendid opportunity so far so ill. But I hope what has begun so badly may end better. I will consult with the National Spiritual Assembly. And my prayer is that I may learn from this experience how to serve the Cause better and may live long enough to make good amends in one way or another.

This deeply touching letter fills us with compassion but also begins to reveal the high spiritual attainment towards which he was progressing. It is an extraordinary expression from a man of sixty who has attained high office in his profession. (He became Archdeacon in 1933).

Shoghi Effendi's reply (through his secretary) of April 17 was balm to his heart:

> As it stands your essay is very impressive, convincing, and its moderate tone will greatly appeal to the British mind. Sir Francis Younghusband liked it very much indeed, and was specially impressed by the method you had followed in presenting and clarifying the Twelve Basic Principles of the Cause.
>
> Enclosed you will find twenty-three different poems written by believers. The Guardian wishes you to carefully read them, and to mark for him the *fifteen* best which he is planning to have published in the next issue of *The Bahá'í World*.

The Guardian wrote in his own hand:

> With the renewed assurance of my deepfelt and abiding appreciation of the valued assistance you have extended to me in my labours, and praying for your health, your welfare and spiritual advancement, Your true brother, Shoghi.
>
> I would deeply appreciate a poem, however short, from *your* pen, for *The Bahá'í World*. Shoghi.

George sent his poem *Recognition*[1] and noted that another of his, *Prelude*,[2] was one of the twenty-three. 'I like the old one to 'Abdu'l-Bahá better.' 'I am no judge of my own poem 'Prelude' . . . which is not among the fifteen selected.' *Recognition* had already been printed in *The Bahá'í World*, vol. VI and the Guardian included *Prelude* in vol. VII under the title *The Day of God*. George continued:

> I am glad to think the Ground-Plan isn't so inadequate as I feared. To me at present it is infected by the painful conditions under which it was written. The date for reading it is fixed as July 16, the last day of the Congress. I am in hopes that in contrast to the suave generalities of the other papers this more concrete scheme may strike a new note and gain special attention. The Secretary of the Congress reports that *every* religion thinks it has the solution of today's problem. My primary idea therefore of avoiding any statement such as 'My prophet is better than your prophet, my creed than your creed, my church than your church' (which is what the rest will all be saying) and of putting forth instead a definite code of reform practically

[1] See p. 49.
[2] See pp. 98–9.

fitted to the emergency, seems to be justified, and will I trust make God's Plan appear at once as different from all the others. (April 30, 1936)

As the great day approached the Guardian wrote in his own hand:

I trust and pray that at the forthcoming meetings of the Congress you will be guided and assisted to contribute a notable share to a better and wider knowledge and appreciation of the Cause. I hope that the day may not be distant when you will have been freed from every shackle that impedes your work in the Divine Vineyard. May the Almighty enable you to become an instrument for the execution of His inscrutable Purpose. (July 3, 1936)

This was the first clear statement from the Guardian of his hopes that George would be free and must have uplifted him and given him great confidence.

But George's path was never smooth. He had offered to read an unofficial paper describing the contribution of the Bahá'í Faith to world fellowship and had agreed with the officials of the Congress that his paper would bear his name and titles. To his dismay he found, when he got to London, that the Proceedings named the Guardian as the author of the paper which, of course, made it completely official. For the Venerable Archdeacon Townshend to read an official Bahá'í paper on such a public occasion was a very different matter from the same dignitary reading his own unofficial presentation as an interested observer. The latter course was provocative enough; he had already described it as 'outrageous' and 'unheard of indiscipline on my part'. To act officially would, he believed, leave him open to legal action and would be construed as disloyalty to his ordination vows.

He met this challenge with true spiritual statesmanship. He consulted 'some of the most earnest and experienced Bahá'ís in London and was strongly advised to drop out and let someone else read the paper. But I had promised you to read it and I could not follow this advice. I arranged with Sir Francis and Sir Herbert that as you were not present they would ask me as a member of the Congress to read the paper.' A few days later he attended the Nineteen Day Feast[1] in London and explained his resolution to read the paper as he had promised, albeit against advice and on his own responsibility, and then to await developments. 'The sympathy and kindness of the Bahá'ís has been to me a great support and comfort.'

On the morning of July 16 Sir Herbert Samuel, in the chair, called

[1] The regular gathering of Bahá'í communities the world over. A devotional session is followed by open discussion between the Local Spiritual Assembly – the elected body in charge of Bahá'í affairs – and the members of the community, and the meeting ends with the time-honoured custom of friendly association and the serving of food.

on George, and he went to the rostrum and read his paper. In the afternoon he wrote to the Guardian:

This morning the Bahá'í paper 'The Ground-Plan of World Fellowship'[1] was read to the World Congress by an Irish clergyman, and was received without a dissentient voice. The appointed leader of the debate who followed began his remarks with the words 'I think there is nothing to discuss in the paper as it expresses what is in the hearts of us all.' Miss Sharples, the chief secretary of the Society that is behind the Congress, told me later in the day that everybody in the hall felt the unifying influence of the paper. Sir Herbert Samuel was in the chair and stated he knew no movement which concentrated its efforts so much on the promotion of world fellowship.

So – that is that . . .

I regard this as the end of my clerical career and, if God permit, the opening of a more useful life of service to the Cause of Bahá'u'lláh. Soon the authorities will ask me for explanations and for apologies which I shall be unable to give. I have no idea what shape things will take. I am just in the hands of God. There is no more to say.

I am, loyally yours in His service.

It seems incredible to us in the 1980s that so much heart-searching and anxiety should have attended such a simple act as was contemplated. But the feelings were unanimous, not just George's own, and when his determination was apparent he was surrounded with 'sympathy and kindness'.

An account of the Congress and this session in particular is found in *The Bahá'í World*, vol. VII; George's paper appears in *The Bahá'í World*, vol. VI and in *World Order* magazine, volume 2, No. 8, November 1936. Forty years later, Mr Douglas Martin of the Canadian Bahá'í community would address the Congress at its anniversary meeting in Canterbury, reading a paper entitled 'Bahá'u'lláh's Model for World Unity', in which he referred to George's initial presentation. In the intervening years Bahá'í speakers had addressed a number of smaller meetings of the Congress at which Sir Francis Younghusband, whenever present, invariably asked the speaker to say more about the Báb.

The Guardian's reply to George's letter was:

Your heroic determination to face the consequences of your fearless act on behalf of our beloved Cause has touched my heart and enhanced my admiration for what you have already achieved in the service of His Faith. I will pray for your guidance, strength and success. You will no doubt be reinforced by the hosts of the Abhá Kingdom. The Beloved is well pleased with the spirit that animates you. (August 14, 1936)

---

[1] It was actually entitled *Bahá'u'lláh's Ground-Plan of World Fellowship*.

George fully expected the morning papers of July 17 to carry banner headlines, 'Irish Archdeacon Supports New Religion' and the like. He had steeled himself for the personal horrors of publicity and swarming reporters and for immediate demands for an explanation from 'the bishops'. The latter he could deal with, but placing himself in certain danger of the former is a gauge of his courage and of the intensity of his desire to place all his time, effort, talents and energy at the disposal of the Guardian. 'The shrinking' not only did not go as deep, but was obliterated by 'the ardour'.

Nothing happened! Nothing! He was congratulated on all sides for his splendid contribution to the purpose of the Congress, and the press was occupied with Edward VIII and Mrs Simpson. George always maintained that he was scooped by the constitutional crisis, although it had not yet got beyond the point, in England, of rumour. It is, however, at least curious that *The Times* made a feature of the Congress and faithfully reported every day's session, *except the last one*, when George read his paper to a packed audience of distinguished people. There was no scoop to report on July 17, pre-emptive of space; it was just ignored.

No one will ever know the feelings of bitter disappointment, frustration and failure which assailed him. After he had built such hopes of gaining his freedom, to be ignored was humiliating. It was as though some *enfant terrible* had performed his most outrageous trick only to be applauded and given a penny for being a good boy. He went back to Ahascragh, and perhaps consoled himself with the knowledge that he had proclaimed Bahá'u'lláh and won the loving admiration of the Guardian.

By now his desire to leave the Church had become an overwhelming necessity, and in less than three weeks he had devised another plan for accomplishing the freedom he so longed for.

Chapter 9

THE FIRE THAT RAGETH

THE original of George's letter of August 4, 1936 to Shoghi Effendi has not come to light. We know its date from the reply on September 20, which George considered of such vital import to his purpose that he made a transcript in his own hand and sent the original to the National Spiritual Assembly of the British Isles with his own covering letter of November 13. These two letters were to have a profound effect on the fortunes of the Faith in the British Isles and eventually upon George himself.

The Guardian's letter reads:

> Our beloved Guardian has duly received your letter of August fourth, and has carefully noted and considered its contents. He cannot, indeed, but profoundly appreciate your determination to break away from the Church, and to henceforth consecrate all your time and effort to the service of the Cause. The spirit which is prompting you to take such an action is highly praiseworthy, and it is hoped through it you will be guided and assisted in fulfilling the fondest and dearest wishes of your heart. Your intention is certainly meritorious in the sight of God. May Bahá'u'lláh give you the means as well as the strength necessary for its realisation.
>
> As to the plan you have suggested as a possible solution to your family problems in case you decide to leave the Church, the Guardian while ready to extend to you whatever help he can, would suggest that you first refer the matter to the British N.S.A. for their consideration. He would be only too glad to cooperate in enforcing any decision which that body may reach in the matter. He earnestly hopes, nay he feels confident, that the N.S.A. will give your views their most careful and sympathetic consideration, and that their deliberations will result in opening before you a clear way out of your present cares and difficulties. You should be confident and persevere. But you should also take care lest any hasty action may lead you into

further complications. Your success depends on the loyalty, courage and wisdom with which you strive to solve this most delicate and challenging problem of your life.

In the meantime, the Guardian will ardently offer his prayers to Bahá'u'lláh on your behalf, that He may confirm, bless, guide and reinforce every step you are taking in this connection.

Shoghi Effendi's personal note reads:

Dear and valued co-worker:

I fully realize the difficulties with which you are faced, and am only too pleased to extend my share of assistance to you in your noble and courageous stand on behalf of the Cause of Bahá'u'lláh. I will, pending the decision of the National Assembly, pray that you and they may be guided to handle this delicate and vital issue with all the courage, fidelity, wisdom and self-sacrifice it requires. Rest assured that I will do everything I possibly can to enable you to adjust your personal and domestic problems in such a manner as to render the most effective service to our beloved Faith,

Affectionately
Shoghi

George's covering letter to the National Spiritual Assembly is as follows:

I am writing to you by direction of the Guardian given in a letter which I enclose and which will explain in a general way the situation.

I have been anxious for some time to escape from the restrictions under which I work and to be able to give all my time and effort, such as it is, to the propagation of the Faith of Bahá'u'lláh. Lately I have felt this desire more strongly than ever. The matter for me is difficult and delicate. It means for one thing the renunciation of a tradition I have served all my life, and for another thing the sacrifice of my livelihood, my home, the major part of my insurance and the whole of my pension.

The only possibility I can see of providing means for the support of my family is through writings and publications on behalf of the Bahá'í Faith. I want and expect to write and speak for the Cause during the rest of my life; and if in this work I am strengthened by Bahá'u'lláh and my endeavours are endorsed by the Guardian and by the N.S.A. I have no doubt that as the Cause grows, the sales will be more than sufficient to meet our modest needs, particularly when the demands of education are over.

George then enumerates the work he had in hand, includes *The Promise of All Ages* and 'material for *The Heart of the Gospel*, on the life and teachings of Jesus Christ as revealed by the light of Bahá'u'lláh. It seems to me a most moving story and it is planned to produce a revolution in the Christian churches.' He continues:

My suggestion is – would any members of the Bahá'í community consider the purchase of the copyright of these volumes, and perhaps of other prospective writings, and so provide me with enough to keep my family. I cannot tell what arrangements might be made about this; or how much manuscript the Bahá'ís would require to have in hand first; or whether the proposal is feasible at all. But only along this literary line can I ever reach freedom; and the method I suggest would lessen delay and would produce from me a larger amount of Bahá'í literary work. Urgent desire impels me to lay this proposal before the Guardian and you, and I hope it will not seem presumptuous.

I trust you will give this letter and my ardent hope your kind and sympathetic attention. It is my prayer that through this effort the fulfilment of my great desire will be attained. I feel supported by the Guardian's wisdom and kindness and cheered by his confidence that 'a way out of my present cares and difficulties' will be found.

He received a sympathetic reply from the secretary of the Assembly which assured him that copies of his letter and enclosure had been sent to every member and that his proposal would be considered at the next meeting of the Assembly on December 20.

George was on tenterhooks and did his best to abide by his new determination of patience. On December 6 he wrote to the Guardian thanking him for his most kind and helpful letter and saying that he had 'thought carefully over all you said, and then submitted the matter as you directed to the British National Spiritual Assembly'. He gave the gist of the Assembly's reply and continued: 'I am sure heaven will protect and strengthen me through the difficulties that now cannot be far away. There has been definitely some change in me and a corresponding outer change must take place. I have no doubt at all that the material weight of things will bring about my liberation.' He then related that he had begun writing *The Heart of the Gospel* (perhaps under the impulse of this new proposal and as a sedation to his impatience). 'If I can publish it as a Bahá'í its effect will be timely and its use may be considerable. For it is (so it seems to me) the book the churches have clamoured for for seventy years but could not write because they did not turn to Bahá'u'lláh. But when He pleases He makes it all so utterly simple.' But his heart was with the main issue and he concluded, 'No doubt the British National Spiritual Assembly will report to you direct after December 20th. Yours in hope and longing . . .'

Ten days later, on December 16, four days before the Assembly was to meet, he wrote again to its secretary:

I am so glad to hear from you and to know the Guardian's letter to me is well cared for; and I am also glad to know you are so sympathetic about my effort to serve the Bahá'í Faith with all my strength, uninterruptedly.

I now enclose two letters (copies) from 'Abdu'l-Bahá to me which bear on this personal crisis and which possibly may be of use when the matter is under discussion on the 20th. The underlinings were made for another occasion and have no reference to the present question. Please return later.

This effort is the sequel to some three years of acute trial and distress. The approval and support of the British National Spiritual Assembly is essential for the normal development of my desire to serve the Faith; and without it nothing very good can happen. But I am now in the psychological position that if I were quite alone I should still have to stick to my guns and confess my Faith in Bahá'u'lláh whatever the consequences. I have somehow reached the end of the old uncertainties and got into Tranquillity Bay. The journey pretty nearly destroyed me, but not quite; and I'm not going back again.

You will see 'Abdu'l-Bahá refers definitely to my present endeavour in His first letter page 3, line 3: I did not realise this till I read 'Abdu'l-Bahá's phrase 'consecrate' used by the Guardian in his letter to me in this connexion.

May God guide and empower us all.

The phrase in 'Abdu'l-Bahá's letter to which he referred is *consecrate thy life to the diffusion of the Divine Fragrances*. (See p. 47)

The National Spiritual Assembly of the Bahá'ís of the British Isles at this time (1936), rested somewhat insecurely upon the foundation of two Local Spiritual Assemblies, London and Manchester (sometimes three if Bournemouth managed to conduct its election)[1] and a tiny community of believers gathered mainly in these three centres with a few scattered in isolation in other parts of the country, numbering all told little more than a hundred, of whom only a few were active. In later times, when this community found itself 'in the sometimes difficult position of being a cynosure for all eyes,' the Guardian would refer to 'a certain lethargy which seemed to have retarded its progress in the past.' However, a new wind had lately begun to blow through the British Bahá'í community which George had noticed and upon which the Guardian of the Faith had commented. Indeed the summer of that year had witnessed a very important achievement, the successful organization and conducting of the first Bahá'í Summer School in Britain, a feat, which, accomplished against 'difficulties and obstacles which may have first appeared, to many at least, to be quite unsurmountable'[2], delighted the Guardian and established the institution firmly; it has flourished ever since. But the matter now placed before the National Spiritual Assembly was of greater

[1] The Bahá'í Administrative Order comprises elected institutions at local, national and international level which are in charge of Bahá'í affairs in their respective areas.

[2] Letter written on behalf of Shoghi Effendi to the National Spiritual Assembly of the Bahá'ís of the British Isles, October 17, 1936.

magnitude, complexity and delicacy than any which it had yet faced, and offered a challenge both exciting and daunting. The Assembly's response would be critical, not only for George, but for the Bahá'í Faith in Britain, which is doubtless why the Guardian so insistently placed responsibility for its resolution squarely upon the National Assembly's shoulders. Were the Assembly to fail in face of its first major challenge, the new stirrings of life would probably die down again; were it to meet the opportunity vigorously and imaginatively, the sparks which had begun to glow might well be fanned into a flame of activity, which could launch the British Bahá'ís on a course whose future could only be dimly imagined, but whose glories and triumphs, if the promises of their Faith meant anything, would outshine in splendour the most brilliant achievements in the remarkable history of their country.

Some such thoughts as these had entered the minds of all members of that National Spiritual Assembly. Its secretary still remembers the high spirit of awe, solemnity, cheerfulness and temerity with which they faced the problem. In addition to the items of George's submission, given above, they had the immeasurable bounty of direct guidance from the Guardian, who had written to the Assembly on December 2:

> Regarding Mr Townshend: the Guardian is pleased to hear that he has written you, and offered a method whereby he could be freed to serve the Faith. He is confident that your National Spiritual Assembly will give this matter their most careful and sympathetic consideration, and fervently hopes that they will, as a result, be able to find some way that would relieve Mr Townshend of his many domestic cares and troubles which, as you know only too well, seriously impede the progress and expansion of his activities for the Faith.
>
> It is a matter of deep regret, indeed, that our dear friend's material position is such as to make it quite impossible for him to devote his full time and energies to the Cause. The friends in Great Britain, who are in special need of his able assistance in their teaching work, should, therefore, consider it their responsibility to find some solution to this urgent problem facing one of their most distinguished and competent fellow-workers.
>
> Any suggestion which your National Spiritual Assembly could offer would certainly be deeply appreciated by Mr Townshend, and the Guardian would be only too pleased to assist your Assembly in insuring the success of any plan you may propose and decide upon in this matter.

The Assembly's decision was remarkable – almost unbelievable at the remove of forty-five years – and its immediate implementation a plain impossibility to this age of computers, electronics and the whole array of modern gadgetry. Under the heading A CALL TO UNITED

SACRIFICE a two-page letter, setting out the whole proposition, the Assembly's decision, the Guardian's comments and appealing to the entire British Bahá'í community (all hundred of them) for immediate and continuing support, was in the hands of every believer in time for informed discussion to take place at the Nineteen Day Feast[1] on December 31, eleven days after the meeting of the National Spiritual Assembly. This historic document reads, in part, as follows:

> Beloved Friends: the National Spiritual Assembly has before it a matter of supreme and vital importance to the Faith and wishes to take into consultation and enlist the wholehearted support of every believer in this land.
>
> The critical period through which our beloved Cause is now passing has brought forth an opportunity for sacrifice, for renewed endeavour and for the uniting of all our resources in a common aim. We may well be thankful to God for this task, which will strain our every nerve and effort and test our devotion and faith.
>
> The Reverend George Townshend, known to many as Christophil, author of *The Promise of All Ages*, has signified his desire to abandon the church and to devote the remainder of his life to the service of Bahá'u'lláh. In coming to this decision he has chosen a sacrifice which we are not able to measure. In his own words it means 'the renunciation of a tradition I have served all my life, and for another thing the sacrifice of my livelihood, my home, the major part of my insurance and the whole of my pension'.
>
> It was suggested that if a few members of the Bahá'í community would purchase the copyright of Mr Townshend's books, of which there are two ready and others in process of composition, he would be in a position to take care of his family and to devote his full time to Bahá'í writings, from which he is confident sufficient income could be derived for his needs. This suggestion was communicated to Shoghi Effendi and to the National Spiritual Assembly.

Then comes the Guardian's letter quoted above, followed immediately by:

> Dear Friends: bearing in mind that the Guardian has made the solution to this problem our responsibility, remembering the assurance of his support and considering the pressing needs of the Faith in this land, the National Spiritual Assembly, after deep discussion, has formulated the following plan.
>
> To form a Publishing Company for the purpose of meeting the publishing requirements of the National Spiritual Assembly. The company will acquire the rights and publish the works of Mr Townshend and of all other literature upon which the National Spiritual Assembly may decide.
>
> The need for some such organisation within the Cause has been felt

[1] See footnote p. 131.

more and more strongly during the past year and the National Spiritual
Assembly believes that this matter of Mr Townshend has precipitated the
necessary action. Not only will the successful outcome of this project
secure for us the full-time co-operation of our dear and distinguished
friend and the valuable fruits of his labours, but the friends will have built
by their sacrifice, a new and powerful instrument for the service of the
Faith. In this common task our unity will be immeasurably strengthened
and visibly demonstrated. May we not compare it, in proportion to our
numbers and resources, to the task of building the Temple which the
American friends so nobly shouldered?[1]

The Guardian expressed his 'admiration and gratitude for the quick
action' and commented that

The plan you have conceived is certainly bold, knowing how limited are
the numbers and resources of the believers in England. But it nevertheless
offers great possibilities of development and success, provided your
Assembly gives it full moral and financial support, and succeeds in
stimulating the interest and obtaining the assistance of the believers
outside Great Britain for its immediate and effective prosecution.

The National Spiritual Assembly had taken a greater step than it
knew. The Guardian not only approved solicitation of funds from
Bahá'ís abroad ('those countries who normally order literature from
them') but felt it

to be the duty of every believer who has the means, and has also the interest
of the Cause at heart, to assist in any capacity, and to any extent he can, in
carrying out the British National Spiritual Assembly's project . . .
London . . . commands an importance which few other centres in the
world can equal and should consequently be raised to the status of one of
the leading outposts of the Faith . . . And it is quite evident that the
formation of a Publishing Company along the lines suggested by the
British National Spiritual Assembly is the greatest asset to such a
development and expansion of the Cause in London and throughout
England as a whole.

He hoped that the response from the friends would be such as to 'mark
the inauguration of a new era of expansion of the Cause throughout
the British Isles, and the rest of the far-flung British Empire'. His
personal note to this letter (March 5, 1937) after acknowledging letters
and minutes and a copy of the *Bahá'í Journal* (the news-letter of the
National Spiritual Assembly) said that they

---

[1] The Mother Temple of the western world, built on the southern shore of Lake
Michigan just north of Chicago. Its foundation stone was laid by 'Abdu'l-Bahá in
1912; see *A Compendium of volumes of The Bahá'í World*, compiled by Roger White,
George Ronald, Oxford 1981, p. 113.

filled my heart with joy and gratitude for the splendid services of your Assembly and the efforts they are systematically and vigorously exerting for the initiation, the expansion and consolidation of Bahá'í administrative activities and enterprises at this auspicious stage in the evolution of the Faith in your country. I fully approve the publication in your Journal of the passages quoted in your letter of February 26th. I am enclosing the sum of £50 as my contribution towards the Fund which is being raised for the establishment of the Publishing Company for the success of which I cherish the brightest hopes. I will especially pray for the removal of every obstacle that may impede its formation and development, and for the realisation of your highest hopes in this connection. Persevere in your great enterprise, and rest assured that the almighty power of Bahá'u'lláh will, if you remain steadfast in your purpose, enable you to attain your goal.

The story of the founding and development of the British Bahá'í Publishing Trust belongs to British Bahá'í history, but deeper consideration of George's part in it enables us to perceive in some measure the profound influence which his life and striving had upon that history. Ireland will for ever claim him, but the Irish Bahá'í community is the child of the whole community of the British Isles and was within that matrix throughout George's life and for sixteen years thereafter, until in 1972 it established its own National Spiritual Assembly. We may hope that the happy, indeed loving relationship which now unites two independent Bahá'í communities may one day characterize the entire population of both countries and that old bitterness will be forgotten in the acknowledgement that England atoned for its wrongs to Ireland in the only way possible, by inducting it, through the sacrifice of its pioneers, its administrators and teachers, into the World Order of Bahá'u'lláh, the long anticipated, Christ-promised Kingdom of God on earth.

The last paragraph from the British Assembly's circular 'A Call to United Sacrifice', cited above, opens with mention of a 'need'. That need was for Bahá'í literature in English. Apart from the *Hidden Words* by Bahá'u'lláh, which had been published in an elaborate edition by the National Spiritual Assembly, *Paris Talks of 'Abdu'l-Bahá*, printed privately by Lady Blomfield, and Dr Esslemont's *Bahá'u'lláh and the New Era*, the basic books of the Faith and even introductory essays and pamphlets had to be obtained from America. They were expensive and not suited to English taste. There was, of course, Christophil's *The Promise of All Ages*, but that was a scholarly work and merited deep study. Even prayer books were in short supply. What was wanted, in addition to the sacred text, was a spate of short, attractive, simply presented introductory books, pamphlets, study guides for use in teaching. The National Assembly's sense of providential influence precipitating, through George's *cri de coeur*, action to meet this vital need is clearly intimated and is highly pertinent to George's story.

It was George's steadfastness which, only a few weeks earlier, had upheld him, in the face of strong contrary advice from the leading Bahá'ís in London, to read his paper to the Congress of the World Fellowship of Faiths, as he had promised the Guardian he would. The failure of that episode to provoke any reaction from his Church or to alter in any way his desperately anomalous position, led him on to make in his own mind and heart the sacrifice to which, so soon after, he dedicated himself. It was that sacrifice which motivated the National Spiritual Assembly to embark on a course fraught with such historic consequences as the Guardian described.

The confluence of the two processes, George's final determination to embrace every sacrifice which his recognition of Bahá'u'lláh might require of him, and the stirring of new life within the Bahá'í community to which he belonged, provoked in the year 1936, an activity which was to 'mark the inauguration of a new era of expansion of the Cause throughout the British Isles, and the rest of the far-flung British Empire.' Who will say that it was fortuitous or deny the guiding hand of 'Abdu'l-Bahá Who had Himself sown the potent seeds of Bahá'u'lláh's message in the soil of Britain? Within a few decades the two Assemblies had become two hundred, the hundred believers several thousand; Bahá'í pioneers from the British Isles had taken the message of the New Day to Asia, Africa, the Americas, Australasia, the islands of the Pacific and the Mediterranean; and George Townshend had become a Hand of the Cause of God.[1]

The Hand of Providence used George's desperate spiritual need as the lever to finally prise loose the Bahá'í community in Britain from the inertia into which it had relapsed. The Cause moved forward. But that same guiding Hand withheld from George, for another ten years, the freedom for which he so ardently longed and for which he was ready to give everything he had. The ways of Providence have always been, and still are, hard to understand; we can but observe, and marvel at the results.

What we can appreciate in this spiritual saga of George Townshend is his own developing understanding of the change in the structure of human society which its coming of age, signalized by the appearance of the revelation of Bahá'u'lláh and the proclamation of the oneness of mankind, would entail.[2] The apocalyptic vision was clear, but the actual changes which the establishment of the Kingdom of God as a world order

[1] See Ch. 19.

[2] See *The Goal of a New World Order*, Shoghi Effendi.

Not in Utopia, – subterranean fields, –
Or some secreted island, Heaven knows where!
But in the very world, which is the world
Of all of us, [1]

would impose on the multitudinous and conflicting systems and
establishments in the legal, social, religious, political, educational,
scientific, artistic – indeed all realms of human endeavour, had not yet
been given his earnest consideration. All things would be made new,
but a world order which would be the spiritual and social expression of
the oneness of the human race could not be vivified by a dozen major
religious establishments, all claiming exclusive salvation, all
separating the masses of their adherents from the rest of the human
race in the most vital aspect of their lives, all shredded into sects often
far fiercer in their exclusive claims than the parent bodies themselves,
all laying great emphasis on traditional rites and ceremonies which
reinforced divisiveness and from which spirit had long since departed.
Christ had promised 'there shall be one fold, and one shepherd.'[2] How
did all these considerations affect a single country clergyman holding
high office in one of the most firmly entrenched and best organized
sectors of one of the major exclusive religious groups of the planet? He
found his answer gradually, through deeper and deeper study of the
new Revelation, of the Bible (comprising two revelations), of Islám,
by deeper and deeper meditation, but chiefly through the ceaseless
promptings of his own inner spirit.

George was 'thrilled and uplifted' with the National Assembly's
'stirring and magnificent response to my appeal', news of which was
conveyed to him by letter with a copy of the statement 'A Call to
United Sacrifice': 'I deeply felt that appeal to be on my part
presumptuous and I only made it because I was determined to carry
through this change-over in spite of any kind of obstacle. Your
answering enthusiasm and action, so earnestly supported by the
Guardian, strengthen that determination. It will *have* to happen somehow. The sooner the better.' He expressed his warmest appreciation
of the Assembly's attitude: '. . . the sense of companionship and good
will in this is infinitely precious.'

A stream of correspondence now flowed between George and the
Assembly in an attempt to work out a practical plan which would
enable George to sever the ties which bound him to the ecclesiastical
order, continue to provide for his family, and assure security to Nancy
after his passing. Once the commitment had been made on both sides,

[1] Wordsworth, *Prelude*; cited by George at the end of his life in his 'crowning
achievement' *Christ and Bahá'u'lláh*, Ch. 10.

[2] John 10:16.

as it had, utterly and joyfully, it was a question of money: 'I have
virtually no private means left, I regret to say. Our outlay here is more
than the Bahá'ís could rise to; but if we lived in a flat near schools,
without a car or appearances to consider, the expense would be greatly
reduced.' The Bahá'ís wanted the full-time benefits of George's pen,
scholarship, experience and spirituality; George was eager to make
any sacrifice which would permit him full, untrammelled association
with his fellow believers and give him the unquestioned right, as a
recognized member of the Bahá'í community, to join in all their
activities for the promotion and establishment of the new Day of God.
The Guardian looked forward to the day when he could be to him a
general at the Front, and he offered his support for this new plan to
secure George's freedom. All the omens were favourable and this
must surely be the time.

But – and it was a great but – that mysterious, critical point in the
development of an organic process when all the operating forces
conjoin to produce an event – the birth of a baby or the setting of fruit
on a tree – had apparently not yet been reached in George's struggle for
freedom. It was no *force majeure* or 'killing frost' which now prevented
the fruition of his hopes but an unintegrated factor in the equation,
Nancy's adamantine opposition. Characteristically, George blamed
himself and recognized the failure to win her over as his own.

The first proposal was for the company to buy immediately the
copyright of *The Promise of All Ages* and of other books as George
produced them. George pointed out that American sales had been and
for some time were likely to be at least double those of all others, and
the vigorous, expanding American Bahá'í community should be
consulted. He also noted that as the Faith grew, the value of his books
would increase, and it was therefore impossible to place a true
commercial value on them at the present time. Furthermore, by
selling his only assets now he would be losing future income, the very
thing both he and the National Assembly wished to preserve. 'I wish
to goodness I could give it all for nothing at all to the Cause.' The
upshot was a definite offer, made to George by the Assembly in its
letter of February 3, 1937, of £750[1] for the copyright of *The Promise of
All Ages* and an undertaking to make an offer for other books as they
were submitted. George was urged to complete the books he had in
mind and particularly *The Heart of the Gospel*. When the purchase
price, which was really an advance on future sales, had been recovered
from those sales, a royalty on further sales would be paid to George
and his wife during their lifetimes.

George accepted this offer 'gladly and wholeheartedly'. He

[1] The modern equivalent is about £13,400.

characterized it as a 'magnificent and generous effort. Really, it seems like a miracle! I hope your expectations will materialize satisfactorily, and look forward to hearing soon of their progress. *I have begun cleaning up the house for departure*' [Author's italics]. (February 9, 1937)

Meanwhile the National Assembly had invited subscriptions from other Bahá'í communities, had written to the National Spiritual Assembly of the United States and Canada, specifically asking them to advance £500 for *The Promise of All Ages*, and had engaged a lawyer to manage the proper formation of the company.[1] The Guardian's encouragement was constant. There was plain sailing ahead and it seemed as though George's struggles were over.

As early as January 13, 1937, while he was still in the euphoria of the National Spiritual Assembly's whole-hearted response to his proposal and before any real plan other than the general one to form a publishing company had been suggested, he had written:

> My wife is really a good Bahá'í but does not accept yet the Administration. I may say frankly there is a danger of the home's breaking up over this. I wish to bring her over with her whole heart, and I'll succeed: but it is a difficult problem. Would you, in any important letter on this matter, avoid any remarks which the kindness of your heart might prompt about sacrifice or cost or risk on my part which might alarm a wife? This would make my task easier.
>
> No doubts or opposition will alter my resolution; but I wish to help her, and to make all this advance the Cause in every way as much as possible.

In the letter of February 9 in which he accepted the assembly's offer he added: '. . . my poor wife is very unhappy, has rather gone to pieces and one can't tell what may happen. It is very painful. Difficulties harden my resolution; there is no yielding in me – just as well, for more troubles, though smaller ones, lie ahead. But it's a heart-breaking business just now. The sooner we can end it and get away and shake the dust off our feet the better. But there is need of caution as well as firmness. I can't do this very quietly; it will turn into open *war*. And if my home is to be divided violently against itself the problem will be harder. But I've no serious misgivings at all: not a scrap.'

George knew, none better, that to renounce his Orders in an atmosphere of scandal, such as would have been created had Nancy carried out any of her threats – to denounce him to her family, to leave him – would do the Faith of Bahá'u'lláh no good at all. The breaking

---

[1] It eventually was established as the Bahá'í Publishing Trust under the direction of the National Spiritual Assembly, which itself became an incorporated company during the summer of 1939. Its first publication was an introductory booklet by Dr Esslemont, *Bahá'u'lláh and His Message*; it was printed by Herbert Simon at the Curwen Press and the cover was designed by Mark Tobey.

up of his home would destroy everything he had done to win confidence and respect for his beliefs. But he would not allow his family, or any other consideration, to change his determined course: '. . . if I were quite alone I should still have to stick to my guns and confess my faith in Bahá'u'lláh whatever the consequences.'

It was only too easy to point out, as George did under Nancy's prompting, that the company had yet to be formed, its capital provided and in any case the sale of Bahá'í books was not likely to be affected to any measurable extent by the company's establishment. All this was, of course, begging the question, for no one supposed that there would be any adequate income from the sales of George's books for years to come; the capital of the company would be used to buy an interest in the future of his books as he provided them, and on these sums he could provide for his family for a number of years, albeit in lesser style than they enjoyed at Ahascragh. George put the objections in characteristically mild manner in his letter of January 30, before he received the definite offer for *The Promise of All Ages*, 'thinking aloud as it were', and indicated that he would have to call off the proposal; he was obviously greatly embarrassed:

> I am awfully grateful for all the trouble you have taken over this problem and I appreciate more than I can say your attitude of sympathy and fellowship and helpfulness. I do hope my work for the Cause will prove to be worth such an expenditure of your valuable time and energy. And I am sure some way out for me will be found, though it may not come so quickly as I hoped and may need all my determination and patience. It *must* happen, that's all. Do please make my mind a little clearer as to what your proposals involve.

As we have seen, when a firm offer was made to him he immediately accepted it and started to clean up the house for departure, although no details or logistics had been considered. The whole undertaking was based on mutual faith in the future of the Cause of Bahá'u'lláh and mutual confidence between George and the National Spiritual Assembly. Unfortunately Nancy shared in neither. George realized only too well the prospects for benefit or ill to the Cause and had frequently stated his high hopes for resounding and favourable publicity – from which he shrank insofar as it affected him personally (although the shrinking did not go so deep as the ardour!) – whenever his resignation would take place. The break-up of his home would not only be disastrous for the Cause but he would at the same time lose his prestige and the strategic position from which he hoped to accomplish 'Abdu'l-Bahá's hope of bringing his church into the 'Heavenly Jerusalem'. Resignation as a firmly united family would be at least a nine-days' wonder and might well be more, while no odium –

rather the contrary – would attach to George himself. Nancy was in a commanding position and George withdrew, gracefully, but more than ever determined to win her over and achieve his goal, 'though it may not come so quickly as I hoped and may need all my determination and patience. It *must* happen, that's all.'

The ever-present irony in George's life is nowhere more apparent than in the fact that when, only a few months later, he was in a position to meet Nancy's demands for some degree of financial security, his jubilant hopes were again blighted by her direct threats to leave him, should he persist in his intention. 'And she means it.' The irony becomes even more ironic when after a further ten years involving the inevitable attrition of his capital, he eventually achieved his aim with the loving support, spiritually, morally and financially of the entire Bahá'í world – and with Nancy's co-operation. Clearly financial security was never the insuperable obstacle.

There can be no doubt however that to a practical man of the world (no such individual being engaged on either side) the Assembly's plan was 'certainly bold', doubtful and visionary, and offered poor security to a man with two children still to educate. But the same could be said of the Revelations of the Prophets. Christ's teachings, to the hard-headed practical men-of-the-world of His day, were so bold, doubtful and visionary as to earn their scorn and ridicule. A *fortiori* the Revelation of Bahá'u'lláh, for even at this late date many of His principal teachings, such as the oneness of mankind, the oneness of religion, the federation of the world, are diametrically opposed by the policies, preachings and practices of separatist establishments in the political, religious and social spheres of human activity. Countless enterprises have been killed by the dull blunt instrument of common sense; the uncommon sense of the twice-born constantly reasserts that it is the invocation of spiritual power through sacrifice, love, devotion and prayer which makes the world go round and promotes the onward march of mankind. If Nancy had understood the message of Bahá'u'lláh, George's resignation could have taken place at this time instead of ten years later.

George bore within himself, and wrestled with, the conflicting attributes of patience and impatience. His patience in the face of opposition, humiliation, hardship and trial was saintly; his impatience when 'enterprises of great pith and moment' were afoot was both galvanizing and worrying to the participants. He displayed both at this juncture; the former in his response to defeat (what an enormous disappointment it must have been to him!); the latter in his prodding of the National Spiritual Assembly for action and results, a clear indication of the temporary nature of his retreat; the sooner the proposed company could be established and its assets built up, the sooner could he try again. Reconciling himself to the fact that this plan would not bring an immediate result, but might well be his salvation in the future, he went to work with a will on *The Heart of the Gospel*, convincing himself that this would promote such a response from Christians as to make his income from its sales and those of *The Promise of All Ages* adequate to his needs.

George's persistent over-optimism was never checked by any realization of the true decline which had taken place in men's interest in religion. His remote Galway parish, even Ireland itself, was no position from which to assess the enormous inroads which materialism, agnosticism, 'science' and finally atheism had made into the religious outlook of the western world. He knew nothing of the great massed populations in the industrial centres and almost nothing of the prevalence of Marxist philosophy in the universities and among the intelligentsia. None of these conditions was apparent in the country district of Ballinasloe, where everyone was either a Roman Catholic or a Protestant. And so he still believed that there were vast numbers of apathetic, yet true, Christians, who only needed a new, vigorous, uplifting presentation of the real truth of religion and the fulfilment of its promises (specifically those of Jesus Christ) in the appearance and teachings of Bahá'u'lláh, for them to rise in their thousands and millions and remake the world. His disillusionment was slow and bitter, but, when it came, full and realistic, and he knew where to place the chief blame, and did so, in his castigation in *Christ and Bahá'u'lláh* of the false prophets and of the obscurantism of the churches in his essay *The Old Churches and the New World-Faith*.

George constantly referred to the slow processes of his apprehension; it is an important factor in understanding his slow realization that he would have to leave the Church and relinquish his Orders in order 'to be loyal to Christ as I know Him'. The chief factor of course was the work he was destined to perform, and the influence he was to exert on the founding and rise of the Bahá'í Faith in Ireland, an immeasurable portion of which was accomplished during the course of his twenty-eight years in Ahascragh. Nor can his own personal development be left out of this equation; it can only be regarded as the divine training accorded him in preparation for the final lap when he was not only 'thereabouts at the finish', but breasted the tape in a blaze of glory.

The evolution of George's realization of what his commitment to Bahá'u'lláh would require of him falls into three distinct periods. In each the measure of his understanding affected the type of action he took to fulfil the task which he believed to have been laid upon him by 'Abdu'l-Bahá, and to obtain a greater and greater degree of freedom to promote and identify himself with the Faith of Bahá'u'lláh. These two objectives constituted the positive, motivating force of his life from the time, in November 1921, when he wrote his 'Surrender' to 'Abdu'l-Bahá. The limiting and frustrating factors were, at the beginning, his own non-realization of the independent character of the Order which Bahá'u'lláh had founded (a condition general to the entire Bahá'í community before the Guardian disclosed the full purpose of Bahá'u'lláh's Revelation), and later Nancy's inability to share his faith in Bahá'u'lláh and her consequent refusal to leave her settled home and 'go out into the darkness'[1] putting her complete trust in God. Whether the Master intended His expressed hope for George's church to enter the heavenly Jerusalem to be his shield against precipitate action, a divine decree delineating the course of his life, or a mandate laid upon his shoulders, can only be surmised. Certain it is that George took it as a mandate which he must discharge. Equally certain is it that the Master was fully apprised of George's character and reality. It seems impossible to believe, in the face of the evidence of the two Tablets, that He had no pre-vision of the course of George's life, a belief which finds support in the fact that the Guardian, who had made clear to the Bahá'ís around the world that membership of the Bahá'í Faith was incompatible with membership of ecclesiastical organizations, never once, in the whole course of George's relationship with him, ever intimated that he should leave the Church – until George himself came to that realization. Then the Guardian welcomed him and, as we have seen, greatly supported his efforts to do so. This particular point is considered more fully in Chapter 10.

These are some of the imponderable and unknown factors affecting George's situation.

Mr Adib Taherzadeh,[2] a close friend and admirer of George's who rendered him loving service after his resignation, has discussed this aspect of George's life from his informed and perceptive consideration of it. He recorded, for use in this volume:

[1] In his Christmas broadcast of 1939, George VI quoted Louise Haskin's lines:

> I said to the man who stood at the Gate of the Year,
> 'Give me a light that I may tread safely into the unknown.'
> And he replied, 'Go out into the darkness and put your hand into the hand of God.
> That shall be to you better than light and safer than a known way.'

[2] In 1976 appointed Counsellor, the highest rank to which Bahá'ís may be elevated by the Universal House of Justice.

George related to me that in his early days in Ahascragh, Bahá'í pilgrims to the World Centre of the Faith in the twin cities of Haifa and 'Akká, would sometimes come through Ireland on their ways to or from, in order to call on him, and these visits were a great joy to him. One of them told him that while in the Holy Land he had heard Shoghi Effendi talking about George Townshend, saying quite confidently that he would eventually resign from the church. George was greatly surprised to hear this and did not understand it. He said to me, 'I didn't understand at that time why I should resign from the Church.'

Taherzadeh continued:

I am sure that in the early years of Shoghi Effendi's ministry (1921–57) George's understanding of the Faith was that it would enrich, purify and rebuild Christianity. I am sure that at that time he had no perception of an absolutely independent Order, and therefore none that he would ever leave the Church.

This view is entirely borne out by George's own letters to the Guardian, circa 1925, already quoted, about his plan to 'infiltrate from the rear'. (See pp. 94–98)

This was the first period of his developing understanding, when he would give Bahá'u'lláh's teachings as the modern version of Christ's message, and under Christ's name, thus preparing people for the knowledge of Bahá'u'lláh. To it belong *The Altar on the Hearth* and *The Genius of Ireland,* and in it he is convinced that his work is to be done as a Christian clergyman. On invitation he was willing to assume the work of the International Bahá'í Bureau in Geneva, but still as a clergyman with no thought of renouncing his Orders. This period came to an end in 1928–9 when the Geneva project fell through, and we find him on April 16, 1931 writing to the Guardian, 'I have begun to realise lately that unless some of us over here make some sort of a breakaway nothing will ever happen. We shall all perish. I for one am impelled to take this step.' (See page 110)

There is no doubt that his visit to Geneva, where he saw Emogene Hoagg and other devoted Bahá'ís giving their full energies to Bahá'í service, made a deep impression on him. His subsequent letters to Julia Culver, Emogene and others disclose this. Life in Ahascragh could offer nothing of the excitement of the international atmosphere of Geneva and certainly none of the companionship of Bahá'ís. The self-imposed restrictions on openly sharing the great and wonderful soul-stirring news of Christ's return in the glory of the Father, involving such things as the anonymity of his contribution to the Guardian's English translation of *Hidden Words,* were beginning to chafe his spirit. The old forms and practices were a dead letter when compared with the brilliant light of the new sunrise. He could not hide this light for ever. He started to speak of the Cause by its proper name and to mention Bahá'u'lláh and 'Abdu'l-Bahá. He began his great work *The Promise of All Ages*, and forced through its publication, albeit under a pseudonym, in the face of apathy, non-cooperation and suspicion. More and more he openly proclaimed his allegiance to Bahá'u'lláh and always hoped that his actions would provoke the Church authorities into forcing his resignation. He sent his book to senior clergy; he spoke of 'Abdu'l-Bahá in Bible classes, and read a paper about Him to the Ballinasloe Clerical Union (April 26, 1932); he contributed articles to *The Bahá'í World*; the *Church of Ireland Gazette* published his *'Abdu'l-Bahá: A Study of a Christlike Character*; he printed and circulated his *Reflection* on the *Hidden Words* of Bahá'u'lláh as well as the composite pamphlet of the two essays; and finally he wrote and presented the Bahá'í paper, on behalf of the head of the Bahá'í Faith, to the World Congress of Faiths in London. All to no avail; the rock remained unmoved. That was the end of his hopes that his freedom would be gained by a request from the Church authorities for his resignation, or even an impeachment for heresy; he was ready for anything. Henceforth all his energies would be devoted to bringing about the circumstances which would enable him to resign of his own accord, whether authority liked it or not.

In that second period he rendered prodigious services to the Guardian in relation to his translations of *Kitáb-i-Íqán*, *Nabíl's Narrative*, *Gleanings from the Writings of Bahá'u'lláh* and *Prayers and Meditations by Bahá'u'lláh*. There can be no doubt that the perusal and detailed work on these three volumes of the sacred text of the new Revelation and the heroic saga of the Dawn-Breakers wrought profoundly in his mind and heart. He reached such a deeper understanding of the claims and mission of Bahá'u'lláh that on April 23, 1933 he was impelled to write to the Guardian: 'I trust and pray that very soon God will release me from my clerical position and permit me to serve His Cause openly, and do nothing else. I am ready now to go anywhere and do anything for Bahá'u'lláh.' (See page 112) The Guardian's personal note of May 6 in reply to this was,

I will, I assure you, pray from the depths of my heart and will supplicate the Almighty to liberate you from anything that prevents you from proclaiming the Cause of God and from establishing its principles in the hearts and minds of your countrymen. I deeply appreciate the offering you have enclosed on behalf of the Bahá'ís of Ireland. May the book you are publishing be a prelude to still brighter and greater services in the days to come. You are indeed a pillar of the Faith not only in your country but in Europe, and are endowed with capacities and attainments which few can equal in all the Bahá'í world. More power to your elbow! Your true and grateful brother, Shoghi.

In sending George his suggested amendments for the Introduction to *The Promise of All Ages*, Shoghi Effendi wrote:

> I do appreciate, and feel deeply grateful for, the spirit, the determination and willingness to sacrifice your all and accept the consequences which the publication of your valuable book may entail. God is no doubt preparing the way for the spread of His Faith in a strange and mysterious manner. You are, it seems, His chosen instrument and this should, alone, greatly encourage you in the crusade you are so bravely initiating for the proclamation of His Faith.

So George entered the third and last period of his life in the service of the Church of Ireland. In it he continued to serve the Guardian with his pen and his literary skill; he republished *The Promise of All Ages* under his own name and titles; he completed and published similarly *The Heart of the Gospel*, and, as his freedom drew near, the outline of *Christ and Bahá'u'lláh* began to formulate itself in his mind.

This period covered the years of the Second World War and once again we can only marvel at the way in which he was protected, trained and given the opportunities to proclaim the Name and Cause of Bahá'u'lláh to the whole Church of Ireland. What could he have done during the long, bitter years of unrest, food shortages, isolation, away from the safe haven of his country rectory and the prestige of his position? From that background he proclaimed the Faith as never before. His books were published, openly advertised and reviewed in leading newspapers; he engaged in a written dialogue with his Bishop, announced to him his association with the Bahá'í community (he had attended the British Summer School in 1939) and declared his allegiance to Bahá'u'lláh. He sought an interview with the Archbishop of Dublin and 'told him about Bahá'u'lláh and His Promise'; he preached a sermon in St Patrick's Cathedral, Dublin, proclaiming Bahá'u'lláh by name; he addressed the Synod of the Church of Ireland to the same purpose. And all through the eleven years he strove mightily to win Nancy's full co-operation. He would not give up seeking his freedom from office, by whatever means he could, but he was determined to maintain the unity of his home. Both were necessary and he would achieve both.

The enlargement of his vision resulting from his work on the Guardian's translations and general World Order letters was not a static condition, halted at the realization that he must leave the Church, but a spiritual understanding that continued to grow within him. As late as June 1943 he wrote to the Guardian: 'I have had an experience more impressive than anything since I came into the Cause long ago, and have reached the condition of certainty and realised the separateness of this Revelation. Now, everything is different: a new assurance and stability has possessed me, and a new motive moves me. I want to tell these people the whole truth because they ought to hear it. There is no use my writing now: I must get out first – that is the next step. Anything I write, like all I think, is now pure Bahá'í. I have in view a book different from anything I've attempted yet, based on your World Order essays and centering round Bahá'u'lláh's Tablets to the Christian Kings. It gives the message in a new and I believe uniquely apposite and timely way and with a penetrating directness – so I think!'

His concession to Nancy over the offer of the Publishing Trust was no more than a *reculer pour mieux sauter*, as is disclosed in his letter of October 21, 1937 enquiring how 'the Book Company has progressed – if you secured the capital and if the company is incorporated?' He realized that 'My fortunes are bound up in some way with it or anyway with the National Spiritual Assembly so I have a special interest.'

Now occurred an incident which was to provide some immediate light relief and give rise to a story which would travel the Bahá'í world and be repeated down the generations, apparently, as long as George is remembered. Why he decided to bring Nancy to London at this particular time (September 1938) is not known. He mentioned some medical needs of his own, which proved to be no more than the purchase of some foot bandages from a shop in Regent Street, which could easily have been sent to him by post. He was in the throes of writing *The Heart of the Gospel*[1] from which, as usual, he expected the fulfilment of his highest hopes and he wanted 'a private talk about the book and its publication sometime . . . perhaps when my wife is shopping'. The most likely explanation is that having conceded momentary victory to Nancy over the offer from the National Spiritual Assembly, he hoped that a trip to London, where she could meet some Bahá'ís, would soften her attitude. Above all he longed for association with some Bahá'ís and the opportunity to discuss his position and the new possibilities which would arise with the publication of *The Heart of the Gospel*. I was the BBC's male television announcer[2] at the time and was so far 'with it' as to have one of the

---

[1] See Chapter 15.

[2] Before World War II the BBC operated the only public television service in the world. There were three announcers, Jasmine Bligh, Elizabeth Cowell and myself, and two programmes a day. Leslie Mitchell had been 'the first' but he went off to the newsreels and I took his place. It was the 'thing' of the moment, a four-years' wonder which closed down immediately war was declared.

estimated five thousand sets in use – lent by the BBC in the hope that it would provoke constructive ideas in my mind for the development of television. I suggested to George a party in my flat. His reply supports the above supposition, and reveals his constant preoccupation with 'the way out' and his equally constant optimism over each project upon which he pinned his hopes. His letter of September 10, 1938 reads:

> I am more than delighted to hear I can see you in London. A party in your flat would I think be the most enjoyable thing possible, on 21st if possible and if not on the 22nd. Or the 20th would be free. Let us know as soon as possible as our days are very few.
>
> I am eager to get free and away to Bahá'í business exclusively and openly at once and I'm sure *The Heart of the Gospel* is the way out, and I want to urge you to help me all you can. I want the Bahá'í Trust *as such* to publish it so as to commit me and also because the book is from Bahá'u'lláh and I must acknowledge this . . .
>
> I am sure my wife will back me up when the break comes and stand by me with all her heart.
>
> I will do anything to have a talk with you . . .
>
> Very busy. Longing to see you all and fix something definite.

I had been in close touch with George for two years and knew well his growing fame in the Bahá'í world. I telephoned his hotel and when a rather subdued male voice answered his room number I enquired in my most respectful tone, 'Is that Mr Townshend?' A full-voiced cheery reply came back: 'Is that yerself? It's meself speakin'.' This story, related to a large gathering of Bahá'ís in the old Bahá'í Centre at 4 Market Street, Manchester on the occasion of the National Teaching Conference in 1950, with George himself present, a free man and fully fledged member of the Bahá'í Faith, was a tremendous success. I can never forget him, in the middle of the back row, laughing his head off. He was so happy! Ever afterwards, in Africa, Pakistan, Canada, the United States, and by pilgrims from many parts of the world to the Bahá'í World Centre in the twin cities of Haifa and 'Akká, I have been asked about this incident. Persian Bahá'ís particularly have always seemed interested and amused by it.

We arranged to meet next morning at the bank in Harrods, and I was there early, suddenly realizing that we had never met and had made no arrangements for identification. But as soon as he came through the doors I knew him, and he seemed to recognize me. Of that meeting I have no memory save of a very special event and a sense of excitement and pleasure. Of what we talked about or planned there is no recollection.

The party in my flat I do remember. In addition to George and

Nancy there were present Hasan Balyuzi,[1] Marguerite Wellby, St Barbe Baker,[2] who shared the flat with me, and two others whose names I cannot recall. The television set was not even switched on. Sitting round the fire we read prayers and discussed the work of the Faith. Later, as refreshments were brought in and there was general movement, Nancy turned to me and the following exchanges took place.

NANCY:	Why don't you keep Christmas?
D.H.:	Why don't you keep Passover? Jesus did.
NANCY:	Why do you wear that ring?
D.H:	Why do you wear that cross round your neck?
NANCY:	Why don't you say the Lord's Prayer?
D.H.:	How can I pray for something that has already happened? What would you have done if you'd been living in, say, Ephesus about AD 75, a devout Jewess, married to a rabbi who had accepted Jesus as the Messiah?

Fortunately this was broken up by the arrival of coffee. George was standing behind Nancy and slightly to one side and I could look straight at him. He was obviously delighted, though like Brer Rabbit 'he lie low'. The next day he told me I had done well and later that it had been very helpful. Except for accompanying him to Regent Street to do his shopping I remember nothing more of that visit. But Nancy and I remained friends.

George returned to Ahascragh to work on *The Heart of the Gospel* and to receive, not long after, a letter from his old sweetheart Nellie Roche.

The remarkable story, already outlined in Chapter 4, now unfolds. It is played out by two mature, highly developed characters against the background of the greatest spiritual drama in the history of the world and is as different from the general modern concept of romance as the dime novel from *Paradise Regained*. It restores selfless idealism and exalted spirituality to human relationships. There are elements of classical inevitability about it.

Our sources for this episode are Nellie's own notes, Miss Watkins's letters and recorded memoirs, thirty-nine letters from George to Nellie, two from Nancy to Nellie, ten from Nellie to George, a photograph of Nellie and other invaluable material.[3]

[1] Appointed a Hand of the Cause in 1957; distinguished Bahá'í scholar and author.

[2] Founder of the Society, The Men of the Trees.

[3] See Appendix 2. Miss Watkins wrote that there were other letters but feared that when moving house they had been lost. Those we do have run from April 25, 1939, which by inference is George's second, to October 14, 1947, which was obviously not his last. There are many gaps, the longest being of four years, from 1943 to 1947.

Nellie became a Bahá'í in October 1937, and travelled with Dorothy Baker[1] in the South in 1938. By this time George had contributed to several volumes of *The Bahá'í World*, to *World Order* magazine, a number of his essays had been published in pamphlet form (two: on *Hidden Words; 'Abdu'l-Bahá, a Study of a Christlike Character*, and others), and *The Promise of All Ages* was widely circulated among Bahá'ís, in the United States. It is not surprising therefore that Nellie read something he had written about the Faith. She recognized him instantly of course and wrote to him – from Knoxville, Tennessee, her notes suggest.

Her first few letters to George after the long break of nearly a quarter of a century in their relationship, and George's replies, are unfortunately lost to us, but it is apparent from Nellie's notes that she received one on March 29, 1939, (her fifty-ninth birthday), and from Miss Watkins's letter that 'it made her weep'. This is the letter referred to below (p. 157) in which George gave some account of his life since their separation (in later letters there are references to his Tablets from 'Abdu'l-Bahá, and of other matters about which Nellie was obviously informed) and recounted his situation of having had to refuse the proposal of the British National Spiritual Assembly in order to maintain the unity of his family. Nancy's objections to his resignation appeared to be on financial grounds. It was then that Nellie wrote, insisting on his spiritual destiny and offering her newly-received inheritance of five thousand dollars to enable him to enter fully the service of Bahá'u'lláh and thereby achieve his goal. But let Nellie's own memorandum tell the story. This remarkable document is a series of pencilled jottings, in her own firm strong hand, of a chronological sequence of notes relating her memories of George and the extraordinary intimations which she received in Knoxville while travelling with Dorothy Baker in 1938. The memorandum is dated May 28, 1957, two months after George's death, and fourteen months before her own.

The first notation after the breaking of their engagement[2] is a strange indication of some extra-sensory perception at the very time – September 1936 – when George was making his proposal to the British National Spiritual Assembly for the working out of a method by which he could resign from the Church. Her staccato jottings read:

> Strong urge September 1936 – National Spiritual Assembly here in January 1937 (met H.H.[3]) – accepted Faith October 1937 – D. Baker to Knoxville – 1938 – asking for light – any light – no thoughts of George –

[1] Appointed by Shoghi Effendi a Hand of the Cause, December 24, 1951.

[2] See Ch. 4.

[3] Horace Holley

told George my messenger sent me by God – quite overcome . . . lying in bed on sleeping porch – back to door – eyes closed – saw grey gossamer sack coming through the air – enveloped me completely – was told I was completely within George's protection.

The only possible action after such an experience was to write to George, her messenger sent by God and within whose protection she was completely enveloped. This was the letter which George received in the spring of 1939, a few months after his return from London.

Nellie's notes continue:

March 29, 1939 – in office 713 N.T. – just received letter – queer feeling as if thin plate had turned over inside – intelligence conveyed to my mind – day for which I was born – everything had gone exactly as planned – rebirth into value of selfless love – George had to suffer – whatever I had to give had been held in reserve until then – new funds[1] – insisted on spiritual destiny – poured out ardor – also funds – final break – (with the Church) – last book climax of career.

Nellie's memory was good, for George's letters of April 25, May 15, June 7 and September 8, 1939 all refer to the five thousand dollars or one thousand pounds as an emergency loan to enable him to solve his family crisis, ensure publication of his new book, and 'settle in' and support his family in the interim of building up an income from writing. He asked the British National Spiritual Assembly to hold most of this sum for him to be called on at an instant's notice if needed. He still expected disciplinary action or a trial for heresy, the latter, he states in one of his letters, having been mentioned in ecclesiastical circles.

George's comments on Nellie's extra-sensory experiences are interesting. 'One cannot tell what Intelligence, as you say, communicated with you but assuredly the thought came from 'Abdu'l-Bahá . . . Your gift is the most soul-compelling thing – the sense of sacrifice in it gives it a power to penetrate and grip that otherwise nothing could have and its spirit creates a similar spirit in the recipient. You can imagine!'

Nellie's note, recorded above, that she insisted on George's spiritual destiny and gave whatever she had to assist him to accomplish it, is reflected in many of his letters to her. He also expresses again his conviction that one's spiritual condition affects material circumstances: 'Everything is changing within me and will soon change immediately round me.' His pleasure and gratitude are expressed from a full heart:

This is all a wonderful experience – it long has been and still is for me a

[1] The inherited $5,000 which she sent to George for an emergency fund.

spiritual crisis searching, rending, convulsing. I've aged twenty years in the last eight – but it's worth it. I hope and believe happiness, long forgotten, is now about to come back to me. And you through your self-sacrificing gift have now brought it to me. I suppose it's the sacrifice in it gives it the power it has to animate me – how extraordinary and unforseeable it all is!

George lost no time in taking advantage of the new situation resulting from Nellie's generous offer, and of building his hopes anew. He wrote to me personally on April 13:

> I have been offered as a gift or a loan £1,000 by some Bahá'í friends to tide me over my passage out of the church: the money would be paid to the British National Spiritual Assembly for my benefit if they would accept charge of it, so that the name of the donors need not be known. All you would write to me would be you had the money for me. I have not accepted this help; but if it meant my getting out I would do so in all probability. I should then have the proceeds of two books, £1,000, and my pen (such as the poor thing is) to start a new life on with my family.
>
> I have no qualms about it and I expect to do it anyway. It will however be easier as a family man if the National Spiritual Assembly thought the prospect of my making some sort of a livelihood out of Bahá'í authorship were reasonably good.
>
> If I remain a clergyman I shall not live one year, and should hope to die much sooner! So my family don't really stand to lose much.
>
> I had hoped and still hope to be free in July.
>
> If I hear from you in a favourable sense I shall write at once to the U.S.A. to accept the money offer and ask for a portion of the sum to be remitted to you . . . If all goes according to plan I shall take the first excuse for declaring my adhesion to the Cause and for resigning my post and get out of this. It has to happen; and the sooner the better.

This was followed on April 20 by 'The offer of money from a friend in the U.S.A. to help my transition may enable me to move out quicker. I wish I knew where to move to. These are days of great delicacy and strain for me.' He started collecting his Bahá'í papers to put 'in the care of the National Spiritual Assembly for safekeeping'. Eight days later (after writing to Nellie on April 25):

> Things are moving fast for me now! I feel like a man engaged to be married, who fixes the day for twelve months hence, then advances it to six and to three. Now that it is to come, the sooner the better. This most generous financial help from U.S.A. hurries up my liberation, and I hope the National Spiritual Assembly by the end of May will have in hand for me £500. I am ever so much obliged to them for consenting to handle the money.
>
> I will post off registered 'Abdu'l-Bahá's letters now in my keeping for

the National Archives. And I'll send also some contemporary London papers giving accounts of 'Abdu'l-Bahá's doings and sayings in 1911 (sent me long ago by Martha Root) and other similar newspaper cuttings concerning the Bahá'í movement and its progress. Whatever is of interest for the Archives is yours. As regards my own Bahá'í library (which is very extensive and some of it probably now rare) perhaps I may be glad to ask you to keep safe a little of it if you can. I hope to keep most of it by me for use and reference.

My imagination often lately has run to the point where the family waves adieu to Ahascragh and starts off on its new adventure: but there I stop, for I haven't the smallest idea where to go or what to do. This *does* leave a hiatus in one's picture and I had it in mind to write and ask for some suggestions on the matter and also what prospect there is of my getting a sale for what I may write. At present I do not know definitely *how* I can serve the Cause which I am leaving Ahascragh to help; and on that point I should be glad of any information or counsel or opportunity the National Spiritual Assembly can give me. I *urgently* need to know *where* the National Spiritual Assembly thinks I can be of most use as a professed and active Bahá'í. On my location, my family plans must depend and the sooner I know for sure the better. I may think it wiser to leave the family in comparative safety here in Ireland – or some members of it – and myself go to the field of action alone. And my family may have definite views on the matter.

This long letter also discussed publishing plans for *The Heart of the Gospel* which he had asked me to manage for him, and for the re-issue of *The Promise of All Ages*, under his own name and titles. It reveals the enormous strain under which he had lived for some time, writing *The Heart of the Gospel*, with his usual nervous concentration and constant revision, discharging his own Church duties and those of his Bishop who was ill, writing an incredible number of letters, writing for the Guardian, fighting a bout of influenza and eventually being forced to stay in bed by a scalded foot. This final calamity may well have been providential for it forced him to rest and realize that he had been on the verge of a breakdown. 'I am relaxing and rather glad of the rest. My health is altogether different since I had that enforced rest in bed. I was very near a nervous breakdown.'

Now with renewed vigour and hope he entered into detailed discussion of publishing plans, resignation plans, plans for removal to Bournemouth, which the National Spiritual Assembly had suggested as the best place for him to settle.

It's hard to imagine any device for a resounding advertisement of the Cause over here more telling than this book written by a 'dignitary' (heaven forgive me!) in active church work, followed by attacks on him and by his scandalising rebuttals and his withdrawal from office and so on, provided he raises a big enough row over it. And *that* must depend a great deal on the real value and force of *The Heart of the Gospel*. If it is, as you and I think, a truth whose time has come: then all somehow will be well.

I wish it could all happen quickly; however, it can't, and I must be patient for a few weeks.

He decided to show the authorship of *The Heart of the Gospel* as 'simply George Townshend, M.A.(Oxon.) leaving out clerical titles (which may not be mine any longer when publication takes place).' The magnitude of the task began to worry him; 'I fear the job of finding a suitable little house in South England may be a long job and cause delay and expense. Can you put me in touch with any land or house agent in or near Bournemouth or ask any of the Bournemouth friends to help me at once to get information. I can't stir till I have a place to move to. This matter is urgent and I do hope you will help me. Weeks may be lost over it.' Five days later, on May 17: 'These are stirring days for me, I can assure you! . . . I do trust that by the special aid of Bahá'u'lláh I can bring over a united family.' The definite views on the matter which he foresaw are obviously being expressed. However, 'My present plan is to resign as soon as I have that £300 in hand and have the contract signed for *The Heart of the Gospel*; and leave not later than the end of July. I ought to give fully that much notice, especially as the diocese is shorthanded and my leaving even at that date will cause much inconvenience. But if I can get any reasonable excuse for getting out sooner I will seize it!' But on May 31:

> Since I last wrote you I've been away on a few days holiday and have had an opportunity for calm reflexion . . . I will publish the book as a clergyman, addressing my fellow-Christians and urging them to accept this new interpretation and to find it embodied in practical modern form in the Bahá'í Teachings. As an officer of standing with a lot of acquaintances and friends in the church, and congregations to whom I've preached in various parts of the country, I have a large audience already gathered. I hope that my standing my ground and taking as a clergyman the consequences of my book, will cause a greater stir and will give greater strength and effectiveness to my appeal.
>
> I am sure this is right and I feel I had a narrow escape from making a serious mistake and from throwing away the special opportunity which Bahá'u'lláh gave me.
>
> I hope you will keep me informed as to how things are going. There is at the moment nothing for me to do but to cool off and rest up and prepare for future eventualities. When the book is out that 'clear way out' which the Guardian predicted for me as a result of your National Spiritual Assembly's action will open up.

Were we not aware of George's utter commitment to maintaining the unity of his family it would be only too easy to see him as a

Hamlet-like figure, unable to take the dreaded action and finding cogent reasons for procrastination. But George was not like that; he was neither half-hearted, vacillating nor retreating. His was a two-fold task: to resign and maintain the unity of his family. His determination not to concede defeat on either count never wavered and eventually he won them both.

He pursued his campaign of more and more openly declaring his belief in Bahá'u'lláh and his allegiance to His Cause, a course which he felt must sooner or later bring down upon him the wrath of the ecclesiastical establishment whose servant, albeit of high rank, he was. He believed that if he were attacked or his position became untenable, Nancy would stand by him, a confidence which was well founded and was to be proven in the event.

After much discussion and clarification George accepted the publisher's terms for *The Heart of the Gospel* as well as for a re-issue of the unsold copies of *The Promise of All Ages*. The title page of the latter was reprinted so that both books came out under his own name and with his titles.

George had been invited to give a talk at the Bahá'í Summer School to be held during late July and early August at Hoddesden in Hertfordshire and great efforts were made to have the first copies of *The Heart of the Gospel* available there. When, as a sop to Nancy, he had changed his plan to resign first and then publish, he had also thought it better (against his heart's desire) not to attend the school, but Nancy was so delighted that he was not going to give up Ahascragh and all it meant to her life that she agreed to accompany him if he could get a locum tenens. He lost no time in doing so and wrote joyfully on July 27 that he had bought railway tickets for himself and Nancy to cross from Dublin on August 4 and be in Hoddesden the afternoon of the 5th. On August 1 however he wrote, 'There was not a berth to be had on boat or train for Friday night (excursion day) so I have to advance my going, and go alone on Thursday night, sleeping in Holyhead harbour till a later train than the mail and finally reaching Euston at one o'clock or so. It would be ever so nice if you could meet me there (on Friday 4th, 1 p.m.) and I will look out in hopes.' So he came alone. But he appeared on the programme as the Venerable Archdeacon George Townshend, M.A. presenting a paper on 'World Religion and World Unity'.

This venture is a clear proof of the unassailable position of the Establishment at that time. A senior clergyman attending such a function of what was generally regarded then as an obscure sect,[1] not

[1] On Oct. 22, 1934 George had written to the Guardian that the Church authorities and others in England supposed to be informed definitely regarded the Bahá'í Cause as a dead issue. George's comment to the Guardian was, 'We'll see'.

only would raise no eyebrows but would be taken as an indication of the personal interest of the visiting dignitary, which would lend some cachet to the occasion and foster friendly relations with a rather far-out group.

This was a totally different matter from the writing of expository books in favour of a new Messiah. More than one bishop, dean or archdeacon had attended socialist conferences, Buddhist or Quaker gatherings – indeed, the Dean of Canterbury, Dr Hewlett Johnson[1] was generally known as 'the red Dean' on account of his predilection for communism – but there was nothing challenging to the ecclesiastical order in such activities. George's writings would condemn him; his attendance at the Bahá'í Summer School in the full panoply of his 'Venerable' would only show his intellectual vigour and liberalism.

Furthermore, the doctrines of the Churches of England and Ireland were, and still are, so amorphous as to permit its members any number of unofficial beliefs, interpretations of Scripture, practices and membership in other associations. The Church itself is heterodox and not united on its own teachings.

In the meantime, publication of *The Heart of the Gospel* went ahead. George, recovered from his exhaustion and full of euphoria at the prospect of freedom held out by Nellie's generous help, eager to see the new book ('I am ever so much pleased with the printing, format and all that'), and thanking God that 'My wife is heartily with me in this, with all her vigour and resolution of character', stimulated by approach of the day when he would attend his first Bahá'í Summer School, appeared in his correspondence of the time at the top of his form, genial, happy, cheerful.

He had asked that the cover of *The Heart of the Gospel* be in Irish blue:

> I should like the book to be St Patrick's blue the exact colour of which I enclose. But in this I should defer to the judgement of the publisher who may think this too weak a colour. But it's the colour of heaven and of Ireland; and with a touch of Celtic ornament somewhere on the page before the title page or at the head of the introduction, a character might be given to the appearance of the book. But let the publisher, an expert in the business, say the last word.

I had confessed in reply that I had always thought Ireland's colour to be green. He replied:

> No, Ireland is *not* green. Nor yellow. Nor white.
> She is sky blue.

[1] 1874–1966. Dean of Manchester (1924–31), of Canterbury (from 1931). Author of *The Socialist Sixth of the World* (1940); published in America under the title *The Soviet Power*.

And her emblem is a harp: some day a nine-pointed star will be over the
harp.

Cheerio.

The earth darkens. Heaven brightens.

George was the lion of the Summer School in spite of such
distinguished visitors as Chief Jomo Kenyatta, who had just
published his book *Facing Mount Kenya* and would later become first
president of the independent Kenya; Reg Turvey (1882–1968), the
South African artist; Richard St Barbe Baker, the 'Man of the Trees';
and Lady Blomfield (1859–1939), 'Abdu'l-Bahá's hostess during His
London visits. He wasn't worried by the attention he received but
glowed with love of the friends and happiness to be among them. He
signed copies of his book for them; he played tennis, (borrowing my
'bags' and racket and shoes and still, at the age of sixty-three, showing
signs of the prowess of his Oxford days). The snapshots in Plates 21 and
22 show the informal and easy atmosphere, and only the tennis player
is posed. Of this one he later commented, 'I recognize the bags, but
who owns the ankles in the foreground? I can't quite remember'.

But let him speak for himself:

> I wanted to write to you as soon as I got home to tell you how much I
> enjoyed my days with the Summer School and how much I got out of it;
> but I waited till I could have a copy of *The Heart* to send you . . .
>
> That Summer School filled a void in my Bahá'í experience, for I've not
> had for many years, not since Miss Rosenberg's time, any personal
> association with a number of believers together. Accustomed to living in a
> lonely countryside, I appreciated this companionship all the more and I
> hope to goodness I'll soon find a means of getting out of this and living
> among Bahá'ís in future.
>
> Converts will have to be made in tens of thousands to do any real good.
> Amazing that a Prophet should have come nearly a century ago, should
> have turned history upside down, and scarce a hundred Britishers should
> know anything about it.

And a postscript, referring again to Summer School: 'I'm living in
hopes of the next one: all my family will be at it.' And later still: 'Since
the Summer School I have had wonderful spiritual experiences: if
these continue I shall be able to do my part.'

George wrote to Nellie telling her

> I've decided not to resign my incumbency before the publication of the
> book. (The National Spiritual Assembly hope it will be out at the end of
> July or early in August.) If I resigned it would look as if one had to give up
> Jesus Christ in order to follow Bahá'u'lláh as the Christ; and of course as a
> clergyman I ought to be the *connecting* link between the two. To my delight
> I've just received from the British National Spiritual Assembly a letter of

the greatest relief and happiness at this decision. They had been dismayed at the idea of my resigning but had not wished to influence me; and now they're tremendously pleased and full of confidence for the outcome. So am I; aren't you?

Everything is shaping right in the most extraordinary manner. But I'm not satisfied that the publication arrangements are right: the publisher seems to be driving a very hard bargain with the Bahá'ís. We'll know more soon . . .

George, although disclaiming any business ability, was by no means gullible, and his legal training stood him in good stead. We have already seen how, in the matter of the financial valuation of his books he realized that their worth in 1936 was no criterion of their future value. He queried closely the terms of the publisher's contracts, conceding points which he understood, but refusing to accept what he felt unfair. He was very aware of the great advantages of American copyright and of the far larger market in the United States and he insisted on full attention to both matters.

He continued to Nellie:

I'm keeping the balance of the money safe for the present to provide for eventualities as there is no telling what steps the Church will take when the book is out. They'll *have* to come into the open and make a decison instead of continuing to ignore the matter, and of course my own material future will be very much involved.

So it's a moment of keen crisis and impending change; and I do hope so much your most generous and self-sacrificing help will prove to be of vital service. I hope too it won't be long before I can return it to you in full; if the books sell well this ought to happen quite naturally . . .

His over-optimism was always proof against shrewdness!

The Second World War was declared on September 3, 1939, and on September 8 George wrote to Nellie, 'Nothing yet has moved or is taking shape. No reviews or notices of the book. All thoughts are of war and fear and horror. But something must happen though prophecy indicates the spiritual breakaway will not occur till *after* the war has come to an end. Your enthusiasm and devotion to the Cause are wonderful – wonderful. I do hope I will now do my bit and I am *ever* so glad I have your prayers.'

This was followed shortly by a very revealing letter to her, describing his own inner struggle and clarifying his repeated thought that when he was ready, God would act. He is apparently writing of *The Promise of All Ages* and *The Heart of the Gospel*:

The reason these books have been so late in appearing is not that I found it difficult to connect up Christianity and Bahá'ísm and express the

17. *Summer School, Hornsea, 1947*

18. Groups at Summer School, Cottingham, 1951. In the lower picture Richard St Barbe Baker, the 'Man of the Trees', is amusing the friends.

19. *A group at the first British Bahá'í Summer School, held at Hoddesden in 1939. George is sitting and wearing a hat; second to his left is Jomo Kenyatta.*

20. *Summer School, Bangor, North Wales, 1952. George is sitting, holding the picture of 'Abdu'l-Bahá.*

21. *A group at Hoddesden Summer School, 1939. George is signing something for Kenneth Christian (white collar), American pioneer to Greece.*

22. *Hoddesden, 1939: 'I recognize the bags, but whose are the ankles in the foreground?'*

connexion in literary form but rather the need for action on my part. To sever yourself completely from your past, your training and tradition, environment, friends, Church, university and your own old self is no small job if effected thoroughly. Then I have to come forth alone as a pioneer and stand at the meeting of two ways of thought and call Christians to come along over and face the consequences and be prepared to answer all conundrums: one has to be very sure of oneself and one's cause before one is equipped for that. This task is especially onerous to me who hate publicity and wish only for a quiet life among my friends. To equip myself for this has been the main difficulty.

The worst is now over but there is plenty of trouble to come, of course.

I am delighted beyond words to hear your favourable report of opinions on *The Heart*, and I'm glad too you think *The Bible and the New Age* a better title. My expectation is that the Churches will accept a measure of Bahá'u'lláh's Teachings and will be confused and divided on this. They will not accept the Teacher: at least for a long, long time. I shall have to stay here for a bit but only some months, please God; and I need never denounce my Orders. They are no harm. But the Church authorities may denounce me, or try to!

Nellie now suggested that she should try to find an American publisher for his two books, an offer which filled George with excitement and inspired him to send the necessary authorizations at once. In this instant call to action he displayed business knowledge, shrewdness and practicality, which presents us who know him with something of an enigma and his Irish friends with an utter impossibility.[1] He gave Nellie the relevant details of the contracts with Drummond, his English publisher, explaining that if Drummond found an American publisher first, Nellie would have to give way ('he was in the field before you. But he is not likely to get anyone'), advising her to consult Horace Holley, secretary of the National Spiritual Assembly of the United States of America for exact terms of their promise to the British National Spiritual Assembly to buy five hundred copies from any interested American publisher ('Better have a clear undertaking from the National Spiritual Assembly about this.'), he offered to put up £100 if need be, ('but the publisher will not push the book unless he himself risks something on it.'), he suggested she tear up two printed copies to make a text for the printer since making typescripts would be inefficient, ('My chief counsel is to consult Holley: I'll write to him and I've no doubt I'll fall in with any plan he suggests or approves'). This is a man of action, not a bumbling philosopher.

Nellie co-opted Winston Evans, a young Bahá'í business man in Nashville, who worked on the project to such effect that both

[1] See Ch. 12, 'The Archdeacon'.

Macmillan and Prentice Hall, two of the leading and most reputable of American publishers, discussed it at two board meetings of each firm. They both regretfully declined but asked to see the next book from George's pen. Macmillan, as George wrote to the Guardian, 'very nearly took *The Heart*'. He covered his own disappointment with messages of encouragement and gratitude to Nellie and Winston: 'Ever so many congratulations to you and Mr Evans for your original and splendid propaganda work among the big publishers. To have introduced the Faith to them is a great service; and will bear its fruit in due time.'' . . . Mr Evans' work and yours in bringing the book before so many publishers is continually in my mind as a splendid piece of propaganda. I hope to offer you something soon they will be more likely to accept. I am cogitating a real live subject. Any suggestions for an essay or book from you and Mr Winston Evans will be most acceptable: I mentioned this to him . . .'

On November 18 he wrote saying, 'A letter from Horace Holley came this morning promising the National Spiritual Assembly would buy five hundred copies of *The Heart* at wholesale prices from the American publisher.' 'We expect to feel the war acutely even in Eire: but I wonder if we are the small afflicted people who the Bible prophesies will not be submerged in the catastrophe?' This sentence is extremely interesting in the light of his view of prophecy:

> A prophecy in the full sense of the word means much more than any mere prediction. It refers to a foreview of the future seen by an inspired Prophet by the light of eternity and is a vision of the future purpose of God laid up beyond mortal ken.[1]
>
> . . . the prophets of Israel. Those seers wrote – as a great poet might write – with their minds turned towards God and their hearts lighted and warmed by ardent faith. They could not control the vision that was vouchsafed them: they could not complete it nor set it in its own environment and perspective, nor plumb its meanings nor yet count the years which should elapse before it descended from the realm in which they saw it to the realm of actuality.[2]

George continued his plan of action. He sent a copy of *The Heart of the Gospel* to his Bishop, hoping at least to be questioned, but he received a letter from his Lordship expressing warm interest, commending its ideas and suggesting that George should try for a D.Lit. degree on the strength of it! Irony was ever present in George's life! Later, at a luncheon, he told George that the lack in *The Heart of the Gospel* was that he 'should have told much more about Bahá'u'lláh for His Teachings were wonderful.'

[1] *Christ and Bahá'u'lláh*, Ch. 2
[2] *The Promise of All Ages*, Ch. 1

George's next move was more than bold; in any other man it would have been defiant. He replied expressing disappointment over the reviews and continued:

> There is and must be something very wrong indeed about a world in which religion is not in the van of progress: no wonder we've got to an impasse, for religion ought to show the *direction* of progress. As I said in *The Heart of the Gospel* I have found today no original spiritual leadership for the time except in the writings of Bahá'u'lláh: but plenty there. For myself I have accepted His teachings in their entirety, have identified myself with His Cause and joined the Bahá'í fellowship. I am trying to get published in London in an effective form a book which may prove what can be done along that line, under the title *The Promise of All Ages*. I hope it will appear quite soon and when it does I will if I may send you an advance copy.

A few days later he wrote:

> The Bishop has replied ignoring my declaration but saying he will be glad to read *The Promise*. (I wonder!) His breadth of mind, so far, is splendid and I honour him for it. Some other clergy agree with him, too.

This seems the appropriate moment to comment on what might appear, from the passion of George's longing to be free of the Church, to be a lack of gratitude for the very warm friendships which he enjoyed with his colleagues and neighbours, and the affection in which he was, and still is, held by his parishioners and those further afield. The subject is dealt with more fully in Chapter 12, *The Archdeacon*, where Una herself comments on it. Suffice it for now to say that George, the most humble of men, warmed himself at the hearth of friendship. Even after he had committed the appalling act of rejecting the Establishment, it was only a few of his colleagues who saw fit to slight and blackball him. The great majority, though not understanding his reasons, respected his integrity. He himself retained his affection for Ahascragh and its people and more than once went to stay with former neighbours. His longing was to be a free and openly-declared disciple of Bahá'u'lláh bearing witness to and working for Him.

> I want to see that Order started at least as an experiment in this country soon.
> I want to attend Conventions and other such meetings . . . with Una . . . as voters and eligible for all privileges . . .

In the spring of 1940 Drummond's new edition of *The Promise of All Ages* came out with George's own name and ecclesiastical posts on the title page and 'Abdu'l-Bahá's statement in His second Tablet to

George: *It is my hope thy Church will come under the Heavenly Jerusalem.* In London, Allen and Unwin Ltd., publishers of Dr Esslemont's *Bahá'u'lláh and the New Era*, were about to issue a new revised edition. It was suggested that the two firms should undertake some co-operative advertising, and this was done. Allen and Unwin sent a circular letter to the literary editors of a large number of newspapers calling attention to their own book and saying:

> At the same time, the firm of Lindsay Drummond Ltd. will re-issue *The Promise of All Ages* by Archdeacon Townshend. Special interest attaches to this book also because the author, having now identified himself with the Cause of Bahá'u'lláh, reveals the authorship of this book, which he formerly published under a pseudonym. Archdeacon Townshend submits this statement of the Bahá'í Faith in order to indicate what is in his opinion the radical cause of the present religious unsettlement and to show the direction in which there is to be found a full deliverance from our tribulations.

George had written this paragraph himself and was insistent that whatever amendments were made there should be no weakening of the position he had taken.

People in Ireland were beginning to talk about this new religion and George was becoming recognized as the authority on it, but it was, as yet, no more than curiosity about a matter of passing interest. An ex-missionary from Persia, the Reverend Lord, of Cork, wrote an angry letter to the editor of *Church of Ireland Gazette* 'assailing Bahá'u'lláh apropos of a review of *The Heart*. The editor did not publish the letter but sent it to me to deal with. I shall try to make a Bahá'í of the chap. If I fail, he may prove to be the match to the powder.' George sought and obtained an interview with the Archbishop of Dublin, and, as he disclosed to Nellie

> told him about *The Promise* and the new world religion and my hope our Church would adopt at any rate a large part of its teachings and so on; and he never turned a hair. I was disappointed. I wanted him to flare up. The fact is he did not take it in, I expect. I went away saddened; but on reaching the Cathedral found this furious letter from the ex-missionary, and I was greatly relieved, for then I realised the controversy would come along all right.

His high spirits were upheld by this apparent interest.

> Here in Ireland the prospects are miraculous. Marvellous responses in every way on every side all of a sudden. *Anything* may happen within one year, if these present symptoms develop!

One of his letters to me at this time (April 1940) about *The Promise* reads:

The Bishop is reading it and is seemingly struck dumb. I told the Archbishop about it. Some of the clergy are expressly looking for light from the East now. This book will *get* them. Mrs ...., the intellectual light of the Mother's Union in Ireland is deeply interested and has asked Una to stay with her. She is our feminine Archbishop! The atmosphere in the family is changing. The Guardian has written to me to stay in Ireland. Everything is happening from every direction at once. There is a good chance of *great* publicity for my two books in U.S.A.

I expect a volcanic outburst of the Bahá'í propagation very soon. It may begin any week any day now, in this country.

As for a livelihood, God will take care of us. I must go ahead with this anyhow. I am too full of hope to fear . . . I am very busy – planning – thinking – writing. I push my book and talk about the Cause: but the next Big Move is with the Bishop or the religious press or my warlike ex-missionary Lord of Cork.

Write soon, and write circumspectly.

He was writing now an enormous number of letters; three and four a week to me alone; others to the Guardian, to members of the clergy, to Nellie, to individual Bahá'ís who were beginning to write to him in gratitude for his books. He was to address the assembled Irish clergy (of the Protestant Church of Ireland) immediately before the opening of the Synod on May 7, his subject being 'Personal Experience of God', '. . . and shall tell 'em of Bahá'u'lláh . . . Then what!' He related later that he opened his address by saying that he had learned all he knew of Christ from 'Abdu'l-Bahá. His reception was apparently 'mixed' for he mentioned 'many snubs and disappointments'. But nothing could dampen his enthusiasm or lessen his purpose.

The fact is the Cause is utterly new over here, I am a very, very lonely pioneer and to expect quick results on any scale is to be too optimistic. But *The Heart of the Gospel* has done and is doing great work and people are beginning to talk and ask about Bahá'u'lláh – a few of them.

There is little chance of my being, as I expected to be, had up for heresy over *The Promise*: they ignore it . . . I am going now to put forward every effort on *Builders of a New World*[1] and shall float out on it. Positive initiative is necessary . . . The Guardian is eager about it. *This* will be the book to get me out.

An offer now came from Lindsay Drummond, the publisher with whom I was dealing on George's behalf, which seemed very advantageous in view of the rapidly developing restrictions on paper supplies due to the war. It involved an expenditure of more than £100 – a large sum in those days – and needed an immediate decision. I rang the Ahascragh Post Office and asked for Archdeacon Townshend.

[1] See pp. 175, 176.

George takes up the story:

> I am just back from the Post Office and now that half the village is not
> listening to me I want to tell you . . . I was sick in bed when the message
> came of a telephone call from London, and as the day was fine I got up and
> rushed into my clothes and biked down; I am none the worse – just a chill
> or something. A telephone call from London, probably Bahá'í, was too
> out of the way to miss!

He showed again shrewd judgement by not accepting the offer in
view of his need to conserve every penny he could raise to ensure that
he could move swiftly immediately he secured Nancy's agreement.
He wrote about this:

> The Bishops apparently will not attack me over *The Promise*. I then made
> ready to attack once again and arrange on my own initiative for a
> resignation.
>   My wife told me, if I moved she would leave me definitely and finally.
> She meant it, too. To have her even seem to reject the faith was intolerable;
> if I had been a better Bahá'í the situation would never have occurred. I am
> sure I can get her in. So is Una . . . I am trying all I know to make my
> family the nucleus of the first Spiritual Assembly. Meanwhile the name of
> Bahá'u'lláh is becoming well known among the intellectuals of the Church
> of Ireland and Una and I are not hiding our belief in the Cause. This
> morning a clergyman wrote me that he 'enjoyed' *The Promise*
> 'immensely'.
>   Of course the books are spreading too much for this to go on for many
> weeks: I shall be attacked somehow. If I am, I believe my wife would stand
> by me and fight to the last ditch. But more and more I want to take the
> initiative and get out by my own voluntary act.

But he counselled: 'Don't speak of this in any letter or any wise! It is
anxious work. The end will be all right.'
He kept up his high spirits and ended his letter of May 1, 'I hope to
ring *you* up some day with news of a new heaven and earth for my
family!'
Again,

> Oh, it is so lovely here, I wish you all could see it and enjoy the flowers
> and bursting buds and sunshine: we all now are so happy – and the birds are
> happy and New Jerusalem is only a little over our heads almost within
> reach!
>   Still no threat of a heresy trial for publishing *The Promise*. It has however
> been spoken of. The effect of the book on those who read it is wonderful –
> but so far they are very few . . . People are reading *The Heart* and talking of
> Bahá'u'lláh (on a small scale)!

He kept sending for more copies of *The Heart*, which he sent to
people all over Ireland, and when the new edition of *The Promise*, with

his own name and ecclesiastical rank on the title page, was ready, he sent copies to fifty senior clergymen of the Church of Ireland. This open proclamation reached its boldest moment on Sunday, June 30, 1940, when he preached the sermon at the morning service in St Patrick's Cathedral, Dublin, of which he was Canon in residence at the time. He recounts, with characteristic diffidence, in the middle of a letter about less important items,

> By the way, last Sunday in St Patrick's Cathedral I spoke of harmony and concord as the purpose of Christianity and all true religion, said the religion of Bahá'u'lláh was today the only religion I could find living up to this, and pleaded that we should follow suit and closed by affirming that the future belongs to the Church that did follow suit.
>
> My son Brian who was listening (I did not know he was there) wondered what would happen. The only thing so far is that the Dean of the Cathedral did what he never did to me before – volunteered how much he liked the sermon and what a change it was from what they had been listening to of late!

Brian wrote in the beautiful memoir of his father which he contributed to *The Bahá'í World*, vol. XIII,

> . . . in 1940 he concluded a sermon on world perplexities by saying that he personally had found no answer to the problems of the modern world except that given by Bahá'u'lláh, the sound of Whose Name I can still hear as it was uttered by my father's voice that day amid the echoes of the great cathedral of the pioneer of Christianity in Ireland.

Mr Adib Taherzadeh, whose memoirs we have already invoked, recalls that on one of their companionable rambles about Dublin, after George had left the Church, George took him to St Patrick's and showed him the exact pulpit in which he had stood to proclaim the Name of Bahá'u'lláh.

He sent more books to eminent people – Sir Francis Younghusband, Archbishop Temple (Canterbury), many others: – 'Sir F. did not acknowledge it, the "Arch." did.' He was thrilled with a large spread in *The Irish Times* for March 1, 1941 reviewing both *The Promise of All Ages* and Lady Blomfield's *The Chosen Highway*.[1] The headlines were the ones he had expected in the London newspapers in 1936: 'A NEW RELIGION FROM THE EAST – An Irish Churchman on Bahaism'. The reviewer made some attempt at objectivity but both books are rather more than damned with very faint praise. The crux of the whole reaction is stated in one paragraph:

[1] Her personal accounts of 'Abdu'l-Bahá's visits to London and the stories of His sister (Bahíyyih Khánum) and His wife (Munírih Khánum) which they related to her during her long stay as a guest in the Master's house in Haifa.

The Christian is not asked to give up going to church or reading the Scriptures, but he is to do these things in a sort of symbolic manner. He no longer can hold the orthodox teaching concerning the Trinity, the Incarnation, the Sacraments, or the Mystical Body of Christ – but, if he makes the trifling sacrifice of these Christian mysteries, he is welcome to go on praying in his old formulas, and is as good a Bahaist as any Mohammedan in Turkey.

George didn't mind the sarcasm, or the mild criticism of himself which closed the review:

Archdeacon Townshend's book also is enthusiastic, and is more gracefully written. The Archdeacon lays great stress on the goodness of character, so evident in this revolt from Islám, but he does not show how diametrically it conflicts with Christian dogma and Western philosophy. Some readers will think that, while a sympathetic account of a well-meaning movement outside the Christian world is commendable, it ought not to appear without qualification in the light of its essential irreconcilability with the Christian faith.

George commented:

. . . it has the historical interest that it is the first public broadcast of the Cause in this country by the Press. Of course I've published articles and preached and spoken over here about 'Abdu'l-Bahá, and the Cause of Bahá'u'lláh and so on; but I never got anything on this scale – it must have been read by thousands, being in our most important Irish newspaper.

The reviews of *The Heart of the Gospel* were much more favourable and will be considered in Chapter 15, in the literary context of his book. Although few, it was the leading papers which noticed it: *The Times Literary Supplement*, *The Irish Times*, the important Quaker journal *The Friend*, *John o'London's Weekly* a much loved review which has, alas, fallen to modern progress, *The Baptist Times*, *The Birmingham Post*, *John O'Groat Journal*, *The Aryan Path* and *The Church of Ireland Gazette*.

This mild success of his books together with their enthusiastic welcome from the Bahá'ís, contributed to his cheerfulness. His plan of action was bearing fruit: 'Meantime the knowledge of Bahá'u'lláh spreads slowly but continuously through the country.' The financial help and spiritual backing from Nellie gave him an assured position from which to obtain his freedom. But the source of his greatest happiness was undoubtedly Una's sudden realization of the truth of Bahá'u'lláh and her immediate identification with the Bahá'í community. George's joy knew no bounds. For months afterwards his letters spoke of it. 'Una's declaration is infinitely precious to me: a tree of fresh spring leaves in a sandy waste. It is an end to my loneliness. Nothing can express my gratitude and delight.' 'But I mustn't write of her for my heart just bursts into pieces with happiness and gratitude when I think of her.'

In occasional whimsical vein he thinks 'Una and I might buy a caravan and travel rent free as the "Bahá'í Gipsies" and teach and preach the New Message everywhere through the country.' He recalls his visit to London and the Summer School and asks after 'The Mollys and Margarets', members of the very active youth group. On March 21, 1941 he wrote in a postscript: 'I kept the Fast fully and strictly: the first time to do it thoroughly. None the worse.'[1] He concluded a letter to me at a time of overwork, 'R.I.P. now old chap but keep alive while you do it.'

It would be wearisome, though not to the degree it was to George who lived it, to follow in detail the course of his persistent efforts during the war to obtain Nancy's co-operation and to arouse more than a passing interest in Bahá'u'lláh. But the war, in spite of the physical difficulties and increased isolation which it imposed,[2] was a time of great activity for him, and of advancement towards his goal, both spiritually and practically. He was by now wholly and utterly committed to the Cause of Bahá'u'lláh. His thoughts, his energies, his aspirations were all for its promotion and his service to it. His correspondence dealt with nothing else. It was during the war that his work for the Guardian on God Passes By, Shoghi Effendi's monumental history of the first hundred years of the Bahá'í Faith, was done, including the writing of the Introduction.[3]

On February 17, 1940, barely six months after war was declared, he wrote to the Guardian listing the items of his active and open proclamation of the Faith of Bahá'u'lláh, relating in detail his statement to his Bishop. He continued:

> I shall take the earliest possible opportunity of resigning rather than stand a trial for heresy in which I have no defense to offer. Probably the Bishop will approach me very soon: the sooner the better. I am impatient to be gone, awaiting with eagerness the moment of release. But the next move is not with me.
>
> I have thought much over the situation that must now arise in a very few weeks. Though I am quite tranquil in my mind the difficulties are serious. I can only make a living by teaching English; this is precarious and will leave me little time or energy to carry out my purpose of devoting myself to the

[1] Bahá'u'lláh prescribes daily prayer and an annual fast. The latter takes place from March 2 to March 21 when Bahá'ís abstain from food and drink between the hours of dawn and sunset. March 21, Naw-Rúz, is the first day of the year in the Bahá'í calendar and is a festival.

[2] See Ch. 10.

[3] See Ch. 6.

propagation of the Cause of Bahá'u'lláh. To be diverted from this now, after all my effort, would be a catastrophe, and I feel sure Bahá'u'lláh will save me from it.

But when I get free (let us hope in April) I do not know what I can do for the Cause. Of course I'll work under the National Spiritual Assembly but they don't seem to have very much that suits my rather specialized training and confined abilities. I want to do and must do my *utmost* during the few remaining years of my life. I therefore venture to hope that you will be able to give me some work that I can do. So far as my time, my strength and my ability go, I will if I can be of any use, be henceforth always at your service. I have no greater hope nor other aspiration than to work for you in any way you say for the benefit of the Cause which now has become so dear to me.

In writing of the new edition of *The Promise of All Ages* under his own name and title he had added: 'My wife has undertaken to stand by me in upholding everything I have written in this book, whatever the consequences.' This was an old promise made by Nancy to which she remained firm, in spite of her refusal to agree to George's resigning, and he built upon it.

Shoghi Effendi's reply was immediate and contained clear guidance to George for his future services to the Faith. By his secretary:

As regards your general work for the Cause; Shoghi Effendi strongly feels that whatever the action which the Church authorities may decide to take as a result of your recent published declarations dissociating yourself from the Church, you should not leave Ireland, but instead should endeavour teaching openly the Cause, and make every effort to attract and confirm as many souls as you can, thus paving the ground for the establishment of a Bahá'í Assembly, nay of a number of such assemblies throughout Ireland. This is indeed the main task on which he wishes you to concentrate your energies, while also he would recommend that you devote as much time as you can to your literary activities on behalf of the Cause. As the first and only pioneer of the Faith in Ireland you should consider it your unique and priceless privilege to undertake so vital and sacred a mission, and you should rest assured that success will crown your efforts, as it has already crowned your services in the years past.

This was the letter in which the Guardian asked George for an essay on Queen Marie of Rumania and the Bahá'í Faith.[1] His personal note was balm to George's troubled heart:

Dear and prized co-worker: I was overjoyed by your letter, and admire the spirit that animates you and your dear wife in His service. The Beloved indeed watches over you, is well-pleased with the stand you have taken, will reinforce your high endeavours, and will inspire you and bless you in

---

[1] See Ch. 6.

your future activities and services. May He graciously enable you to champion His Cause, to proclaim its verities, to establish its truth, to defend its interests, and to consolidate its Administrative Order. I will continue to pray for you from the depths of my heart. Persevere, be confident, happy and grateful.

George's deepening isolation in his remote Galway parish, which at one time would have been a source of pleasure to him, now provoked a longing for the company of Bahá'ís with whom he could discuss and promote the new Revelation. Nancy was of no help to him here, being extremely wary of all his Bahá'í interest which she knew threatened her secure life, and George turned more and more to the Guardian and a few Bahá'í correspondents. Nellie not only discussed his books with him but supplied him with news of the Conventions, fireside meetings, seminars and teaching journeys undertaken by the American believers, and proposed subjects of her own for investigation. Her picture of the active Bahá'í life, in an America which had not yet entered the war and which he remembered with nostalgia, awoke in him a growing interest in the Administrative Order of Bahá'u'lláh to which he had, as yet, given little attention. As he explained to Nellie:

> . . . you always keep me informed about a side of the work that otherwise I know very little of. More and more the value and interest of the social and personal side comes home to me: here, living a sort of a hermit life and being of a meditative sort of habit of mind, *that* side of the life has been out of my reach. I am longing for more of it in the near future. My dream is that when the war is over I shall contrive to get off to Palestine and then to Baghdad and Persia (I wonder what will be left of us and all these places then!) and spend long enough in those Sacred spots to get intense and much needed inspiration. A visit to the U.S.A. sometime might be possible, to learn about the Administration and to meet you and all the good people I know so well by name. What oppresses me is the thought of what a lot I have to do and how few years remain to me to do it in! And during these months now I can accomplish so little.

Inevitably he began to plan a new book and mentioned it in a postscript to his letter of February 17 to the Guardian. He described it as short and of a practical and popular nature on the Administrative Order, probably under the title 'Building the New World'. The idea received a tremendous impetus from the Guardian's reply:

> Regarding the book you are planning to write on the Administrative Order. The Guardian heartily welcomes your idea, as the subject he feels is most vital and challenging. He would, however, suggest that you should not confine the work to a mere booklet, but treat the subject as extensively and thoroughly as possible, basing your studies on his World Order letters

which, as you may know, are now available in one book entitled 'The
World Order of Bahá'u'lláh'. A copy of the book is being mailed to you
under separate cover.

This now became the central theme of George's immediate
aspiration, and he endowed it with all the hopes and visions which he
had previously given to *The Promise*, his appearance at the World
Congress of Faiths, *The Heart*, his public association with the Faith of
Bahá'u'lláh and his declaration to the Bishops. But it was a new subject
to him and he approached it with careful study and forethought.

Nellie gave him every encouragement and assistance. She sent him a
compilation entitled *Bahá'í Procedure* and a book *Bahá'í Administration*.
The latter contains excerpts from the Will and Testament of 'Abdu'l-
Bahá, which is the Charter giving authority for the administrative
structure of the Faith, and a compilation of letters and statements by
the Guardian addressed to the American Bahá'í community in which
he guided them along the path of the evolving Order of Bahá'u'lláh, an
Order whose roots are planted deep in the soil of His Revelation and
whose structure is the organic embodiment of those spiritual laws and
principles which nourish its life. George, to his own surprise, was
captivated by the subject and was not slow to perceive its outstanding
feature – the perfect blending of the spiritual and the practical which
must inevitably characterize all the works of the Creator.

> We can begin to form a picture of civilization as it will be even one
> generation from now. One's own outlook changes in a way no one could
> imagine or describe once one gets really busy inside this Order: who can
> tell what the development will be when thousands march forward
> together in every land and are able to mould society to express their new
> ideals and understanding?

The book had now become 'Builders of a New World' and the
subject filled his mind. Not a word would be written for more than a
year, but notes and study and research, meditation and expression of
his thought in letters, wrought a continuing development of the whole
plan. It finally emerged, seventeen years later, as his 'crowning
achievement', *Christ and Bahá'u'lláh*.[1]

In May 1940 he wrote to Nellie,

> I am only so far at the stage of thinking over the material of the new book.
> It is perfectly astonishing to note how much there is in this Administrative
> Order and how it answers so *many* of the problems. The study of it has
> been a real eye-opener to me. I am in strong hopes its publication will be
> timely and it will be recognised as showing *how* all these questions of
> democracy and totalitarianism and world-organisation are to be
> answered.

[1] See Ch. 16.

Nearly a year later, on March 13, 1941, he wrote a progress report to the Guardian, telling him about the American publishers, his sermon in St Patrick's, the growing interest aroused by his books and complaining that 'People tell one another of their interest but they avoid telling me'. He mentioned hard and continuous work on 'Builders of a New World' and the beginning of the first draft. When finished he would send it to 'Winston Evans and Nellie Roche, who got the two companies aforesaid interested in my work . . . The leaven is working hard.' The Guardian's personal note in reply read:

I am delighted to learn of your continued activities to which, as you well know, I attach great importance and for the extension of which I continually and fervently pray. The new work you are preparing to publish, to which I am looking forward so eagerly, will be another laurel which you will be adding to the glorious crown you have deservedly won in the service of Bahá'u'lláh. May His spirit guide, sustain and protect you and your dear daughter, and your dear son for whose recovery I will specially pray when visiting the Holy Shrines.

His persistence was beginning to take effect, slowly but surely. He was able to tell the Guardian:

My clerical friends rather naturally won't commit themselves very much. Some are scared even of *The Heart of the Gospel*. But they have begun to ask about Bahá'u'lláh. I have begun to get an audience in the Church now, and am trying to get an opening for articles on general religion in the Church paper and *The Irish Times*. If I succeed I can teach the Bahá'í point of view as in *The Heart*, and the whole Protestant population of Eire will have these articles before them. This will both advertise my Bahá'í books or at least their author, and will put people in the right attitude of mind to approach the argument which these books present.

It is very difficult but *very* interesting to be the only Bahá'í in the country (save Una) and to have to begin everything from the very start. There is no sign yet of a heresy trial though it has been mentioned.

Among those to whom he sent *The Promise of All Ages* (the new edition under his own name) was the Rev. Norman Guthrie, who had engaged him for the University Extension Courses at Sewanee. Guthrie acknowledged the book but had not read it, 'and perhaps he won't, for his interest in the subject has quite evaporated'. He excused himself on the grounds that the Faith had been made 'such a petty thing'. George commented to Nellie on the sacrifice necessary to really accept the Messenger of God in His Day. But some three years later he reported, 'I have just had a great letter from Mr Guthrie. I am wondering what has prompted him to renew communications with me. I hope some day I may again go to America and see him and have a try if I cannot renew his interest which began so promisingly many years ago.'

He recorded that 'The Heart of the Gospel and The Promise have brought me many lecture engagements and I am trying to prepare the ground for fuller teaching later on . . .' 'I begin next month to do a certain amount of touring and speaking and shall make it all work into my newly assumed responsibilities: Dublin, February 5, Cork early April for one week; Derry [Londonderry] in June for four days – i.e. East, South and North of the island.' 'I always speak now on such occasions with a view to the near future when I shall be out and preparing minds for the larger and progressive outlook of Bahá'u'lláh.'

Pope's immortal line, 'Hope springs eternal in the human breast,' was never more greatly exemplified than in George. His resilience, his optimism, were inexhaustible. He began making plans for widespread teaching and begged Nellie to send him materials; study courses, pamphlets, introductory booklets:

> Your wisdom and your American experience will be of great service to Una and me, and soon to others of us here, in developing teaching work in the near future; and I hope you will help us. At present I am trying to unify the family, to spread generally a knowledge of the Cause in Ireland, and to write The Builders of a New World which will – for me – open the campaign full throttle when it is published. Una is doing great work in her neighbourhood; but all this now is preparatory only.

George's continual over-optimism can never overshadow the reality of his great achievement in spreading throughout Ireland the knowledge of Bahá'u'lláh and the message of the New Day. The clergy of the Church of Ireland were informed personally and by his addresses to the Synods, and many read his books. Thousands of laymen read the reviews and notes in The Irish Times and Church of Ireland Gazette; others attended his lectures. As the first, and for many years the only pioneer in Ireland, he conducted a one-man programme of proclamation which brought the Bahá'í Faith to the attention of his fellow countrymen.

Yet despite all this constant, vigorous activity for the Cause of Bahá'u'lláh he was restless and unsettled spiritually. There could be no peace for him until he became a fully recognized member of the Bahá'í community, bearing witness to the Revelation of Bahá'u'lláh fully and openly with pen and heart and life itself. He wrote to Nellie:

> I have pretty well made up my mind to resign my incumbency here as soon as the war is over, move the family to a little flat or house in Dublin and seek my fortune as a Bahá'í freelance. I can't do anything for the Cause so

long as I have a parish; and except to serve the Cause I have no interest in life. Something will turn up. Even the expectation of this new freedom fills me with exultation! Lately, great 'confirmations' have come to me.

He discussed methods of teaching and continued:

Do tell me what you, with your greater opportunities, think or know of these things. They are very much in my mind, with a practical purpose in view – when I leave my home to work for the Cause I want to have some effective approach in view that I may achieve results!

But not all his agitation was caused by the frustration of his position. His own visions and expectancy of wonderful things to come, 'the immense positive attainments that will burst upon us when the strife is done and peace reached and the price of our evils is paid and justice appeased and the Divine Mercy opens its gates,' excited his imagination: 'the vision of it eclipses the light of the sun and the beauty of the stars'. 'One is always ill at ease. For years I have suffered from too much darkness. Now I suffer from too much light – I am dazzled! My job is now to tune up my spiritual eyes to see by the new light. The plain prose of which is for one thing I must remake myself, and particularly so unite this family that we shall all go out together with radiant joy.'

Nancy's anxiety increased with George's sense of frustration, and she made great efforts to accommodate to him. Again irony raised its head when she suggested that after the war the whole family might start a school, run in sympathy with Bahá'í principles, 'in England or Switzerland'. George knew he could not leave Ireland, nor, if such a project were to succeed, could he abandon his ecclesiastical dignities, which would be its essential bona fides. But he was delighted that Nancy should make the proposal and wrote off to Stanwood Cobb[1] for ideas 'in spite of evident difficulties about carrying it out'. He was cheered and took it as a good omen.

It was possibly this evidence of Nancy's willingness to co-operate in his giving up the work of the Church that encouraged him to strike while the iron was hot and go to Dublin, determined to find a place to which he could move the family and then immediately resign. His letter of October 28, 1942 from Power's Hotel, Dublin tells the story:

Things are moving and changing fast. I feel I have to tell you!

I have [been] up here since Monday investigating; and by the aid of Bahá'u'lláh I have the offer of a suitable abode at what is regarded as a reasonable price, and have arranged provisionally for transport if and

[1] A well-known member of the American Bahá'í community who had met 'Abdu'l-Bahá and who maintained a school operated on a principle of progressive education; author of many books about the Bahá'í Faith.

when needed, and studied the cost of living. It is all a difficult proposition but the way has opened to me.

Before I left home a miracle happened and Nancy suddenly took a conciliatory attitude. If when I go home tomorrow she accepts the situation and will run up to Dublin and examine the residences I've selected from her point of view and approve, nothing remains but to tell the Bishop, summon the furniture vans and say goodbye to parish, Church and all – and become your full Bahá'í brother in an independent home in the beautiful suburbs of Dublin! Then every hour and every thought till I die must be Bahá'u'lláh's and His only. I pray now for hours daily. I wrote again to the Guardian explaining I did not really seek any material work but welcomed the opportunity of proving my detachment and letting my deeds surpass my words.

I write full of hope, relieved by the easing of many difficulties and trusting the way will continue to open step by step as we push forward. The problem of the <u>Home Front</u>[2] is now all that endangers our advance. Goodbye. Remember us!

The picture of this brave, dedicated, elderly man, coming up alone to Dublin, where he would normally stay in a canonry of the great cathedral, driven by an all-compelling necessity to abandon his secure position, his honours, his comfort, in order to serve fully and freely the newly revealed Christ, evokes the most poignant feelings of admiration and compassion and even awe. He was sixty-six, and, save for Una, the only soul in all Ireland to recognize the manifested King of Glory, to work for Him and proclaim His name. His lonely, persistent, passionate effort catches the rays of that splendour and reflects it again to our duller mirrors.

Meantime at home, George's announced intention had brought Nancy to such a pitch of desperation that she took the extraordinary step of appealing to Nellie for help. This is but one of the remarkable tales in this utterly remarkable story. Her letters (two) are among the most valuable documents we have, reflecting the greatest credit on herself while revealing her total incomprehension of George's all-consuming passion. The first is dated September 27, 1942:

Dear Miss Roche, I do hope you will forgive my writing to you about what may seem 'personal affairs'. I have known of you from George for some years and of your common interest in the Bahá'í Faith, and that is why I write to you.

From time to time George becomes restless and emotional about his work here and he feels that if he could go off to an unknown place and say he was a Bahá'í, life would be just perfect. But then George has always

[2] The wry pun is to the great war effort of the civilian population in Britain; the Home Front was synonymous with the Home Guard and the work in the factories to keep the Forces supplied.

been a restless highly-strung person loving change and variety continually. He has never stayed for so long in any one spot as here. Anyway, at the moment he wants to hurl himself out of the Church, thereby losing all the funds to which we have been contributing all these twenty-five or twenty-six years. Doing things this way, the Church will wash its hands of me too and I don't like this. In three years' time George could retire and he could then do what he liked . . . The only money George has available to carry out this scheme of his is whatever you sent him a few years ago. (I wish you would ask him to send it back!) George's plan is a small house in Dublin in a row . . . I am not a snob but I love the country and my garden. The cost of living has gone up enormously. Here we only just pull through on all his emoluments with a free house, cheap electricity and our own food and firing. In Dublin the food and firing for the poor and others is negligible and we have no right to put ourselves on top of them.

I appeal to you not to encourage George to break up his home now, but to be patient . . .

For myself I love my home; I got it together. My family fill my whole life and I just live for them. But I feel George is forcing me now to go with him and be a Bahá'í. While I admire the teachings and the lives of the Bahá'ís, especially 'Abdu'l-Bahá, I cannot in my heart accept Bahá'u'lláh as Christ come again. Therefore I am resolute that I must go out into the unknown alone as I could not possibly share something that I would not honestly accept.

I am no longer young, I have been more or less brought back from the grave many times having many operations. Living with Saints is not a bed of roses!!! Forgive this hurried letter but I felt I had to write it.

Nellie's reply is, alas, missing, but it was apparently wise and understanding, for Nancy's acknowledgement is an outburst of relief and gratitude, even more revealing than her appeal. It is dated November 20, 1942:

I want to thank you from the bottom of my heart for writing so promptly and wisely as you did. I shall always remember how magnificently you rose to the occasion and by doing so saved George from doing something which would have been a failure and it certainly would have killed him. He went to Dublin to investigate houses and cost of living and if anyone had prevented him he would have just collapsed here. He simply can't take these brainstorms which he has periodically. He seems to be pursued by some fear and he feels he has to run and hide and he feels all will be well once he is in a new place. But all his family do the same thing – they are either pursued or pursuing some new home. I know George would not be so happy anywhere as here. The quiet country suits him, he is able to write all day long; he gives his whole time to work for the Bahá'í Faith. I feel how much better to live for something than to die for it. I think he will never have such opportunities as he has here. He is so highly-strung and nervous that he is not the type for human contacts and I think by giving his books to the world he has played a great part. However, as he never himself will make use of his opportunities, Una and I planned we should organise fireside chats. We suggested our (or his) asking a number of people from our own neighbourhood to come in and have a group discussion round the fire. This he was willing to do and he became awfully keen and asked the people, and Una and I made sandwiches and cut bread and butter, etc. We brought it off quick as we felt George urgently needed the outlet. So we had a happy gathering and George gave the message as he felt so inspired at the moment. Una spoke and I acted as 'Questionnaire' at the psychological moment. It all went off very successfully and happily and we had coffee and apple juice and other home-grown eats and drinks and they went away interested taking Bahá'í literature with them. We were nine that first evening. We have met once every week since and last evening our number was sixteen. The number gradually grew. We have now set aside our most beautiful room in the house – the library – for these meetings. We all sit round informally and George tells us as much as he thinks fit and we try to foster discussion and interest in the Bahá'í Teachings. George is much happier, absorbed in preparing his talks and loving it all. He now realises how hopeless his plan was. Here he can use his position which is a unique one – he has access to all homes. Everyone expects him to do things and no matter what he does or what he says, they all feel he has exceptional authority for it and they all respect him for himself. This isn't just local. It is in the whole Church of Ireland. Our Bishop, who is very broadminded and has read all George's books, says 'when the Archdeacon speaks he deserves to be listened to by all'. Then George is asked more than any other clergyman to speak at refresher courses of the clergy and lecture at Trinity and for two weeks he is the resident Canon of our national cathedral – this is the highest honour the Church could bestow on him. Now I've always said that these opportunities were not given for nothing – especially when they all *expect* to hear something new from George. But the funny thing is that I think these opportunities have not been made the most of and it is this that unsettles George from time to time. It is fundamentally some fear. Outside the Church he would never have any influence but would antagonise everyone in this little island. He is so surprised to find how keen and interested his own people – ordinary people – are for news of the Bahá'í Teachings. But I've realised that all these years here the people have been gradually prepared by George without his or their knowing it for something new. What a tragedy it would have been to have gone away and not even given them a chance. I do hope George will now, when he feels the foundation is sure here, gradually build on it and then extend it little by little, so that people are won over imperceptibly and because they themselves desire it. Forgive this outburst. George must never know I appealed to you and your letter has helped and strengthened us now in our effort to bring George's 'Church under the New Jerusalem' which I think follows the most important sentence in 'Abdu'l-Bahá's letter to him: 'I pray that thy Church may come under the Heavenly Jerusalem'.

Perhaps you will come to see us when the war is over. Gratefully . . .

George's account of all this was given in a letter of November 10:

A line to tell you that my wife and Una and I have arisen to give the Bahá'í message personally in our own home to neighbours whom we ask to come and chat at our fireside. We had our first meeting on November 3rd at 8 p.m.; they were all interested and took away Bahá'í literature, and some of them promised to bring friends they thought would be interested to our next meeting, and all expect to be with us again on Thursday at the same hour.

I have mentioned the Message round the parish, too. So the effort is started openly here by all three of us with one voice, and Mrs Townshend is working, organising and planning away with her usual vigour and efficiency . . . To me it seems a miracle! But I could not think of it nor do it till I was fully prepared to abandon everything, even home and family, and be quite alone in trying to give the Message in Ireland.

I saw that if I now rushed out of the Church I would alienate everyone and be condemned by all; I would break a hundred old ties and be in no position to make new ones or make new friends; I would break up the home and the family and would altogether utterly misrepresent the friendliness, concord and union the Faith stands for and do the Cause in Ireland immense damage.

Then I thought of this plan. To my profound delight and joy my wife welcomed it, has thrown herself into it and made it so far a success. This action of ours has brought us reconciliation and happiness and opened up avenues which we all can travel together. How we shall miss dear, precious Una! Her faith has had such an effect on her mother.

What, pray, could be more suitable than that here, where 'Abdu'l-Bahá's letters came, where we have lived for more than twenty years and are known to everyone, here by our own fireside we should as pioneers personally give the Message and start a movement which some day (whoever carries it on) will beatify all the people of this little island!

No more now. We are so happy and so hopeful!

In February he wrote that 'our Bahá'í meetings have been an astonishing success and have laid a local foundation for future building.'

These Bahá'í meetings were the first ever to be held in Ireland and are therefore historic. George was the first ordained priest[1] of the Christian Protestant persuasion to renounce his Orders so as to become a fully accredited member of the Bahá'í community. He was not the last, either Protestant or Roman Catholic, to do so. Clergymen, monks, nuns, theological students from Christianity and the other great religions are recognizing in Bahá'u'lláh the Promised

---

[1] See p. 205.

One of all ages and civilizations and are coming out of the old exclusive systems to enter the universal fellowship of the 'one fold, and one shepherd' promised specifically by Christ.[1]

Indeed, Bahá'u'lláh Himself had called upon the Christian priests and monks to come forth from their churches,[2] and He referred to the fact that in this Revelation, unlike earlier ones when the first believers were mostly from the poor and humble (e.g. the fishermen Apostles of Christ), a great many learned and exalted divines,[3] supported by their understanding of the Scriptures of the past, recognized the new Messenger and joyfully embraced the trials and harassments and martyrdom meted out to His followers. George led the way to the clergy of Christendom as the youthful Mullá Husayn and his fellow Letters of the Living had led the way in the time of the Báb, a hundred years before.

George was now the unconscious centre of a situation which, ignoring the spiritual and dramatic character of his struggles, has all the appurtenances of a Restoration comedy, bordering on farce. Sheridan could have written it. George convincing himself that Nancy's sudden 'conciliatory attitude' to his Dublin foray was a volte-face on her part and gave him the all-clear signal for resignation; Nancy appealing to Nellie to restrain him; Nellie's satisfying reply, which may well have arrived at Ahascragh while George was in Dublin; Nellie's letter to George (we must assume its existence from Nancy's second letter to Nellie) which has not come to light but was a prime factor in the development of 'the plot', leading to the happy ending of Bahá'í meetings in the Rectory with the family united and George satisfied, for the moment.

Such an entirely superficial reading of the situation can only emphasize the spiritual drama which the outward appearances concealed. The worldly comedy was produced from the interaction of desperate spiritual need and the common-sense aspect of the realities of daily life, and was never far from tragedy. It was one more occasion when all the omens, concentrated by George's positive action, were favourable. Nancy, alas, was not his spiritual partner and George again accepted defeat in the cause of family unity.

The Second World War dragged wearily on; George continued his work for the Guardian, for the most part at this time on *God Passes By* (see Chapters 6 and 13). He suffered for months from arthritis in both arms, and his writing – the breath of his real life – had to be curtailed to

[1] John 10:16.

[2] *The Proclamation of Bahá'u'lláh*, Bahá'í World Centre, 1967, pp. 94–5.

[3] *Kitáb-i-Íqán*, Bahá'í Publishing Trust, Wilmette 1974, pp. 222–3. British edn. pp. 142–4.

what he could do with his left hand. He commented to all his correspondents 'Not so bad with the left hand, is it?' or some such. In freer moments he managed to discuss with Nellie abstruse or mystical subjects in the Bahá'í sacred Writings, or the art of religious teaching, or to ask about the practice of the American Churches in relation to racial discrimination; '. . . do they have separate Churches and services, any black parsons, and so on; and do they promote any social existence?' Nellie continued to send food parcels which they shared with neighbours and which caused George to add, 'greetings from us all' to his usual signature, 'Your old friend and fellow believer'.

But Nancy, as her letter of thanks to Nellie clearly shows, was a great deal closer to an understanding of the Faith than any arbitrary or dictatorial action on George's part (however unthinkable) could have brought about. Una records that when she herself became a Bahá'í, in January 1940, Nancy was very angry and accused George of having led her into an obscure oriental cult. Now, nearly three years later, he could write as above of the effect of Una's faith on her mother. He sent Nellie 'a little gift from us all, a copy of my first Irish book *The Altar on the Hearth*,[1] inscribed to you by all the four people concerned in it.'

In 1944, at the British Convention held at the end of April, an action was initiated which was to gather up, concentrate and direct all the new energies which had recently been released in the British Bahá'í community, and to exert a profound influence upon the destinies of that community. This was the adoption of the historic Six Year Plan, whose achievement was to bring its promoters to the forefront of the Bahá'í world. That is another story. Its pertinence to us is that among the objectives of the Plan was the formation of Local Spiritual Assemblies in Eire and Northern Ireland. George was not slow to notice this, although the British Bahá'ís were characteristically slow to get started (and impossible to stop once they had). Dublin was chosen as the goal city in the Republic; the first pioneer, Una Townshend, arrived in September 1946, and the whole British Bahá'í community was committed to the establishment of the Local Spiritual Assembly.

George's excitement, and pride in Una, renewed his spirits and once more raised his hopes for himself, this time, at long last, to be realized. The Guardian, in a letter acknowledging an article George had written for *The Bahá'í World*,[2] expressed his longing for the establishment of a Spiritual Assembly in Eire and sent George to the seventh heaven with his personal note 'more tuneable than lark to shepherd's ear':

The work so splendidly initiated by your dear daughter is unique, historic

---

[1] See pp. 98, 99.
[2] *The Call To God*, vol. X

and of vital importance. I admire her courage, zeal, devotion and perseverance. I will pray for her success from the depths of my heart. I urge you to help her in any way you can, and to encourage her constantly in her labours. How glad and proud you must feel that a member of your family has arisen to enrich the record of services associated with your name!

George needed no urging to help and wrote, 'Una has an unsuitable job in Dublin . . . We drive up frequently with supplies of fuel and food and have a glimpse of her.'

He continued his campaign of proclamation to the senior clergy, and wrote to the Guardian in August that he was sending *God Passes By* to other Bishops (his own, Killaloe, having shown no interest in it) and to the Dean of St Patrick's with letters 'proclaiming Christ has come. Once begun, the enterprise will go on (and I shall go out!) [Change to left hand.] The sooner the better.' He dwelt again on family unity and asked for the Guardian's prayers.

Did he sense that the end was near?

> I will write again when I have anything worth telling.
>
> I am longing to serve the Cause fully. Jumping out of the aeroplane takes a bit of doing; but it has been not so much family opposition as something in my self that has hindered me.

We must not take this at face value. George was ever ready to attribute failure to some lack in himself. It was part of his deeply felt conviction, noted before, that personal success was dependent upon spiritual progress, which attracted the confirmation of God.

Now the threads were beginning to draw together and George's release was at hand. Let him tell his own story as he related it to the Guardian in his letter of March 12, 1947:

> Now something new has happened. After a business meeting on March 4th the Bishop[1] showed me an air letter addressed by an Anglican missionary to the Archbishop of Canterbury complaining of *The Promise of All Ages*, a book which, he said, exalted Bahá'u'lláh at the expense of Christ and was otherwise objectionable, being written by a Canon of one of our Cathedrals. The Archbishop forwarded the letter to the Primate of Ireland. He sent it to my Bishop, to investigate; and the Bishop said all he wanted to hear was if the book lowered Christ. I said certainly not; but that I had much more to tell him. I myself believed Bahá'u'lláh was Christ returned and was the Father prophesied by Isaiah, and that this was the Day of Judgment. I had said more in my Introduction to *God Passes By* than in *The Promise of All Ages*, and had sent it to him; I intended to say more still and was ready to leave the Church. I withdrew nothing and

[1] of Killaloe

modified nothing I had written. He is *very* kind, and very narrow; and was utterly perplexed. He asked a number of questions, like a child not like a judge. Finally, he suddenly in much distress of mind, went off to his car, and was driven away.

I came home and told my wife.

That is the position at the moment. My departure now is certain and near and as soon as anything develops of a definite kind I will write to you.

My wife still does not take it all in; but she will come with me, I am sure, and will be a tower of sense and strength when she does.

I feel a great peace and happiness beginning to well up within me.

With endless thanks for your long patience and help and wisdom, I am yours, George Townshend.

The Guardian's reply was a cable: 'THRILLED YOUR NEWS PRAYING MIGHTY RESULTS DEEPEST LOVING APPRECIATION COURAGEOUS STAND SHOGHI.'

Chapter 10

RENUNCIATION

NOW that the great moment had come at last, George acted with the same statesmanship he had displayed in the crisis over reading the paper at the World Congress of Faiths in 1936. It was characteristic of him that when faced with crisis and the need for decision he became assured, reliant on God and effective in action. However vague or absent-minded he might appear generally or whatever emotions and tensions, hopes and fears might be surging within him at the critical point, once the die was cast he remained calm and, whatever would come, inviolate to the world.

Having informed Nancy and the Guardian of the position, he wrote to the National Spiritual Assembly of the British Isles, welcoming its recent proposal for a meeting to discuss the future of the teaching work in Ireland, a future fraught with possibilities of such great consequence for the Faith, and inevitably for himself. He commented on the timeliness of the proposal in view of the enquiry (news of which he now imparted), started by the Primate of Ireland through the Bishop of Killaloe, on reference from the Archbishop of Canterbury.

Immediately on leaving the Church he would become a recognized member of the British Bahá'í community, whose governing body was the National Spiritual Assembly. He had kept that Assembly generally informed of his Bahá'í teaching activities (though he made no mention, to anyone, of his great work for the Guardian) and more particularly so since the inauguration of the Six Year Plan in April 1944, which required the establishment of at least one Local Spiritual Assembly in the Republic and one in Northern Ireland.[1] Ever since his

[1] The Church of Ireland was in an anomalous position politically. It was the Protestant Episcopal Church of the entire island and having been disestablished in 1871 took no notice of the political division in 1922. The Archbishop of Armagh in Northern Ireland remained Primate of All Ireland, senior to the Archbishop of Dublin, Primate of the Republic. George was an Archdeacon in the whole Church of Ireland and carried authority and rank in both parts of the island.

approach to the National Assembly in 1936 the Assembly had been well aware of his longing to come out of the Church. Now that it had the clear intention of establishing the Faith in Ireland, George realized that his activities and his delicate position in relation to its own programme were of the greatest concern to it. It was therefore wise and proper to act now in consultation with the Assembly and under its guidance.

The National Spiritual Assembly in 1947 was a very different body from that of 1936. It had grown in experience, capacity and stature. It had aroused and led the small community of British Bahá'ís into active promotion of the Faith of Bahá'u'lláh and the teaching work had already been extended to Ireland, Scotland and Wales; the Six Year Plan was in process. The two Local Spiritual Assemblies were now nine, not many as yet but more than four times the starting number. The Publishing Trust was active and growing and three rallying points of the community, Convention, Summer School and Teaching Conference, had been firmly established on an annual basis. The National Assembly itself had become an incorporated body under the Companies Act and had guided the friends in negotiations with the authorities over their applications, as Bahá'ís, for non-combatant service during the war. It had, in 1944, in company with its fellow National Spiritual Assemblies throughout the world, organized befitting celebrations of the Centenary of the Faith.[1] Through its own secretariat, through its committees, and through its encouragement of the Local Spiritual Assemblies and scattered groups and single believers, it was conducting a campaign of extension and consolidation of the Faith, in which the seeds of the unfolding destiny of the British Bahá'í community were already beginning to swell.

It was to this body that George turned with confidence and complete faith, well aware of its youth and inexperience in the eyes of the world, its lack of the historical and traditional associations or the great prestige accumulated by the age-old Church, but knowing too that its foundation rested clearly and explicitly on the sacred text of the Revelation itself, an authority which no Christian institution could invoke.

The appointment was made for Sunday, May 11, 1947 at the Bahá'í Centre in London. George wrote that he would bring Nancy with him 'for the particular purpose of protecting the unity of the family in this enterprise: a delicate and most important matter.'

This new development placed Nancy in an equivocal position. The complaint which sparked the investigation was made against *The*

[1] See *The Bahá'í World*, vol. X, pp. 188–201, or Roger White's *Compendium of Volumes I–XII*, pp. 188–91.

Promise of All Ages, and Nancy, long ago, had promised to stand by him should he be attacked because of it. The absence of any complaint during the thirteen years since the book was first published, in 1934, had enabled George to pursue his persistent programme of proclamation of the Message of Bahá'u'lláh to the whole Church of Ireland. But now the die was cast, and Nancy, though unhappy, stood by her word. George informed the Guardian on April 9:

> The Bishops as yet have made no move. I expect them soon to offer me some terms which will be unacceptable; I shall in reply resign and leave the Church of Ireland. My wife has come round wonderfully to consent to this action. Una of her own volition has promised to share our lot, to live with us and so far as she can to contribute to our support. She is now with us for a little while. The British National Spiritual Assembly invited me last month to go over and interview them: I hope to meet them on or about May 9th in London . . . I am very grateful indeed for your prayers. This is an hour of crisis within crises.

On May 4 he wrote from Dublin: 'My wife and I are on our way to the National Spiritual Assembly in London and have seen a good bit of the Bahá'í nucleus here whose prospects now seem good.'

Although the Bishops had made no move, George was expected to attend the Synod in Dublin during the week of May 4–10. The National Spiritual Assembly offered to send me over to be with him 'through these probably critical days' as he put it. George wrote:

> You can get into the Strangers Gallery at the Synod: and when I am not in the meetings I hope to spend the hours with your good self.
> Please avoid all controversial topics with my wife. She is very unhappy over this development, and it is worse than useless to try to argue. I have faith Bahá'u'lláh in His own way will bring the matter out to a harmonious and joyous end.

So Nancy had not yet come to terms with the situation.

At the last moment I was unable to go for more than the weekend, when the Synod would not have started, and George sent a cable advising not to come.

The National Assembly advised George that it had asked Miss Ursula Newman,[1] a Bahá'í pioneer to Dublin and a member of the National Assembly, to give him every possible support on its behalf during the time of the Synod.

Mrs Samandarí kindly gave this account of the proceedings:

> Doris Gould (afterwards Morris) and I were the truly strange strangers in

[1] She later married Dr Mihdí Samandarí; they pioneered in Somalia and in other parts of Africa and are now in the United Republic of Cameroon. Dr Samandarí was appointed a Counsellor in 1968.

the gallery, silently praying during the extraordinarily dull meetings. Nevertheless we listened to every word, expecting any moment that our beloved Uncle George would be attacked – but never a word was said to him or about him! The time was mostly spent in one dreary old man after another getting up and complaining that the churches were empty! George Townshend looked very distinguished in his gaiters and shovel hat – like some 18th century learned divine.[1]

All George's letters at this time were full of gratitude for the sense of comradeship and support which he felt extended to him. He described the fellowship he sensed with the National Spiritual Assembly as a 'light and warmth to me in my loneliness here', and 'that sense of Bahá'í companionship for which I am longing with all my heart and soul'; 'I am tired of loneliness and long for my fellow believers'; 'However great the delight of trying to serve the Cause in this, there is a strain, and the sense of friendship lightens the strain'; 'I am longing to meet you all on the 11th, and I hope all the right things will happen in the right order meantime!'

The Minutes of the National Assembly's meeting, though bare and factual, are of interest; and are cited with its permission:

Although Mr Townshend would prefer to leave the Church at once by resigning, he thinks the more effective plan would be first to write a pamphlet identifying the Cause of Christ with the Cause of Bahá'u'lláh in relation to the present crisis, which would be circulated by him to the officials and members of the Church, in order to reinforce the challenge contained in *The Promise of All Ages*. The Assembly records its agreement with Mr Townshend.

The Assembly advised Mr Townshend, as suggested by him, to withdraw from the Church, his resignation to become effective from September 30th. The Assembly recommend that every effort be made to have the pamphlet distributed before his resignation is submitted. The following time limits are suggested: pamphlet printed by June 30th, resignation [submitted] by July 30th.

Mr and Mrs Townshend were both invited to attend the Summer School this year as the Assembly's guests.

The financial aspects of the situation arising when Mr Townshend left the Church were discussed, and the Assembly explained the help given to Bahá'í settlers. The Assembly agreed to take up the financial aspects with the Guardian. Mrs Townshend was assured that if anything happened to Mr Townshend after he left the Church the Assembly would consider itself responsible for her welfare.

[1] For modern readers who may never have seen an Archdeacon in full regalia, Mrs Samandarí's later note may be interesting: 'Mr Townshend wore all his clerical trappings for the Synod – which included black knee-breeches, gaiters, and a sort of tunic under a black coat *and* the shovel hat.'

Mrs Townshend expressed a strong desire to leave Ireland and establish a home in England, preferably in the South.

The Assembly ascertained that Mr Townshend has no assets beyond his income from the Church, and whatever may be derived from the sale of his books. When he leaves the Church he will forfeit his superannuation and insurance and so will Mrs Townshend. We therefore record that in our opinion Mr Townshend will need at least £500 a year.

It was agreed to send copy of the minutes relating to the consultation with George Townshend to the Guardian by airmail asking for his comments by cable.

We recognise Mr Townshend as a declared Bahá'í, and record that immediately his resignation from the Church takes effect he will have voting rights in the Bahá'í community in the British Isles.

The above were sent to George with a copy of the Assembly's letter to the Guardian on the subject. George wrote a hurried note of thanks and concluded, 'I thank God for having a wise and a very brave wife!' from which we may gather that Nancy had been much reassured by the meeting with the National Assembly. A longer letter followed immediately, expressing his happiness at meeting the members and his hope of being always in the closest touch with them in the future. He commented:

The important matter is the date of my Manifesto. The dates I proposed were to send the manuscript in a month's time; i.e. the middle of June or so and later circulate it before my actual resignation. Printing it by June 30th is surely impossible. I do not remember assenting to any other dates than those I proposed. Consider the position if I sat here as rector for three months while circulating what would be thought an heretical pamphlet criticising the Church and while carrying on a controversial correspondence with the authorities and others who counter-attacked me. I would seem to be taking a mean advantage. My action would estrange those I hope to conciliate and would compromise the Bahá'í Cause throughout Protestant Ireland. On the other hand, there is no gain of any kind in thus advancing the date of circulation. The opportunity opening to me is very great but the position is delicate – I do not want to begin with a false step and I hope the Assembly will consent to leave the dates as originally proposed and let me withhold circulation till my actual resignation draws near – I shall still hold my ecclesiastical posts, and they can be on my pamphlet. . . . Can you now begin to imagine the relief you have given me, and the hope of life and happiness which after years of darkness you have brought again to me. With loving gratitude and good wishes . . .

Now came a letter from the Guardian to the National Assembly written on May 8, three days before the consultation with the Townshends took place. George's growing fame in the Bahá'í world had prompted the American National Spiritual Assembly to invite him to the United States, where they hoped to use his services as a teacher of the Faith. The Guardian's secretary wrote:

> He has already informed the American N.S.A. that he feels Mr Townshend's services to the Faith can best be rendered by his writing about it, as he obviously has an outstanding ability in this direction, combined with knowledge and zeal, and can render a very valuable service this way; also he feels that Mr Townshend, now that his church association seems about to be broken, could be used as part of the pioneer force in Eire. It is his own land, he knows his own people, and the need for workers there is very particularly great this year. Naturally, if Mr and Mrs Townshend have received a personal invitation to go to America and care to accept it, they are quite free to do so.
>
> If Mr Townshend has not as yet been registered as a voting believer he certainly should be immediately. Every one knows he has been a most devoted Bahá'í for many years and his contributions should certainly be considered those of a voting Bahá'í.[1]

By the time this letter arrived in London, the Guardian had received the minutes of the Assembly's meeting of May 11 with the covering letter asking for his cabled comments. His cable arrived at the same time as his letter of May 8 and began: 'TOWNSHEND'S RESIGNATION IMPERATIVE.'

The above extracts from both the letter and the cable were immediately forwarded to George, and the Assembly recorded in its minutes of May 31 that George was recognized as a voting member of the British Bahá'í community. It also recorded: 'The National Spiritual Assembly believes that although Mrs Townshend expressed a personal wish to the Assembly to leave Ireland, in view of the Guardian's letter of May 8 the National Spiritual Assembly should ask Mr Townshend to establish his residence in Dublin.'

All was now turmoil in the rectory at Ahascragh. George, used to an unhurried schedule of life with ample opportunity for long hours of concentrated work on whatever was engaging his attention, was suddenly plunged into a maelstrom of urgent tasks. He had to prepare his letters of resignation from the Church of Ireland and of renunciation of his Orders, his longer manifesto for circulation to

---

[1] Contributions to Bahá'í Funds are accepted only from recognized believers, and the Assembly's secretary had questioned whether a contribution which George had sent could be accepted. This was the first time he had contributed to the National Fund, although he had sent small sums – two or three pounds at a time – to the Guardian for the last twenty-five years. On one occasion when he was, literally and factually, the only Bahá'í in the whole island, he sent his contribution from 'the Bahá'ís of Ireland'. At another time he described it as 'the monthly contribution from the Irish Bahá'ís'. No one knew of these contributions except the Guardian and George, and the Assembly's query may not have been as pedantic as it may seem.

several thousand people, addressing all Christians and explaining his action; he had to find a home in Dublin; and he had to prepare his retirement, in a decent and friendly manner, from the many ecclesiastical positions he held, chief of which were Archdeacon of Clonfert, Rector of Ahascragh, and Canon of St Patrick's Cathedral (there were many others, such as Diocesan Secretary). Leaving the rectory and disposing of the accumulations of thirty years of a family home were no small task for a man of seventy. Eventually it was the finding of a house which defeated his planned programme and postponed the publication of his appeal to Christendom, but not his resignation and removal to Dublin.

A tremendous brouhaha ensued, embroiling the two Bahá'ís in Dublin, the secretariat of the National Spiritual Assembly in London, the members of a committee appointed to plan and execute a large public relations programme, described in our next chapter as 'Operation Townshend', visiting teachers to Dublin and, of course, George, Nancy, Brian, who was studying at the Guildhall in London but now appeared in Dublin, and Una.

Housing was undoubtedly very difficult to find in Dublin at that time and the cost of living was soaring. 'For himself,' as Una wrote in a letter some three years after his passing, 'he would have chosen to live in a back room on bread and cheese,' where he could write and write and write. But such an unworldly attitude found no echo in Nancy's mind and George knew its impracticability. He lost no time in writing to house agents, whose offers only increased his sense of the difficulty and Nancy's gloom. He had agreed with the National Spiritual Assembly to resign from the Church by the end of September, which put him under pressure to leave the rectory and to move to Dublin by that time. He quickly realized that renting a house was out of the question and on June 9 sent a telegram to the National Spiritual Assembly suggesting purchase: 'CAN I TAKE THIS STEP?' The Assembly, with remarkable dispatch, agreed that it was committed to backing George to the hilt and enlisted the support of the two pioneers[1] in Dublin in the search for a house. Ursula Newman, whom we have already met, and Doris Gould set about finding a house for George either to rent or to buy, and the Assembly started approaches to building societies in case purchase became inevitable. Mary Basil Hall, Lady Blomfield's daughter, went for a week to give what help she could, and Brian Townshend started an active search of his own. The excitement and hope of the Dublin friends knew no bounds. They were committed to establishing the first Bahá'í Assembly in Eire, and

[1] Bahá'í pioneers are believers who leave their homes to settle in some other town or country for the sole purpose of establishing or maintaining a Bahá'í community there.

the possibility of so distinguished a believer as George, with members of his family, coming to help them filled them with delight. Ursula Newman wrote to the National Spiritual Assembly, 'Of course, if *only* the Townshends could and would come to Dublin – life would be too wonderful. They *might* have a house, and might let me live in an attic or cellar of it, and in return I would be cook, housemaid, gardener, what-you-will.' George was urged to go to Dublin to inspect possible places, but Nancy was not accommodating; she still wanted to live in southern England. Ursula wrote on July 11 to the National Spiritual Assembly suggesting that the Townshends be asked to live in a hotel, storing their furniture, until a suitable place was found. She continued, 'My impression from all Townshend's letters to me, is that he is willing to live anywhere and only anxious to carry out the Guardian's wishes. My impression from Mrs Townshend's letters, is that she is very reluctant to live in Dublin . . . I am convinced that George Townshend *wants* to live in Dublin.'

Mary Basil Hall reported: 'I very much doubt if Mrs Townshend will be satisfied with any house in her present frame of mind, and unless she becomes more reconciled to the idea of living in or near Dublin, it will be very difficult for the settlement to take place harmoniously . . .' and added 'Let us hope and pray a delightful house at a possible price (or rent) may miraculously appear – one which Mrs Townshend could not help liking, just outside Dublin with a garden and garage and everything she wants.'

Nancy fought a strong rearguard action against Dublin; it was too late in the season now to move; there was no fuel available, except turf (a fact confirmed by all visitors); there was no time to dispose of their own furniture; she refused even to consider the first two houses proposed and was not willing to store their belongings and live in a hotel for the winter.

George relayed Nancy's feelings to the Assembly but let it be seen that he was not to be deflected: 'Dublin is not the smoothest place to go to, for it means social ostracism to my wife and walking into the lion's mouth for me; but it is assuredly a strategic point, and I've no objection to the lion's mouth.'

In the midst of all this George sent his letter of resignation to the Bishop of Killaloe, and advised the Assembly on June 20, 'I posted my resignation on June 12th, naming September 30th for its coming into effect. The Bishop accepted it but sent a form to fill; which I filled, signed and sent to him yesterday.' (See p. 196)

The National Assembly informed the Guardian by cable: 'JOYFULLY REPORT TOWNSHEND RESIGNED INTENDS SETTLE DUBLIN FACING SERIOUS HOUSING PROBLEM' and received the following reply: 'OVERJOYED

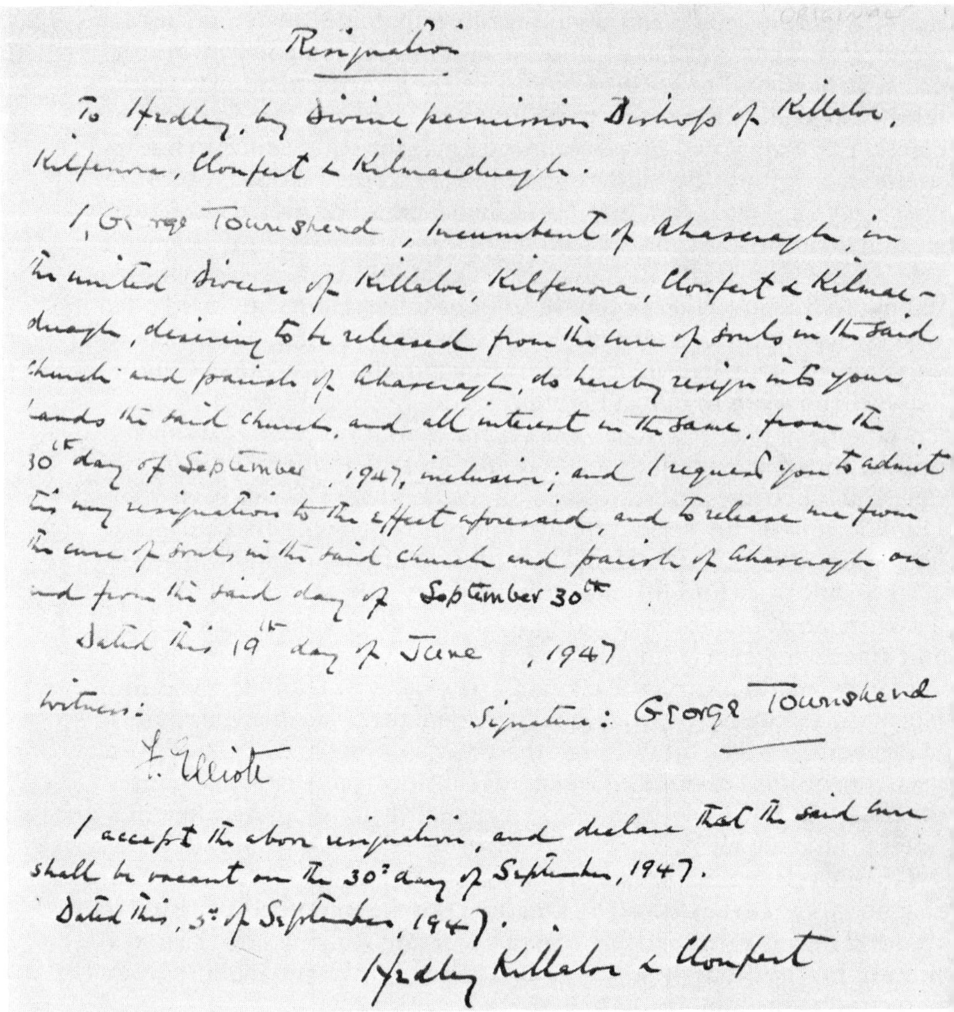

Resignation

To Hedley, by divine permission Bishop of Killaloe, Kilfenora, Clonfert & Kilmacduagh.

I, George Townshend, Incumbent of Ahascragh, in the united Dioceses of Killaloe, Kilfenora, Clonfert & Kilmacduagh, desiring to be released from the cure of souls in the said church and parish of Ahascragh, do hereby resign into your hands the said Church, and all interest in the same, from the 30th day of September, 1947, inclusive; and I request you to admit this my resignation to the effect aforesaid, and to release me from the cure of souls in the said church and parish of Ahascragh on and from the said day of September 30th.

Dated this 19th day of June, 1947

Witness:

Signature: George Townshend

F. Elliott

I accept the above resignation, and declare that the said cure shall be vacant on the 30th day of September, 1947.

Dated this, 5th of September, 1947.

Hedley Killaloe & Clonfert

George's letter of resignation

TOWNSHENDS MEMORABLE DECISION NOBLE EXAMPLE COMMENDABLE DETERMINATION SETTLE DUBLIN ARDENTLY PRAYING SUCCESS PROTECTION REMOVAL DIFFICULTIES.' The texts of both were immediately sent to George, who expressed lasting pleasure.

He was full of gratitude and energy now that it was happening at last. He wrote of the dismantling of his house and severing of thirty-year-old ties. 'It's all a thrilling job with such a purpose as the service of Bahá'u'lláh in view.' But the determination to conciliate, not to antagonize, was ever present. 'The Bishop of Killaloe and the Bishop of Cashel[1] know clearly my reason. But I am not going at present to give the reason to others. It would cause misunderstanding. It will come out in good time; and soon enough, and in a creative manner and not in a critical or divisive spirit.'

Committed to leaving the rectory within three months, and no accommodation in Dublin yet being in sight, George asked the Assembly to consider an alternative place. Ursula Newman's letter, cited above, clearly shows that this was not his own wish. The Assembly repeated the proposal to the Guardian, feeling itself unable to go against his expressed guidance for Dublin. It had, meantime, taken into its confidence a few believers in England who it was thought would be willing to help finance the purchase of a house. It also arranged to send Philip Hainsworth, a young and vigorous member of the Assembly, to Dublin so soon as it seemed possible to acquire an agreed house, to complete the purchase and help the Townshends move into it. At this point a cable was received from the Guardian: 'ADVISE TOWNSHEND TRANSFER RESIDENCE OUTSIDE IRELAND IF NECESSARY.' Whether George ever shared this with Nancy is not known, but the idea was never heard of again, and no further reference to it appears in the records.

There were still a number of ups and downs involving an enormous mass of correspondence but on July 26 a telegram was received by the Assembly from Brian: 'IDEAL BUNGALOW AVAILABLE PROBABLE PRICE £3000 PARENTS COMING VIEW MONDAY SUGGEST WIRE INSTRUCTIONS.' The reply read: 'IF FAMILY LIKE BUNGALOW OBTAIN OPTION ASSEMBLY WOULD THEN ADVANCE DEPOSIT STOP PHILIP PROCEEDING DUBLIN ASSEMBLYS REPRESENTATIVE.' This was followed on July 30 by a telegram from George: 'FAMILY UNANIMOUSLY APPROVE ONLY POSSIBLE BUNGALOW £3400 STILL AWAITING PHILIP YOUR APPROVAL AND DEPOSIT NECESSARY FOR AGREEMENT.' The secretary of the Assembly cabled George: 'MANY THANKS WELCOME TELEGRAM LOAN AVAILABLE UP TO £1000 IF NECESSARY PHILIP INFORMED.'

[1] His old friend Arnold Harvey, whom he had served as curate in Booterstown.

Despite this unanimous family approval Nancy made her last stand. She had already, on June 20, asked George to explain to the Assembly, 'We do not want to have an official house (as we have had here) where we'd be expected to entertain all visitors, much as we should sincerely like to: for this would give my wife more work than she is able for and would probably interfere with my efforts to write. In our home, we want quiet! There is no pleasure like that of meeting the friends, all the same.' Now she raised this same point again, that the house, if bought by the Assembly,

> would be considered as official and Mrs Townshend would probably be expected to entertain at all times.
> Her independent spirit would not like this; and she is not strong enough to undertake it anyway.

But George had the final trump in reserve, Nellie's gift of five thousand dollars. Nellie now emerged as the *deus ex machina*, and after consultation with her by cable, George telegraphed the Assembly 'PLEASE CONSIDER AMERICAN MONEY[1] MY PERSONAL CONTRIBUTION TOWARDS PURCHASE I WILL UNDERTAKE REFUND BY MY YEARLY ROYALTIES BALANCE RAISED BY YOU STOP RESULT UNITED FAMILY CONSULTATION.'

The upshot was that 'Ripley', Mount Annville Road, Dundrum, a double-fronted bungalow in a suburb of Dublin and within sight of the Irish Channel was purchased. George put up £800, the Assembly £1,000 and a building society £1,600.

This might have been thought to have concluded the affair, but the bedevilment which seems to attend so many Irish undertakings, harried every step of poor George's negotiations. The purchase of Ripley involved the purchase of most of its furniture, a fortunate circumstance since the large pieces of the high, airy rooms of the rectory could not have fitted into the bungalow. Philip, who had prodded and pushed easy-going solicitors, estate agents and the Building Society, had also assisted in arranging an auction in Ballinasloe of the Townshend 'moveables', from which it was confidently expected to receive enough to pay for the furniture of Ripley. But the sale was delayed on the auctioneer's advice, because of 'Lord Ashtown's big auction in the next parish' on the date fixed for George's. This meant that payment to the owners of Ripley could not be made at the date agreed and the apparently simple matter of agreeing to pay a couple of weeks later provoked a veritable hurricane of letter-writing, anxiety that the deal might fall through, unnecessary worry and harassment all round. In the event the sale realized

[1] see p. 157.

approximately the amount required and the storm died down. It was the same with the simple matter of booking passage for England to attend the Bahá'í Summer School in Hornsea, to which the Townshends had been invited by the Assembly. George wrote on July 13, 'After endless wiring and worrying with no good result at all, when as a last resort we had arranged to drive to Dublin to try for a ticket for at least some of us somehow, suddenly this morning a wire from the L.M.S. "Four sailing tickets in post" put an end to our disappointments.' That should have been that (as George was fond of saying). But then it became apparent that return passages might not be immediately available. The National Assembly had agreed to consult George and Nancy at the school on all matters affecting their future and it authorized Philip to bring them both by air.

Eventually they moved to Ripley on October 6, 1947. Both George and Nancy had wanted to keep the resignation as quiet as possible until it had taken place, for the good reasons we have already considered. But the British Bahá'ís inevitably heard rumours of what was afoot and on August 6, 1947 the National Spiritual Assembly sent the following letter to all members of the British community:

> With greatest joy the National Spiritual Assembly communicates to you the following news. Very soon our dear friend George Townshend will be free to devote all his energies to the service of the Cause. Archdeacon Townshend is too well known to you to need any introduction. The services which his able pen has rendered to the Cause are monumental. Now he has offered his resignation from the position he holds in the Church, thus forfeiting all his sources of income including his pension, which at 71 is indeed a great sacrifice. Before long he will be in the pioneer field.

The letter then related the exchange of cables with the Guardian, mentioned above, and continued:

> Dear Friends, these are great days in the life of our Community. Let us keep in front of our minds 'the noble example' of our dear Bahá'í brother and pray for the unfailing bounties of Bahá'u'lláh. To George Townshend we send a message of love and gratitude. You will see him at Summer School.

We must now try to complete the tale of George's becoming a layman. As in so many facets of this simple man's life, the matter was complicated. He had been ordained in the Protestant Episcopal Church of America by Bishop Spalding of Utah, the ceremony taking place in St Mark's Cathedral, Salt Lake City, in 1906. He served that Church for four years in Provo and then taught high school for a year before joining the faculty of the University of the South in Sewanee.

But he remained an ordained priest of that communion. When in 1916 he entered the service of the Church of Ireland he was not formally transferred from the American to the Irish Church. The certificate of his American Orders was accepted as valid by the Archbishop of Dublin who forthwith appointed him to a Dublin curacy (Booterstown). In 1918 the Bishop of Killaloe instituted him to the incumbency of Ahascragh. Therefore, in spite of his becoming a dignitary of the Church of Ireland he held no Orders from it. He later commented, 'I was advised by a Church lawyer at the time that the action of the Archbishop in accepting me, and of the Bishop of Killaloe in instituting me to a parish in his diocese, was irregular; but was also advised to "let sleeping dogs lie".' And he concluded, 'The only way in which I can renounce my Orders and become a layman is to send my resignation to the Church in which I hold them.'

He therefore penned the following letter to the Bishop of Utah, Bishop Moulton:

> In the year 1906 I was ordained to the priesthood of the Protestant Episcopal Church in America by the late Right Reverend F.S. Spalding, at that time Bishop of Salt Lake. I took charge of Provo Mission near Salt Lake City, but after some years returned to Ireland where I entered the service of the Church of Ireland and became incumbent of Ahascragh, Archdeacon of Clonfert and Canon of St Patrick's Cathedral, Dublin.
>
> I have now identified myself with the Faith of Bahá'u'lláh, and that I might do so have resigned my place in the Church of Ireland. In order that my position may be unequivocal I send this letter to you to relinquish the American Orders which I received in 1906.
>
> It is with very real regret that I loosen in any way my old and precious associations with the American Ministry. My motive is to be loyal to Christ as I know Him and to give to His Church the best service which in the special circumstances I have to offer. It is my settled conviction that the Glad Tidings brought by the Prophet of Persia, Bahá'u'lláh, represent the promised return of Christ; that Christ is and has ever been through all our difficulties in our midst though we have recognised Him not; that the Christian Churches in recent years have missed their way, and have lost their hold on human hearts because they are out of touch with their Lord; and that the path back to Him and to His Father lies wide open before them though they have chosen not to walk in it. I feel I must make any sacrifice in order to be free to help in transmitting to my fellow-Christians a Message which presents the one and only hope of respiritualising mankind and rebuilding the social order.
>
> I published some years ago two books on the relationship of the Bahá'í Teaching to Christianity: *The Promise of All Ages* and *The Heart of the Gospel*. With this letter I enclose a shorter statement on the subject, directed especially to yourself as head of the diocese in which I was ordained. It is really addressed to all Christian people since its message

vitally concerns every one of them, and I propose to send copies of it to a number of representative members of the two great Communions for which I have had the high privilege of working.

George intended, as the final paragraph of the above shows, to enclose with this letter a copy of his Manifesto. The delay in sending both is dealt with in the next chapter, but he commented, 'The law will be complicated on the point as there is (I understand) no precedent for the Church of Ireland's accepting American Orders. So the Bishop of Utah may have to write to the Archbishop of Armagh! Let them worry it out – the more publicity, the better for us.'

The thread of irony in George's life wove its way even into this episode. At the end of 1949, more than two years after his sacrificial act, he wrote:

It turns out that my effort to give up my American Orders conferred in Salt Lake City was based on a mistake. The ecclesiastical position is a simple one: when I left the States and became an officer of the Church of Ireland and changed my allegiance I severed my connexion with the American ministry. I held nothing which I could resign.

So my renouncing my Orders on September 30th 1947 was the final act and completed the official severance. I then ceased to be a clergyman of a Church anywhere.

He received a reply from his old colleague the Venerable W.F. Bulkley, DD,[1] Archdeacon of Utah, which is so relevant to the confidence which George inspired in all with whom he worked that it cannot be omitted from any account of his life.

Dear Townshend,

Bishop Moulton has just turned over to me as the Secretary of the Convocation of Utah two of your letters asking for deposition. I have read them with deep interest as messages from a fellow worker in Utah whom I knew long years ago and whom I also knew as a deep student and thinker. You know, by the way, I came to Utah in 1908 and succeeded you in Provo going there in 1914 and remaining there till 1929 when I returned to Salt Lake City to give all my time to the work as Archdeacon. Bishop Clark has just this month retired me after 41 years of service.

I am sure that any step you take or have taken, is based on real and deep thinking. It is a hard thing to give up old associations and I know you have done so only after having thoroughly convinced yourself that you are taking the right step. I am sure that you will have a devotion for your new phase of life that is very real for you have entered it through great searchings of heart and soul.

I am sure that I fully agree with you in your feeling regarding the real presence of God, and the living Christ in the life of this world. I am sure

[1] See p. 23.

you will agree with me when I say, that the greatest hindrance to God in his leading, through our living, this world of His into becoming the Kingdom of God, is the failure of Christian people – their leaders especially – to realize the real presence of the living Christ and to yield their lives to His will. We could make life right and Godlike in no great period of time if we accepted that belief and put it into action in living. You are looking outside the Church to find the way to accomplish this – I respect you greatly for I know you honestly are convinced that the lethargy and indifference within the Church renders it inoperative. I am trusting and hoping and working to accomplish this within the body of the Church and through the Ministry of the Church. I am sure it can so be done. I am sure that you and I would work along well together as we have the same ideal, the same idea and purpose. Though some of our methods and hopes might differ, still our aims are one.

As an old fellow-worker with you in Utah I wish to state my confidence in you and your conscientious withdrawal from our Church to accomplish better the purpose of that Church. God be with you and bring you happiness in success.

This seems to be the right place to clarify that George's resignation and renunciation of his Orders were not made at the instruction of the Guardian. Neither had the Guardian requested him to remain in the Church.[1] As we have seen, his approach to the National Spiritual Assembly in 1936 was made in the hope that some way would be found for him to leave the Church then and devote his free time to the service of the Bahá'í Faith. The Guardian fully approved.[2] When, eleven years later, his resignation took place, it was done on his own initiative and timed in consultation with his National Spiritual Assembly. The Guardian was advised of the facts and asked for his comments. His reply, 'TOWNSHEND'S RESIGNATION IMPERATIVE' was his comment, as Guardian of the Bahá'í Faith, on the situation as presented to him which comprised George's clear decision to resign. There was obvious danger to the infant Faith of Bahá'u'lláh in the possibility of a dignitary of the Church being unfrocked, on representations of the Primates of both the United Kingdom and Ireland, for adherence to an obscure heretical sect, as the Bahá'í Faith was considered to be by the ecclesiastical leaders. Historically the comparison is again with St Paul, the eminent member of the established religion who embraced the Cause of Jesus Christ, crucified as a heretic and blasphemer. Today, barely thirty-five years after George's transition, it is hard to imagine an unfrocking even being noticed, much less causing a scandal, such is the decline which has taken place in the prestige of the Church.

[1] Both these mistaken ideas have gained some credence among Bahá'ís.
[2] See letter to George cited pp. 134–5.

Even more important perhaps was the consideration of the damage which a trial for heresy, with all its attendant ill-feelings, would have done to George's own programme of conciliation and gradual presentation of the new Revelation in a manner which would not offend the traditional beliefs or susceptibilities of devout Christians. Adamantine in his faith and determination to proclaim Christ returned in glory, he was ever the most conciliatory of men and gentle with others. His own concern for the preservation of friendly relations with the leaders of that community which he hoped to guide into the light of the new day, thoroughly understood by the Guardian, is reflected in his letter to the National Spiritual Assembly cited above, protesting the suggested advancement of the date of his 'Manifesto'(see page 192).

This factor is important for the apprehension of George's spirit and character, and of the persistence with which he pursued his objective through all the years of his incumbency of Ahascragh, when he was straining at the same time to achieve his freedom. His resignation was essential to his destined work, but it implied no antagonism towards Christianity or to the members of the particular communion which he served so faithfully and with such distinction. Rather was it the ultimate sacrifice in the bridge-building from one Dispensation to another which his greater vision imposed on him and which he was trained by Providence to bear.

On August 1, 1941 the Guardian's secretary had written on his behalf to George, 'Wherever the Cause is being spread, as it grows in strength, people increasingly will take sides both for and against it. Therefore he is not surprised to learn that you are finding yourself in this position, sometimes being upheld and sometimes being attacked! It is a great bounty from God that you have had a training in this world which so admirably suits you for a champion of His Faith and an exponent of His doctrines.' In his reply to the Guardian's cable, 'THRILLED YOUR NEWS PRAYING MIGHTY RESULTS . . .' George echoed this idea. He wrote, 'I realise my training calls on me to try to build a bridge for my fellow-Christians to pass over into the Bahá'í Order, and I am now endeavouring to "consecrate my life to the diffusion of the divine fragrances" (as 'Abdu'l-Bahá wrote me) in this difficult, delicate and perhaps dangerous field.'

A letter from Una to the National Spiritual Assembly of the British Isles, more than three years after his passing, expresses concern

for something my father worked for long and hard: 'Abdu'l-Bahá wrote to my father, 'It is my hope thy Church will come under the heavenly Jerusalem' and Dad did his best to bring this about; the Church of Ireland has been very sympathetic to the Faith and Dad's tact and wisdom have done a lot of good spade work towards realising 'Abdu'l-Bahá's hope.

BALLINASLOE CLERICAL UNION.

::

A Meeting will be held on April 26 Tuesday

at 3 *o'clock, in* O'Carroll's Hotel
Ballinasloe

Greek Testament Rev. G. W. Murray

Paper by Canon Townshend : "Abdul
Bahá

G. Townshend

Hon. Sec.

An invitation to a meeting of the Ballinasloe Clerical Union

She is distressed about a report that George's former colleagues have been referred to as his enemies:

> This is very far from the truth. They were always good friends who had a genuine admiration for him. He used to enjoy meeting them regularly once a month in Ballinasloe when they would talk together of spiritual things; they were interested in mystical and metaphysical things and loved the Bahá'í writings which he loaned them, but they didn't seem capable of understanding the station of Bahá'u'lláh. The broadness and all-encompassing nature of the Faith appealed to them. When Dad wrote *The Promise of All Ages* his bishop was very pleased; 'We must do away with all this orthodoxy,' he said. He [the bishop] wrote to *The Irish Times* and asked them to review the book which they did. After preaching a sermon on Bahá'u'lláh in St Patrick's Cathedral, (the Church of Ireland's national cathedral) for which the Dean congratulated him, Dad sent a copy of *The Promise* to him which was subsequently placed in the cathedral library. When Dad passed away, a memorial service was held in Ahascragh church at the suggestion of the clergyman who has taken his place there; the present Archdeacon preached on that occasion, expressing his

understanding and admiration of my father. He said that some narrow-minded people might think George Townshend had been disloyal to the Church by leaving it as he did, but that his loyalty was to that larger Truth which could be contained in no church. He ended by quoting, in full, Dad's poem to Bahá'u'lláh . . . While George Townshend and all he stood for is remembered and admired by the Church of Ireland the Bahá'ís have a door open which will be gradually closed if the opportunity is lost. 'Abdu'l-Bahá was not a wild dreamer and He wouldn't have said what He did had it not been possible. Think what it would mean to have a whole Church come into the Faith en masse! . . . I do hope it will be possible for Dad's work in the Church of Ireland to be brought to a (or rather turned into a) tremendous triumph for the Cause of Bahá'u'lláh.

Una's point is well illustrated by George's enquiries about the possible recovery of some part of his contributions to the Church of Ireland's insurance scheme. They were unsuccessful, but give us a valuable document from the Bishop of Killaloe, whom we have met before. His letter of November 5, 1947, while explaining very reasonably why George's application could not be entertained, is very friendly and sympathetic and a clear indication of the regard in which he still held his former Archdeacon. Unlike the Archbishop of Armagh, Killaloe still addresses him 'My dear Archdeacon' and concludes 'I am indeed very sorry not to be able to help you in such an important matter. Ever yours sincerely.'

This also seems the opportune moment to comment that George's renunciation of his Orders had far greater significance than the simple act of retiring from Church service. Howard Colby Ives, a Unitarian minister who had founded The Brotherhood Church in New Jersey, became one of the early heroes of the Bahá'í Faith in the United States, and achieved immortal fame by his description in his book *Portals to Freedom*[1] of his association with 'Abdu'l-Bahá during His visit to North America in 1912–13. But Howard was not an ordained priest. I am indebted to Mr William Hellaby, an English Bahá'í, who was himself a Unitarian minister prior to his identification with the Bahá'í Faith, for clarification of this point. He cites the ordination service of the Church of England, which is also used by the Church of Ireland and the Protestant Episcopal Church of the United States of America (all three of the same hierarchy; see Chapter 3), which reads: 'When the prayer is done, the Bishop with the priests present shall lay their hands severally upon the head of every one that receiveth the Order of Priesthood . . .' The Bishop then says, 'Receive the Holy Ghost for the office and work of a priest in the Church of God, now committed unto thee by the imposition of our hands. Whose sins thou dost

[1] George Ronald, Oxford

forgive, they are forgiven; and whose sins thou dost retain, they are retained. And be thou a faithful dispenser of the Word of God, and of His holy Sacraments; In the Name of the Father, and of the Son, and of the Holy Ghost. Amen.' This is clearly a much weightier and more solemn mandate than that given to a graduate from a theological college who has been accepted by a liberal-minded congregation to manage the proceedings of its church. Mr Hellaby comments: '. . . the priest is clearly a person with special gifts, empowered to act as an intermediary between God and man. The concept most emphatically does not apply to Unitarian ministers either in these islands or in the United States of America so that if you describe George Townshend as "the first *ordained priest* in Christendom" to become a Bahá'í you will be describing him correctly.' It was no small matter to renounce such Orders, particularly after forty years in their service.

At the Clonfert Synod of September 2, 1947, George's Bishop, Bishop Webster of Killaloe, paid this tribute:

> Soon we are to lose from amongst us our Archdeacon. It is almost 28 years since the Archdeacon came to the Diocese as Incumbent of Ahascragh; for the past 20 years he had filled the office of Diocesan Secretary, and for the past 14 years the office of Archdeacon. Last year I was glad to have the opportunity of appointing him as Canon representing the United Diocese in the National Cathedral, he having previously held a Chapter Canonry in that Cathedral for some 13 years. The Diocese has been indeed fortunate to have had his services in all these important offices, and this Synod would, I am sure, desire to place on record its appreciation of his faithful and efficient work during these many years. But it is for himself as a man, even more than for his work and service, that we value the Archdeacon most. His constant kindness, his unfailing courtesy and his singleness of purpose have endeared him to Clergy and laity alike, and have made him a respected and beloved figure in these parts. We shall miss him far more than I can say, but I can assure him that he carries with him our earnest prayers and good wishes for the welfare and happiness of himself and his family in the days to come.

On October 1, 1947, George wrote from Ahascragh Rectory to the secretary of the National Spiritual Assembly, 'Today, October 1st, is my first day as *Mr* not Rev. G. Townshend!'

Chapter 11

OPERATION TOWNSHEND

GEORGE had agreed with the National Spiritual Assembly to send the typescript of his manifesto 'by the middle of June or so', for printing, and to circulate it immediately prior to his resignation, which was to take effect from September 30, 1947. He had been thinking about it since that day in March when the Bishop of Killaloe had discussed with him the complaint referred by the Archbishops of Canterbury and Armagh, and the issue seemed joined. On April 9 he told the Guardian 'My pamphlet, "Calling All Christians", has a strong argument and I believe promises well. I hope my resignation will give me an opening for a press campaign, publicising the Cause.' As late as May 24th he expressed confidence that he could complete it by June 30, and noted that 'the title will probably be "Examine My Cause" (from Bahá'u'lláh's letter to the Kings[1]).'

However, it soon became apparent that the turmoil and upset, physical, mental and spiritual, attendant upon his resignation and removal from the rectory, created a distinctly unfavourable atmosphere for the composition of the weighty, well-planned and incisive document which he had in mind. On June 19 he wrote to me, 'I have not succeeded in writing to my satisfaction that pamphlet I projected to the National Spiritual Assembly, though I have composed three or four alternative versions; and I have concluded it must be postponed for the present, indefinitely perhaps. This I greatly regret except that I feel clearly the Almighty does not approve. If He did there would not be this trouble.'

The final statement in this passage cannot be taken as an excuse or

[1] *'Examine Our Cause ...'* See *The Proclamation of Bahá'u'lláh* to the kings and leaders of the world, Bahá'í World Centre, Haifa 1967, p.10.

the invocation of a cliché by an ageing clergyman. George knew the reality of guidance, whether resulting from prayer, meditation or consultation or any combination of them, and had seen statements from the Guardian to the effect that while we can never be certain, even after our most ardent supplications, that our inner promptings are true guidance, if 'the doors appear to open' then by all means go through. Conversely, if no gleam of light appears and difficulties show no sign of dissolving, then it would seem reasonable to conclude, as did George, that divine approval is withheld.

While the hardships of his new circumstances made it no easier for him to write, the freedom to proclaim himself, fully and openly, a Bahá'í, mitigated for some time the unaccustomed harassments of reduced circumstances. It was the usual artistic dissatisfaction with first attempts at new compositions which further delayed the work. In April 1948, he related, 'My early efforts at a pamphlet were too light. This last one is like a small book and won't do either.' It eventually emerged as *The Old Churches and the New World-Faith* and is one of his finest masterpieces.

But the hiatus in writing his manifesto by no means implied the cessation of all literary work. On the contrary, that process of healing and restoration of energy for a particular creation, well known to artists in all media, came to his assistance, and he was able to complete, in the first months of 1948, when the springs for his open letter were running dry, one of his most valuable works.

The distinguished publishing firm of John Murray had on its list a series called *Wisdom of the East* which presented, in a small book form, annotated compilations of the sacred scriptures of the world's great religions, and expositions of oriental philosophy. As early as 1909 it had published *The Splendour of God* by Eric Hammond, described as 'Extracts from the sacred writings of the BAHAIS.' (Reprinted in 1911) The current editor of the series, Cranmer-Byng, felt the need of a new Bahá'í representation and approached the National Spiritual Assembly, which immediately recommended George for the task.

He was very pleased and expressed gratitude for the opportunity. 'All this begins to look like business!' He was able to complete a compilation 'developing one theme, one thought: the regeneration of the individual soul and that of mankind, and then the building of the Most Great Peace which is the outward expression of a humanity inwardly regenerated.' He wrote an Introduction and explanatory notes and sent it to the National Assembly for review; it was published by Murray under the title *The Glad Tidings of Bahá'u'lláh* in October 1949 and was reprinted in January 1956, and again by George Ronald in 1975. He sent signed copies of the first edition to the Guardian and the National Spiritual Assembly. The Guardian was delighted with it and cabled 'GLAD TIDINGS BAHÁ'U'LLÁH GRATEFULLY RECEIVED. HEARTFELT CONGRATULATIONS LATEST EVIDENCE UNIQUE MAGNIFICENT SERVICE FAITH.' A letter written on his behalf referred to it as 'another feather in your cap'.

This task accomplished very satisfactorily, George returned to his manifesto and sent it to the National Assembly on August 12, 1948, a year and two months after the proposed date. He commented, 'I do not think I ever shall write anything as significant as this.' He asked for five hundred copies which he would post to the Irish clergy and key men in the English church. 'Further: I have *American* Orders and therefore have a special right to address the authorities of the Episcopal Church in U.S.A.'

By now George's demission was no longer 'hot news'. A proposal was put to the National Assembly that circulation of his open letter, as it was now called, be further delayed until his new book with the provocative title *Christ and Bahá'u'lláh* would be ready. The book would back up the letter and the two together, given widespread publicity, would make George's action again topical. Early in 1950 was suggested and George signified his approval.

But the Assembly was thrilled with the challenge in George's open letter and recorded its opinion that it had before it 'the weightiest single matter that we had yet had to handle, because of its potential significance throughout Christendom in the West'. It did not want to delay, knowing very well how tentative was the publication date of any book not yet completed, and particularly one from George, who grieved that he was 'a slow worker'.

The Assembly had other good reasons for not delaying. The British Bahá'í community was now approaching the peak of its tremendous effort to win the Six Year Plan to which it was committed. The community was on its toes, united as never before, its appetite for victory 'whetted', as the Guardian described it, by the successes already achieved in establishing nine new Local Spiritual Assemblies (not the least astonishing being Dublin, in 1948, with three Townshends as foundation members). The first four months of 1950 would be the last lap of that history-making, destiny-compelling Plan. It would be a time of desperate activity for all Bahá'ís in Britain, with every evening and weekend pre-empted to ensuring success by Riḍván[1] (April 21). Now the community was still building up its powers and able to take this new task in its stride.

[1] The pre-eminent festival of the Bahá'í year, commemorating the Declaration by Bahá'u'lláh, during twelve days in the Garden of Riḍván outside Baghdád, of His Prophetic mission.

A committee was appointed, composed of four members of the Assembly, and 'charged with the responsibility of making the best possible use of the statement, to help Mr Townshend himself in a personal release of copies to senior clergy, and to organize a national release to a maximum of some 10,000 leaders of thought in religious, educational, social and cultural fields.'[1] The committee was empowered to seek the help of Local Assemblies, individual believers and others and to form subsidiary committees; it was given a budget and required to plan and execute the operation and to study and suggest ways of dealing with repercussions. With the Guardian's approval every other National Spiritual Assembly was sent a copy of George's statement and invited to assist financially in the project and to distribute the statement. The response was unanimous and 'Operation Townshend' was launched.

The story of the committee's discharge of its task is its own and is documented in the minutes of its meetings and in those of its subsidiary committee and in its reports to the National Spiritual Assembly. It was an enormous task for already heavily engaged people. Ten thousand envelopes had to be prepared; George's open letter had to be printed and dispatched to those who would insert it in the envelopes; covering letters had to be printed, (separate ones for the Press, for George's personal release, and for 'leaders of thought'); local Bahá'í communities and individuals had to be co-opted and instructed, and the closest co-operation maintained with George himself and the National Spiritual Assembly. There was no time for hiatuses or post-war delay. The whole project had to be completed within three months from the day of the committee's first meeting. Its success was in large measure due to its only officer, Richard Backwell,[2] who acted as secretary, maintained adherence to a strict timetable and brilliantly co-ordinated the entire project.

George's statement *The Old Churches and the New World-Faith* was printed as a pamphlet of twenty pages with a dignified cover and the title-page bearing the legend

[1] From the National Assembly's report to the Bahá'í Annual Convention, April 1949.

[2] He served during World War II as an education officer in the R.A.F., became a Bahá'í in Malaysia, returned home to England on discharge and was a member of the National Spiritual Assembly during the Six Year Plan. He then pioneered to British Guiana where he became Personnel Officer of the great sugar company there and rendered sterling service to the Bahá'í Faith. His review of *The Promise of All Ages* was published in the principal newspaper. His family became Bahá'ís, his mother and father both serving on the sub-committee for distribution of George's pamphlet, and rendering distinguished services in other fields. Richard came home to England, married and returned to British Guiana where both gave fine service. They later pioneered to Northern Ireland. Richard died of cancer October 4, 1972. (See 'In Memoriam', *The Bahá'í World*, vol. XV, pp. 525–7.)

George Townshend, M.A. (Oxon.)
*(Sometime Canon of S. Patrick's Cathedral, Dublin
and Archdeacon of Clonfert)*

The Bahá'í Publishing Trust took over 7,000 copies and immediately dispatched 5,000 to Australia and 2,000 to the United States. Four thousand were later sent to Canada and a number to Egypt for distribution to the churches there. Germany expressed its intention to translate and distribute as widely as possible. Over 8,000 were sent out in the British Isles to the categories listed below from dispatching committees in Dublin, Oxford and London. One was sent to the King and was acknowledged by the Home Secretary.

Where Posted	*Categories of Recipients*	
DUBLIN	English clergy	800
	Irish clergy	150
	Personal to Mr Townshend	50
OXFORD	Press and periodicals	319
LONDON	Bahá'ís	282
	House of Commons	660
	Selected peers	58
	Ambassadors, governors, envoys, and consuls-general	200
	Heads of universities and colleges	450
	Permanent civil servants	150
	Matrons of principal hospitals	200
	High and Appeal Court judges	100
	Senior Army, Navy, RAF officers	190
	Leaders of thought in Scotland	100
	Leaders of thought in Eire	450
	Leaders of thought in Wales	500
	Lords-lieutenant, sheriffs, chief constables	150
	Members of learned societies	150
	Members of world order organizations	150
	Members of Royal Institute of International Affairs	50
	Secretaries and presidents of religious societies	48
	Selected social service members	46
	Headmasters and headmistresses	468
	Philanthropic industrialists and professionals	266
	Secretaries and presidents of social service organizations	30
	Leading musicians	18
	Selected writers	615
	Librarians	480
	Submitted by LSAs, groups etc.	940
	Added by Distribution Committee	52
	TOTAL	8122

Once again George was the mainspring of an operation affecting, this time, not only the British Bahá'í community but extending around the world. In 1936 the National Assembly had considered the matter of his withdrawal from the Church to be the greatest problem it had yet faced,[1] and the action then taken, though bringing no release to George, unified the British community and established the British Bahá'í Publishing Trust, an institution vital to the future expansion of that community.[2]

Now, in 1948, the National Assembly considered the wide dissemination of George's statement relating to his resignation 'the weightiest matter that has yet come before it . . .' and so informed the British Bahá'í community in the following letter sent to every member.

6th December 1948

Dear Friends,

There has come from the pen of our dear friend Mr George Townshend a clarion call to all Christians entitled *The Old Churches and the New World-Faith* or *The Day of Judgement is Come*. This takes the form of a statement in some 3,500 words, of the Bahá'í challenge and summons to Christendom.

In the first instance it will accompany a personal letter to the Bishop of the diocese in the U.S.A. where he took Orders.

So excellent is this statement that we think the chance must not be missed of making the fullest use of it by having it printed and distributed.

   1. by Mr Townshend himself to senior clergy.

   2. by the British Bahá'í Community to the Press and to leaders of thought tentatively numbered at some 10,000 recipients in all.

Indeed the National Assembly regards this as the weightiest matter that has yet come before it and feels that it is our first opportunity to proclaim the Faith to the Christian World. As such, it is of international importance and our plans have been developed bearing in mind the Guardian's hope that from Mr Townshend's resignation would come 'Mighty Results'.

Before launching this mighty project the National Assembly deemed it proper to write specially to the Guardian, who cabled his reply: 'APPROVE TOWNSHEND'S ADMIRABLE STATEMENT CONVEY CONGRATULATIONS PRAYING SIGNAL SUCCESS APPROVE APPEAL FUNDS OVERSEAS.'

A committee has been appointed to get the job done. Its members are: Marion and David Hofman, Alma Gregory, Richard Backwell (Secretary). It has met and outlined its plans which may be summarised:

   1. Release date will be February 15th 1949 (provisionally).

---

[1] See Ch. 9.

[2] The Publishing Trust not only made available new and authentic translations of the sacred Scriptures, the Guardian's writings and introductory works and pamphlets but, for example, during the Ten Year Crusade (1953–63) provided a basic booklet in forty-one African languages.

2. Distribution Committees will be formed to prepare with ample systematised assistance a full list of names and addresses of all leaders of thought in these islands.

3. Individuals and established Communities will be invited to send in names and addresses of people of special eminence in their own area, outstanding in social, educational, literary, religious spheres.

4. Other National Assemblies will be invited to co-operate, to state their needs for copies of the statement, to contribute towards the estimated cost.

As you will see at once, this project, for the outcome of which the Guardian prays a 'signal success', has a great many other ramifications which need to be considered – teaching and follow-up, press releases, repercussions, to name but three.

We are sure however that you will all wish to take a hand in this work by actually researching, listing, indexing, addressing, enveloping and by contributing to the special fund we are setting up to defray the financial cost which we estimate at about £200. Our Committee plans also to approach certain individuals and communities because of the special assistance we believe they can give.

Rightly and boldly handled this project will serve to establish the Faith still more firmly in the eyes of the world. Its full results will surely be cumulative, but will just as surely lend a great impetus to the work of the Cause in these islands.

We feel impelled to call on each and every believer to join in prayer for the success of a work which has already been blessed by the prayers of our beloved Guardian.

Might not this project help us to play that 'distinctive part in the threefold crusade' amidst the races and nations of Europe, 'whose fate' as the Guardian puts it, 'now hangs so perilously in the balance'?

Yours in His Service,
National Spiritual Assembly

The community seized whole-heartedly this opportunity to reinforce its strenuous teaching campaign and launched a nationwide programme of proclamation of the Faith of Bahá'u'lláh, remarkable in relation to its numbers and resources. It was a community project, led and fully supported by the National Assembly and its committee, and as the Committee's final report stated, 'All Local Assemblies and Groups and some individual believers in the British Isles, supplied lists of local influential people as recipients. Many also assisted in listing those who came under special categories.' Many envelopes were addressed by a mail agency firm and sent to Dublin, London or Oxford where they were filled, stamped and mailed by the friends. Many were addressed by individual believers working at night over and beyond their activities for the Six Year Plan. In Dublin alone the handful of believers completed and sent out, under George's direction, a thousand envelopes, and George himself sent out more than two hundred with his personal card. It was a magnificent, unified operation, accomplished by a hard-pressed community, newly awakened to the excitement, joy and satisfaction of united service.

There were nine National Spiritual Assemblies in the world at that time[1] and every one of them contributed financially to the project and five undertook distribution of George's open letter in their own areas. But beyond that, every one of them signified their willingness, indeed happiness, to contribute to the fund for George's support, and all did so. The American National Assembly was particularly interested in view of George's ordination in the Protestant Episcopal Church of the United States, and his letter to the Bishop of Utah which accompanied a copy of *The Old Churches and the New World-Faith*. Already known throughout the Bahá'í world community, George now became an international figure in the Faith.

We have already seen George's letter to the Bishop of Utah.[2] The letter accompanying the copies of his statement sent to editors, 'Press and periodicals', was imposed on a letterhead:

BAHÁ'Í PUBLIC RELATIONS
(National Spiritual Assembly of the Bahá'ís of the British Isles)

used for the first time by the British National Spiritual Assembly. It reflected the new designation of the 'Townshend Committee' which was now authorized to deal with repercussions. George's utter modesty was revealed in a postscript to a letter he wrote to the committee about the circulation of his manifesto.

> The point of approach which I think it would in a general way be wise to make central and vital is not so much the personal one about a clergyman's turning to Bahá'u'lláh as the fact that the Bahá'ís are vindicating, justifying, magnifying Christ in contemporary history and in this world crisis while the churches for all their credal protestations are letting Him down and utterly failing to connect what is happening with the promises of Christ or the divine power the New Testament assigns Him.

This advice was not received until the Committee's letter had already been printed. It read:

February, 1949

Dear Sir,
              The Resignation of Archdeacon Townshend

The relinquishing of high office for reasons of conscience is always a

---

[1] Australia and New Zealand; British Isles; Canada; Egypt and Sudan; Germany and Austria; India, Pakistan and Burma; Iráq; Persia; United States of America. At Riḍván, 1981, 132 National Spiritual Assemblies were elected.

[2] See p. 200.

matter of interest. But in the case of George Townshend the circumstances are so challenging as to provide news interest to everyone.

An Archdeacon of the Protestant Church of Ireland and Canon of S. Patrick's Cathedral, Dublin, he has resigned not only his offices, but has relinquished his Orders as well, his reason being as he says 'to be loyal to Christ as I know Him'.

Nor is this mere whim or dissatisfaction, but a positive proclamation to Christendom that 'the Glad Tidings brought by the Prophet of Persia, Bahá'u'lláh, represent the promised return of Christ'.

The Bahá'í Faith is not unknown in the world. Lord Curzon, Jowett, Tolstoy, Younghusband, all called attention to it while Queen Marie of Rumania openly proclaimed herself a believer. Its message of peace, Divine guidance and world civilization through the promised 'return of Christ', is of concern to every human soul.

Mr Townshend has penned a remarkable letter called *The Old Churches and the New World-Faith*, copies of which are being sent to all senior clergy and to several thousand responsible people. The publication day is February 15th. We feel sure it will engage your interest and only ask that no comment should appear before publication day.

Faithfully,
Bahá'í Public Relations

In addition, a leaflet, printed by George Ronald, my own firm which had become George's publisher, was included in the envelopes of librarians and the press and also circulated to the major booksellers in Britain. It referred to George's resignation and his reasons being 'clearly and boldly set out in an open letter *The Old Churches and the New World-Faith*;' it described *The Promise of All Ages, The Heart of the Gospel*, and indicated future publications.

The impressive plans made to deal with repercussions, which included the setting up of a bureau in London, supplied with Bahá'í literature to deal with mail enquiries, organization of reception times at the London headquarters for personal enquiries, arrangements for George to make a lecture tour, readiness to arrange a Press conference, all proved unnecessary. The response of ten thousand leaders in the nation's life was less than meagre – almost nil. The committee summed it up in its report embodied in the National Assembly's Annual Report to Convention in April 1949, and although granting it was a little early to make a full assessment, nothing was added later.

A fine full-page article appeared in the Birmingham *Sunday Mercury* on February 20th, . . . a bare mention of the Faith was reported made from an Edinburgh pulpit, an enquiry from an author engaged in compiling an encyclopaedia of religious matters, a small number of private letters and many formal acknowledgements passed through the London Centre. Mr

Townshend received a 'remarkably kind' reply from the Bishop of Utah.[1]
He also had questions from the Primate of Ireland, an invitation to speak to
a religious society in London with offer to print the Address, and a few
private letters.

Perhaps the response of the Primate of Ireland, the Archbishop of
Armagh, to whom George had previously sent *The Promise of All
Ages*, indicates the general spiritual awareness of the time.

> THE PALACE,
> ARMAGH.
> February 21st, 1949.

Dear Mr Townshend,
I have to acknowledge receipt of the brochure you have kindly sent me.
But having read it, I can find nothing there to make me understand the
appeal which Bahá'u'lláh has apparently made in various parts of the
world. I do not observe in the letter he addressed to Rulers and Popes
anything that either fills out or elucidates or carries further the Gospel of
Jesus Christ for those who are believers in the revelation made in and
through His Person.
    If the Prophet really seeks to *commend* Him and not to replace Him, why
is he outside the Society which He founded?
    I do not see how he has advanced much further than the Persian mystic,
Jalal-addin-rumi.

> Yours faithfully,
> (Sgd) John Armagh

To this George replied:

Your Grace,
It was good of you to acknowledge the pamphlet I sent you and to ask
these thoughtful and important questions.
    In illustration of 'this appeal which Bahá'u'lláh has apparently made in
various parts of the world', I may quote Tolstoy's statement 'the teachings
. . . now present us with the highest and purest form of religious
teachings.' Dr Jowett (of Balliol) thought 'Babíism might prove the most
important religious movement since the foundation of Christianity.' Dr
Cheyne (of the Encyclopaedia): 'If there has been any prophet in recent
times, it is to Bahá'u'lláh that we must go.' Lord Curzon: 'Tales of
magnificent heroism illumine the bloodstained pages of Bábí history . . .
Of no small account, then, must be the tenets of a creed that can awaken in
its followers so rare and beautiful a spirit of self-sacrifice.' Queen Marie of
Rumania: 'The Bahá'í teaching brings peace to the soul and hope to the
heart.' These are samples.
    It is true – as you write – that the short passages from Bahá'u'lláh quoted
in this pamphlet do not fill out and carry further the Gospel of Christ but

[1] Actually it was Archdeacon Bulkley who replied on behalf of the Bishop. See p.
201.

they were chosen to illustrate another theme, and Bahá'u'lláh elsewhere deals with this topic largely. For instance in His 'Iqan' or 'Book of Certitude' He develops at length the principle of Incarnation (or Manifestation) on which the Christian and Bahá'í Faiths are alike based, and describes and analyses the historical reaction of mankind to it. Among the humanitarian principles which are explicit in His teaching and not in the Gospel are the equality of the sexes, the prohibition of slavery, the obligation of Universal education, the harmony of religion and science, the duty of independent investigation of truth, the duty of every man's having and practising a trade or profession, the forbidding of monasticism and encouragement of matrimony, the adoption of an auxiliary universal language, the attainment of a world conscience, and other like injunctions, as well as economic teachings and plans and patterns for universal peace and the unification of the human race.

These, like all His teachings, were given between 1853–1892 by One who lived among a backward and degraded people and was kept throughout His entire ministry a prisoner and an exile.

You wonder why, if so appreciative of Christ He should have remained 'outside the society which Christ founded'. It may have been a difficulty that there are so many such societies and that He could not join one of these without excluding Himself from all the others.

You write that He does not seem to have advanced much further than Jalal-ud-din Rumi. The range of Bahá'u'lláh's writings is vastly wider, for they deal with all aspects of human life and fill one hundred volumes. The book of *Gleanings from the Writings of Bahá'u'lláh* by Shoghi Effendi (though not chosen for the purpose) gives some idea of the variety of His teaching. John Murray of Albemarle Street will be publishing in the late autumn a smaller volume of selections from Bahá'í sacred writings in his 'Wisdom of the East' series.

I happen to have by me a booklet of such selections which I hope you will accept, such as it is. It contains on page 14 one of Bahá'u'lláh's tributes to Christ, and to the powers of His atonement, and some passages on the *status* of a Messenger of God, etc.

I remain,
Respectfully yours,
George Townshend

The Archbishop wrote again:

Feb. 28th, 1949.

Dear Mr Townshend,

I have to thank you for the 'Selected Writings' you kindly sent me. I have looked through the book but have to confess that I find nothing in it to change my estimate of the subject.

The Prophet pours out a succession of excellent moral sentiments, not one of which goes anything beyond what Christians are familiar with, but gives us nothing but an appeal to man's spiritual sense, to help for the putting his advice into practice. Inwardness of the same kind marked the American Transcendentalists of the middle of last century, Emerson, Thoreau, Lowell, Holmes, in whose writings I find much more to bite on than I do in those of Bahá'u'lláh.

I even found more in the writings of the India Swami Vivekananda. But to forsake the Risen and Ascended Christ for *this* is to me an incomprehensible step.

Faithfully yours,
(Sgd) John Armagh

George also reported that 'The Editor of *The Irish Times* when I called was *not* sympathetic about the contents of the press package, and I don't know what he will say, if anything.' George was delighted with everything that had been done, the production of his brochure, the world-wide support accorded him, and summed it up: 'nothing like it has ever been dreamed of by the British Bahá'ís before, or I suppose by any Bahá'ís'.

The National Spiritual Assembly's evaluation read: 'Bahá'u'lláh's call to Christendom was reiterated; a great project, sponsored by the entire national community, and supported by its Sister Bahá'í communities of East and West, was launched; the principal leaders of thought in the British Isles were offered yet another chance to respond at this eleventh hour of humanity's progression towards the final harvest of what it has itself sown.'

The final summation came from the Guardian in his letter to George of August 8, 1949. His secretary wrote on his behalf: 'Your challenging letter to the Christians – so well conceived – has shown clearly how deep is the sleep of the heedless these days. It is like knocking on a grave; the dead make no response!'

The text of the message, *The Old Churches and the New World-Faith,* which Britain's religious, political, social, educational, and intellectual leaders ignored, may be read in Appendix 3.

Chapter 12

THE ARCHDEACON

BEFORE leaving Ahascragh altogether, we ought to attempt some account of George's life there. The twenty-eight years of his incumbency occupied, in his varied career, the longest episode, the first ten of which were certainly the most settled and probably the happiest of his life. All the events described in Chapter 5 took place there. In Ahascragh, newly married, occupying a position of honour and dignity among his own people, engaged in a profession well suited to his training and predilections, with unlimited scope for advancement, he achieved the object of his quest, that search upon which he had embarked fifteen years ago in the Rocky Mountains. His two Tablets from 'Abdu'l-Bahá were received there. His recognition of the Promised One of all ages, expressed in his poem *Hail to Thee, Scion of Glory* and in his spiritually passionate *Surrender*, filled with exaltation the opening years of his new life and was the best possible of all auguries for the future. No conflict of loyalty to the 'Old Church' and the 'New World Faith' was conceived, for the World Order of Bahá'u'lláh was as yet undisclosed in its larger implications. The most wonderful, the greatest 'Glad Tidings', the ineffable, had taken place. Bahá'u'lláh *was* Christ, in the promised glory of the Father, and George had a mandate to bring his church into the New Jerusalem, now descended from heaven for man to occupy. What more had life to offer!

He had already read, in the books sent to him from America, albeit in poor translation, Bahá'u'lláh's call to the Christians[1] to take the lead

[1] See *Lawh-i-Aqdas* (sometimes called *Tablet to the Christians*), *Tablets of Bahá'u'lláh*, Bahá'í World Centre 1978; *Tablet to Pope Pius IX, The Proclamation of Bahá'u'lláh*, Bahá'í World Centre 1967. Now available in these better translations. See also Shoghi Effendi, *America and the Most Great Peace*, in *The World Order of Bahá'u'lláh*, Bahá'í Publishing Trust, Wilmette 1938.

in guiding mankind to its fore-ordained fulfilment, and therefore his service to his Church, to Christ, to Bahá'u'lláh, would be performed 'as a Christian clergyman'[1]. His developing understanding of this issue is traced in Chapters 7–9.

The parish of Ahascragh is a small village six miles north of Ballinasloe, itself a small county town with one main hotel and a weekly market. The setting is the eastern part of Galway on the edge of the central bog of Ireland. The river Suck and the railway meander through the countryside, and Ballinasloe boasts a station on the main line to Dublin. On George's side of Ballinasloe there were two large landowners, the Dillons and the Mahons. Sir George Mahon, the present baronet, assured me that although they had no such thing in Ireland as a lord of the manor, if they had had, that's what his father would have been!

Dillon was the family name of Lord Clonbrock, whose title died out at his death. His daughter, Miss Ethel Dillon, became head of the family and a personage in the neighbourhood. She died in her ninety-ninth year, having been a source of information and anecdotes about George. She lived at Clonbrock and entertained Nancy, Brian and Una there for a few days when the memorial service to George was conducted in the parish church by his successor, Archdeacon Burrows.

The Rectory was approached by a curved drive heavily wooded with enormous copper beeches, ash and oak and their attendant scrub. It was a large three-storey house set off from the village along a side road which continued past the Protestant church and up to Castlegar, the Mahon's estate. The outlook was across a vast meadow, bordered by the road from Ballinasloe, and on to the 'distant bog' whence the curlew's cry was often heard, and along whose paths turf-cutters and 'travelling people' would be met, the former plying their skill and the latter camping for a few days at a time on some small strip of green in the shelter of an occasional tree. The distant horizon was the blue of Ireland, azure in the morning and deepening to purple as the shadows lengthened. There was a five-barred gate in the hedge separating the rectory grounds from the adjoining meadow, and Nancy maintained that George, although forty-two when they first went there, would frequently clear this in classical hurdling style, chiefly for the delight of the children, Brian and Una, who were born at the Rectory in 1920 and 1921 respectively.

George's parish duties were not burdensome and even when he became Diocesan Secretary he seemed to find time for his personal pursuits, chiefly reading and letter-writing. The church and the

[1] Letter to the Guardian, October 16, 1925, see p. 96.

23. Porch of the church at Ahascragh, before the fire in 1922. George is in the foreground.

24. *Views of the Rectory, Ahascragh*

25. The driveway to the Rectory

26. Family picnic

27. *Ahascragh Parish Church rebuilt after the fire in 1922*

28. *Canon Townshend*

rectory were in his care, and he had to perform the normal duties of parish priest, that is, hold the services designated by the Church of Ireland, instruct and present to the Bishop for confirmation the Protestant youth of his parish, conduct the marriages, christenings and funerals of his parishioners and preach the sermon on Sundays. This latter duty was the source of one of the numerous stories about him, retailed by Miss Dillon as late as 1976, twenty years after George's passing. It appears that for his first Sunday in office he had made all arrangements for the celebration of Matins (Sunday morning service of worship for all comers) which was likely to be well attended out of curiosity to see the new parson, but had forgotten to prepare the sermon. This omission suddenly occurred to him as he made his way along the church driveway to the vestry and was repaired by the inspiration afforded by the sight of sheep grazing in the neighbouring field.

A later story recounts that on walking in the village one morning he met one of his lady parishioners and greeted her with his usual hearty geniality, 'Hello, Mrs ...., you old sinner; how are you?' Unfortunately the lady took umbrage and it was some time before she could be convinced that the Rector was not impugning her moral character.

Sir George Mahon recalls that one evening at dinner when the prospective new rector was being discussed, his father, Sir William Mahon, enquired whether he spelt his name with an aitch or without. On being informed that it was with the aitch, he pronounced, 'Very well. We'll call him Shend!'. And Shend he became, and still is in the memory of his personal friends. Nancy even signed herself to Miss Dillon 'Anna S. Shend'.

Una relates that George and Nancy were a fairly happy pair for the first few years. It was Nancy who explained to Brian and herself that the photographs in the living room and George's study were of 'Abdu'l-Bahá, 'a very great and holy man, and that Daddo would soon be working for Him and His Father and we would be living in Geneva.'[1]

George's mother died in 1919, shortly after he had become incumbent of Ahascragh, and he returned to Enniskerry for a few weeks to settle up affairs. She lies in the churchyard there, a few yards from George himself.

Some of Una's earliest recollections of George are

> of riding on his shoulders and of being taken for bicycle rides on the front of his bike, in a little basket seat. He was always lots of fun and very kind.

[1] See pp. 102–5.

He used to take my brother and me for walks, and he told us stories which he made up as he went along. The continuing story of Satchy, Watchy and Patchy – three little African children – seemed to last for years, and their adventures became more exciting as we grew bigger. When we reached the stage of wanting to have frogs and insects for pets he explained that this was cruel; part of loving things was to love their freedom ... 'You don't need to touch things in order to love them.'

Daddo, as we called him, used to be the one to give us our baths and put us to bed. He taught us our first prayers and brought us up to think of religion from the Bahá'í point of view though we were members of the Church of Ireland and knew nothing about Bahá'u'lláh. His reason for not telling us was that he was working with great care and tact to bring the Church of Ireland into the Bahá'í Faith, as 'Abdu'l-Bahá had mentioned in His second Tablet to my father. He felt that it was very important that nothing should be done to antagonize the members of the Church of Ireland and he was afraid that Brian and I, who were little chatterboxes, would really upset the applecart and that the goal toward which he was working, to please 'Abdu'l-Bahá, would fall through.

We learnt the three R's from Daddo before we were finally packed off to school.

He loved to go for walks and would say, 'Let's go out and commune with nature'. Our favourite walk was to a place called the horse park; this was a large area of grass, mainly for grazing cattle and sometimes horses. There was a small lake and migrating birds used to stop there. It was a lovely place, surrounded by woods and in the spring there were lots of bluebells. There was a high part where there were mostly beech trees and there was a little round tower; it seemed to be solid, but it was made of limestone, and Daddo said it was authentic Irish architecture. The entire place was covered in bluebells, and ferns used to be coming out, and the fresh green of the beech trees, and there were some wild cherries along the edge – it was, I suppose, about a mile and a half from where we lived. We used to love to sit there and look down the hill towards the little lake, and then we would go back home.

This particular scene apparently impressed George as deeply as it did Una, for in *The Altar on the Hearth* we find this lovely apostrophe:

TO A LITTLE GIRL ON HER THIRD BIRTHDAY

O little one, my Una, April's child, thou breath of the spring wind embodied!

The bluebells cluster about thy knees; overhead the giant beech-trees spread their half-unfolded leaves; across the meadow the cuckoo calls, and from the distant bog comes the curlew's lonely cry.

How happy art thou, leading the revel of the woods, their native queen, for whom a thousand springs have come and gone to weave thy flower-beauty, and to find their meaning and perfection in these fresh lips and laughing eyes of thine.

O little one, joys more rare than these await thy wakening heart! A richer spring has cast its bounty at thy feet, a greater glory shines from another Heaven. And never morning breaks nor evening falls but lovers' prayers go forth to beg the early vision of God's Golden Age for thee who playest here thinking all happiness is already thine!

George's sense of parenthood and his attitude to its responsibilities were, as would be expected, highly spiritual and are well reflected in the following items from the same book:

A FATHER'S REFLECTION

While they are at your side, love these little ones to the utmost. Forget yourself. Serve them; care for them; lavish all your tenderness on them. Value your good fortune while it is with you, and let nothing of the sweetness of their babyhood go unprized. Not for long will you keep the happiness that now lies within your reach. You will not always walk in the sunshine with a little warm, soft hand nestling in each of yours, nor hear little feet pattering beside you, and eager baby voices questioning and prattling of a thousand things with ceaseless excitement. Not always will you see that trusting face upturned to yours, feel those little arms about your neck, and those tender lips pressed upon your cheek, nor will you have that tiny form to kneel beside you, and murmur baby prayers into your ear.

Love them and win their love, and shower on them all the treasures of your heart. Fill up their days with happiness, and share with them their mirth and innocent delights. Childhood is but for a day. Ere you are aware it will be gone with all its gifts for ever.

THE FIRST LESSON

We are thy teachers because God has appointed us. You are to hear us because God wishes you to do so. He made us your father and mother, because He chose that you should be taught by us.

We provide you with food and clothing and warmth. This is good; but the good of it will not last forever. The truth we teach you is the greatest of all the gifts we have to give you. Nothing else is important compared with this. Truth and the effects of truth last for ever: not only for a little time. The teaching which God has told us to give you will make you more happy than clothes or houses or pleasure or money. People cannot be happy without truth, even on this earth: in the next world we shall be very unhappy without it.

Remember, these teachings are of more value than all else we have to give you. We teach you because we wish to obey God. We teach you not only because we love you very much, but for God's sake.

To teach you as God would have you taught is not easy. We are not so wise nor so good as we should like to be; nor even so wise and good as we hope soon to become. God Himself alone is a perfect teacher. We pray God constantly to help us; and because we so truly wish and strive to please

Him He strengthens us with the power and wisdom of His Spirit. Whatever is true in our teaching, and whatever is good and right in it comes not from us, but from God.

Una continues her reminiscences:

Sometimes the family used to go out for bicycle rides, just the four of us, along various lanes, and we often used to take a picnic lunch with us. In summer we always used to go to Galway,[1] at least twice a week, provided the weather was fine, and we would go out along the bay and have a picnic and swim. And then, for summer holidays, we used to go to different places. My father would sometimes take a rectory, perhaps Ross's Point – he was there a couple of times; that was in County Sligo. Sometimes we would just take a caravan and go to Connemara. He always dreamed of returning to the United States some day for a visit. He wanted to take us all with him and he said above all he wanted to see Yellowstone Park again. Of all the places he had ever been to, this was his favourite. He spoke of the magnificent scenery and all the wild creatures, the friendly bears who loved chocolate, the eagles, and all sorts of other wild life, and the rivers and the waterfalls and the forests. He told us one time about fighting a forest fire – this was not in Yellowstone, though – this was up somewhere in the Rockies, I think. And he told us about how wild a lot of the men were, and that a horse's life was considered more valuable than a man's. Once he just missed being called out on a posse; but he said posses weren't any good because the bad men always got away anyhow.

Life in Ahascragh was a good life for my father and for all of us. Daddo had lots of time to pursue all his interests. The only thing, really, he had to do was prepare for the Sunday service and hold it and to see his parishioners; and he really loved that and seeing all the people around. Everybody in the neighbourhood, Protestants and Catholics alike, all loved him and they used to go to him with their troubles and ask his advice. As a lawyer, he was able to give them a certain amount of legal advice as well as other kinds of counsel. Oh, everybody was very fond of him. And he was able to do things for the community, too. He was able to start a tennis club. He organized dances in the diocese – each parish would take it in turn to entertain the other parishes. And he organized other outings and things for people in the parish and the diocese. He was diocesan secretary for twenty years or more and he did all the accounts and I suppose ran things. And everybody all around in the diocese and around the whole neighbourhood, they all loved my father. We heard a lot of praises and things about him after he died that we didn't even know anything about at the time – a lot of things he had done, how he had helped people.

This idyllic picture was marred by one incident from among the

---

[1] The charming seaport on an inlet of the Atlantic, on the west side of County Galway.

many violent activities of Sinn Fein in its efforts to terminate British
rule and achieve an independent Irish republic. George's church was
burned down during the night of July 19, 1922. *The Irish Times* of July
25 contained the following factual report:

BURNING OF PROTESTANT CHURCH
Roman Catholics' Protest

A meeting of the Roman Catholic people of Ahascragh and the adjoining
parish was held at Ahascragh, Ballinasloe, on Sunday, at which the Rev.
P.J. Shanagher, P.P., presided, to condemn the recent burning of the
Protestant church there.

The Chairman said that he was so affected by this outrage against God
and man that he could scarcely speak of it without being overcome by his
feelings. It was the work of demons in human form. It was a challenge not
only to human authority, but to God Himself, and the criminals would
soon stand before an outraged Saviour, who would take up the challenge.
It was the climax to many crimes, including public and private robberies
previously committed in the parish, not one of which would go
unavenged.

The following resolution was passed unanimously: 'That we, the
Catholic people of Ahascragh and adjoining parish, in public meeting
assembled, hereby express our horror and indignation at the unchristian
conduct of the wicked individuals who burned the Ahascragh Protestant
church; and we beg to offer our profound sympathy to the Rev. Mr.
Townshend and every member of his congregation, with all of whom we
have lived in the most friendly relations.

The more circumstantial and emotional account in *The Church of
Ireland Gazette* of July 28, although unsigned, is clearly from George's
hand; his style is unmistakable.

KILLALOE, KILFENORA, CLONFERT AND KILMACDUAGH
Ahascragh

Many of us in this part of the West have lived of late the life of the hunted.
We have suffered many things, and have been afflicted with the uneasy
sense that there was worse to come. But that which has happened is what
no one expected. Nobody dreamed of the malicious destruction by fire of a
church. And if there are any churches which might well look for special
immunity from such a fate or such a fear, Ahascragh Church is surely one
of them. Protestant and Catholic in this quiet Galway village have always
lived in amity, and have co-operated with one another in many ways. The
large landowners of the parish enjoyed always a reputation for justice and
generosity to their tenants, second to none in Connaught. 'They never
quenched a hearth,' is the current tribute to their record. Yet on the night
of Wednesday, July 19, the parish church was maliciously set on fire, and
the Protestants awoke in the morning to find their beloved and beautiful
church burned to the ground. Nothing remained of the edifice, of its

hallowed equipment and costly adornments, save the tower (its woodwork badly damaged), and the stark, blackened walls. While it stood, the church was one of the most beautiful in this part of Ireland, and was kept with the most scrupulous care. It has been enlarged and richly adorned in recent years, particularly through the tireless devotion and generosity of Lady Clonbrock. The west entrance with its archway of carved limestone and marble, the handsome roof of pitch-pine, the stained-glass windows, the organ, and the rare and wonderful mural mosaics, contributed to give the building its air of ornate and dignified beauty. The large entrance doors in the tower were a memorial to the late Rector, Canon Hunt; and the interior was embellished with many special gifts and with memorials to the chief families of the parish, notably to the ancestors of Lord Clonbrock and of Sir William Mahon, Bart. Now, the accumulated offerings of generations of worshippers have been destroyed in a couple of hours by a gang of miscreants. The Catholic Priest and the respectable Catholics of the neighbourhood lost no time in making known their amazement and horror at the crime, and a meeting of protest is reported to have been held. The outrage is attributed to republicans, but no evidence is forthcoming, and no charges are likely to be made. No repudiations, no convictions, no amount of compensation can ever restore the beautiful and beloved church as it stood a few days ago, with its treasure of old associations and hallowed memories.

George, the gentle, kindly heart was appalled at this tragedy. Sir William Mahon professed himself stunned. There appeared to be no personal vindictiveness in the action, which was motivated by simple hatred – British and Protestantism being identified as synonymous. Irony once more enters George's story, for the Irish Free State had already been agreed upon and was established that same year and it was the Free State Government which supplied funds for rebuilding this Protestant Church.

Church services had somehow to be arranged. Further along the road towards Castlegar, the Mahon's estate, there was a derelict school house on part of Sir William's property called Weston. George seized with gratitude the offer of the use of it and parishioners moved in and cleaned it up. A trestle table and small platform served as altar and pulpit and George limited his sermons to ten minutes – with his watch on the table. The congregations endured this makeshift for four years and seven weeks.

The Church of Ireland Gazette of September 17, 1926 has the following account of the consecration of the new building. It is again written by George, unsigned, and with no mention of himself by name or the great part he must have played in holding his congregation together, maintaining friendly relations with the Catholics of the neighbourhood and getting the church rebuilt.

KILLALOE, KILFENORA, CLONFERT AND KILMACDUAGH
Consecration of Ahascragh Parish Church

Ahascragh Parish Church, which was destroyed by fire on July 20th, 1922, and has been re-built with funds supplied by the Government of the Free State, was consecrated by the Bishop of Killaloe and Clonfert on Tuesday, September 7th. The new building was designed by Mr R.C. Orpen. Erected on the old foundations, but remodelled in important particulars, the building has more than fulfilled the hopes of the community. In spite of the smallness of the funds available the church is a monument of artistic taste, and the architect's plans have been carried out with remarkable skill and conscientious care. The opening ceremony was impressive and in its main features had been carefully prepared. Certain details of the Sarum use were added to our very simple form; and the procession round the church, the approach to the west entrance, the Provost's opening of the door and carrying the key to the Holy Table, the Bishop's invocation of the Peace of the Father, the Son and the Spirit upon the House as he passed through its portals, contributed to the solemnity and dignity of the ceremony. There was a large attendance of clergy, who all took part in the Service, and the congregation gathered from the surrounding country filled the church to its utmost capacity. The music, under the direction of Mrs Townshend, was a special feature of the Service, the parish choir being supported by members of the choirs of Ballinasloe and Portumna. The strong and ardent emotions of gratitude and thanksgiving felt by all present and most of all by the parishioners of Ahascragh were voiced in the striking sermon of the Bishop, who drew his audience's attention to the deeper significance of the day's Service, and also found expression in the reverence and enthusiasm which marked the entire cermony throughout. The first Service to be held in the new church was that of Confirmation, which was administered by the Bishop on the day following the consecration. The candidates were presented by the Rector in the presence of a considerable congregation, and were confirmed by the Bishop, who delivered two impressive addresses.

During the time that the church was rebuilding, George wrote and produced a play for children entitled *The Fairies of Killupaun*. It was performed in the school house and Brian and Una were among the fairies. It is a charming piece of Irish folk-lore drollery, involving a leprechaun, an old man of the woods, the Fairy Queen and her attendants and the entanglements they manage to weave for three mortals, a girl, a boy and his mother – a sort of children's *Midsummer Night's Dream*. Today's children, knowing nothing of God, let alone fairies, might find it dull old stuff, but Ahascragh enjoyed it in 1926. Sir George Mahon's sister, the Hon. Mrs Crofton, made by hand a beautiful illustrated edition, the text in careful copperplate and every page illuminated by coloured drawings of country scenes, flowers, birds and insects, sprigs of leaves and the *dramatis personae*. The illustration on page 228 is of the title page.

THE FAIRIES OF KILLUPAUN

A PLAY IN 3 SCENES BY THE REV. GEORGE TOWNSHEND

DRAMATIS PERSONÆ

NORA CREINA   an Irish girl

DERMOT KAVANAGH   an Irish boy

Mᵣˢ KAVANAGH   his mother

MAD TEIG   an old man of the woods

THE FAIRY QUEEN

TROOPING FAIRIES

THE LEPRECHAUN.

SCENE 1.   KILLUPAUN WOOD   EVENING

SCENE 2.   SAME   NEXT DAY

A later episode gives another picture of happy family life. In 1935 George and Nancy felt it was time for Brian and Una to see London, so George undertook a locum tenens for the Vicar of a West Kensington church and the family moved into the vicarage at 29 Oriole Road for six weeks. Una again is our informant:

> When we arrived we found flowers in washbasins and jugs all over the place and lots and lots of fruit, particularly cherries. George Mahon had put all these things there for us. And then he phoned and told us he had bought a £5 car so that he could take us around. He had just come back from New York where he had been studying banking for a year and now was with some bank in London. He gave us a great time; he took us around all the various places and showed us London by night, took us to a Prom. concert and down to a beautiful little village in Surrey called Sheen; and took us to Cambridge, Eton, Windsor and I don't know where – we saw quite a lot of him.
>
> One time we were driving through Piccadilly Circus and George [Mahon] said, 'Oh, we're out of petrol'; he managed to coast into Piccadilly itself I think, and then we got out and pushed it into a side street and there was a policeman watching us and we were all laughing and we didn't know whether the policeman thought we were stealing the car or not, but he walked up and asked us what the trouble was and we told him and he told us where we could get some petrol. So my father and Brian walked off to get it, and I'm not sure if George went with them – I think the three men must have gone – and my mother and I were looking at shops around there. Fortunately it was daytime.

They called on Aunt Geraldine, who had married the poet Wilfrid Gibson (see page 15), and found them poor and happy in Hampstead. Aunts Hill and Mill (Hildegarde and Mildred), George's younger sisters, had teamed up to act as cook and housekeeper to a 'rich Jewish lady', Miss Lawrence, in hopes of saving enough money from their limited private means to make a trip to the Holy Land. Miss Lawrence took Brian and Una to the zoo. 'She was very generous and gave us lots and lots of tickets.' They were able to share this largesse with the children of a family whom they had known in Galway. Brian and Una were taken to see Lady Blomfield, who showed them the room Abdu'l-Bahá had occupied in her house in Cadogan Gardens.

George made the most of his considerable leisure. He read voraciously and his notebooks are filled with quotations and comments on the successive 'books of the day'. Einstein, Weigall, Toynbee, Carrel, Jung, anthropology, history, many Christian apologists, mystics – all were grist to his mill. His favourite historian seems to have been Lecky, whom he describes as 'careful'. He indulged his love of poetry, both study and composing; his criticism of Yeats in *The Genius of Ireland* won the approval of Bernard Shaw.[1] The fruits of his study of the romantic movement are seen in *The Dawn-Song of the Kingdom*, Chapter 10 of his final work *Christ and Bahá'u'lláh*, while Chapter 9 of that same book, *The Rise of Modern Europe*, is a brilliant condensation of his reading and perception of the forces leading to the present state of confusion and chaos.

One of his letters to Nellie gives a clear intimation of the comfortable, well-ordered life of study and contemplation which his position enabled him to pursue. 'My present daily routine is to start work with a cup of tea in bed very early [brought by a housemaid or other servant] to meditate or read till seven, write from 7 to 8 (still in bed) and then get up and start on domestic or professional jobs.' We shall revert to this when viewing his life in Dublin, after his resignation.

The Bishop of Killaloe's diocese was the united one of Killaloe, Kilfenora, Clonfert and Kilmacduagh, the cathedral being in Clonfert, of which George became Archdeacon in 1933. The many ecclesiastical offices he held during his twenty-eight years at Ahascragh, in addition to the incumbency of the parish, were:

1926 to 1932   Canon and prebendary of Kilteskill in Clonfert Cathedral; Canon of Kilquane.

1927 to 1947   Diocesan Secretary.

1932 to 1945   Canon of Tassagard in St Patrick's Cathedral, Dublin.

1933 to 1947   Provost of Kilmacduagh (the last to be appointed); Archdeacon of Clonfert.

1946 to 1947   Canon of Tipper Kevin.

It is apparent that he was heavily involved in Church administration, and not only in the diocese. The *Diocesan Magazine of Killaloe, Kilfenora, Clonfert, Kilmacduagh*, giving notice of George's retirement mentioned that 'He had the distinction of being twice appointed as Canon of S. Patrick's Cathedral, Dublin, once by the Cathedral Chapter and on the second occasion by the Bishop as Canon representing the Diocese of Killaloe.' These appointments imposed upon him the obligation to be 'Canon in residence' for two weeks every year, to preach a sermon in the cathedral, and he was expected to attend the national synods in the capital, as well as the diocesan, which were held in different parts of Galway.

In June 1942 he wrote to Nellie: 'The last weeks have been rather fussy. I've had a lot of business and committee meetings to attend to, and have had to do duty for sick neighbours and spend two weeks in

[1] See p. 244.

Dublin.'

In spite of all these appointments he found time for his prodigious work for the Guardian, for the writing of his own books and essays, and for an enormous correspondence. The volume of his correspondence is incalculable; fully a thousand letters, originals or copies, are in my possession. He was known as a dreamer, absent-minded, 'dear, vague, impractical Shend,' and yet in his letters and literary work he was the exact opposite. In writing he lived a different life from that known to the remote world of Galway. The astonishing thing is how he found time for it all.

There is no doubt that in his outward life he could have been cast as the archetypal absent-minded professor, so beloved of schoolboys. On one occasion, when Nancy was away, he asked Miss Dillon, before the Sunday morning service began, whether he could come to her for lunch afterwards. He was welcomed, but on arrival at Clonbrock informed her that he was keeping the Bahá'í Fast (which required him to abstain from food and drink from sunrise to sunset)! He apparently wanted to explain something to her, but as she confided to her friend, Mrs Crofton, she couldn't make head or tail of it. This anecdote perfectly illustrates the point emphasized earlier, that George, shy and overly-concerned for others, was often unable to pursue in person the relationships which he fostered so successfully with his pen.

On another occasion he forgot a christening which had been arranged and the anxious parents had to call at the Rectory to get him. Fortunately the church was only a minute's walk away and no great delay ensued.

His addresses to the diocesan Synods more and more became Bahá'í in character, in relation to the station of Christ and Christian teaching; he earned a few 'snubs and disappointments' but in general was listened to with respect and interest. We recall Nancy's second letter to Nellie in which she quoted the Bishop of Killaloe as saying, 'When the Archdeacon speaks he deserves to be listened to by all.' The many appointments and the demand for his services at refresher courses for the clergy and for lectures to the divinity students at Trinity clearly show his standing with the senior men of the church. His first books, *The Altar on the Hearth* and *The Genius of Ireland* had endeared him, not only to Church of Ireland people but to many Irishmen, Protestant and Catholic alike, who recognized his love for Ireland and his identification with its traditions and people. The printing in *The Church of Ireland Gazette* of his little booklet *'Abdu'l-Bahá: A Study of a Christlike Character*, with the subsequent request for its reprinting,[1]

See p. 122.

and the later publication of his two great books *The Promise of All Ages* and *The Heart of the Gospel* added to this sentiment admiration for his intellectual and literary achievements and for his presentation of new ideas, strange as many of them apparently seemed. This growing prestige was greatly increased by the brilliant review in the *Church of Ireland Gazette* for January 1940 of *The Heart of the Gospel*.[1]

This affection in which George was held generally is apparent from the charming note which he wrote for the November 1947 issue of the *Diocesan Magazine*. It appeared under the sub-heading, Ahascragh parish.

> It is not without much sadness that the Rector and his family leave the parish and the home and the neighbourhood where they have lived happily for so long a time: Friendships and acquaintanceships stretching over nearly 30 years create ties which are not lightly broken. And a clergyman's work is often connected with those emergencies (sometimes joyous, sometimes very much otherwise) in people's lives which strike very deep chords in our feelings.
>
> This little note is written as one way of expressing our appreciation and our gratitude for the many words and signs of real friendship which we have received and which have warmed our hearts very much. Especially we wish to thank very cordially those members of the parish and also those good friends and neighbours who are members of another Church than ours, who have organised and so generously contributed to the Presentation we have the privilege of receiving.
>
> It will be a lasting pleasure to have in our new home keepsakes of old friends, whose memory will always be cherished.

As the Second World War followed its destructive and horrible course, Ireland, though not a belligerent, began to suffer from shortages of fuel and food. George's letters to Nellie were eloquent of the distress: 'Supplies are rapidly getting shorter in Eire but we ourselves have not yet suffered in any way: my little store of tea and paraffin isn't quite exhausted! Imagine however the prospect – a country with no coal, no gas, no trains, no paraffin, no tea, and not enough fuel of any kind to go round, and a grave shortage of foodstuffs and of petrol.'

Nellie sent parcels of food[2] and small luxuries; some beads for Una

---

[1] See Ch. 15.

[2] One of the happy phenomena of the war was the wonderful outpouring of generosity from individual Americans. This began with the reception by people in Britain, who had friends or relatives in the United States, of parcels of rationed or unobtainable food. It soon became a planned war-time operation and eventually there was scarcely a household in Britain which did not receive some of these very acceptable 'gift parcels' from unknown Americans. It did more to promote friendship between the people of both countries than has ever been recognized. Spam became, among other things, the symbol of Anglo–American kinship.

and *Reader's Digest* 'which we all love'. One parcel arrived at the Rectory on November 12, the anniversary of Bahá'u'lláh's birth in Ṭihrán in 1817. George wrote at once:

This morning – an hour ago – your parcel arrived – wasn't it an appropriate day for a Bahá'í gift from overseas? And this letter is starting off at once to thank you. We've had great excitement over it. First, the long weeks of waiting, and now I assembled the family and made an occasion of it and we opened together the package and took out the contents one by one. The sweets ('candies') we'll reserve for Christmas (which is still a high family festival with us) but the tea won't last long. I hope to have some in my next brew, this afternoon. My wife is delighted with the paraffin which she never bought in this country, but which she once saw with a friend home from India. All the gifts will be very greatly appreciated, and you have given us a lot of pleasure over it already!

Early in 1942 he wrote:

Here the shortages are getting more serious, neutral as Eire is. The poor in the cities are suffering greatly and as the country is not well organised they don't get the relief they might. In the rural parts it is better: but tyres are now unobtainable, wheat is getting scarce, and cotton and even medicines and indeed many things, including tea! We've not been inconvenienced to any extent and I feel rather selfish over it: but one does not see much one can do. The want is off in the cities. One cannot send money, food or clothing out of the country. What a terrible plight! The poor faithless world!

By February the position had worsened:

Well, we are threatened with a bona fide famine in Eire now, a hundred days with no prospect of any flour at all before next harvest; and if you can send a few cargo ships of wheat they will find a welcome. But there's nothing at present we need, thanks indeed for the generous offer.

In May:

This country though neutral is suffering sadly now: tea rationed for a year and a half past at $\frac{1}{2}$ oz. a week (and the poor live on tea and bread, or used to!); fuel hardly obtainable in the cities, little cooking and little warmth possible; gas severely rationed; a flour famine threatened; electricity rationed and perhaps withdrawn from many uses; petrol short and all road transport except heavy commercial practically ended; the trains reduced to one each way a day, using turf and sticks and some bad coal for fuel and travelling at fifteen miles an hour with frequent rests along the way! . . . The transport difficulty is very grave; clergy and doctors are allowed a minimum of petrol so far but only for strictly professional calls, so we are all badly in the soup together! It may be impossible to move the harvest – the shortage is getting worse and worse: but the Government is beginning to look around, and I am sure nothing catastrophic will happen to us. The moral effects so far have been good, for our divisions are being exposed and removed and we are uniting in a common effort to save health and life as we never were united before.

His letter of June 29 related:

Public transport is reduced to a minimum; the trains have no coal and run on turf and wood, with the result it may take twelve hours or more to travel 100 miles. The engines get blocked up every few miles, and the train has to stop to let them cool off and be cleaned out. There are hardly any trains anyway. Private motoring is prohibited, and the electric supply is almost nothing. We now are all hermits, living almost as they did before the wheel was invented.

George's conviction that Ireland had a destiny to fulfil in guiding mankind to the 'Heavenly Jerusalem' brought to earth by Bahá'u'lláh, is clearly stated in the following prayer. It was originally published, in a different form, in *The Altar on the Hearth*, in the days when he was attempting to prepare the minds of Christians for the incredible news of Christ's return and the revelation of the Kingdom of God on earth, – without ever mentioning Bahá'u'lláh. This is his version of 1952, greatly revised for his collection of essays, poems and 'other literary pieces' published under the title *The Mission of Bahá'u'lláh*.[1]

FOR IRELAND

Look Thou, O Father, upon this land where once Thy Son's name set hearts on fire and His light shone in lonely splendour across the darkness of the west.

Now in this Advent of a mightier Day awake anew that power of vision, that readiness to answer Thy clear call. Make us on whom the fullness of the times has come, prove ourselves true heirs of all that is most heroic in our past. Use once again, but now for a yet larger end, the spiritual gifts Thou hast vouchsafed this people. Let them swiftly arise as one in common acclamation of the Day of Glory.

Thou hast in this Great Age ordained the nations of the west to bear to the world the Message of Thy regeneration of the whole human race. Guide, O Father in heaven, the people of this land to the path Thou hast appointed them. Kindle the flame of adoration in our hearts; teach us the joy of the soul's surrender to its God. Speed us on our forward way. In our share of service to this crowning Day of Days let us find at last the challenge and the meaning of our country's ancient title, Inisfail, the Isle of Destiny.

Ireland's present-day Bahá'ís have accepted George's vision of their destiny as a duty which they intend, and strive with all their might, to

[1] George Ronald, Oxford

accomplish. They are convinced that he sustains their effort from that constellation of 'three luminaries' described by the Guardian in his cable mourning George's passing.[1]

It seems fitting to conclude this chapter on George's life as a Christian priest with the following excerpts from the tribute paid to him by his successor, Cecil Burrows, Archdeacon of Clonfert, in the little church at Ahascragh, which George had had to rebuild after the fire and which was the centre of his professional life for twenty-eight years:

. . . one who not only held the love and respect and trust of all who had the privilege of knowing him and working with him, but who carried with him all our good wishes and affection when he went away. We all knew George Townshend as 'The Archdeacon', and it is as such that we continued to think of him even after he relinquished that office . . .

. . . at heart he was a student, ever searching for the truth of God as revealed in this world – in creation and in the hearts and minds of men. He believed that God revealed His Truth in many ways and through many channels. He believed that no one particular Church or system of religious thought contained the whole of that vast Truth – that each system of thought had its own particular revelation to help its followers to reach the Eternal God. He studied those systems exhaustively, and from them gained much that illumined his own thinking. He was, in fact, an authority upon what we call 'Comparative Theology'. Some shallow people might possibly conclude from that that he was disloyal to the Church that gave him birth – the Church in which he held Holy Orders – but no one who knew George Townshend could possibly accuse him of either disloyalty or insincerity. The horizon of his thinking was far above and beyond any stereotyped system of thought which we popularly call religion. Generous in his attitude to all philosophies he extracted from them all that was best and noblest and most satisfying, and added it to his store of Truth. Most of us, in our search for God try to interpret our revelations in terms of the particular system of thought which bears our own specific label. We are, in fact, more concerned in loyalty to our Church than in loyalty to the great God which can be confined in no Church. We set out with fixed ideas and try to relate what we find *to* those ideas – to bend and mould and prune them till they fit into our own ready-made system. But not so George Townshend. He set out with an open mind – free and unbiased – and was himself moulded by the Truths that were revealed to him. Each new thought he sifted carefully and examined meticulously before he finally accepted or disregarded it. Each one that he accepted was like a new window through which more and more of the glorious light of God filtered into his mind and soul. He was, in fact, one of those rare thinkers, – an honest searcher after Truth. The Psalmist says in our Text, 'Blessed are those who seek him with their whole heart'; and that is what George Townshend did.

See p. 365.

Chapter 13

THE WRITER

THE world has not yet recognized George Townshend's literary achievement because it does not read him, being uninterested – for the moment – in his subject. The Bahá'ís love him for his sacrificial life, learn from him and rejoice in his spiritual attainment; but how many realize that we have had among us a major literary figure, undoubtedly to take his place, one day, among those other Irishmen who form so large a company in the pantheon of English letters.

This neglect is the world's response to George's renunciation of it, and will surely be repaired when the world comes to know that he chose the better part. Even then it is likely that his spiritual station will overshadow his scholarship and greatness as a writer, though, like St Paul or the Psalmist, he may ever be read for edification and delight.

His *oeuvre*[1] comprises three major works, a vast number of essays, prayers, meditations, commentaries, reviews, a few poems, and his Introductions to Shoghi Effendi's *God Passes By* and edited translation of *The Dawn-Breakers: Nabíl's Narrative of the Early Days of the Bahá'í Revelation*. The association of these Introductions with the works of the Guardian of the Faith is an even firmer assurance of the immortality of George's memory, but in themselves they would add distinction to any anthology of that most brilliant coterie, the English essayists. They are among his finest work.

His great literary ability was compounded not only of love for the English language and a gifted style but a deep knowledge of literary forms, of construction, of the great works in classical and European languages and a long training in the ways in which language could be used.

[1] A list of George's known works is printed as Appendix 5.

His literary style was no artificially developed technique but the natural expression of the man himself, and the perfect vehicle for his thought. Like himself, it was subjected to the discipline of his training and refinement. It is orderly, persuasive, orientated and smoothly running. Indeed, so easily does he read that the most tremendous concepts, whether of dire warning or heavenly vision, are received into the mind without a murmur. Only upon reflection does the reader realize that he has entertained such transcendent ideas, not as rhetoric but realistically. His expression is a remarkable reconciliation of spontaneity and restraint, forthrightness and moderation, impassioned outpouring and mildness. And in these reconciliations are seen two of the greatest qualities of this totally dedicated man, namely his senses of balance and propriety. He was relentless but never aggressive; longing for progress, impatient of delay, but never rebellious; distressed by the slights of a few former colleagues but never embittered; careful of his family responsibilities to the brink, but not beyond, of sacrificing his own integrity to their needs and desires; steadfast to the end but never unreasonable. His writing reflects these qualities.

The first ingredient of his style is his command of and facility with the English language. Ireland has for long written and spoken the best English and George upheld and enriched this tradition, developing an individual and characteristic style which is at once recognizable. Like his fellow-countryman George Bernard Shaw, he perfected a rhythm of triads:[1]

'Once, and only once, and for One only . . .'
'He was misrepresented, humiliated, frustrated . . .'
'Whatever the subject, whatever the occasion, whatever the need . . .'
'. . . wonders greater, mightier, more beneficent . . .'
'The theme on its human side is that of Love and Struggle and Death.'

At times he used it contrapuntally:

'As Nature, having borne with patience the lightning and thunderbolts and storms of winter, is afterwards rewarded with the season of blossom, flowers and fruit . . .'

He put this phrasing to many purposes – dramatic impact, flowing rhythm, heightened effect, and not once does it seem a technical device

[1] Dr Seasamh Watson of the School of Celtic Studies, Trinity College, Dublin, informs me that this is an ancient Celtic form, particularly the alliterative triad. A splendid example is seen in Shaw's *Pygmalion* where Doolittle tells Higgins: 'I'm wantin' to tell yer, I'm willin' to tell yer, I'm waitin' to tell yer.' George's 'Once, and only once, and for One only' is the opening sentence of his brilliant essay 'The Genius of Ireland'.

but always the clear-flowing river of his thought.

His early letters to the Guardian have already revealed his intense interest in language itself,[1] but we must turn to his essay *The Language of the Commonwealth* to obtain a clearer picture of his deep scholarship in the subject and his keen apprehension of the forces affecting the development of any particular tongue. English was his own language and he accepted its discipline to the full, never conceding the debasement and bowdlerization it has suffered as an unofficial world language. But he was no pedant or diehard purist, as the following passages show:

> A modern language, if it is to meet the increasing requirements of this complex life of ours, must be a highly elastic and expansive thing. There is no language which has been put to so severe a test as English, nor is there any which has stood up to its work more stoutly or more successfully . . .
>
> Those words which form the core and heart of the language date back far beyond any known events of history. They go back to a time before the ancestors of the Germans and English and Dutch and Scandinavians had separated and while they still spoke a common language: back yet further to a still more distant age when all the European peoples (Celts and Latins, Slavs, Teutons, and Greeks) lived together; back ultimately to a period out-dating Babel, when the Hindus and Persians and the peoples who now inhabit Europe shared a single primitive language, and a single civilisation.
>
> Those distant ancestors whom we have in common with so many now sundered peoples, lived somewhat as the patriarchs of the Old Testament lived, and had words to cover all they knew of nature and human life: such words as 'night' and 'star', 'dew' and 'snow', 'wind' and 'thunder', 'father' and 'mother' and 'daughter' and 'sister', 'hound' and 'ox', and 'wheel' and 'axle', and 'door' and 'thatch'. These primeval words, and a few dozen more of the same simplicity, have come down through all the unrecorded changes of time to this present day and hour. They form still part of the common vocabulary of many nations of the East and the West. And their presence in the vernacular of peoples now divided bears witness to the closeness of kinship which for long lay neglected and forgotten.
>
> This continual expansion of our vocabulary has often roused misgivings in the minds of scholars and of purists. It has not always been so managed – especially in recent years – as to be an unmixed advantage . . .
>
> Errors in word-formation have, too, called forth protests from those jealous for the purity of our English speech . . .
>
> The additions made during the last century, and especially during the last generation, have not been such as to rejoice the heart of the poet or to lend themselves to the use of the stylist. They have contributed nothing to the aesthetic quality of the language, and have, in fact, rendered it less euphonious than the 'English undefiled' of an earlier day . . .
>
> Nobody could say they were pleasing to the ear or to the eye. They are

[1] See pp. 55–8.

not suited for literary or aesthetic purposes but are blankly utilitarian. They illustrate the undoubted fact (now recognised more generally than ever before) that the development of a language through the influence of circumstance has its drawbacks and its dangers. The result may be at times to mutilate and to debase rather than to improve. If the intelligentsia could exercise more control than in the past they might in a degree prevent deterioration and increase effectiveness. Recent study of the processes of thought and of speech has indeed suggested that science may do more for a language than our forefathers knew or than conservative scholars to-day are ready to admit . . .

May not experts build a means of communication more simple, economical, and possibly more beautiful than any of our inherited forms of speech? . . . All modern languages are moving along the same path . . . All modern languages, for example, are learning to express meaning by the easy method of word-order rather than by that of changing the form of words. But English has carried this further than any other . . . To a greater extent than any other nation we have discarded many grammatical forms, have given up inflexions of nouns and verbs, using (instead of cases and tenses) prepositions and auxiliaries . . . More and more we succeed in expressing each separate thought by a separate word, and so lead other nations in achieving that exactness of language which is the product of a high civilisation.

He understood thoroughly the need for change, but, as the above extracts show, wanted it not simply for the sake of change but to answer the need of men, as their lives became ever more complex, for a more serviceable tool with which to express themselves, and therefore to think. For we think linguistically. He preferred to follow the way of 'all modern languages', rather than the rake's progress of using words to mean what you will or of inventing new ones with no basis in philology or tradition.

George had followed a rigorous training; he trod no royal road but knew the rigours and ardours and struggle of literary creativity. He worked almost in textbook fashion; made his outline, set the boundaries of the work, recorded his notes under each heading, established a sound foundation of content and fact and devised a structural form to bring all into relatedness and unity. Yet no technique could relieve the artist from the labour of living and wrestling with the plasticity of theme and language and form; but when the hoped for inspiration seized his pen, living English flowed from him like water from a mountain spring.

His approach to any theme is revealed in a letter of August 13, 1940: 'I find the administrative order a *much* richer topic than I ever imagined, but I have now got to the stage of sorting out ideas and composing a picture which is the necessary preliminary to actual writing. It is very hard . . .'

When an aspiring writer sought his advice about a new general introduction to the Faith, George replied:

> Your plan seems good but all will depend on how you carry it out. I would strongly advise you to plan the restricted area within which the whole narration and exegesis is to move. The subject is so rich, the material so immeasurable, the stage so full of striking figures and tremendous action, that unless you plot out the whole thing in its height and in its depth and in the round before you start you may get your argument confused. Plot out, too, the *proportions* of your material.
>
> Your sketch of the Teachings, e.g., should anticipate the chapter on the Administrative Order, and be largely in that plane; and avoid straying off into metaphysical mysteries.
>
> I wish you great joy in the composition and great success with the book.

The Professor of English speaking!

Writing was his natural medium, like water to a fish. In it he was uninhibited by shyness, conventional manners, humility or over-sensitivity to others. He knew his way with the written word and could make it serve his purpose. He made and nourished enduring friendships through hundreds of letters, intimate relationships he never could have made in person. With this natural facility and his legal training he was able to marshal his argument on whatever theme he was discussing – were it *Irish Mythology* or the mysticism of *Hidden Words* – and present it in a clear, persuasive and attractive manner. In speech his modesty and shyness inhibited him; the thought processes were doubtless the same but without pen and paper he was a painter without a brush, a potter without clay.

He never underestimated the magnitude of the task facing a would-be writer. He knew the physical labour, the constant conscientious effort, the discipline, which all artists must accept before the god smiles on them. As early as 1910, in his essay on Mormonism,[1] he wrote of the 'considerable business of literary composition'. Thirty years later he commented in a letter about a new book he had in mind, *Builders of a New World*, 'You will like it! (An author has to think this or he could not face the physical effort of writing!)' About the same time, 'I have written two pamphlets, both bad and torn them up.'[2] Very typical is his letter of December 9, 1938, relating to the final chapters of *The Heart of the Gospel:*

---

[1] See pp. 24–5.

[2] Not everything he discarded suffered so precipitately. His letter of September 29, 1934, to Mrs Stuart French, Secretary for many years of the Editorial Committee of *The Bahá'í World*, records: 'Yes, certainly, I will be glad later to submit something for the *World* vol. VI. I am longing to see vol. V. My little article in it was the first chapter written for *The Promise*; but it didn't seem to suit the occasion, so was sent up for the *World*.' In vol. V it was entitled *The Descent of the New Jerusalem*. This is an excellent

I am toiling over them with great delight but progress is slow chiefly because the notes I made some months ago prove to be very inadequate.

Truths flash on one quickly; but one then must find their bearings, and then coordinate them – and this can not be done except by patience and persistence. It is useless to try to hurry. The labour of welding things together into a continuous flow of argument and of putting them in such a way that they will become clear to other people, cannot be avoided.

On top of this cause of slowness, I am constitutionally a slow worker: more's the pity, but I can't help it.

'I am a slow worker' was confided to many correspondents; to one or two, he described the more harassing experience of the results of slow and painful work being upset by the unexpected emergence of a new conclusion or a slight shift in viewpoint. Other troubles beset the ardent author; he wrote on August 16, 1939 'I strike out some great theme and then write a trivial book on it. I have great fun while I am working and then only disappointment and humiliation when I see what I have done.' However, he wrote to Nellie a year later, 'I need not tell you it is very hard work: but when it is done it will look quite simple, as if I wrote it straight off the reel.'

Shoghi Effendi's opinion of George's style, often expressed, is nowhere better revealed than in his personal postscript to a letter of late January 1931. George had sent the Guardian a copy of *The Genius of Ireland* and in thanking him Shoghi Effendi wrote, 'I wish the style of the narrative [*The Dawn-Breakers*] and particularly my rendering of it were half as vivid and appealing.'

Mrs Dorothy Ferraby has kindly permitted the use of notes made by her husband, the late Hand of the Cause John Ferraby when he was on pilgrimage during January 1955, two years before George's death. Among the Guardian's comments, recorded by Mr Ferraby are the following:

> I want you to give a message from me to George Townshend. He must take care of himself, husband his strength, and not exhaust himself with his writing. His services are greatly valued.
>
> He is the best writer we have. He must be taken care of. He is the best living Bahá'í writer. It is good that in spite of his frailty he is still able to write.
>
> He is the pre-eminent Bahá'í writer.

The great, the overwhelming vision of his life, the centre of his thought, the pole-star of his soul, was the appearance of the Promised

example of the 'considerable business of literary composition'. The first essay is a fine didactic presentation of the Bahá'í message, and stands by itself; it could never have led so majestically into the 'grand redemptive scheme of God' as does *The Epic of Humanity*, which is the eventual first chapter of *The Promise,* written after more reflection and wrestling with his theme.

One of all ages, and all his writings on this theme, or even connected with it, pulsate with a higher tempo, a spirit of excitement, an intimation of impossibly glorious things which have yet been vouchsafed to men on earth. When dealing with the vast kaleidoscope of history, which he saw as the 'grand redemptive scheme of God' to bring mankind to its fore-ordained destiny, he wrote in transcendental and apocalyptic terms, perfectly suited to his high theme. Never grandiloquent, rhetorical or turgid, this grand manner is always clear and understandable, easily read and uplifting to the mind. The words are simple but the concepts sublime.

Every event, process, invention, development on this planet is related directly or indirectly to the unfolding of God's plan. This was George's subject, central to all his writings, and dazzlingly illumined for him by his knowledge that he, unbelievably, impossibly, was alive in the birth time of its fulfilment, recognized its truth and could dedicate his life to its witness. The theme is heavenly and only the transcendental concepts of apocalypse befit it.

That he could, and did, write in less exalted terms is happily demonstrated by the veritable spate of his shorter works, not yet gathered definitively but including a number of poems in various forms, one of which, his poem to Bahá'u'lláh, 'Only Beloved',[1] would alone ensure him eternal fame. The rather long essay, *The Genius of Ireland,* is a superb literary piece which, together with some others, *Irish Mythology, A Kinship in Genius,* his two Introductions to works of the Guardian's, *'Abdu'l-Bahá: A Study of a Christlike Character, The Hidden Words of Bahá'u'lláh: a Reflection, The Sufferings of Bahá'u'lláh, Bahá'u'lláh's Ground Plan for World Fellowship,* and *The Old Churches and the New World-Faith,* shine out like stars in the firmament of his literary works.

Early in his marriage he wrote a poem, in the style of Milton's *L'Allegro,* celebrating the birth of his son, Brian, and paying a nice compliment to Nancy. Its lines are captivating:

> Often with enchanted pleasure
> Have I sped an evening's leisure
> Taking to me for a guide
> From my lonely fireside
> Homer or Scheherazade
> And the wondrous tales they made
> Of a world beyond the dawn
> Where magic and her brood were born.

[1] See p. 318.

Or:

> Marvel treads on marvel's heels
> Till the dizzy Reason reels
> And e'en Fancy is perplexed
> Wondering what can happen next

Nature was ever an inspiration to George:

> And a thousand harmonies
> Softer sweeter more endeared
> Than my heart had ever heard
> Gush fróm every bank and rise
> Fill the woods and touch the skies.
> Wind and cloud and leaf and stream
> Notes of purest music seem
> And all Nature like a choir
> Tunéd to the sun-God's lyre
> In new hymns of jubilee
> Chants her ancient ecstasy.

This is not far from the great master's '. . . notes, with many a winding bout, of linkéd sweetness long drawn out.' But all this is preliminary to the main theme:

> Yet the flowing cup of bliss
> Holds more precious wine than this.
> Our sweet rapture did but screen
> Brighter glories yet unseen;
> 'Twas a distant fragrance blown
> From a Garden yet unknown.
> Love has pierced the mystery
> Hid within the prophecy
> Of the heavenly poets who said
> 'By a child shall they be led,'
> 'From a babe is wisdom gained
> From the weak is strength ordained.'
> By some mightier miracle
> Than any feigne'd charm or spell
> A little smiling newborn boy
> In his gift will hold more joy
> Open glimpses of a heaven
> More remote from earth than even
> That enchanted land we knew
> Where all fairy-tales came true.
> Now when e'er I gaze upon
> This my loved and loving son,
> When beside his bed I keep
> Watch o'er his elysian sleep

> When I fold him in my arms
> Nestling safe from all alarms
> Or behold his innocence
> With a sinner's reverence –
> Lo, an infinite high hope
> On my longing 'gins to ope!
> With this tiny hand to guide
> We will leave the cold earth's side
> And faring far and far away
> Beyond the springs of night and day
> Will travel to the end the road
> That bears all lovers up to God.

Only a true poet can make rhyme and strict rhythm serve his purpose in such a seeming easy flow of highly disciplined couplets, almost all of which can stand by themselves; for instance,

> 'Twas a distant fragrance blown
> From a Garden yet unknown.

or:

> 'From a babe is wisdom gained
> From the weak is strength ordained.'

George's essay *The Genius of Ireland* is a model of distinguished excellence which might profitably be studied by all aspirants to English authorship. It excels in four aspects. The contents are fascinating; the craftsmanship makes it a work of art; it contains brilliant literary criticism; it is beautifully written. Bernard Shaw commented on the last two items as *The Irish Times* reviewer noted: 'It shows some courage on the author's part to have submitted his work to the discriminating, if sometimes devastating, genius of Mr George Bernard Shaw; but Mr Shaw is emphatic with regard to its merits.' Shaw wrote to George, 'It is very well written in our Irish manner (the only classic manner still in use), and the critical part about the poets is excellent, with the right quotations.' The reviewer himself declared, 'The appreciation of Yeats and A.E. is noble, and the insight of the criticism entitles it to attention.', so we had better examine it. But first the theme, to which the literary criticism is contributory.

'Once, and only once, and for One only' has Ireland been the leader among the nations of Europe. Her 'one constructive achievement in international history' was neither in the fields of politics, economics, commerce or administration, but was distinctively religious. The story of her pre-eminence in the spread of Christianity during the sixth, seventh and eighth centuries, is briefly told, enlivened with a

From Bernard Shaw.

4, WHITEHALL COURT 1:30 LONDON, S.W.1
PHONE: VICTORIA 3160
TELEGRAMS: SOCIALIST. PARL-LONDON.

14ᵗʰ Novʳ 1930

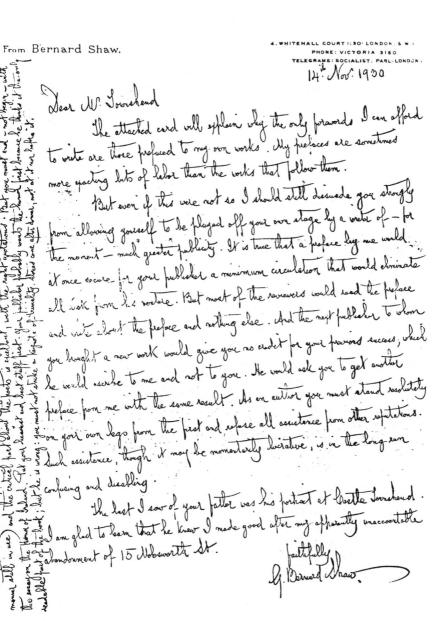

Dear Mʳ Townshend

The attached card will explain why the only forewords I can afford to write are those prefaced to my own works. My prefaces are sometimes more exacting bits of labor than the works that follow them.

But even if this were not so I should still dissuade you strongly from allowing yourself to be played off your own stage by a writer of — for the moment — much greater publicity. It is true that a preface by me would at once secure for your publisher a minimum circulation that would eliminate all risk from his venture. But most of the reviewers would read the preface and write about the preface and nothing else. And the next publisher to whom you brought a new work would give you no credit for your previous success, which he would ascribe to me and not to you. He would ask you to get another preface from me with the same result. As an author you must stand resolutely on your own legs from the first and refuse all assistance from other reputations. Such assistance, though it may be momentarily lucrative, is in the long run confusing and disabling.

The last I saw of your father was his portrait at Castle Townshend. I am glad to learn that he knew I made good after my apparently unaccountable abandonment of 15 Molesworth St.

faithfully
G. Bernard Shaw.

P.S. I have had time for only a very hasty glance through the book. It is very well written in our usual manner (the only decent manner still in use) and the critical part about the facts is excellent, with the right questions. But you must and in not begin with the essay on the human of Ireland. Tell your leader and best stuff first. Your publisher probably wants the usual first because he feels it the only readable part of the book; but he is wrong: you must not shirk a height of humility. Dried ore, after dinner, not at our breakfast.

A letter from George Bernard Shaw to George

hundred human and historical anecdotes. But historical circumstance
was only half the cause of this great efflorescence of Irish genius; the
other half was the Irish temperament, which

> was – and is – markedly spiritual. Had there not been latent in those Irish
> tribesmen mental potencies of a rare order, the Message which St Patrick
> brought could never have kindled so quickly so great a fire, nor could a
> religious achievement so brilliant ever have been accomplished nor
> undertaken. To-day, as then, the Irish character – taken at its truest and
> best – is of a mystical cast. This special gift is not confined to any one class
> or to any one school of thought. Sometimes it is developed; more often it is
> not. But the sympathetic observer may, without search, see it as a
> tendency, an inclination, a dormant power, on every side, even among the
> most poor, the most obscure, the most remote.
>
> That ancient gift of spiritual intuition is with us still, though there
> would be little wonder if it had vanished. For what is there remaining to us
> from those old days – what but the hills and the winds and the ruins of
> sculptured stone? . . .
>
> But the old spirituality has not been dissipated. . . .
>
> The world at large is ignorant of the true character of the Irish. . . .
>
> It allows to the Irishmen and Irishwomen quickness of mind and gaiety
> of spirit. In its romances, it likes to give to its heroines a dash of Irish
> blood. It regards humour and drollery as the peculiar national
> characteristic, and it has fixed into its imagination as a type to set beside
> John Bull and Uncle Sam the figure of the stage Irishman. . . .
>
> But these false impressions are rapidly disappearing. . . .
>
> For the past fifty years or so we have had in Ireland a brilliant revival of
> letters, which has been written about in many lands as an Irish
> Renaissance. And in the work of this Renaissance no human quality has
> found such general or such felicitous and ardent expression as that of
> spirituality.

Now comes 'the critical part about the poets':

> A country's poets give the highest expression of the national character
> [and] one of the traits which is seen at once to mark the Irish writers is the
> vividness and ardour of their religious feeling . . .
>
> The two finest and most famous of Irish poets are, however, those in
> whose works this spirituality shines out with the greatest brilliance and
> power. It is to both Yeats and A.E. the one dominant thought, the one
> central theme. The hero of their verse is not man the mortal, but man the
> immortal, and their sadness is that of a spirit ill-content to dwell in a house
> of clay amid a world of illusions. Yeats has spoken of 'the disembodied
> ecstasy' of A.E.'s verse, and no two words can better describe its special
> quality . . . His verse is, in an extraordinary degree, aetherial, and its ideals
> of human life noble and august. He loves his country, but has no patience
> with those who are slaves of the embittering traditions of history. Of
> himself and those who think like him he says:

We are less children of this clime
Than of some nation yet unborn,
Or empire in the womb of time.
We hold the Ireland in the heart
More than the land our eyes have seen,
And love the goal for which we start
More than the tale of what has been.
We would no Irish sign efface,
But yet our lips would gladlier hail
The first-born of the coming Race
Than the last splendour of the Gael.
No blazoned banner we unfold,
One charge alone we give to youth,
Against the sceptred myth to hold
The golden heresy of truth. . . .

A.E. looks out upon a world full of unhappiness, and he sees human sorrow as springing always from men's forgetfulness of their divine origin and of that high estate which once was theirs before they descended into this world of matter. 'We dwindle down beneath the skies, and from ourselves we pass away.' They who forget they are from everlasting spiritual beings invoke misery. The remembrance of this truth brings an inward joy which lies 'far beyond earth's misery' and is the one road to real dominion and self-completion . . .

A.E.'s *Collected Poems* include more than two hundred and thirty pieces, and George comments that

The treatment of a theme so vast and rich in so many brief lyrics leaves, perhaps, on the reader a sense of fragmentariness . . . The view of life and of the universe which A.E. presents is taken from the Upanishads. The mythology which he employs is Celtic. Those readers, therefore, who are trained in the classical tradition of the West may find themselves here in a strange world. But the poet's facility, the splendour of his language, the delicacy of his colour-sense, the occasional magic of his descriptive phrases, attract and charm; and no reader can be unmoved by the magnanimity and loftiness of the poet's thought. Technically the work does not always show infallible clarity and finish. The poet seems a genius first, an artist in the second place. Yeats, on the other hand, is a genius in the second place, an artist first . . .

George devotes the major part of his essay to Yeats, a consideration befitting Ireland's premier poet. He tells of his passionate devotion to Beauty, whose dwelling places he portrays in his larger works as 'some imaginary land beyond the known borders of the world – in *The Wanderings of Oisin* it is the Isle of the Blessed; in *The Land of Heart's Desire* it is the realms of Faery; in *Where There is Nothing* it is the heaven of the mystic's faith . . .' Man's striving to reach this other world of beauty is the perpetual plot of these poems, but George does not fail to trace and comment upon Yeats's changing perspective: 'In his youth his fancy broke its leash, and he revelled in the delights of his dream-Elysium. His hero of this period, Oisin, escapes forthright from earth and rides with a fairy bride to the Isle of the Blessed, and the poet fills almost the whole of his poem with enraptured descriptions of that wonderful world.'

Approaching middle age, *The Land of Heart's Desire* is not so easily attained; Maire Bruin only escapes 'this dull world' after hard and bitter struggle and renunciation of earth's ties. When he is 'come to fifty years' the brightness of his vision has faded and the hero of *Where There is Nothing* has an even harder journey to a Paradise of which he knows nothing and of whose existence he is sometimes in doubt; his goal remains unknown until the final moment when 'as he drops dying beneath the stones of the mob, he cries "I go to the sacred heart of flame," and finds his soul's desire through martyrdom.' Yeats's attempt to find some gain in this dimming of his vision was poignantly expressed in his lines,

> Through all the lying days of my youth
> I swayed my leaves and flowers in the sun;
> Now I may wither into the truth.

George asks pertinently, 'What, then, is this truth which has come when joy is gone?' Can the pen which charmed all hearts with a story of that 'Land of Heart's desire where beauty has no ebb, decay no flood', have written,

> How shall I know
> That in the blinding light beyond the grave
> We'll find so good a thing as we have lost?
> The hourly kindness, the day's common speech,
> The habitual content of each with each,
> When neither soul nor body has been crossed.

Apparently so. But he knows his loss and cries out, 'O, who could have foretold that the heart grows old!' George laments, 'What is an Irish poet who has lost his idealism? He is as a saint without the knowledge of heaven, as a scholar without the knowledge of the earth.'

But George, as always, was optimistic and encouraging, and Yeats was a mere sixty-five. 'But Mr Yeats has not spoken his last word . . . Before he lays down his pen he will, of a surety, see once again the gates of pearl cast wide, and, in fuller, stronger tones than ever before, will sing in his old age the glories of the Land of the Ever-Young.'

He now brings his argument to its highest pitch and launches into a splendid peroration, which discloses the whole purpose of his essay, and leads into the final paragraph which, however moderately stated its premises, however restrained the expression of its hopes, rings like a peal of bells calling the believers to victory. Not only have A.E. and Yeats brought honour to the name of Ireland throughout the English-speaking world but they have, 'in a dark and doubting age, upheld, with power and persuasiveness, the cause of idealism and of spirituality.' By their identification with the revival of letters in Ireland, the special qualities of their poetry have been regarded, not merely as personal, but as typical of the genius of the Irish people.

Their greatest and most splendid quality is one which they inherit from Ireland. Their power of vision is an Irish gift. It marked the Irish long ago, and it marks them now. . . . It is not their privilege to sing of themes unknown or strange to the Irish people, but rather to give utterance to aspirations which many among the Irish felt, yet none but themselves can put in music or in words. Indeed, what these two men have achieved might well be impossible had they not had the spirit of the people with them. For they have done something which, in the realm of letters, is comparable with the work of an ancient Irish missionary in the realm of religion. In an age when the Philistines have captured the Ark of Beauty, when most poets sing of earthliness and shadows and despair, here are two Irishmen singing, in strains of rapture and desire, tidings of joy and light and loveliness.

> Men yet shall hear
> The Archangels rolling Satan's empty skull
> Over the mountain tops.

is continually the burden of their song. And where else in the wide world to-day will this be found as the characteristic and dominant note of a nation's contemporary verse?

The Irish have long desired a place among the peoples of the world and an opportunity for national self-expression. That opportunity now has come. It has come, indeed, in almost extravagant measure . . . The Roman poet long ago proudly voiced his country's renunciation of the pursuit of Beauty and of Truth, of the arts and the sciences, and proclaimed that the imperial glory of the Caesars lay in the military conquest of the world. The larger nations of to-day may – if they will – pursue some such ambition. For the humble and the weak, such as ourselves, another path invites. If this little land of ours is to play, indeed, a useful part among mankind, it will not be in the field of commerce, nor in the arts of administering vast areas or complex commonwealths. Rather it may be – if anywhere – in the realm of the mind and the spirit. No service to mankind can be higher than that which may be rendered by religious intuition and the faculty of vision; and now there lies before the Irish such an opportunity of using these gifts as has not appeared for a millennium. If they fail, the blame can no longer be laid on hostile conditions nor on other people. If they succeed, they will prove themselves not unworthy heirs of a great tradition. That which has been done in Ireland during the last ten years will not permit anyone to sentimentalize the Irish character. The name of honour which Ireland once won is used often now in mockery of our present state. But a high and rare capacity for spiritual attainment is assuredly ours. It has but to be used. Our poets have led the way; they have sounded the *reveille*. Now it is for others to walk by the path of the Spirit into heavenly places, and continually to see and declare a fuller and fuller vision of God and His truth.

To consider that this great gift of spiritual sensibility belongs in a marked degree to the Irish: to look back on a distant past and see how the religious genius of the people made this lovely island once the shrine of Western Europe: to realise that still there burns deep in the dumb heart of the people that ancient fire: to hear to-day in our midst the voice of poets beginning to raise again the strain so long unheard, and the chant in the ears of a forgetful world the praise of eternal beauty and eternal truth: thus to watch, to listen, and to reflect is to be filled with hope that Ireland may not be slow to catch the vision of a breaking day, or to hear the tidings already breathed from on high, and that she may do for mankind now such service as her saints and scholars did for Europe long ago.

The Irish Bahá'ís know full well the meaning of that 'vision of a breaking day', the tidings breathed from on high, and have taken as their mandate George's hope that Ireland will now do for mankind 'such service as her saints and scholars did for Europe long ago'.

The Genius of Ireland has been examined at such length as being the most brilliant of all George's brilliant essays. But the others which comprise his eponymous book must certainly be mentioned. We have already dealt with *The Language of the Commonwealth;* the remainder are *Irish Humour, The Beauty of Ireland* and *A Kinship in Genius: The English Poet-Prophets*.

Irish Humour, though replete with funny stories and incidents, is by no means a mere compendium of such. It opens in George's mild satirical vein, calling upon the Ministers of State of the new, free, independent, protectionist Ireland to examine the rumour that Irish humour is vanishing, and if found to be true, by some further measures of protection prevent its total disappearance. This is the only known instance in all George's work of even so slight an incursion into political persiflage. Perhaps this essay may become renowned as the repository of the best of his own half-conscious 'bulls': 'We do not think of Milton as an hilarious person . . .'!

The Beauty of Ireland was published serially one summer by *The Church of Ireland Gazette*. It deals not so much with the sensuous

beauty of the Irish countryside as with the distinct advantages for men
of living in the country, and does not fail to suggest the greater
spiritual health conferred thereby. 'Jesus Himself was country born
and country bred . . . His images are taken from the occupation of the
farmer, the vine-dresser, the fisherman, from the sunset or the veering
wind, from the beauty of the wild flower or the happiness of the birds.'
But he will have none of the 'God made the one and man the other'
nonsense – 'the most deceitful of truisms'. Towns are necessary to
man and he emphasizes that the Author and Designer of both Eden
and New Jerusalem is God. 'A town, as well as a garden, may be a
Paradise,' and the Bible shows 'that the Archetypal City is as beautiful
as Eden.' A time will come when men will build a city worthy of the
name, fit place for men to dwell in, but those 'who design and build it
will have gone to school to the Original and Supreme Architect and
will have learned how to turn the principles of His consummate
workmanship to the everyday uses of mankind.'

This last is perhaps George's most recondite allusion to the World
Order of Bahá'u'lláh, made in the days before he proclaimed it openly.

A Kinship in Genius: The English Poet-Prophets presents one of
George's major themes. Like a wide tributary swelling the flow of the
great river, the romantic movement in English literature, which
spanned the nineteenth century, was always, to George, 'The Dawn-
Song of the Kingdom', as he called it in *Christ and Bahá'u'lláh*. The
'soaring and majestic song' of the English romantic poets was Western
man's unconscious response to the dawning light of the new Day of
God. The brotherhood of man, the spread of universal civilization, the
happiness of nations was their joyful note, sounded by Burns and
Blake in the latter half of the eighteenth century and rising to a
tremendous crescendo as Wordsworth, Shelley, Byron, Browning,
Tennyson, hailed the rising sun whose growing warmth they sensed,
all unconscious of its actual appearance in the Revelation of
Bahá'u'lláh. From Robbie Burns's 'It's coming yet, for a' that,'
through Blake's *Jerusalem* 'In England's green and pleasant land' and
Wordsworth's 'Bliss was it in that dawn to be alive' to Tennyson's
vision of a united world 'When the war drum throbs no longer and the
battle-flags are furled / In the Parliament of man, the federation of the
world,' George traced this sensitivity of the poet soul to the New Age.
'Kinship in Genius' was written in the days when he was attempting to
'infiltrate from the rear' and not once does he mention the new
Message or the name of Bahá'u'lláh. But he declares forthrightly that
it was the long-anticipated Kingdom of God whose advent the poets
chanted. As in *The Altar on the Hearth* he showed that the conditions
foretold in the Bible had actually come about.

Tennyson died, and since his time there has been no open vision. The heavens are shut up. Instead of making peace men made a universal war. Nation rose against nation, class against class, children against their parents, wives against their husbands and husbands against their wives. Society was resolved into its constituent atoms and whatever discipline or order had existed was swallowed up in a raging chaos. Hope fell away, and a sense of impotence bred despair. The young took refuge in dissipation, and the old imitated, as best they might, the young. Instead of the progress and development the Prophets foresaw, Time has brought us decadence.

So dark are the portents of the time that the hearts of many thoughtful men fail them for fear. They are tempted to despair of the future, even of human nature. Satire and destructive criticism have become the vogue.

But the poet-prophets never doubted their perception; they wrote with assurance and clear vision.

That which they saw, that which they sang, that which filled their souls with joy and empowered them to thrill the hearts of all who 'had ears to hear' was the ancient and everlasting truth. The veritable victory of Him whose smile kindled the Universe, the beating of the sword into a ploughshare, the transmutation of men into sons of God, the appearance of a new heaven and a new earth, make up an Event which prophets have upheld in more ages than Blake's. But in the present age it is on the eve of accomplishment. The prophet now sees it in greater fulness and shows it forth in greater detail. The spirit which moves him is the same spirit, the vision is the same vision, the rapture which fills him is the same rapture, but now the destined transformation takes shape and outline. The changes that are involved, and the method by which these changes are to be effected and maintained, these now are left no longer indefinite or obscure. The unification of the peoples, the establishment of a world-order and of a central Parliament, the substitution of social justice for force, and the attainment of this universal metamorphosis not by an arbitrary decree but as the climax of an age-long process of race-education and race-development: all this, set forth of old in ecstatic images by the seers of distant times, is now proclaimed with a new precision and exactitude.

Christians will recognize the biblical references and Bahá'ís the phrasing of the Guardian's letters.

George's book quickly sold out and is now out of print, though the name essay was included in a compilation of some of his essays, poems and devotional pieces entitled *The Mission of Bahá'u'lláh*.[1]

Using this theme in *Christ and Bahá'u'lláh*, George attempted no literary criticism or analysis of the poet's mind, as in the essay under review. There his presentation, both of poet and quotation, is perspicuous, pertinent and brief. And the entire romantic movement, whether seen in the literature of Europe and America, the revival of

[1] George Ronald, Oxford 1952

adventism, the removal of age-old restrictions imposed on the Jews leading to their return to the Holy Land or 'the impulsion of a new spiritual force . . . a new spirit of hope and enterprise and happiness and creative vision' is directly attributed to the dawning influence of the Revelation of Bahá'u'lláh.

We have four of George's essays written before ever he heard of the Bahá'í Faith. They are: *Why I am not a Mormon, The Conversion of Mormonism, England's Atonement for Old Wrongs* and *Irish Mythology*. The first two are dealt with in Chapter 3. The latter two were contributed to the *Sewanee Review* when he was Professor of English at the University of the South. *Irish Mythology* is a superb piece, placing him at once among the greatest English essayists.

One of the finest qualities in all George's literary work is its integrity. Books have always been compiled from the work of research teams and attributed to one author who has done little more than put it together, and there is no great harm in that. But if we are to believe the current literary reviews, authors, now that publishing has been largely taken over by the financial combines, write what they are told. And that is very bad. George never wrote anything for publication from superficial knowledge. It was not just a case of 'doing his homework' but of becoming steeped in the subject, meditating upon it, considering the conditions and circumstances surrounding it, attempting to penetrate to the heart of it and grasp its reality. This approach to his work is strikingly apparent in his early essays on Mormonism, and even more so in the beautiful *Irish Mythology*. One feels his identification with those ancient people. He knows why they created those stories, what purpose they served; he grasps their inner spiritual truth and is able to relate it to universal, eternal principles. He frequently referred to his own spiritual preparation for writing on some particular subject, a process which became more necessary to him as he progressed on his mystical path. The nearer he attained to Truth or the knowledge of God – synonymous terms in his lexicon – the more profound became his study and the simpler the final exposition. Witness *Christ and Bahá'u'lláh*,[1] his 'crowning achievement', with which, over the years, he wrought and struggled and re-wrought and struggled again and of which Shoghi Effendi, on the testimony of the Hand of the Cause Amatu'l-Bahá Rúḥíyyih Khánum, said: 'lucid, readable, sound, convincing and challenging'.

We recall the doubts and difficulties he experienced with writing the Introduction to Shoghi Effendi's *Dawn-Breakers*,[2] because of his inability to identify with the social and religious assumptions and

[1] See Ch. 16.
[2] See Ch. 6.

conventions of a society so remote and unimaginable as nineteenth-century Persia. He had read every word of the manuscript, 'englished' it, responded to the Guardian's request for his advice and comment, and yet felt inadequate to the task. He would not refuse the Guardian and set out to build a bridge between the dark, cruel, fanatical heart of Asia and western concepts of progress, democracy and human rights. By revealing the close similarities between the Great Hero of Nabíl's Narrative, the Báb, and the Great Hero of Western civilization, Jesus Christ, he accomplished his task. His essay is an unqualified masterpiece.

Because of the anonymity which George requested, and to which the Guardian reluctantly consented, the Bahá'ís understandably thought, until 1980 when the Universal House of Justice announced the truth of the matter, that the Guardian had written the Introduction himself. Even so great a scholar as the late Hand of the Cause Hasan Balyuzi quoted a paragraph from George's Introduction as the dedication of his great work *Bahá'u'lláh, The King of Glory*[1] and attributed it to Shoghi Effendi. A closer consideration of the English manner of both writers makes it immediately apparent that neither could have written in the style of the other. The Guardian's vigorous, vibrant, galvanizing sentences, influenced by the majestic periods of Gibbon, are the antipole of George's urbane, gentle, softly flowing stream. The paragraph quoted by Hasan Balyuzi, when compared with a paragraph by the Guardian of similar length and on a closely related, if not identical theme, clearly illustrates this. The Guardian's paragraph is quoted on page 111, 'The call of Bahá'u'lláh . . .'; George's is the following:

> The humanitarian and spiritual principles enunciated decades ago in the darkest East by Bahá'u'lláh and moulded by Him into a coherent scheme are one after the other being taken by a world unconscious of their source as the marks of progressive civilization. And the sense that mankind has broken with the past and that the old guidance will not carry it through the emergencies of the present has filled with uncertainty and dismay all thoughtful men save those who have learned to find in the story of Bahá'u'lláh the meaning of all the prodigies and portents of our time.

Perusal of the four pre-Bahá'í essays noted above, reveals not only a developing style, culminating in the impressive maturity of *Irish Mythology,* but a difference between them and everything he wrote as a Bahá'í.

Of the first two essays which we have from his pen – the two on Mormonism – the second, *The Conversion of Mormonism* is by far the

---

[1] George Ronald, Oxford

more appealing. It has been discussed in Chapter 3, but is of interest now for its advance in literary values over the preceding *Why I am not a Mormon*. The first essay is a legal argument, clear and compelling but with none of the warmth or pleasure in his subject which characterizes all his other work. He may have written it from a sense of duty, appropriate to a missionary. It is dated 1907, a mere year after his appointment to the Provo Mission and before he could have cultivated the warm friendships among Mormons which he refers to in his second essay (1910). It has points of interest for us, however. His opening words, 'I would turn a Mormon today if I could believe its doctrines true,' is a resounding statement of what became, after his enlightenment, the motivating principle of his life – the search for Truth. He perceived other basic Bahá'í tenets through his Christian faith: the equality of men and women was to him a 'necessary corollary' of the universal Fatherhood of God, although when Bahá'u'lláh taught it, it was revolutionary to both East and West; he perceived in his study of history a progressive revelation of God to men, and knowing nothing of Muḥammad or the Báb or Bahá'u'lláh thought the process had culminated in the appearance of Jesus; he was convinced that God is one and would have none of the Mormon doctrine that 'man was also in the beginning with God'.

The Conversion of Mormonism is more mature, not only in a literary, but in every way. There is positive purpose as well as authority and one senses that the first four years of his new life and of real responsibility had brought to focus the undoubted powers of his natural endowment. A clever sixth former or theological student could have written *Why I am not a Mormon*; a mature man is the author of *The Conversion of Mormonism*.

England's Atonement for Old Wrongs is of the same quality as his second Mormon essay. He is erudite, objective and believes in the value of his bridge-building. But not until *Irish Mythology* do we feel the joy of his subject, his deep absorption in it, the warmth of his identity with 'the wide extent of human nature and human activity' which these ancient stories cover. 'Unless my judgement be misled by my kinship with the myths of my native land, we need an Aeschylus to give the myths of Lugh back to us again; a Homer to create anew the Red Branch heroes; a Euripides to write of Finn and Grania. I have faith enough in Ireland and Irishmen to believe that one day these poets will appear.'

The only reason that *The Genius of Ireland* may take precedence over *Irish Mythology* is that their author was able to predicate for the Irish genius an infinitely greater destiny than the renewal and celebration of the ancient Irish legends. The later essay is informed with a new knowledge. No longer need Irishmen turn to their distant past for inspiration. A glorious future beckons them, and the Day is at hand. They are called now to render again such service as they performed in Europe at the dawning of its youth. But *immensely exalted is this Day above the days of the Apostles of old.*[1] Now the wide world is open to them and the entire human race, at its coming of age, is in need of the genius of Ireland. Their own Hand has led the way.

This is the difference between George's pre-Bahá'í writings and everything he wrote after he had sent his *Surrender* to 'Abdu'l-Bahá. In all these latter works there is an air, a confidence, an overtone of informed purpose, no matter how indirectly pursued. His readers are encouraged to believe in wonderful things, that they have great capacities, that 'the power of God is now abroad among men in its fulness'[2] and will help them. 'What the early Christians did we can do.' His sole purpose in writing became to proclaim the Name and Message of Bahá'u'lláh and to do it in such a way as to relate His teachings to what people knew already, to their holy books and the fulfilment of the promises contained in them; to announce the actual initiation through the Revelation of Bahá'u'lláh of the new heaven and the new earth, and to arouse Christians to the special service expected of them by Christ, returned, as promised, in the glory of the Father.

The theme of a special summons to Christendom is one of his major ones, equal to the unity of history or the dawn-song of the Kingdom. His Introduction to *The Dawn-Breakers* had stressed the many similarities between the Revelations of the Báb and Jesus Christ, and noted the sympathetic attitude of the Christian physician, Dr Cormick. His Introduction to Shoghi Effendi's *God Passes By* takes up this theme in greater detail. He notes 'a conscious sympathy of Christians with the New Teaching, which was in marked contrast with the attitude of their Muslim neighbours.' He relates how the colonel of the Christian regiment detailed to carry out the execution of the Báb begged Him for relief from so heinous a task and tells of the 'remarkable miracle by which this prayer was granted, and the martyrdom of the Báb carried out by another regiment under a Muslim officer . . .' He shows how Bahá'u'lláh 'took the most vigorous steps possible to bring the Truth of the Age to the knowledge of the West and its leaders.' He summarizes the specific messages sent by Bahá'u'lláh to the Christian kings of Europe and His 'appeal to Christians', voiced in the Tablet to the Pope, to come forth and acclaim their Lord. He dwells on 'Abdu'l-Bahá's three-years' tour of

---

[1] From the Báb's address to His Letters as he sent them out to herald the Promised One. See *The Dawn-Breakers*, pp. 92–4 (US).

[2] *The Altar on the Hearth*

Europe and America after He was released from prison by the Young Turks, and His laying of the foundation-stone of the first Bahá'í House of Worship in the West, at Wilmette, on the southern shore of Lake Michigan, the heart of the North American continent.

He stressed this theme in nearly all his works. Chapter 1 of *Christ and Bahá'u'lláh* is *God's Call to the Christians* and the final paragraph of that book is his own impassioned appeal to Christian believers, made earlier in *The Old Churches and the New World-Faith* to cast away their conflicting dogmas and interpretations and throw themselves, heart and soul, into the Cause of Bahá'u'lláh. (See Chapter 16)

He sounded it again at the conclusion of his Introduction to *God Passes By:* 'But for the leading of the peoples into the Promised Land, for the spiritualizing of mankind, for the attainment of the Most Great Peace the world awaits the arising of those whom the King of Kings has summoned to the task – the Christians and the Churches of the West.'

Foremost Bahá'í writer, master essayist, critic, poet, teacher, George Townshend concentrated all his great talent, scholarship and fire of devotion to the realization of 'Abdu'l-Bahá's message to him: *It is my hope that thy Church will come under the Heavenly Jerusalem.*

Chapter 14

THE PROMISE OF ALL AGES

THE *Promise of All Ages*[1] has strong claim to be George's greatest work. It is written in his grand, apocalyptic style and benefits from the polishing – that process which he described as resulting in an appearance of easily flowing prose – which he bestowed upon it in his more leisurely days. It has the supreme advantage of having been edited for Bahá'í concepts and presentation of Bahá'í teaching by the Guardian of the Faith himself.[2]

Consider some of the chapter headings: *The Epic of Humanity; The Vigil of the Day of Days; The Entrance of the King of Glory.* It is entirely characteristic that he should depict the great climax of human history in such terms, for the whole story of humanity was to him the unfolding of the Divine Plan. The concluding chapters, *The Light of the King's Law* and *The Fire of the King's Love* describe correctly his own vision of the purpose of that vast organic process, culminating in the establishment of the Kingdom of God on earth, when God Himself shall rule His people, His will shall prevail here as it does throughout the universe, and the earth shall be filled with His knowledge and radiant with His love.

None of these terms was rhetorical. By the Kingdom of God on earth he meant not some vague, unrealizable green pasture in the far distant future, but a real world social order, now to be established according to God's age-old plan and Christ's promise and whose beginning he, George Townshend, wanted to see. The grand redemptive scheme was the sending forth of the Prophets, the Founders of the world's religions, to promote the spiritual evolution

[1] George Ronald, Oxford
[2] See pp. 112, 117.

of the race; *The Epic of Humanity* is the story of its evolution under the influence of the spiritual impulses released successively by these Manifestations of God; *The Vigil of the Day of Days* traces the vicissitudes of the eternal and universal hope of the appearance of that Great One who would establish the Kingdom four-square on this very earth which is our home; *The Entrance of the King of Glory* is the grand climax of the entire saga, the appearance of Bahá'u'lláh, Who took the government upon His shoulders and addressed the kings and rulers of the nineteenth century; *The Light of the King's Law* is Bahá'u'lláh's revelation of that World Order, with some indication of its principles, laws, social economy, constitution and *modus operandi* embodied in the *Kitáb-i-Aqdas,* His Most Holy Book; *The Fire of the King's Love* describes the dynamic of that glorious age of human felicity and fulfilment.

Consider the title itself. *The Promise of All Ages* is a statement of a known fact of history – the universal hope and vision in societies and civilizations of all times and stages of a great day when peace would reign and men would live as true brothers. This has been expressed more academically as 'Messianic hope' or 'the millennium' or such, but George's phrase rings with the simple hope of simple millions throughout the ages.

George was always ready to seize upon everything which would help bridge the gap between Eastern and Western assumptions and conventions and particularly anything which would present the new revelation in terms familiar to Western Christians. We have already seen how he pursued this path in his brilliant Introduction to *The Dawn-Breakers*, and that it was one of the main reasons why the Guardian was so eager for him to write it.[1] He followed the same course in his Introduction to the present work where he presents in some detail the appreciations of the new Movement expressed by so many of the intellectual, social and religious leaders of Europe around the turn of the century.[2] E.G. Browne, Sir Thomas Adams's Professor of Arabic and fellow of Pembroke College, Cambridge, had already achieved a front place among orientalists and was generally regarded as the foremost authority on Persian literature and history. George drew heavily upon him, as indeed must any writer on the origins of the Bahá'í Faith, for Browne recorded the only known account by anyone from the Western world of an interview with Bahá'u'lláh. This unique honour was conferred upon him in Bahjí in 1890.[3] George quoted the

[1] See chapter 6.

[2] See p. 260.

[3] See H. M. Balyuzi's *Edward Granville Browne and the Bahá'í Faith*, George Ronald, Oxford 1970.

full passage from Browne's introductory notes to *A Traveller's Narrative,* from which the following extract is taken:

. . . a second or two elapsed ere, with a throb of wonder and awe, I became definitely conscious that the room was not untenanted. In the corner where the divan met the wall sat a wondrous and venerable figure, crowned with a felt head-dress of the kind called *táj* by dervishes (but of unusual height and make), round the base of which was wound a small white turban. The face of him on whom I gazed I can never forget, though I cannot describe it. Those piercing eyes seemed to read one's very soul; power and authority sat on that ample brow; while the deep lines on the forehead and face implied an age which the jet-black hair and beard flowing down in indistinguishable luxuriance almost to the waist seemed to belie. No need to ask in whose presence I stood, as I bowed myself before one who is the object of a devotion and love which kings might envy and emperors sigh for in vain!

A mild dignified voice bade me be seated, and then continued: 'Praise be to God that thou hast attained! . . . Thou hast come to see a prisoner and an exile . . . We desire but the good of the world and the happiness of the nations; yet they deem us a stirrer up of strife and sedition worthy of bondage and banishment . . . That all nations should become one in faith and all men as brothers; that the bonds of affection and unity between the sons of men should be strengthened; that diversity of religion should cease, and differences of race be annulled – what harm is there in this? . . . Yet so it shall be; these fruitless strifes, these ruinous wars shall pass away, and the "Most Great Peace" shall come . . . Do not you in Europe need this also? Is not this that which Christ foretold? . . . Yet do we see your kings and rulers lavishing their treasures more freely on means for the destruction of the human race than on that which would conduce to the happiness of mankind . . . These strifes and this bloodshed and discord must cease, and all men be as one kindred and one family . . . Let not a man glory in this, that he loves his country; let him rather glory in this, that he loves his kind . . .'

Such, so far as I can recall them, were the words which, besides many others, I heard from Behá. Let those who read them consider well with themselves whether such doctrines merit death and bonds, and whether the world is more likely to gain or lose by their diffusion.

George cites Browne as listing twenty-seven accounts of the early days of the Bahá'í Faith published in the capitals of Europe, and he himself adds to this another dozen, including Lord Curzon, Tolstoy, Jowett, Forel, Vámbéry, Younghusband and 'an English princess', Queen Marie of Rumania. He quotes some of them. Professor Forel for instance, 'C'est la vraie réligion du Bien social humain . . . Je suis devenu Bahá'í. Que cette réligion vive et prospère pour le bien de l'humanité; c'est là mon voeu le plus ardent.'[1]

[1] 'It is the true religion of the Social Good . . . I have become a Bahá'í. My most

Having thus introduced his subject to Western audiences with such august references, he concluded with a brief account of 'Abdu'l-Bahá's journeys to Europe and America and an exposition of the Master's presentation of Bahá'u'lláh's message. He showed how greatly appealing was this presentation to Christian people, in confirming the divinity of Christ and setting out the teaching of the Gospel in modern terms, particularly and emphatically in relation to 'the most vital of all the causes in the world: the cause of peace . . .' Bahá'u'lláh's announcement that 'God had in this age fulfilled his ancient promise to mankind . . . that . . . universal peace would be attained and all nations would unite in founding a new world-civilization . . . has been taken as the subject of the present essay. It is worked out with special reference to our Christian religion, and is expressed in our Western idiom with sufficient clearness and candour (it is hoped) to represent faithfully the teaching of 'Abdu'l-Bahá.'

After his Introduction, Chapter 1, *The Epic of Humanity*, opens in his most exalted vein:

> Bahá'u'lláh revealed a sublime vision of human history as an epic written by the finger of God and proceeding along an ordered course to a climax, the nature of which was exactly defined before the story opened and the appearance of which at the date ordained by the Author no human misunderstanding nor opposition could prevent or postpone.

How beautiful! One single flowing sentence describing the origin, course and purpose of human history. It is a masterpiece of prose, and with it we are away on a new path, irresistible and exciting:

> He taught that human history throughout its entire length was an intelligible and connected whole, centring round a single theme and developing a common purpose. From the beginning of the cycle to the present day and beyond the present to the cycle's distant end, one master-scheme is by set degrees disclosed. The stage upon which the action moves forward is the entire globe, with all its continents and all its seas; and there is no race nor nation nor tribe nor even individual who has not a designated place in the unfolding of the Grand Design of God.
>   . . . The idea that the course of human events is directed by a stronger will and a clearer eye than man's to a predetermined end is found in more revelations than one. It is said to have been mentioned by the founders of all the world-religions.

He cites the Gospel, the Qur'án, the Bhagavadgita, which, 'long before there was a word for evolution, taught the God-guided

ardent prayer is that this religion may live and prosper for the good of humanity.' Forel had founded a 'scientific religion of the Social Good' and explained that when he met the Bahá'ís he let it slide and became a Bahá'í.

progress of history towards a distant but certain culmination,' declares that 'the Hebrew allegory of the creation of the world in seven days made a cryptic allusion to the procession of the world-religions and to the final consummation of God's full purpose in the Seventh Day, the day of maturity, completion and rest.' He shows how the prophets of the Old Testament 'lifted by inspiration into the eternal realm, would descry some sign or feature of the far-off Day of God, the fore-ordained climacteric of world-history' and attempt to describe in whatever terms their generation knew, or in metaphor, the unimaginable glories of their vision: '. . . they shall beat their swords into plowshares, and their spears into pruning-hooks: nation shall not lift up sword against nation, neither shall they learn war any more.'[1]

The Self-Manifestation of God, Chapter 2 of this brilliant book, attains the highest achievement of George's combined literary ability, legal training, intellectual force, moderation and scholarship. He is presenting a theme virtually unknown to the Western mind, which was bound to be anathema to its religionists, yet essential to the development of his book. He had used great subtlety in his Foreword in predisposing the reader to a favourable view of Bahá'u'lláh, Whom he described as a 'Great Seer', ahead of His time, misunderstood, 'proscribed, anathematised, and cruelly persecuted,' promulgating from prison 'noble peace-aims that now increasingly find utterance in western lands'. Having documented in Chapter 1 the eternal vision of the Kingdom of God on earth, he now approaches the vital question, 'Who is Christ?', and takes three chapters to expound – always supporting his argument from the Bible and the teaching of Jesus – Bahá'u'lláh's principles of the unity of religion and the progressive nature of revelation.

> For the development of civilisation does not proceed in a manner parallel to that which science discovers in the evolution of material life. Humanity does not advance in wisdom, virtue and happiness through the inward urge of some anonymous force or the uplift of some original inborn power of its own. Far otherwise. For all that raises him above the level of a human animal man depends upon a new and special principle that is not found on the lower stages of being. This principle is a part of the creative process, and is the cause of all that is noble and gracious in life. It is active today as it has been active since the time of Adam, and men depend on it now for their well-being as completely as they have done throughout the past.
>
> This is the principle of God's Self-Manifestation in the human degree of existence.
>
> The operation of this principle is the force that gives to history its

[1] Isaiah 2:4. This theme is presented in great detail in *Christ and Bahá'u'lláh*, Ch. 2, *The Kingdom in the Bible.*

direction and its continuity. The part that man's will plays in the perfecting of civilisation is a minor part. His dependence on the will of God is more complete than his ignorance realises and more abject than his pride inclines him to admit. Were it not for the special intervention of God in human affairs, so teaches Bahá'u'lláh, the earth would be the cockpit of base desires and raging appetites and man himself would appear as the most disagreeable and dangerous of the animals. History (if the annals of such a race could be called history) would have neither coherence nor meaning and the elevation of mankind would be impossible. Did not God show himself in this human realm, bringing down gifts from heaven, man would lack both the power and the will to develop. There would be no spirituality, no vision, no true life: the minds and the hearts of men would be wrapped in infernal darkness. For God not only leads mankind onward by his grace to a predetermined goal but in addition empowers them to follow his lead.

This theme of 'a succession of Great Souls . . . who inspire the onward movement of mankind' being established, he moves into his next chapter *The Succession of the High-Prophets.* And here George is really subtle:

> The advent of a Divine Messenger does not seem to be represented in the canon or the sacred writings of any world-religion, and is surely not represented in the Christian Scripture, as an isolated phenomenon, simply an angelic adventure; nor is the Messenger shown as a solitary figure. He comes expressly as one of a line of teachers and is sent on a specific mission . . .
>
> As Moses linked his mission with that of his successor, not less closely did Jesus connect his with that of Moses. He made himself equal with Moses, claimed authority to change the Mosaic law and represented his own work as so much the same as the work of Moses that sincere acceptance of one would involve acceptance of the other: 'For had ye believed Moses, ye would have believed me . . .'[1]
>
> Muḥammad 'recognized the truth of the signs, prophecies, and words of Jesus, and testified that they were all of God'. He declared indeed, 'I am Jesus.' He claimed for himself the position of being the last of all the High-Prophets that preceded the Supreme Theophany. He closed the line – 'I am the seal of the prophets,' he said.

George now describes the rise and fall of those material civilizations resulting from the spiritual and moral education which every High-Prophet confers upon mankind. He likens His appearance to the heartbeat of history and with this simile launches straight into *The Mission of the Lord Christ.*

The whole purpose of this chapter is to show the Christian revelation in its critical place in the unfoldment of God's grand

[1] John 5:46

redemptive scheme. No longer an isolated event occurring at some arbitrary point in history, it is related to what has gone before and essential to what is to follow. It was the mission of Jesus not only to release into the world such an outpouring of spiritual power and love as to change mankind forever, but to announce the approach of the Kingdom. 'From that time Jesus began to preach, and to say, *Repent: for the kingdom of heaven is at hand.*'[1]

> The coming of that Kingdom was by this command to be the prayer of the faithful all through his Dispensation: *Thy kingdom come, thy will be done on earth as in heaven.*

George dwells at some length on the central position in Christ's revelation of this theme – the coming of the Kingdom, 'indeed an earthly kingdom in the sense that it is set down four-square upon the solid earth for all men to see it, know it and inhabit it,' and the undoubted association of its appearance with His own return.

The Vigil of the Day of Days is a scholarly dissertation upon the Christian hope of the second coming of Christ. George traces the vicissitudes of this expectation during the Christian era right down to that remarkable upsurge of adventism in the first half and middle of the nineteenth century.

> So deep was the impression made by the predictions of Christ that from the time of the Apostles onwards for several centuries the expectation of a Second Coming in power held a prominent place in Christian orthodox belief. It was a leading feature in the teaching of Peter and of Paul. It forms the subject of that wonderful series of visions which closes the Canon of the New Testament. It is associated with the names of some of the greatest of the early Fathers of the Church: with Papias, with Irenaeus, with Justin Martyr and with Tertullian. It is found in some of the earliest Christian writings, in the Epistle of Barnabas, in the Testaments of the Twelve Patriarchs, in the Shepherd of Hermas.
>
> In spite of disappointments (for the early believers took in too narrow a sense the promise that the Advent would come to pass soon) the enthusiasm of this hope persisted for some three centuries, and did not begin to wane till the reign of Constantine. Discouraged by the ecclesiastical authorities, it had sunk out of sight by the fifth century, and for a thousand years from that date it appears but little in history.
>
> It never died out of the popular mind, however, and with the Renaissance and the Reformation it once more began to take its old place in Christian belief and thought. As far back as the beginning of the fourteenth century, from the time of Dante and Giotto onward, the art and poetry of Italy depict the Last Judgment in works which are still famous. Orcagna, for example, has a painting of it in the Campo Santo, Pisa, Luca Signorelli

---

[1] Matt. 4:17

in the Cathedral at Orvieto, Michael Angelo in the Sistine Chapel (1541), while Fra Angelico and Tintoretto dealt with the subject more times than one. Thereafter renderings of the same theme appeared in Germany and elsewhere, Sir E. Burne-Jones's 'Dies Domini' holding the position of a postscript to the long series. Old writers, too, of less distinction than Dante sang of the last Judgment in verses that are not forgotten . . .

The English poets of the seventeenth century began to write of the Day that was to be.

And he quotes Henry Vaughan and Dryden and describes how the movement grew through the eighteenth century until 'on one notorious occasion a concourse of votaries assembled at a designated spot to watch the clouds from which before nightfall a white-robed Messiah was to descend to earth'. But

> By the middle of the last century the Christian expectation of the Second Advent had reached its zenith. After that date it began to decline and finally passed out of sight. Even when the sign of the return of the Jews to Palestine was fulfilled so dramatically as to startle the imagination of all acquainted with the predictions of Christ, the former expectancy was not reawakened, and the heart of Christendom was not moved to seek the explanation of so astonishing a phenomenon.

He now relates that this expectation of a new Manifestation of God was shared by the other world religions – Judaism, Buddhism, Hinduism, Zoroastrianism and Islám,[1] and dwells on its decline in Christendom after the mid-nineteenth century. It fell to the Christian churches of the twentieth century – some twenty years after the publication of George's book – to call a world conference in Evanston, Illinois, in the shadow of the first Bahá'í Ma_sh_riqu'l-A_dh_kár (House of Worship) of the western world, to debate whether Jesus meant what He said when He spoke of His 'return' and described the circumstances.[2] History has its own ironies!

George examines in some detail the reasons for the modern world's neglect of the supreme event of history, the appearance of the Promised One of all ages, draws comparisons with the rejection of Christ by the Jews among whom He appeared and to whom He gave His message, cites the Old Testament to support his contention that the 'predictions of the coming of the Kingdom, are set forth in symbol or parable with a deeper meaning hidden underneath the literal significance of the words', and sums up:

> As in Christendom, so throughout the rest of the world. The universal expectation of an august theophany was vitiated by misunderstandings

[1] See also *Christ and Bahá'u'lláh*, Prologue.
[2] Matt. 24

and led to no good result. A rigid traditionalism cramped the souls of men. No organised religion in any quarter of the globe seems to have believed that the coming Prophet would demand radical reforms and lift the people to a higher level of thought and conduct than that with which they had contented themselves in the past. Every religion looked for a Vindicator who should be exclusively its own, who should justify its dogmas, reinforce its institutions and exalt it to a position of complete and unchallengeable supremacy over the erroneous faiths of the rest of mankind.

Nowhere is George's mild satire better demonstrated than in his commentary to this conclusion:

> The world's unanimity, therefore, in looking for a Divine Advent was not so complete as to suggest that when the Deliverer actually appeared all the communions of all races would be at one in acclaiming him. Far otherwise. Not only had each of the great religions drawn in rough outline its own distinctive picture of the Messiah, but some of these religions were themselves subdivided into numerous sects each of which had prepared the Messiah's portrait in yet smaller and more exclusive detail. However ready, therefore, to accommodate himself to the predilections of man the Divine Teacher might prove to be, it is evident that he could by no possibility gratify the expectations of more than a minute proportion of the human race and must at the same time keenly disappoint the hopes of all the other millions of mankind. On the other hand, if the Holy Prophet should come (as all Holy Prophets had done before him), disregarding all human preconceptions, bearing a new Name, bringing a new Book, he would be confronted by the denial of every section of every extant religion. His acceptance would be secured through the private judgment of independent individuals.

The Gate of the Dawn gives an account of the appearance and mission of the Báb, the Prophet–Herald of Bahá'u'lláh. The opening paragraph is reminiscent of that splendid passage which started Chapter 1; it too is a single sentence:

> A few months from that day on which in America the adherents of William Miller stood looking up to heaven to catch the first glimpse of the Saviour returning in glory among the clouds, on the other side of the world the Báb gave forth the Declaration of his Sacred Mission and began his appointed work of preparing mankind for the dawning of the Last Day and the advent of its Lord.

The tragic, bloodstained 'tales of magnificent heroism'[1] which comprise the episode of the Báb, lose nothing in their telling at George's hands, and his portrayal of the Báb, that 'Charmer of Hearts', is attractive to Western readers in spite of the great gulf

[1] Lord Curzon, *Persia and the Persian Question*

separating them from nineteenth-century Persia.

The Entrance of the King of Glory is the story of Bahá'u'lláh Himself, anticipated in the prophecies and traditions of every great world religion and in the poetry and legend of the human race.

Nowhere else than in this chapter is George's literary skill, clarity of mind, ability to weave essentials into a flowing pattern, more happily displayed. Not even the brilliant Chapter 2, *The Self-Manifestation of God,* can surpass it in readability. Its condensation of a mass of information into an ordered whole, without ever appearing to summarize or categorize, is editing and writing of the highest order. In Chapter 2 he was developing a philosophical concept of history; now he is presenting a Person, and a life packed full of dramatic contrasts, indescribable sufferings, exiles, victories in captivity, outpourings of divine revelation and announcements, castigations and warnings to the kings of the earth and its religious leaders. His précis is superb, omitting nothing essential, minimizing no great issues or vital episodes, yet containing within a score of pages the great climax of his book and leaving the reader convinced that it is so and that all that follows can only be exegesis and history.

One sample of the tenor of this chapter is sufficient:

Nineteen years before, when he had first espoused the cause of the Báb, Bahá'u'lláh was in his golden youth endowed with all that fills life with pleasantness and hope: rank, wealth, health, popularity and growing fame. Now when he assumed the full responsibilities of his divinely-given office he had been denuded of all that could be taken from him. He was homeless, destitute, branded, a captive, an exile, with the threat of further punishment held over his head. Only his life (according to the strange predictive dream of his boyhood) had been preserved by God from the powers of his enemies. Despoiled of all those facilities for propagating the cause which originally he had had in so great a measure, and left with nothing on earth but those inalienable gifts of mind and heart which he had from his Maker alone, Bahá'u'lláh was at the same time the victim of active restraints and positive afflictions. He underwent at the hands of the government every variety of punishment: now he suffered from cruel exposure, now from continued and close confinement; now he was subjected to torture, now weakened by long privation. More than once the inhumanities inflicted on him brought him to the verge of death, and a hundred times his life was in peril from the anger of a despotic master or the rage of a howling mob. He was compelled from the time of his exile onward to the end of his life to watch those most near and dear to him endure for love of him calamities only less than his own, and to see them in many instances untimely sink and die under their miseries. Not until his closing days was there any abatement of the rigours of his captivity, and he died as he had lived, a prisoner and an exile, far from that fair and well-loved land in which he and his forefathers had reigned in ducal affluence and splendour.

He concludes on a note sounded many times throughout his life:

> His wisdom impresses ever more deeply its claim on men's admiration as the repeated failure of all superficial schemes drives them back upon the truth that the social order of the world will never now be rebuilt till men subject their personal wills to him who is the Source of all unity and the Cause of all concord.

Having presented the 'Promised One of All Ages', George sets apart the remaining two chapters of his book by interposing a Note which simply lists the 'Cardinal Dates of the Bahá'í Faith' from the mideighteenth century until the passing of 'Abdu'l-Bahá in 1921.

The Light of the King's Law offers a view of 'Abdu'l- Bahá's and the Guardian's expositions of that new civilization which Bahá'u'lláh had adumbrated, 'the brightest emanation of His Mind'.[1]

> We are too near in time to Bahá'u'lláh, too enfeebled by the mental habits of an unregenerate past, to be able to grasp the meaning of his constructive work or to form a picture of the new society that is to arise under his command. But 'Abdu'l-Bahá, out of his father's Revelation, has set forth the main features of the divine scheme, and has explained in clear perspective the central truths and instructions round which humanity is to be reordered and reorganised.

George, naturally, dwelt first on the spiritual principles and attitudes inculcated by Bahá'u'lláh, which all revolve around the axis of unity. Unity of men with the will of God, knowledge by men of the love of God, the oneness of mankind – *Ye are all leaves of one tree and the fruits of one branch* – the unity of the world – *The earth is but one country and mankind its citizens* – and then goes on to mention some of the specifically social, religious, personal, and educational teachings and ordinances. He gives an outline of the administrative order by which the life and work of the Bahá'í world community is ordered and fostered and some account of its growth in America and elsewhere.

He quotes the Guardian's 'exposition of certain passages contained in the Epistle which Bahá'u'lláh wrote and despatched to Queen Victoria in 1868.', which broadly outlines some of the main features of the future World Order anticipated by Bahá'u'lláh, and which concludes with the vision of 'a world community in which the fury of a capricious and militant nationalism will have been transmuted into an abiding consciousness of world citizenship . . .'

The Fire of the King's Love, the final chapter of this great book, deals,

[1] Shoghi Effendi, *The Goal of a New World Order*, 1931

as its title exactly states, with the greatest observable, and at the same time indefinable, power in creation, God's love. The opening paragraph reads: 'Not by divine instruction, not by mind knowledge, nor by the following of a code of law or system of administration is the unification of mankind to be established or inaugurated, but rather by a true abiding love that burns away difference of self-interest, and melts by its flame all hearts into one heart. Each stands for all, and where one is all are.'

George dilates on this theme, quoting lavishly from the talks and letters of 'Abdu'l-Bahá, revealing in simple terms the nature and effects of Divine love. We hear the voice of Bahá'u'lláh uttering the mystical verses of *Hidden Words: 'Veiled in My immemorial being and in the ancient eternity of My essence, I knew My love for thee; therefore I created thee, have engraved on thee Mine image and revealed to thee My beauty.'*

We are reminded that the three central figures of this new revelation exemplified in their lives the all-conquering power of love for God and immolated themselves upon that altar for the sake of an ingrate and self-interested humanity.

> Bahá'u'lláh endured half a century of imprisonment, was four times exiled, underwent year by year and day by day countless afflictions, submitting to all with a radiant acquiescence in the will of that Supreme Sovereign whom for love's sake he served.

The Báb, answering some friends who expressed concern for his personal safety answered:

> . . . Nay, beseech the Lord your God to hasten the hour of My martyrdom and to accept My sacrifice. Rejoice, for both I and Quddús will be slain on the altar of our devotion to the King of Glory. The blood which we are destined to shed in His path will water and revive the garden of our immortal felicity. The drops of this consecrated blood wil be the seed out of which will arise the mighty Tree of God, the Tree that will gather beneath its all-embracing shadow the peoples and kindreds of the earth.

'Abdu'l-Bahá,

> born the heir to high distinction and to wide estates, at the age of nine years followed his father into exile, and from that moment to his death at an advanced age made himself as nothing but the servant of the Great Beloved, and counted his title 'Abdu'l-Bahá, 'the Bond-servant of Glory', as his sword and his crown.

It is the effect of this irresistible outpouring of Divine love which is seen in the world today. The dissolution by self-destruction of the old order of things – separateness, enmity, prejudice, self-interest – and the unfolding of a new, universal order generated by the all-conquering power of that all-embracing love poured out by Bahá'u'lláh, the Báb and 'Abdu'l-Bahá and embodying the principle of the oneness of mankind in all its implications, are both attributed to the influence of the rising sun of the new age.

The portrait of 'Abdu'l-Bahá which emerges in this chapter is that of the Exemplar. He set the example of the true life of man, treading the mystical path with practical feet, as was said of Him, overcoming enmity with love, responding to injury with love, returning love for hatred, for slander, for chains and imprisonment, acting always with love, caring for the poor, the sick, the bereaved, the misfits and outcasts, walking with kings to their benefit, dispensing love and encouragement, happiness and love, love and more love.

George concludes his chapter, 'This love now pouring down from God in fullest measure upon the awakening consciousness of mankind is the power that will regenerate human nature, and will create in deed and in fact a new heaven and a new earth.'

He added a Conclusion, which he revised for each new edition published in his lifetime,[1] but always promoting 'Abdu'l-Bahá's hope that his church would enter the heavenly Jerusalem. The final version, a brief seven paragraphs, notes the progress and consolidation of the Bahá'í Faith in a disintegrating world and stresses the preservation of its unity, 'the integrity and exaltation of its teachings'. His final word is an appeal: 'Will not the religious leaders and thinkers of the West examine thoroughly and without prejudice, the high claims of Bahá'u'lláh? And will they not, discerning the true Source and spiritual nature of this supreme Epoch of Transition, lead their churches into the heavenly Jerusalem, so that all Christendom may arise for the regeneration of mankind?'

[1] See p. 120.

Chapter 15

THE HEART OF THE GOSPEL

'WHAT the early Christians did we can do.' With this challenging statement George began the Introduction to the first edition of *The Heart of the Gospel*.[1]

> The opportunity given to them is repeated in our time. The same strength which was given to them may be claimed by us too. The civilisation into which they were born was cankered at the heart, and was dying of irreligion. They, because they loved God and were possessed with the knowledge of His truth, were endowed with power from on high to convert the world and to build by slow degrees a new social order more near than the old to the divine ideal. We, in a like emergency, are called on to undertake a like task.

The revision which he made for the second edition, although done 'to show more explicitly that the narrative, the prophecies, and the promises of the Bible lead naturally up to the Bahá'í Faith and find their completion only in the acknowledgement of the claims and the Revelation of Bahá'u'lláh,' unfortunately omitted this excellent opening, quoted by more than one reviewer. For the same purpose, he changed the original subtitle from 'a restatement of the Teaching of the Bible in terms of modern thought and modern need' to 'The Bible and the Bahá'í Faith'. These two, and other changes, clearly show how, in 1938, although he was putting his name and full titles to his proclamation of the Bahá'í message, he yet favoured the gentle and indirect approach to his church and Christianity in general.

Indeed it is of interest that his first typescript, sent to a committee of Bahá'ís for general review and advice, contained no mention of Bahá'u'lláh. The committee was unanimous in its admiration for his

[1] Lindsay Drummond, London, 1939

compelling and Bible-documented argument; it was also unanimous that unless he answered the conclusion to which that argument clearly led, the work lost its point and became 'another theory instead of a practical truth'.

It fell to my lot to convey this view to George, whom we already regarded with deep affection and great respect. (As the years went by, both feelings increased until they merged into one and we revered and loved him as our Hand of the Cause.)[1] I wrote that 'each successive chapter leads one farther on to an expected climax, and unless it comes there will be a sense of let down . . . the whole work would be immensely strengthened by the declaration of Bahá'u'lláh as the One indicated by the whole theme of the book.' George, with his usual over-optimism had many times expressed confidence that this book would secure his freedom, would force the authorities to demand his resignation, would terminate his clerical career, and such.[2] I suggested that without a declaration of the Bahá'í Faith it would not bring about his freedom. 'Christianity would accept progressive revelation as a theory but would definitely get vociferous if anyone showed that we are no longer living in the Christian Dispensation.'

George's reply, on January 16, 1939 expressed '. . . great surprise; and when I had thought it over a great joy. I decided I would do as you and the committee suggest; and would go a little further and declare my own acceptance of the Bahá'í teaching.'

His introduction of Bahá'u'lláh gives a foretaste of the closely reasoned, powerful, irresistible manner in which his whole theme is developed.

> As a starting-point, the reality of divine revelation is fully accepted. The whole argument proceeds from the primary truth that God being infinite is in His own Godhead incomprehensible to man's finite mind, and He has therefore (in order that men may know Him and adore Him) established through successive mediators a system of continuous self-revelation measured to man's advancing intelligence. This truth may be gathered from the pages of the Bible, where, chiefly in symbol and parable, it is unmistakably declared. It has, however, been set forth in a more modern manner and with more of philosophic detail in a recent work on comparative religion written by Bahá'u'lláh under the title *The Book of Certitude*.

He then cites the perspicuous and pertinent passages from *Kitáb-i-Íqán (The Book of Certitude)* which declares the transcendence of *God, the unknowable Essence* and the appearance, *in the noble form of the human*

---

[1] See Ch. 19.
[2] See Ch. 9.

temple, of the Manifestations of the Sun of Truth to impart unto the world the mysteries of the unchangeable Being, and tell of the subtleties of His imperishable essence. They are described as *primal Mirrors which reflect the light of unfading glory . . . expressions of Him Who is the Invisible of the Invisibles.*[1]

It was this passage from *Kitáb-i-Íqán*, together with a few paragraphs in the Epilogue developing Bahá'u'lláh's principle of world unity and peace, reinforced by a long quotation from Shoghi Effendi's exposition of 'The unity of the human race, as envisaged by Bahá'u'lláh . . .' taken from *The Unfoldment of World Civilization*, which had impelled the Bishop of Killaloe to remark, as already mentioned, that the only thing wrong with *The Heart of the Gospel* was that it didn't say enough about Bahá'u'lláh, Whose teachings were wonderful. George's plan to make friends rather than enemies was evidently successful.

The single theme of *The Heart of the Gospel* is spiritual evolution accomplished through a succession of divine Revelators. George had already presented the social aspect of this process in *The Promise of All Ages*, but more as an observable historical fact related to the rise and fall of great civilizations and in relation to that thread, running through all history, of the promise and hope of a great Day when men would live in brotherhood and peace in one world society. Now in *The Heart of the Gospel* he is at pains to reveal this principle as the central theme of the Bible, particularly stressed in the New Testament by the teaching of Jesus. This inevitably involves recognition of other revelations of Truth than that given by Jesus and leads directly to our own time and the mission of Bahá'u'lláh. And herein lay George's greatest problem. Somehow he had to expose the falsity of the general Christian assumptions about Christ and His teaching. These he described in his seventh chapter:

> Speaking broadly, the Christian community has not believed and does not now believe in a continuous and world-embracing scheme of Revelation in which Jesus Christ played a part.
>
> The existence of such a vast divine Design might in the past have been denied; and perhaps the idea of it would have been to many without value or meaning.
>
> Nor has the Christian community believed that the Bible teaches a progressive system of Revelation which began with the creation of man and has been constantly guiding the race forward towards the attainment of a spiritual maturity. It has not believed in the gradual spiritual growth of the whole human race down through the ages, aided by a succession of heavenly Messengers.

[1] *Kitáb-i-Íqán, pp.* 98–103

No doubt with the thought of magnifying the position of Christ, and certainly with the effect of magnifying its own opinions, it has suffered Jesus of Nazareth to eclipse utterly all other Teachers; it has regarded His spiritual teaching as exhaustive and final, and has attributed to Him a personal immortality of some such corporeal kind as the pagans of old might have attributed to one of their gods like Apollo.

Such conceptions as these, though not indeed contained in the formal creeds of Christendom, have come down through tradition and are generally held, and either implied or expressed in much of the greatest Christian literature.

But their seeds were sown by men in less enlightened times than ours, and they flourished in the Dark Ages. They are not taught by Christ. They are now difficult to reconcile with known truth. They do not add to the magnificence of Christ's station, and they are seen to be derogatory to the character of Almighty God.

He would not assail these positions with any of the weapons of secularism such as ridicule, harsh criticism, displays of superior intellectual power or the like, but by examining the recorded statements of Christ, about Himself and His revelation, and its relationship to the past and the future. He would try to uncover the origins of those false assumptions, find excuses for their arising, and offer a truer understanding of Christ's message, based on His own words and reasoning therefrom.

Six chapters are occupied with laying the foundation of what the Bible is all about and why it has remained of such enduring interest, in spite of vicissitudes like those of the present. 'The Bible contains no word for evolution; yet evolution is its subject from beginning to end.' 'World-history at its core and in its essence is the story of the spiritual evolution of mankind.' 'Evolution is – in the Bible – a mode of education chosen by God, and it is not shown as ever reaching a final end.'

The unnumbered millenniums during which the Creative Will laid the scene for the appearance of man – the 'days' of Genesis – are accorded 'two pages' in the Scriptures, but twelve hundred are not enough to deal with the spiritual evolution of man, whose physical form, 'the last and finest flower of evolution,' was fit to receive a breath from God's own Being. Not that primitive man is spiritually a complete and finished product. His likeness to God is essential but embryonic, just as the leaves and flowers and fruit of a tree are embryonic in its seed.

Now George begins to grapple with the heart of his problem. He cites the Bible to show that physical evolution was carried through by stages (days) and that the spiritual evolution of man 'from his First

Birth in Genesis to his Second Birth in the Apocalypse' followed the same pattern. Spiritual birth, which is knowledge of God and His law, does not arise from man himself as in the case of physical growth, but is conferred on him by Great Souls especially empowered to reveal those divine mysteries according to man's developing spiritual capacity to receive. The grand climacteric of this process will occur at man's maturity, when he, at long last, becomes a new creation, fit to inhabit the New Jerusalem which will then be revealed for him. But even this is not the end of the process but the opening of a new and more glorious chapter in the life of mankind, a period which according to the analogy of a single life will be several times longer than what has gone before.

The Bible 'gives a clear account of the division of the evolutionary movement into great Eras' generally known as Dispensations but often referred to in the Bible as Days. Five such eras or epochs are mentioned by Christ Himself and George documents each from the text of the Gospel. Jesus' own Day (*Your father Abraham rejoiced to see my day*);[1] His second advent *in the glory of his Father*[2] incorporated into the Christian creeds and canon; the Day of Moses, narrated from its beginning to its close; that of Abraham 'briefly and indistinctly sketched'; and that of Noah, in the long dark age before Abraham, whose unspiritual conditions would reoccur, Jesus said, at the time of His return: *As it was in the days of Noe.*[3]

George now has the argument well in hand, with the authority of Scripture to support it. He has said nothing which is not documented from the Bible and he proceeds to examine closely the relationship between these Dispensations.

> Each Dispensation opened a New Covenant between God and man; each covered a term of years and was succeeded by another Dispensation. Each was inaugurated by a Master Spirit, a man who was specially called by the Most High to the task, and who, after his death, continued to be the supreme sole guide and governor of his people so long as the Dispensation endured.
>
> . . . On these whom God appoints as the Suns of the Days of Spiritual Creation, or Lords of Dispensations, He bestows spectacular power. They stand out in greatness above all other men. The two thousand two hundred years and more of Hebrew history narrated in the Bible are dominated by three heroic figures, and the earlier period of pre-Hebrew history is, in like manner, dominated by the earlier Covenant-bringer Noah. The Dispensations of these four Leaders are treated in a very

[1] John 8:56
[2] Matthew 16:27
[3] Matthew 24:37

unequal manner. The Age of Moses is sketched in its full length, and from its inauguration in Egypt to its close in the epoch of Jesus Christ . . . Only two generations are covered by the New Testament narrative, and the rest of Christian history is written elsewhere than in the canon of Scripture. But the Bible record shows that as Christ in His time overshadowed the peoples, so did Abraham and Noah likewise in their time. Each was supreme in his own Day over the people committed to him, and was remembered and venerated long ages after his Day had passed away. Of Moses, God said to Aaron: 'He shall be to thee as God.'

He goes further and examines the similarities of these 'Overlords of Evolution', particularly in the power they have to accomplish Their purpose of promoting God's 'Grand Design'.

> . . . though they, themselves, submit to violence and wrong and show forbearance and gentleness under every provocation, yet they have a reserve of power which enables them to accomplish fully the work committed to them by God. They cannot be resisted. In spite of every difficulty, in spite of the unworthiness of the world, in spite of the incapacity, the vacillation, the faithlessness of the people, they do not fail. They are the Lords, the Divine Agents of the Spiritual Evolution of the race; and this Evolution is an integral system ordained by the Almighty. The power of the whole is behind its every phase, its every movement. Ignorant and foolish men can bring about their own undoing; they cannot frustrate the purpose of God. Every Dispensation is charged with ample power to fulfil its part and function in the grand Creative Scheme of God.

There follows a chapter devoted to *The Power of Christ*. It is a paean of love and wonder to the magnificence and beauty and glory of Christ, a panegyric obviously poured forth from his own soul which can only warm the hearts of believers and perhaps astonish that great and growing number who know little about Him.

Now, at last, in the central position of his book, having established from the Bible the Grand Redemptive Scheme of God and the succession of Revelations all playing their part in this one process of spiritual evolution, he challenges the false assumptions, listed above, so widespread throughout Christendom.

He then shows that those views, held today by Christians, were exactly paralleled by the views which the custodians of Judaism held, in the time of Jesus, about Moses. The Scribes maintained and taught that Moses' Revelation was complete and final in itself and needed no further aid from God. We condemn in them their lack of open-mindedness and yet there is less excuse for modern men to have so narrow a view.

What knowledge had they compared with ourselves of the vast extent of the globe with all its seas and lands, of the number and variety of the peoples that inhabit it, of the civilisations and religions that had sprung up and flourished and perhaps already decayed in that great continent of Asia in which they dwelt; what did they know of the antiquity of the earth and of humanity, what conception had they of such truths as progress and evolution? . . .

We who compose universal histories, who study comparative religion, who can take a far broader and more discerning view of the ancient world than was possible for those who themselves lived in it, we, thus highly privileged, have no excuse at all for prejudice or egoism in our interpretation of Christ and His mission.

. . . What intelligible or consistent philosophy of world-history can be woven around the idea that the one authentic Revelation of God was given nineteen hundred years ago, and that it was both final and complete? None at all. This idea originated in days of ignorance, and bears every mark of the date of its origin. It contradicts the teaching of Christ and the spirit of the Bible; it is incompatible with the revealed character of God and repugnant to the better instincts and to the fuller knowledge of our time.

George dwells at some length on the reasons for the rejection of Christ and His teaching by Judaism, in order to draw the obvious and vital lesson to be learned by men of our own day *vis-à-vis* the Revelation of Bahá'u'lláh.

Every good Jew, whether a cleric or a layman, whether he came from Judæa or Galilee, believed in the finality of Moses' Revelation and in the everlasting permanence of all the Mosaic rites, customs, sacrifices and laws. He believed that his people were the elect of God among all nations, that the Scribes were the only teachers of true religion in the world, and that the Messiah when he came would reduce the Gentiles to their proper position of subordination and establish for ever the sovereignty of the Jewish people and their theocratic system.

When Jesus appeared and announced that the Revelation of Moses was not final, that its moral precepts were not exhaustive nor the highest possible; that the secular and ecclesiastical laws of Mosaism were subject to modification and to repeal; when He announced that the appointed time for these changes and for a new Independent Revelation had come, He challenged the accepted view and the established belief of every Israelite who heard Him.

They were just as wrong, and in exactly the same particulars, as the generality of Christians today.

But in spite of the crucifixion of Christ by the religious leaders of Judaism, the historical effect of His Teaching has been to spread the knowledge of the Old Testament around the earth and to win for Moses the veneration of countless millions who, but for Christ, would not have heard of Him. 'The enthusiasm of the Scribes and Pharisees did not accomplish this: far otherwise.'

George ascribes the corruption of Christ's teaching to the self-
seeking instincts of human nature. Personal ambition and egoistic
desire for leadership were always present in the Christian community.
Even among the Apostles there were quarrels about who would be the
greatest among them. Immediately after His passing there were
contentions about the interpretation of His teachings, leading to
rivalries and schisms. But the greatest failure of all was the inability to
understand the utterly spiritual nature of Christ's message.[1]

> What Jesus intended in a moral and spiritual sense was taken in a merely
> intellectual sense. Opinion was exalted at the expense of conduct. Heresy
> took the place of sin. Orthodoxy took the place of righteousness. Assent to
> a general theory became the bond of union instead of fraternal love. The
> ground of fellowship was not common obedience to the will of a Father in
> heaven, but the repetition of 'Lord, Lord' according to the same formula.
> The mechanism of government was idealised in order to confirm and
> stabilise the power of those in control. Conformity to pattern was insisted
> on and discipline was maintained by every conceivable resource of fear and
> of force.

George's Epilogue to his first edition declares that the failure, in our
own day, of the traditional religious establishments of the world to
meet the challenge of the new age brought about by the industrial
revolution and the increase of knowledge was due to the same root
cause:

> All our mistakes were rooted in our spiritual infirmity. We ignored the
> supremacy of the spiritual order. We did not subordinate material things
> to it, as the design of the Creator demanded. We did not seek first to
> discover God's meaning and purpose in the unprecedented changes of the
> time, nor yet to gain a fuller understanding of His nature through the
> advances of scientific knowledge. We did not concentrate our efforts on
> uplifting the moral level of Christendom and establishing social justice in
> Christian lands.

Because of this, secular ideas of the organizing of modern life have
been given preference and God's plan has been, and still is, ignored.

> The secularists from their mundane point of view have envisaged this Age
> as a unique and incomparable phenomenon. They have sketched their
> views of its character, have elaborated their ideas of its meaning, and have
> pictured in various forms the materialistic El Dorado to which, through
> their good offices, they suppose the human race now is to attain. In
> science, invention, engineering, commerce and the like, they have made
> brilliant use of their opportunities, and have so changed the circumstances

---

[1] This subject is dealt with more fully in Ch. 4 of *Christ and Bahá'u'lláh*, see Ch. 16.

of life that extravagant weight has been attached to their opinions on matters that lie outside their province – on religion, ethics and the like. They have wrought out of the materialistic data at their disposal philosophies of existence which have fashioned the pattern of much modern thought and conduct; and their revolutionary ideologies have, in some cases, been embodied in widespread social and political changes.

These fabrications of human wisdom built on the sand of conjecture instead of the rock of divine reality were foredoomed to failure; and they would never have deceived and betrayed mankind if they had not had the field to themselves – if there had been any outstanding positive alternative. But there was, or seemed to be, no choice.

Except one: the universal plan of reconstruction proclaimed by Bahá'u'lláh, the only one leading naturally and inevitably from the Revelations of the past and offered in the Name of God as the present stage of His Grand Redemptive Scheme. George reinforces his outline of this new teaching with the well-known passage from *The Unfoldment of World Civilization* in which the Guardian exposes the implications for all fields of human activity of universal recognition of 'The unity of the human race, as envisaged by Bahá'u'lláh . . .',[1] and which concludes with this paragraph:

A world federal system, ruling the whole earth and exercising unchallengeable authority over its unimaginably vast resources, blending and embodying the ideals of both the East and the West, liberated from the curse of war and its miseries, and bent on the exploitation of all the available sources of energy on the surface of the planet, a system in which Force is made the servant of Justice, whose life is sustained by its universal recognition of one God and by its allegiance to one common Revelation – such is the goal towards which humanity, impelled by the unifying forces of life, is moving.

George, the supreme artist, concludes his essay with the same theme which opened it. He refers to the

. . . exaltation and spiritual energy which enabled the early followers of Christ, long centuries ago, to stand firm amid the ruins of a dissolving civilisation and build thereafter a new and better order nearer to their Lord's desire? And now that all our mundane ideologies have so utterly failed, what adequate Plan of Action survives for men to work to, save only that prophetically traced long since by the pen of Bahá'u'lláh?

Other reviewers have commented on the difficulty of dealing with this book except by quoting it entire. *The Church of Ireland Gazette* of January 12, 1940, feared to spoil it by reviewing. It describes it as 'a book of which his fellow-Churchmen may justly be proud.' It quotes

[1] See p. 273.

the opening sentences, as did other papers, and in the course of two columns managed to fill nearly one with quotations, ending with George's pointed comment on the Lord's Prayer: 'He did not teach His disciples to pray that they might go to heaven when they died, but that they might do God's will on earth while they lived.'

The Irish Times (January 6, 1940) was equally complimentary, speaking of George's 'varied experience' as having given him 'so deep an insight into the problems that confront the world today, such as is shared by few ecclesiastics who have looked upon life from one angle only'. 'His teaching owes something to the noble mysticism of the latest of Islam's great prophets, Ali Bahá'u'lláh, whose importance to the religious thought of this generation is slowly becoming known, but there are elements in it which are quite new to theology, and will not fail to bear fruit.' This was wonderful from the Bahá'í point of view in spite of the gaffe about 'the latest of Islam's great prophets'.

The Times Literary Supplement (September 2, 1939) gave it an inadequate two-and-a-half inches, calling it thoroughly conservative and missing the point altogether.

The Friend (October 27, 1939) – the Quaker journal – managed to condense an extraordinary amount of information and favourable comment into its two-inch paragraph:

> The author of this book is a clergyman who has fallen under the spell of the teaching of Bahá'u'lláh, to which he was introduced twenty years ago by 'Abdu'l-Bahá. The many friends who met this remarkable man were deeply impressed by his spirit and outlook. They recognised a fundamental unity between his approach to truth and the Quaker approach. Such Friends in particular – though not only they – will welcome this re-interpretation of the Gospels in the light of the spirit of George Fox and Bahá'u'lláh, and will find much encouragement therefrom. Throughout there runs strongly the note of unity, a world-wide fellowship based upon religion and peace. The author gives a remarkable envisaging of a true League of Nations by this imprisoned prophet of the 19th century.

John o'London's Weekly was kindly if patronizing, and totally irrelevant to the content.

The Baptist Times (August 31, 1939) quite frankly didn't like it: '. . . does not appeal to us.'

The Birmingham Post (September 19, 1939) got the point clearly but shrugged it off with faint praise.

John O'Groat Journal (November 17, 1939), whose editor had formerly occupied that position on *The Rangoon Times* and had become attracted to the Bahá'í Faith there and in India, gave it a splendid review, quoting liberally. 'Truly a remarkable book . . .'

'. . . every page brightened with terse elucidatory thought.'

The Aryan Path (May 1940), in a whole page and a bit, took the opportunity to castigate the West. 'If by Christianity is meant the Gospel for which Jesus lived and died, Western civilization as we know it today is its very antithesis . . . the West, instead of being a menace to humanity in its effort to dominate the earth with its guns would be the servant of all.' However '. . . the author accomplishes with clarity and remarkable success' the presentation of the Gospel message that 'God is in earnest about spiritualising mankind. This message, however, is not the preserve of Christianity alone but the heart of all Religion, whatever its shape or form. [A sentiment with which George would have heartily agreed.] Nevertheless, it is well to have it so ably and so directly put forward by our author in the case of Christianity.'

One local paper, The Ludlow Advertiser (September 22, 1939) mentioned it as a book 'worth obtaining'.

And that was it. Yet no other Bahá'í book had received so many column inches or so wide a critical notice. Only George, from his authoritative position and with his scholarship and spiritual insight, was able to attract so much attention.

George described it himself in a letter to the Guardian: 'The book applies the principles of the Ighan [Kitáb-i-Íqán] to the Bible; and the Introduction makes this statement. The result is new and surprising. I feel sure the correctness of this interpretation of the Bible and of Christ's teaching can't be disproved.' Earlier he had written: 'I am . . . in this book at the limit of my intellectual reach and also of my moral and physical strength . . . It is incomparably beyond anything I've attempted before.'

Some have considered it as surpassing The Promise of All Ages. It is certainly different, concerned with exegesis rather than with narrative and a particular episode in history. Its close reasoning makes it unlikely to appeal to the masses, but to Christians of any and all persuasions it has a profound interest, even fascination in the portrait of the Protagonist, while the variety of 'Biblical subjects', many of them historically controversial and puzzling upon which George comments, gives his discourse a heightened interest. Such matters as 'the chosen people', religion always rising in the East, modern criticism of the Bible, free will (God hardened Pharoah's heart), the origin of morals, their society-building power, the prediction of a period of world travail to precede the realization of the vision of the Apocalypse, the differences between spiritual and physical evolution – these and a dozen others lend variety to the main theme. It is a great book and stands in the vanguard of George's work.

Chapter 16

CHRIST AND BAHÁ'U'LLÁH

The Crowning Achievement

IT WAS the Guardian of the Bahá'í Faith who called this book George's 'crowning achievement'. It was his last literary work, the first published copy of which reached him on his deathbed. The writing of it is a saga of faith and courage.

Shortly after his passing, Nancy sent a copy to Miss Dillon with the comment '. . . the publisher's readers and other experts consider it a masterpiece of condensation'. This is true of most of the book, but there are a few sections which are not so much condensation as non-expansion of his notes. In others, he simply states the facts and documents his references. He was dying of Parkinson's disease and was unable to write decipherably or even to speak in his normal soft voice. But his mind was clear and he would whisper to Una or Brian what he wanted to write; one of them would take it down and read it back to him for approval or amendment. The whole book, as a consequence, is the most terse, factual, and non-expository of all his works. It makes a bare hundred-and-twenty pages, and is indeed a condensation of his entire philosophy, presented in such a manner as to promote the main object of his life.

It was conceived as an essay on the Bahá'í administrative order to be entitled *Builders of a New World*, and gestated in his mind for nearly seventeen years, during which time the seed of his curiosity about that Order gradually developed into interest and then fascination[1] until eventually Bahá'u'lláh's New World Order became the all-glorious fulfilment of his own vision of God's 'grand redemptive scheme', so that instead of a commentary on the Administrative Order we got this remarkable book, *Christ and Bahá'u'lláh*. In it he presents in logical

[1] See p. 176.

equence the facts of the philosophical and historical concepts developed in *The Promise of All Ages* and *The Heart of the Gospel*. It became not only an extension of *The Heart of the Gospel*, as he himself realized, but the third volume of the trilogy which expounds his vision of the unity of history, so succinctly stated in the first sentence of *The Promise of All Ages*.[1]

As early as June 1940 he began to write about it to Nellie and in a postscript to his letter to her of September 16, 1940 said: '. . . of my purpose in the Builders. One aim is to find a new and more telling, more attractive way of putting the Cause with a view to inducing action: it is to be more practical, urgent, immediate than *The Promise* or *The Heart* and is designed to call for active acceptance. So I want to put the argument in a less challenging sort of way, to open a new and apparently easier road. At the same time I want the book to be my springboard giving me a good header into the wide waters of a larger life. *The Promise* does not afford a good excuse for a churchman to change; it isn't a book to make a practical stand and fight on: too philosophic. The Builders is . . .'

By October he had gone a long way to the final concept: '. . . my treatment is not learned nor technical. The book has taken a quite unforeseen shape by degrees, and is now practically settled in its spirit, purpose and outline. It is really, in effect, an effort to proclaim the Cause to the widest public, showing it as a practical immediate answer to a problem which all are trying to solve.'

In January it was 'taking unexpected shape and drawing near the stage of penmanship'. By February he had received a letter from the Guardian expressing delight at the project '. . . and he wants me to get on with this book'. 'The theme itself has opened up before me in the most marvellous manner as I pondered and thought about it and has developed in the last few months in the most marked manner. At any rate I myself have learned from the study much I never so much as dreamed of before.'

Then his eye trouble returned and for some months he was unable to do any literary work at all and apart from a comment about 'beating the air' we hear nothing more for eighteen months, when he wrote to Nellie (with his left hand, the right being crippled by arthritis): 'The objective is to bring the Christian Churches under the New Jerusalem, and the first essential is to begin in the right way on the line that you mean to follow right through. This is why I am pausing over my *Builders of a New World*. This B.N.W. is to complete *The Heart of the Gospel* . . .'

In June and July 1943, three years after we first heard of it, he wrote

[1] See p. 261.

of '*Christ and Bahá'u'lláh* or *Builders of a New World* which I believe is the book the Guardian has been waiting for and the book I was born to write. The theme is topical and practical, and ideas flow easily . . . I am bothered with neuritis in my arms and the doctor is not pleased with my health; if it were not for these physical handicaps the book would not be very long taking shape. It is all planned from start to finish now.' But not a word written yet, although he had sent the promised draft of chapter headings to Nellie.

His letter to the Guardian of July 25, 1945 (see pages 86–7) deplored the physical disability which rendered him unable 'to write a word of it', but the theme was ever in his mind 'and the book will be much better for the delay and the full preparation'.

In January 1947 he was still wrestling with it. 'With infinite labour I have planned a book on Christ and Bahá'u'lláh . . . It is spiritually and emotionally more elevated than anything else I have done before; and is also in an intellectual way and artistically full of hard, hard problems. I am thrilled and enthralled by it.'

It was still maturing in his mind in October 1948, a year after his resignation. He wrote to the National Spiritual Assembly outlining the literary tasks on which he was engaged. Among them was a new edition of *The Heart of the Gospel* designed 'to form a prelude to a volume *Christ and Bahá'u'lláh* which is to follow and is now being planned in some detail. Actually the two books together will deal with the one subject, the first volume being chiefly on Christ, the second on Bahá'u'lláh.'

On July 15, 1949 he reported to the Guardian: 'I have been working as hard as I can on my book *Christ and Bahá'u'lláh:* the unifying kindling idea only came at last in May . . . The patient labour on it has brought me a new vision. Now I seek the high enthusiasm and the physical vigour that will empower me to write it in the manner the theme calls for. The story is one the world needs, and does not dream of !'

In February 1950 he went, with Nancy, to Belfast, on a teaching visit, and wrote from there to the Guardian:

> My work on the 'Covenant' lectures delivered here in Belfast has given me the missing chapters in my book on Christ and Bahá'u'lláh and I think I know now how to complete that book at last. I have been very unhappy and perplexed and ashamed at being so long on the undertaking. I scribbled endlessly, to no good effect. I got lost in the details of a vast and ever opening subject. I was not spiritually up to my job. Now I believe I can work out a thoroughly unified pattern on a level that I can keep up. I hope and pray God in His mercy will overlook my shortcomings and give me vigour and resolution to pursue the task to an adequate end.

By 1951 (January 16) he had begun writing; 'But I do not say it is near completion' nor what the title will be. All I know now is that I will work regularly at it and that it promises to be a richer and more powerful book than any I have done yet. But it opens itself to me as it pleases, not as I please: and there are causes for delay.' In April: 'I am in full cry after the subject and love working on it. The inhibition is lifted. But there is a lot to do yet, my sore weak arm delays me somewhat, and it will be well on through the summer before I can furnish the manuscript in a finished form. The scenario is completed now and much of the rough writing.' By November: 'The writing I have to do is an arduous but thrilling task, and I am hard at it. Pray for me in my effort . . .' A month later he is 'progressing happily', and the following week, '*Christ and Bahá'u'lláh* is difficult, thrilling, promising and moves steadily along . . . The theme is wonderful.' By the 22nd, 'I expect to have *Christ and Bahá'u'lláh* completed within four months . . . The Guardian has shown so much concern about this book that I suggest, when I am through to the end of my theme (not many weeks hence) he should be informed or consulted about the matter of its publication.'

On December 24, 1951, George was among the first twelve Bahá'ís to be elevated, by the Guardian, to the rank of Hand of the Cause of God.[1] This distinction, with all its spiritual implications, had a profound effect upon the progress of *Christ and Bahá'u'lláh*. The first notification of this came in his letter of March 6, 1952: 'I was ill all the winter and got behind on my work for it. What is more interesting is that since I was made a Hand, the theme of it has become clearer and more unified and will need more work. When it is done, you will have a better book than I had been able to devise before. I am busy on it every day. Lots of other things, too.'

He attended the Bahá'í Summer School that year, held at University Hall, Bangor, North Wales, and wrote from there: 'I have not had the life in me you require to write a book. But I have had for some months past the measure of it. I am working on it now in spiritual peace of Summer School where there is none of that housework and work in the garden which have become so laborious now at Ripley. And at long last my heart is pleased with the work I have done and I feel sure the stuff will fill a gap and prove useful.'

His new insight into the theme had obviously unsettled him, for in spite of the above he wrote at the close of the School: 'It has been very pleasant to me and I feel stimulated and refreshed but am looking forward to my home and to work on my writing there.' A few days after getting home: 'This is to say *Christ and Bahá'u'lláh* will not be

[1] See Ch. 19.

ready for some months. There's a *lot* to do on it.'

In January 1953 he wrote: 'For two years I have been going down hill and in the doctor's hands; and this winter I have lost strength and weight. My progress has been slow but I have kept at the work as well as I could and am now doing much better. The Guardian is, as always, encouraging me in my disappointment and I believe now the job will go along the right lines. But I will make no promises, as to date. Spiritual healing may prove a magical process and I believe with all my heart it will.'

Over the past few years I had become George's publisher and we had agreed on the contract for *Christ and Bahá'u'lláh*. Later his lawyer drew a contract covering all his literary works, and later still George signed a document, witnessed by Nancy, Una and Brian, appointing me his literary executor. I was therefore deeply concerned, particularly in view of George's declining health, by the long delay in completing *Christ and Bahá'u'lláh*, which I knew to be his *chef-d'oeuvre* and the final statement of his clear perception of the factual reality of the God-inspired, God-directed unfoldment of human history. It seemed an appalling prospect that this brilliant work might not reach its conclusion in a published book for all to read. I therefore offered whatever help I could – to make available a stenographer, or provide a dictating machine, or go to Dublin for a month and write as he told me and later make a typescript for him to correct. His reply to this offer was, 'I wish I could take it! But the transcribing is not my difficulty which lies in something temperamental inside me . . . All will soon come right! And I shall know how to present the mass of material I have in my head and heart and in my notes. Adib,[1] I may mention, has very kindly offered to transcribe for me, but I hardly expect to call on him. I cannot dictate at all: wish I could!' And a few days later. 'I have no definite ailment at all but remain too weak to do much writing.'

The Guardian encouraged the Hands of the Cause to visit the friends in their communities, whenever they could, and specifically to attend four Intercontinental Teaching Conferences which he had called in Kampala, Chicago, Stockholm and New Delhi. At them was launched the first global teaching plan undertaken by the entire Bahá'í world community. It ran from April 1953 to April 1963 and is known as the Ten Year Crusade. George, in spite of his weakness, undertook a teaching tour in and around Belfast, and made plans to attend the Stockholm Conference in July. The photograph of the fourteen Hands who attended shows him clear-eyed and alert but physically old and feeble. He was seventy-seven and it is very possible that the fatal Parkinson's disease had already set in, albeit as yet undiagnosed.

[1] Adib Taherzadeh; see p. 335.

At all four conferences pioneers were called for to settle in those territories and major islands of the planet where the Order of Bahá'u'lláh was as yet unestablished. Una volunteered for Malta and arrived in October 1953.[1] It was mooted that George's health would improve in the warmth of Malta, and enquiries and plans were initiated for the move. He wrote of the large mass of material he had collected for his book, which he had neither the time nor strength to co-ordinate and expressed the hope that in Malta he would have better opportunities and balmier weather. But the project fell through and added one more frustrated hope to the long list of such in George's life. In November he wrote, 'Yet my health and my writing seem to need Malta – not to mention the Guardian's approval . . . So we are all up in the air.'

All these activities entailed further delay with the book; and then he decided to rewrite it.

> The spiritual first fruits of the Stockholm Conference were for me that I sat down with a new fervour and in August and September redrafted pretty much all of my *Christ and Bahá'u'lláh* giving to it a unity of theme, a direction it lacked before. There was no effort about the work.
>
> Then the cold weather struck me and I dried up, but managed to struggle to the end in a rough way on October 15th.
>
> Since then I have not done much. The cold weather has weakened me and caused me to fall about. There is lots of work remaining to be done but it would all be done with delight if I were well enough in health.

His condition was serious and was described by Nancy in her letter to the Guardian, enclosed with George's of November 26th, explaining why they could not go to Malta: 'George has had a return of his cerebellum trouble which prevents him co-ordinating his movements, so that he just shuffles from chair to chair and has many falls.'

From now on he fought a courageous battle right through to the end. There were no more teaching tours, talks to the British friends, or regular articles for *Bahá'í Journal*.[2] Even his 'precious correspondence' had to be abandoned. His life became a struggle, waged from a series of nursing homes and, for two short interims, from his home, with a nurse in attendance – to achieve one objective, the completion of his book for the Guardian.

At the end of the year a letter came from the Guardian to Mr and Mrs George Townshend saying that he had heard from 'your dear daughter' in Malta and urging George not to worry too much about

[1] For this service she was named a Knight of Bahá'u'lláh.
[2] See Ch. 13, 'The Writer.'

his book but to work on it only as his strength permitted. 'Undoubtedly when finished it will be a great asset to the Faith.' In retailing this George added, '*Christ and Bahá'u'lláh* progresses in spurts, and now promises well – better than ever.'

It may have been this letter which prompted him to write on January 16, 1954, his handwriting still showing remarkable vigour with only a tendency towards the minute and unreadable form it would shortly assume, accepting my reiterated offer of help 'in a new form, and hope you will consent, and Marion as partner'.[1]

> Let us use correspondence only. I will send you bit by bit my notes or manuscript or outline for your examination, expansion, correction or criticism. The manuscript is in disorder, some notes mislaid or lost. But the plan or plot is clear as crystal, comprehensive, direct, urgent. I worked all day on it yesterday and must do the same in future as far as I can . . .
>
> If you will only suggest, copy in full and type my abbreviations, amend and strengthen when advisable, send back my manuscript with your proposed alterations or your remarks, as quickly as possible – I will be kept up to it, and the cost and labour involved will be very much less than coming over here in person. There will be a lot to do! But two months ought to leave little more to do. My appeal is to <u>Marion</u> for help as much as to you, please.
>
> If you agree I will start very soon to send you my stuff in little bits.
>
> You see what an artful dodger I am! If an author can't write a book himself, let him get his publisher to write it for him!!

We accepted this at once and waited for the parcel of typescript, notes and manuscript. But now, even at this late date the familiar artistic dissatisfaction with his work assailed him again and he wrote on April 26, in a barely decipherable hand:

> After some talks with Una[2] whose spiritual views are full of wisdom I find my latest ideas about *Christ and Bahá'u'lláh* are (as so often before) only the old stuff from a slightly altered angle.
>
> I have in fact no book that will fill the need.
>
> But I shall try quite a new theme, and after prayer and meditation a new and far better conception is springing up in my heart and soul – more congenial, more attractive and more potent than history. Something no one has tried yet.
>
> Be patient: and at present do not mention *Christ and Bahá'u'lláh* to me.

While this new concept was developing within him the forefront of

---

[1] In April 1954 the Hands of the Cause were directed by the Guardian to appoint, in each continent, an Auxiliary Board, whose members would be 'deputies, advisers and assistants to the Hands, would work under their direction and report to them'. Marion Hofman was one of the first to be appointed to the European Board.

[2] George had felt compelled to ask her to return home, since Nancy could not cope with the housekeeping and his increasing illness.

his mind became occupied with a compilation he had made of passages from Bahá'í Sacred Writings about Christ. It was called *The Splendour of Christ*. He had sent the typescript to Horace Holley in the United States more than a year ago and now became eager to have it published. He proposed to amend or add to the Introduction which he had already written, and asked me to send for the typescript if it had not arrived by the middle of August. He received it before then and derived several ideas from it which he later included in *Christ and Bahá'u'lláh*, of which there was, as yet, no further mention. But in January 1955, he wrote from a nursing home: 'Meantime I am working on my book though owing to my health, progress is of necessity very slow. I am however determined to go on with it, if my strength permits. It *must* be brought out somehow.' On March 22, still in the nursing home, he sent the typescript of *The Splendour of Christ*[1] but with no mention of *Christ and Bahá'u'lláh*. But he was working at it as his strength permitted, encouraged all the time by the Guardian. In fact it is the correspondence between the Guardian and himself during 1955 which reveals the heroic struggle he was making to complete his book. For instance his letter to Shoghi Effendi of August 1, 1955, typed by Una explains:

> After reading your kind letter of March 3rd I examined the manuscript of my book which you showed anxiety about and found it highly unsatisfactory, lacking unity, clearness and shape. Your letter enabled me to clarify the theme and to unify the whole story. I rethought with ease and happiness the whole thing and only a few days ago reached a clean cut finale . . . It is a song of joy and battle and victory and triumph and happiness. Some is written but most of it is written in short notes or remains in my mind.
>
> I am satisfied, delighted and content with my new work so far. If I had my strength and could use my pen a few weeks of beatified labour ought to complete it and you would be pleased.
>
> But my weakness continues and I can't write and I haven't yet learned how to dictate . . . Brian helps me once a week when he is able. Therefore, progress with my book must be slow however eager I may feel and in my heart may be. I never doubt ultimate success now but I am not able physically to push the work.

At last on January 21, 1956 he wrote to the Guardian, Una wielding the pen:

> For months and years I have longed to send you the letter we are sending now, telling you I have completed the whole argument (in draft) of the book, driving right through it from first to last and coming out at the close with the end of the sentence which began the book. I have a feeling of

---

[1] It was not entirely ready for publication at that time and is still unpublished.

triumph and joy and confidence; but I am not so excited and delighted as
Una is. Her enthusiasm and determination have increased as time went by;
and when yesterday I read the concluding sentence of it all, she said 'We
must have a prayer of thanksgiving' and quoted the Báb's prayer of victory
. . . I have put all I can into it and pray that the mercy of Bahá'u'lláh may
enable it to do its work with irresistible strength so that it will leave no
doubt of its infinite Truth in anyone's heart.

This was good news (conveyed to me by Una on George's
insistence) even though it was only the 'argument' that was
completed, and there was much writing still to do. I arranged to go to
Dublin to collect whatever 'mass of material' he was ready to give me
and to receive his instructions. Even then he cabled at the last minute
'NOT READY, DON'T COME YET LOVE', but two weeks later, on February
6, 1956, he welcomed me from his bed in the Portobello Nursing
Home. Of that meeting I shall write later. For the moment let it suffice
that I brought back a truly huge pile of paper and set to work on it at
once, tremendously relieved to discover how very much he had
written.

From now on the battle raged. He had indeed projected the
complete plan of his book in a Table of Contents and it was possible to
reduce to its order a very large part of the collected material. Three
complete chapters were quickly typed and sent to him for approval or
revision, and from then on a chapter at a time would go to him as it
became compiled from his notes and manuscript. I managed to get
over to Dublin twice in each month to consult him, taking with me a
list of typewritten questions and proposals for him to read and signify
his approval or otherwise. These lists were sometimes sent by mail or
left by me and George would work on them with Anne Chisholm, a
Bahá'í girl who was a good typist. 'They work on the book in the
mornings when Dad is fresh.' His writing and revision were now done
entirely by the method already described, Una and Brian and Anne
attending him as long as he could work.

The chapter on Muḥammad proved the most troublesome and led
me to Oxford for a week where I spent every day in the Bodleian[1]
checking references and obtaining new material. Brian wrote on April
29,

My father wanted me to take him through the Mohammad chapter today
and all I could find was a hopeless jumble of over 50 sheets of handwriting.
I wonder if you could send a copy of what you did of this so that I could
read it to him? I also could not see a copy of the chapter dealing with the

[1] One of the most famous libraries in the world, re-founded by Sir Thomas Bodley in
1603, containing over 4,250,000 volumes and 50,000 manuscripts; the Library of
Oxford University.

nineteenth-century poets when I last looked about a month ago. Perhaps it has since arrived, or were you not able to do this one?

I promised my father I would have the Mohammad chapter to read to him this week. He got quite agitated about the book this afternoon at home when he found he could not talk clearly enough to dictate.

Chapter after chapter was compiled from his own script and notes, enlarged by his dictation, revised and finally prepared for press. By the end of July a complete typescript was ready for final review and I asked Una to tell her father that I was ready to come over and check it with him, 'but from the point of view of expense and time it would be better if I didn't'. The reply was a telegram: 'AS AUTHOR PREFER DECIDE FINAL TEXT AT LEISURE PLEASE POST MANUSCRIPT WHEN READY.' Such was the veneration in which we all held George that I considered this a severe rebuke and realized I had pushed him too hard without considering his feelings in view of the very great liberties I had taken with his text. I wrote lovingly and contritely and sent him the complete typescript with a résumé of the major changes and additions I had made, and a list of the questions.

Anne Chisholm wrote his reply: 'Your manuscript has come in good order, and has already been read with warm approval. There is a lot to be done with it still. (I write in haste.) Please post at once, better and complete version of chapter on Advent Poetry and Jewish Renaissance.' He signed his 'George' more vigorously than for a long time and added a P.S. by Anne: 'Also post other material with Herald.[1] Thank you. Deeply appreciate your interest and help shown in all your work.' This was initialled by George himself, G.T.; P.P.S. was added by Una. This letter, in three handwritings, was not unusual during this entire episode. The listed questions were answered by Anne who added her own note, 'It is a great joy to be able to give even a little help to our beloved G.T.'

Nowhere, perhaps, were George's courage and determination displayed better or to greater effect than in his completion of this book. Often he was too tired to go on, but his love for the Guardian, who wanted it finished, gave him the strength. In July he said to Una, 'You and David will have to arrange about the rest of the book. I am too weak.' Towards the end of that month he seemed to be sinking, but recovered when he heard of the completion of the typescript and was able to send the cable mentioned above.

The press copy was sent to the printer in October 1956 and the first proofs were sent to George, in three packets, during the second week of December. Inevitably, new questions arose and there was some discussion about the title, but eventually all was settled and the

---

[1] The chapter on *Jesus Christ, Herald of the Kingdom.*

production went ahead as rapidly as possible. George was now on tenterhooks and until he left home for the last time to enter the Baggot Street Hospital he sent a number of cards, mostly illegible, asking about progress, expected date of publication and other information 'of interest to the author'. An earlier one had a readable phrase 'Back home again' and another 'Forgive me – I cannot hold a pen these times'.

The letter written on behalf of the Guardian in reply to George's of January 21, 1956 urged him, without taxing his strength, to put the finishing touches to it so that it could be published without further delay, and continued: 'Surely the Master is very pleased with you, and you have added another laurel to your crown.' Shoghi Effendi's personal note read: 'May the Almighty, Whose Cause you serve with such distinction, consecration, love and perseverance, aid you to fulfil your heart's desire, and enrich, in the days ahead, the record of your truly historic and unforgettable services . . .'

On March 14, 1957 Una wrote,

> The book arrived this morning and my father is delighted. Yesterday and today he is *much* better which has surprised the doctors as well as us. His pulse has steadied and his eyes have cleared.
>
> As soon as a clothbound copy arrives he will sign it and we'll send it to the Guardian . . . Dad couldn't say anything but he smiled.

The clothbound copy for the Guardian arrived on March 26th. George died on the 25th.

The Book

Christ and Bahá'u'lláh is George's first and only book written as a proclaimed and acknowledged member of the Bahá'í community and shows on the title page his former ecclesiastical positions. The first paragraphs of the Prologue immediately reveal the direct clarity with which he now states, briefly and without exposition, the truths which in previous works he had been careful to lead up to, to present as the logical outcome of his argument. *Christ and Bahá'u'lláh* is in reality the documentation of his sublime thesis that history is God-directed according to a Plan; it might well be described by an adaptation of Browning's line, 'God's in His heaven, all will be right with the world'.

The one purpose of George's life was to bring his Church into the heavenly Jerusalem, now revealed by Bahá'u'lláh, and to show all Christendom that the glorious vision of the Kingdom of God on earth, which Christ had taught men to pray for, was now to become a reality and Christians were called upon to be foremost in establishing it. His book is therefore addressed chiefly to Christians, opening to them 'the one door leading to the certain prospect of fulfilment of all that is best in their great tradition'.

George's own description of its theme, given in his letter to the Guardian of July 15, 1949 is probably the best: '. . . a reasoned, scholarly but lyrical exposition of the divine purpose of the Supreme Beloved in human history culminating in the Administrative Order, all written with special reference to the West and God's summons to it and its responsibility and its task now.'

He starts off in fine characteristic style:

> 'Briefly but clearly, and with all possible emphasis, facts are given in this little book to prove that the Kingdom of God, as foretold in the Bible with a thousand details, has at last come with those details all fulfilled.'

He refers to the promise in all world religions of a 'World Redeemer, the Lord of Hosts, the returned Christ, the Qá'im, the new Buddha', and immediately states:

> This outstanding pledge, originally given thousands of years ago, has never been taken up by any of the Great Prophets until the nineteenth century, when Bahá'u'lláh, Founder of the Bahá'í Faith, announced to the rulers and religious leaders of the world that He was this Redeemer and the Bearer of God's message to modern man. He proclaimed that He spoke with the Voice of God Himself, that He was the Lord of Hosts, Christ come in the glory of the Father, and that this was indeed the Last Day, the Day of Judgment. The Cause of Bahá'u'lláh and His martyred Forerunner, the Báb, had for twenty years suffered persecution of every form; yet without investigation the kings and ecclesiastical rulers whom He addressed ignored His message. He died in 1892 in the Holy Land, an exile and captive of the Turks. Yet to-day a world-wide community exists bearing His name and following His teachings.

Thus the Prologue. It is interesting that even in the terse, condensed style which he now uses, he maintains the classical form, setting out his theme, presenting it, and in an Epilogue drawing his conclusions and emphasizing his message. So powerful is the impact of this new economy in his writing that it could be easily inferred that he had chosen it for this particular work, were it not known that it was forced upon him.

Chapter 1, two-and-a-half pages, is *God's Call to the Christians:* 'The Kingdom of God has come! The Lord of Hosts has appeared with all the prophesied tokens! His teachings have gone through the earth and He has proclaimed His message to the kings and religious leaders. But the Christians hesitate, the churches will not acknowledge nor even investigate.'

Christ had declared that the interval between His appearance in Palestine, heralding the Kingdom, and His second coming 'in the glory of the Father', would be a period of uncertainty, endless doubt and dispute. He warned of false prophets who would pervert the true meaning of the Gospel (deceive many, even the very elect); He likened the Christian community to a 'ripening cornfield, infested with masses of weeds growing so close and strong they could not be dug out but would have to be left to do their evil work right through to the harvest time' when the reaper would gather the wheat and burn the tares. George laments that the Christians have not noticed the accuracy of Christ's forecast, or realized that the events He foretold have now reached the crisis of that fulfilment. (Matthew 24)

In Chapter 2 he takes up the story of 'the Kingdom in the Bible'. He had dealt with the millenniums of pre-history in *The Heart of the Gospel* and now notes that the teachings of Noah and Abraham, whom Jesus mentions as His predecessors, are lost. Therefore, although the attainment of the Kingdom is promised in the beginning and the vision of it is described in apocalyptic terms at the close, it was 'not until the wonderful and famous prophecy of Moses in Deuteronomy 30 that the real story of the coming of the Kingdom of God to earth begins in the Bible'.

Moses told the Israelites, whom he was leading out of Egypt to the Promised Land, that in the distant future, because of their violation of God's covenant with them they would be rooted out of that land and scattered among the nations of the earth to live in misery and humiliation, until, at a still later date '. . . *the Lord thy God will turn thy captivity, and have compassion upon thee, and will return and gather thee from all the nations, whither the Lord thy God hath scattered thee'.*[1]

The literal fulfilment of these two predictions is too well known to need documentation, but George pointed out that 'the return' provided the Old Testament prophets with their most famous theme. 'It was the chief subject of the greatest of them all, Isaiah,' and other prophets filled out the enraptured picture which he gave of the future restoration. Through their continual song the vision and hope of the return became synchronized with the coming, at the time of the end, of the Kingdom of God through the appearance of the Supreme World Redeemer, the Lord of Hosts. George gives a dozen quotations from eight books of the Old Testament describing the wonder and glory of that time to come, and leaves for future comment that majestic passage from Isaiah which has rung throughout Christendom (and Israel) through Handel's magnificent oratorio *The Messiah:* '. . . and the

[1] Deut. 30:3

government shall be upon his shoulder; and his name shall be called Wonderful, Counsellor, The mighty God, The everlasting Father, The Prince of Peace.'

The New Testament is all about Jesus Christ, 'Herald of the Kingdom', and its final verses repeat in sublime tones the promise and vision of that Kingdom. This passage was probably the best loved by George in the whole Bible. It set the seal on his understanding and vision of the purpose of creation. He quoted it at the beginning of the first edition of *The Heart of the Gospel* and in many of his essays and commentaries. 'And I saw a new heaven and a new earth:

> Behold, the tabernacle of God is with men, and he will dwell with them, and they shall be his people and God himself shall be with them, and be their God. And God shall wipe away all tears from their eyes; and there shall be no more death, neither sorrow, nor crying, neither shall there be any more pain: for the former things are passed away.

The further verse, 'And the nations of them which are saved shall walk in the light of it: and the kings of the earth do bring their glory and honour into it', is the proof that the vision is not some utopian fantasy but the promise of a real kingdom on this earth.

That Kingdom, *The Kingdom,* became in Christ's Revelation 'a living, glowing reality, both within the believer's heart and shortly to be fulfilled in the world.' The supreme quality of love which Jesus' teachings let loose upon the heart and soul of man endowed the early Christians with a spiritual power which enabled them not only to realize the Kingdom 'within them' but to make great strides in the civilizing of social life. They 'taught the sacredness of human life and the dignity of human nature. As soon as they could they stopped the exposure of infants at birth and the practice of gladiatorial shows. Later they promoted education, built hospitals and introduced a juster system of legislation than had been in use in the Roman State before.'

George was adamant in his insistence that Christ's mission was a purely spiritual one, which yet had its profound effect in the world. 'A new and Christian civilization arose, centred on Byzantium, which reached its height in the fourth century.' Thus the promised Kingdom, whose mysteries were so frequently the subject of Christ's discourse and which must first take root in men's hearts, was drawn nearer by the advances in morals, social relationships and welfare which the love of Christ impelled His followers to make.

Jesus testified to that Great One who would establish the Kingdom, as 'he shall testify of me'. George cites Bahá'u'lláh's testimony to Christ:

> . . . *when the Son of Man yielded up His breath to God, the whole creation wept*

*with a great weeping. By sacrificing Himself, however, a fresh capacity was
infused into all created things. Its evidences, as witnessed in all the peoples of the
earth, are now manifest before thee. The deepest wisdom which the sages have
uttered, the profoundest learning which any mind hath unfolded, the arts which the
ablest hands have produced, the influence exerted by the most potent of rulers, are
but manifestations of the quickening power released by His transcendent, His all-
pervasive, and resplendent Spirit.*

*We testify that when He came into the world, He shed the splendour of His glory
upon all created things. Through Him the leper recovered from the leprosy of
perversity and ignorance. Through Him, the unchaste and wayward were healed.
Through His power, born of Almighty God, the eyes of the blind were opened, and
the soul of the sinner sanctified.*

*Leprosy may be interpreted as any veil that interveneth between man and the
recognition of the Lord, his God. Whoso alloweth himself to be shut out from Him
is indeed a leper, who shall not be remembered in the Kingdom of God, the Mighty,
the All-Praised. We bear witness that through the power of the Word of God every
leper was cleansed, every sickness was healed, every human infirmity was
banished. He it is Who purified the world. Blessed is the man who, with a face
beaming with light, hath turned towards Him.*[1]

Having for years attempted to reveal the reality of Christ's message
to the leaders of Christianity, gently and as far as possible according to
their own assumptions and conventions, George is now bent on
shaking them out of their composure. His comment on the above
testimony of Bahá'u'lláh was: 'Wonderful is the story of Christ
indeed! Yet where is the Gospel in the world today?'

He now launched into an examination of the corruption of the
Christian message which, if judged fairly, would shake the most
devout Christian to the very depths. His opening statement is a model
of his new, terse, simple style: 'As Jesus had prophesied, the false
prophets contrived to change the essential meaning of the Gospel so
that it became quite different from that which the Bible recorded or
Jesus taught.'

He deals in swift succession with the major points on which Jesus'
teaching has been corrupted.

1. It has long been generally believed that Jesus Christ was a unique
incarnation of God such as had never before appeared in religious history
and would never appear again. This tenet made the acceptance of any later
Prophet impossible to a Christian. Yet there is nothing in Christ's own
statements, as recorded in the Gospel, to support this view, and it was not
generally held during His lifetime.

Jesus claimed emphatically to reveal God, but equally emphatically
and repeatedly He denied being the Father: *my Father is greater than I; I*

[1] *Gleanings from The Writings of Bahá'u'lláh*, XXXVI

will pray the Father; I do nothing of myself; but as my Father hath taught me.
The Father had knowledge denied to the Son: *But of that day and that hour knoweth no man, no, not the angels which are in heaven, neither the Son, but the Father.* Jesus related His own mission to those of Abraham and Moses before Him and to others to come after Him, notably *the Spirit of Truth.*

George makes the point that every world religion has invented the same uniqueness of their own Prophet, in direct contradiction of His own word. 'The result of this delusive belief has been that the world religions far from unifying mankind have divided it into irreconcilable groups.

2. Christ's teaching is taught to be absolute and final and even if He did withhold many things because they were unable to bear them, it is now taught that Truth in its fullness was revealed at Pentecost:

> But there is nothing in the account of Pentecost to suggest such an interpretation and there is no one who will believe that Jesus would have named the false prophets as characteristic of His age if this warning was to be followed by an immediate release of all Truth to the Church. What the Bible shows is rather a succession of teachers – Abraham, Moses and Christ, each measuring His Revelation to the needs and maturity of His auditors . . .

Neither does the history of the world, and particularly that of Christendom, indicate that all Truth has ever been finally revealed.

3. 'Another universal opinion among the Christians is that Christ was the Lord of Hosts of the Old Testament.' Yet the great prophecies indicated that when He came the Jews would have been scattered among the nations for centuries. The dispersion did not begin until seventy years after Christ, when Jerusalem was sacked under Titus, and the expulsion of the Jews began.

Isaiah's great prophecy about the Lord of Hosts is read in Christian churches on Christmas morning as though it referred to Jesus:

> For unto us a child is born, unto us a son is given: and the government shall be upon his shoulder: and his name shall be called Wonderful, Counsellor, The mighty God, The everlasting Father, The Prince of Peace. Of the increase of his government and peace there shall be no end, upon the throne of David, and upon his kingdom, to order it, and to establish it with judgment and with justice from henceforth even for ever. The zeal of the Lord of hosts will perform this.

But only two of the descriptions given can refer to Jesus; He specifically repudiated the other four 'as if to make such a mistaken reference to Himself impossible'. Wonderful, Counsellor, are certainly 'names' of Christ but He emphatically denied being 'The mighty God' or 'The everlasting Father'; see 1. above. He was the Son and so called Himself. Far from being the Prince of Peace, He said, '*I came not to send peace, but a sword.*' He refused to take the government upon His shoulders when He said, '*My kingdom is not of this world.*'

The effect of these false assumptions is that

> In spite of Christ's promise of further revelation of Truth, through the Comforter, through His own return, through the Spirit of Truth, the Christian Church regards His revelation as final, and itself as the sole trustee of true religion. There is no room for the Supreme Redeemer of the Bible to bring in great changes for the establishment of the Kingdom of God. In fact this Kingdom is often described as a world-wide Church.

Furthermore

> Christ's spiritual mission was, at an early date, materialized, specifically in regard to such things as the miracles, curing the blind and deaf, raising the dead. Even His own resurrection was made physical, missing the point entirely. Moreover, none of the complex order, of the ceremonies, rituals and litanies of the Church can be attributed to Christ. All are man-made, by inference or invention.
>
> Well might Christ warn His followers that false prophets would arise and misinterpret His teachings so as to delude even the most earnest and intelligent of His believers: from early times Christians have disputed about Christian truth in councils, in sects, in wars.

The chapter on *Muḥammad, Builder of Nations* may be an even greater shock to Christians than its predecessor. It is full of information which was until very lately generally unknown to the Christian lay world. George had made a thorough study and cites authorities both European and Islamic.

His first authority is the Bible. Genesis 12 and 17 record how God promised Abraham that the prophetic succession would run through His son Isaac:

> *And as for Ishmael, I have heard thee: Behold I have blessed him, . . . and will multiply him exceedingly; twelve princes shall he beget, and I will make him a great nation.*
>
> He became the progenitor of the people of Arabia and the twelve Princes which he begot are interpreted as the twelve Imams who followed Muḥammad.

Moses confirmed this promise in Deuteronomy (18:15): *the Lord Thy God will raise up unto thee a Prophet from the midst of thee, of thy brethren, like unto me.*

It is a sad comment that in this modern world of enmities one of the bitterest is that between Jews and Arabs, both proud of their descent from the same ancestor. The Qu'rán gives the same circumstantial account of Ishmael's childhood in the desert of Paran as is found in Genesis.

George interpolates here Moses' final prophecy of the succession of Divine Revelations from His own until that of Bahá'u'lláh:

> *The Lord came from Sinai* (meaning Himself), *and rose up from Seir* . . . (meaning Jesus Christ); *he shined forth from mount Paran* (meaning Muḥammad), *and he came with ten thousand of saints* (meaning Bahá'u'lláh).[1]

George devotes four chapters to Islám, its place in world history and its relationship to Christendom. He knew the ignorance and prejudice of the West on this subject, resulting from the misinformation, slanders and utter travesty of fact with which it had been gulled for centuries and in spite of the précis-like presentation of his argument, or possibly because of it, he manages to convey an interesting and even exciting picture of the 'known' world at the time of Muḥammad. (China and Africa south of the Sahara were only known to exist; the discovery of America was still five hundred years away.)

He draws a pointed comparison with Europe in its Dark Ages, where search for knowledge and the idea of progress were anathema to an all-powerful church which condemned the spirit of enquiry and the free use of reason as heretical. In Cordoba, at the height of its prosperity, 'a man after sunset might walk in a straight line for ten miles along paved and illuminated streets – yet in Europe centuries later there was not a paved street in Paris nor a public lamp in London'.

Muḥammad's dispensation dates from AD 622 although He was born about 570. He made three particular contributions to the unfoldment of God's grand redemptive scheme. There is general agreement that the founding of the nation state was the greatest. Another was the promotion of learning and civilization by the erstwhile barbarous and ignorant tribes of Arabia, to such effect that 'In the midst of a dark and stagnant world there sprang up as if by magic a brilliant civilization'. Yet another was the uncompromising declaration of the oneness of God and the progressiveness of Divine revelation.

Muḥammad had made the search for knowledge a religious duty, and historians to this day are fascinated and astonished by the speed with which Islám established its three great centres of civilization. Baghdád in the Middle East, Egypt and the north African littoral, Cordoba the capital of Muslim Spain, became focal points of culture, administration, scientific research, art and commerce, literature, scholarship, in short the poles of a liberal, progressive civilization the

[1] Deut. 33:2

like of which had never been seen before. It extended from Spain to India and covered a greater area than all the dominions of Rome.

The fruits of this great upsurge of energy were not lost as Islám declined, as had been the case with Greece and Rome,[1] but were gradually transferred to Europe, eventually promoting the Renaissance and that subsequent vast extension of the spirit of enquiry which produced the modern age.

George acknowledged that it would seem natural to expect that the Dispensation of the Son, the Herald of the Kingdom, would be followed by that of the Father, Whose good pleasure it would be to give the Kingdom.[2] But before mankind could be ready for so great a bounty major advances would have to be made in arts and sciences involving the discovery and exploration of the planet, and the organization of large associations of human beings. 'Mankind had now had the experience of organizing the family, the tribe and the city state.' The far greater task of ordering a nation must be learned before attempting the government of so vast a commonwealth as world order, which the Kingdom would be. This was the special mission of Muḥammad. George found his authorities at one in regarding the development of the nation state as 'Muḥammad's real and creative contribution to human development'. But national establishments inevitably involved international relationships and, for the first time, the sanctity of treaties became a command from God. Patriotism was an element of faith but,

> be not false in your engagements, with your own knowledge . . . Or if thou fear treachery from any people, throw back their treaty to them as thou fairly mayest, for God loveth not the treacherous . . . And if they lean to peace, lean thou also to it.[3]

Such was the training which Muḥammad gave to a humanity whose most advanced political system was the city-state and which would, in the next Dispensation, have to learn the art and principles of world order.

It was never the intention of the successive Manifestations of God to found separate and alienated communities. Each of the great Revealers built on the foundation of His predecessors and foretold and opened the way for His successor. They came, as Jesus said, not to destroy but to fulfil.[4] They all served the same great Plan of God and are the

[1] The classical arts and sciences, anathema to the medieval Church, were rescued by Islám, which welcomed knowledge from every source, and were eventually restored, greatly enriched and advanced, to Europe.

[2] Luke 12:32

[3] Qur'án 8: 27, 60, 63

[4] Matt. 5:17

'overlords of evolution' as George described Them in *The Heart of the Gospel*. They are the appearances of the one Sun of Truth, the Light of the world. The enmities among religion are the work of men, chiefly the priests.

It was not the populace, thronging to see and hear Jesus, who rejected and killed Him, but the priesthood, led by Annas and Caiaphas. The Christian masses of the earliest centuries were disposed, as the Báb testified, to accept the Arabian Prophet and His message but were prevented from doing so by their clergy. It was the Muslim divines of Persia who attempted to exterminate the Báb and His followers and today are attempting to do the same to the Bahá'ís. God's Messenger is never welcomed by the guardians of religion, the priesthood. Had He been, history would have been different indeed.

If the world's religious leaders of today, particularly those of Christianity, would examine the messages addressed to them by Bahá'u'lláh and follow the guidance offered, the face of the world would change at once. Instead of fighting ever more desperately the losing battle against impending disaster, mankind would be striving with increasing joy and confidence to resolve the constructive problems of establishing world order and the brotherhood of man.

Muḥammad showed 'the greatest kindness' to Christians and took them under His express protection. But alas, Muḥammad's relationship to the Christians did not become the pattern for Islám's to Christianity. The violation of Muḥammad's Covenant, almost immediately after His ascension, deprived Islám of that inspired guidance which Muḥammad had intended it to receive from 'Alí, His appointee and confidant, who was set aside, and before long the powerful Umayyads ruled Islám with little regard for Muḥammad's teachings.

> This heinous violation swept away all possibility of Muḥammad's love for Christendom, so conspicuously displayed in His lifetime, from developing, and thereafter the relationship of these two chief civilizations followed its tragic course, continuing right down to our own day to disturb the order of the world and to prevent the establishment of that unity in brotherhood which was the desire of both Christ and Muḥammad.

George's argument is now approaching the point where the impact of these distant events on modern times is disclosed. He first draws attention to the contrast between the conquering career of Islám and the development of its brilliant, progressive civilization, and the semi-barbarous stagnation of Europe, which because of the Christian rejection of Muḥammad and the violation by the Umayyads of His

Covenant, was shut out from the onward march of history. Inevitably, however, the advanced civilization of Islám, pressing upon Europe from the East and from Spain in the West, began to influence the life and thought of that dark continent.

> Through the Muslim outpost in Sicily and the scintillating brilliance of Muslim Spain, through the intelligence of scholars and the resources of the Muslim universities, through traders, through diplomats and travellers, through soldiers, sailors and reconquered peasants, new ideas, techniques and attitudes passed from Islám to Western Europe.
>
> Then came the day in 1094 when the Pope called on the chivalry and the faithful of Christendom to arouse themselves and go forth and drive the Saracen hosts out of the sacred Christian shrine, which they had seized, and re-establish the Christian Faith in its ancient home. Europe leapt up at his word and for well-nigh two hundred years the vicissitudes of this colossal war between Europe and Asia, the West and the East, Christian and unbeliever continued to cause the loss of millions of lives, to spread infinite misery and to squander immense treasure. The Christians ultimately withdrew in ignominious and complete defeat and Islám remained in possession of all the Holy Places she had owned before.
>
> It was Europe, however, and not Arabia which gained from the struggle, for the Crusades provided yet another channel through which knowledge of the Muslim civilization flowed into Europe.

The Rise of Modern Europe is the heart of George's thesis, for in this chapter he shows that the *joie de vivre* of the Renaissance, 'which Europe learned from the Arabs', resulted in a civilization of enormous and ever extending power, eventually encompassing more than half the world and many of the nations of Islám. It was Europeans who discovered the continents of the Americas and Australia and opened up the unexplored recesses of Africa.

But European civilization, in spite of this tremendous extension of its dominion in economic, political and military matters,

> proved quite unequal to spreading its spiritual influence. Even when, during the eighteenth and nineteenth centuries, it spent large sums of money and sent out hundreds and even thousands of missionaries, its failure to Christianize the world was as conspicuous as its success in establishing its economic suzerainty . . . The Church at the beginning of this period was still the Church of the Dark Ages. Worldly-minded men had got control of it and were determined to hold that control. Uninfluenced by the changing spirit of the age they found themselves in opposition to the whole progressive movement that was forging a new eager, active Europe. They would not tolerate the spirit of enquiry or the free use of reason. These they represented as being definitely heretical . . . They laid it down that the deposit of faith was static. It was once and for all delivered to the saints, and was not to be changed or challenged . . .

Orthodoxy rather than detachment or moral righteousness has been the shibboleth of religious authorities. Their enthusiasm has been confined largely to insistence on teachings, doctrines, speculations which, like their own structure were devised by themselves, and around which controversies were raised which none could finally settle. About the main ethical injunctions of Christ and actual obedience to them there was no such insistence . . . No church, for example, has ever adopted the challenging test for membership used by Jesus Himself for His disciples: '*By this shall all men know that ye are my disciples, if ye have love one to another.*' (*John* 13:35)

Europe in consequence has never been tranquil, full of good will, united, but rather full of oppression, misery, strife and turbulence. The cause of Religion has been supported by the most flagrant breaches of Gospel ethics.

So far did the traditional religion of Europe, in its character and effects, differ from that of the Gospel, that it became the chief cause of unchristian feeling and behaviour. It promoted hatred and schism, discontent, strife, cruelty and injustice, suppression of truth and reason. It has conducted persecutions, burnings at the stake, extermination of heretics, suppression of truth by force . . .

But now another divergence between the attitude of the Church and that of all progressives took shape and grew steadily more wide. The Church objected to that nation-building which had been the main contribution of Muḥammad to human history and which was to be as important to the building of Western civilization as it had been to Islám.

George's exposure of the Church's negative role in the rise of modern Europe is not made for the sake of castigation or criticism. Rather is it a lament for the appalling consequences of the Church's failure to take the lead in promoting the advancement of civilization. Because of that failure the immense advantages won by the development of the nation state were won in spite of the Church, so that European civilization as it spread around the world became more and more materialistic, pursuing only economic and intellectual ideas of progress, uninformed by any knowledge of the Divine purpose, or even realizing any purpose at all except that of greater and greater material comfort:

Not only has the prestige and influence of the Church been thus abased but the prestige and influence of religion with it; and at the same time materialism has been strengthened and exalted. The whole progress of our Western civilization has been, therefore, not the intensifying of Christianity but the opposite.

European man went on his conquering way, misled by his religious leaders and unaware of his true spiritual destiny.

The Dawn-Song of the Kingdom was one of George's favourite themes. It is the subject of the third essay in his book *The Genius of*

Ireland,[1] where he presents the vision of the New Age, entertained by the late eighteenth- and nineteenth-century poets, which they sensed was opening before mankind. In that essay, he describes, in logical terms and in some detail, their expressions of this sensibility but, as was his method in 1930, without ever mentioning the specific event whose near approach so brightened their horizon. In *Christ and Bahá'u'lláh* he clearly relates this joyful outlook to his main theme, the coming of the Kingdom.

This is the chapter which he had referred to as 'Advent poetry and Jewish Renaissance',[2] and in it he describes and documents both phenomena. The emancipation of the Jews from their long centuries of oppression began in the eighteenth century.

> In Europe and America nation after nation began to restore to them by slow degrees rights which for long centuries had been denied them . . . the year 1844 being a time of special importance, since in it the Turkish Government pledged to the Jews protection from persecution throughout the Ottoman Dominion, including of course the Holy Land, though it was not until 1867 that the Sublime Porte gave them the right to own real estate in the land of their fathers.
>
> What could all this mean but the approach of the second coming of Christ?

The exaltation of the romantic poets is well documented although it is possible to think that this part of his book is one of those which he might have written at greater length. The point is clear enough and his argument in no way suffers from the brevity of his treatment, but with greater leisure he might have added to his examples and extended them to European poets and even beyond to those of cultures other than Western Christendom. He cites Wordsworth's marvellous passage from Book XI of *The Prelude* which begins:

> Bliss was it in that dawn to be alive,
> But to be young was very Heaven! O times . . .

and continues for another twenty lines.
Frederick Tennyson's

> The night is ended and the morning nears;
> Awake, look up, I hear the gathering sound
> Of coming cycles, like an ocean round;
> I see the glory of a thousand years
> Lightening from bound to bound.

[1] See Ch. 13, 'The Writer'.
[2] See p. 291.

and two verses of J. A. Symond's

> These things shall be: a loftier race
> Than e'er the world hath known, shall rise,
> With flame of freedom in their souls
> And light of knowledge in their eyes . . .
>
> New arts shall bloom of loftier mould,
> And mightier music thrill the skies,
> And every life shall be a song
> When all the earth is paradise,

a further two from Charles Kingsley's *The Day of the Lord* ('is at hand, at hand') and from across the Atlantic, Julia Ward Howe's 'Mine eyes have seen the glory of the coming of the Lord,' which became popular as the 'Battle Hymn of the Republic', complete his quotations.[1] But he gives some attention to Shelley's 'apocalyptic works' and describes the theme of 'his great poetical drama *Prometheus Unbound*, which many critics regard as the sublimest poem in the English language.'

> Not poets alone but the generality of the people in town and in country, high and low, learned and unlearned, felt this new transcendent power stirring creation . . . For two centuries, it may perhaps be said, this new wave of power affected all the Western world except one section only, the institutions which claimed to be custodians of religious truth, which claimed to have a monopoly of keeping watch for Christ according to His command. The old established, historic churches of Christendom showed themselves irresponsive and uninterested. The false prophets had done their deadly work with full success. So misleading had been their interpretations of religious history that Christ had indeed come and no men had been so utterly ignorant of His presence as those who had appointed themselves to be His special guardians.

George now devotes four chapters to a presentation of the historical facts of the Bahá'í Revelation. He documents the beginning of the Bahá'í era as the evening of May 22, 1844, with the Báb's declaration of His mission, and describes the miraculous happenings 'attested by witnesses on both sides' on the occasion of His martyrdom together with the young disciple 'suspended across His breast'.

Their commingled remains now lie under the famous golden dome of the Báb's Shrine on the slopes of Mount Carmel, facing northwards across the Bay of Haifa to the ancient fortress of 'Akká and beyond to Bahjí, where Bahá'u'lláh, for Whom the Báb gave His life, was imprisoned and ascended.

---

[1] In the essay referred to above he deals at length with Blake, Browning, Shelley and Lord Tennyson. See p. 251.

The two chapters on Bahá'u'lláh are divided into a brief narrative of His life up to the declaration in the Garden of Riḍván – 'Surely this Day must be the greatest day in the history of mankind' – and an account of His proclamation to the kings and rulers of the world, and of His four exiles leading finally to 'Akká.

The narrative is enriched by Bahá'u'lláh's Own account of the fearful dungeon, the Síyáh-Chál in Ṭihrán, into which He had been cast after the attempt on the life of the Sháh, and of what befell Him there.

> The dungeon was wrapt in thick darkness, and Our fellow prisoners numbered nearly one hundred and fifty souls; thieves, assassins and highwaymen. Though crowded, it had no other outlet than the passage by which We entered. No one can depict that place, nor any tongue describe its loathsome smell. Most of these men had neither clothes nor bedding to lie on. God alone knoweth what befell Us in that most foul-smelling and gloomy place! . . .
>
> One night in a dream these exalted words were heard on every side: 'Verily, We shall render Thee victorious by Thyself and by Thy pen. Grieve Thou not for that which hath befallen Thee, neither be Thou afraid, for Thou art in safety. Ere long will God raise up the treasures of the earth – men who will aid Thee through Thyself and through Thy Name, wherewith God hath revived the hearts of such as have recognised Him.'

George showed Bahá'u'lláh's proclamation to the kings and religious leaders of the earth, a summons unprecedented in religious history,[1] as taking place against the background of His second and third exiles to Constantinople and Adrianople and the final banishment to 'Akká, 'the dungeon city of which it was said the very birds fell dead as they passed over it'. The most momentous of these letters, the Súriy-i-Mulúk (Tablet of the Kings) and two others, were written and dispatched from Adrianople, the most northern outpost in Europe of the Turkish empire. In its balmier days it had, for a time, been the capital of that empire but was now as ramshackle as the Sulṭán's dominion itself, in spite of two magnificent mosques which still dominate its entire scene. It has the distinction of being the site of the only occasion in recorded history when a Manifestation of God set foot in Europe.[2]

[1] Muḥammad, according to a generally accepted tradition, sent from Medina a letter to the Emperor of China, and six to neighbouring rulers proclaiming His Prophethood. They were the Emperors of Byzantium and of Persia (the two super-powers of the day), the King of Abyssinia, the Governor of Egypt, the King of Hira and the Duke of Yemen. Cf. *Christ and Bahá'u'lláh*, p. 37.

[2] Mr Geoffrey Ashe, in his *King Arthur's Avalon* (Fontana Books, 1973), puts forward a strong case for the legend that Jesus, in His youth, visited Glastonbury, but it is not widely accepted although Blake's great poem, *Jerusalem*, refers to it: 'And did those feet in ancient time, Walk upon England's mountains green'.

George's book is about the relationship between Christ and Bahá'u'lláh and he therefore lays great stress on those Tablets which are 'of especial moment to Western and Christian readers;' first the Tablet to the kings of the earth collectively, issued in 1864, and secondly the individual Tablets to the four chief monarchs of Europe, Napoleon III, Pope Pius IX, Queen Victoria and Czar Alexander. In His first Tablet, the *Súriy-i-Mulúk*, Bahá'u'lláh summoned the rulers to the Most Great Peace. One and all they disdained or rejected his call. The letters sent to individual monarchs received the same treatment while the Sháh of Persia cruelly tortured and killed Bahá'u'lláh's seventeen-year-old messenger who took the letter from 'Akká to Ṭihrán. Queen Victoria is reported to have said, on reading the letter addressed to her, 'If this is of God, it will stand. Otherwise it can do no harm.' But neither she nor any other Christian ruler turned to Bahá'u'lláh or paid any heed to His counsels and warnings. He said of them that they were so intoxicated with pride that they were unable to discern their own best interests, much less to recognize so bewildering and challenging a Revelation as that of which He was the bearer.

George declares that 'the year 1870 may be regarded as marking the disruption and decline of Western civilization.' In that year Napoleon III, having contemptuously rejected Bahá'u'lláh's summons and subsequent warning of disaster, met his downfall at Sedan. Pius IX, ignoring Bahá'u'lláh's call to abandon his temporal sovereignty, and in fact doing his utmost to maintain it, was forcibly deprived of it and 'became the prisoner of the Vatican'.

The chapter concludes with Bahá'u'lláh in 'Akká and Bahjí, where He spent the last years. E.G. Browne's immortal and oft-quoted description of Him, and the words He spoke on the occasion of one of the audiences accorded the great orientalist are given in full. The final exhortation has acquired added pertinence to the human condition since it was uttered, ninety years ago: *These strifes and this bloodshed and discord must cease, and all men be as one kindred and one family . . . Let not a man glory in this, that he loves his country; let him rather glory in this, that he loves his kind . . .*

'Abdu'l-Bahá is introduced by George in the following terms:

Bahá'u'lláh appointed in His written Will His son 'Abdu'l-Bahá as His successor and with this successorship joined powers to which no successor of any earlier Prophet had attained and which give 'Abdu'l-Bahá a position altogether unique in religious history. Bahá'u'lláh designated Him as the Centre and pivot of His peerless Covenant; as the perfect mirror of His life, to exemplify His teachings; as the unerring interpreter of His Word; as the embodiment of every Bahá'í ideal and virtue.

He visited the western world during the years 1911 to 1913, travelling extensively in Europe, staying some time in Paris and visiting Britain twice. He crossed and recrossed the United States and visited Canada. Newspapers featured His visits wherever He went and crowds surrounded Him and besieged His residences, drawn by the simple majesty of His Person and the overwhelming love for humanity and for all individuals which so powerfully emanated from Him.

George uses this chapter on the last of the three Central Figures of the Bahá'í Faith to lay great emphasis on the contrast between the divine view of civilization and progress as expounded by the Bible and Bahá'u'lláh and the human view as generally held by the people of the West. 'Abdu'l-Bahá well knew the danger facing the Christian West at that time although they themselves had no idea of the awful ruin shortly to overtake their much-vaunted dominion.

> They had no doubt that they at this time were the most enlightened generation of the most enlightened age the world had ever known. Physical science had, they thought, reached the limit of reality and probed all the problems and in fact knew all that was to be known. White man in the plenitude of his power was now established in material control of the weaker nations of the world and would hold the economic, military and political domination of the world indefinitely.
>
> Some such views as these were probably held by every educated person in audiences to whom 'Abdu'l-Bahá spoke in the West; more particularly by those in England; . . .

Knowing this, and knowing too the predictions in the Bible, and specifically that of Jesus that affliction such as the world had never known would precede the victory of God on earth, that none would be left unless the days were shortened,[1] it would have been quite easy for Him to have exposed the Western fallacy and shown the hollowness of the western expectation of a man-made kingdom and the domination of one race over others. But

> 'Abdu'l-Bahá did nothing of the kind. The great ideal which He held before His audiences was at all times and places one and the same: Unity Through Love. His *Paris Talks* are full throughout of a spiritual wisdom, a spontaneous warmth of heart and sweetness and winning tenderness that would be hard to match in the world's revealed religious literature.

George examines very thoroughly, and with deep penetration 'Abdu'l-Bahá's approach to the Western mind. This was not new ground for him, for ever since the receipt of his two Tablets, thirty-five years earlier, he had studied and re-studied the Master's *Paris Talks*, the compilation of His North American addresses – published

[1] Matt. 24:21, 22

under the title *The Promulgation of Universal Peace,* the volumes of His collected letters to Western believers and the famous *Some Answered Questions.* What is remarkable about his presentation in this volume is the clarity of his mind in face of the deterioration of his physical powers. The ordering of his material to combine 'Abdu'l-Bahá's divine philosophy with the overall theme of his book – the coming of the Kingdom – against the background of the hard-headed factual materialism of the West, is masterly. At the same time he reveals that magical fascination which 'Abdu'l-Bahá exercised upon the hearts and souls of men to which George himself had been in thrall for so long.

He showed that 'Abdu'l-Bahá's first aim was 'to create in the minds of His hearers capacity to understand and appreciate this great new Revelation.' He sought,

> as Christ in His day had done, to transform and spiritualize the very hearts and outlook of those to whom He spoke. Unless He could do this the exposure of one error in the minds of the people would only be followed on the next occasion by another error. No remedy was adequate except that of creating a real capacity in the human heart to see and love the truth. This and nothing less was the first and last aim of 'Abdu'l-Bahá.

The 'truth of a new dawning of power in the world', voiced in His address in the City Temple, London,

> became the master thought of all His speeches throughout His work in the West. In America, however, he addressed the Americans particularly as Christians and made an appeal to them not to be listeners only but to become the reapers whom Christ had prophesied would arise in His harvest day. He sought not only to instruct and illumine the minds of His audience but to awaken in them the power of spirituality and enthusiasm which would overcome the materialism that infected mankind and would develop in them a new loving spirituality which would enable His message to get home to their hearts.
>
> He presented a new picture of Christ in contrast to the Christ of orthodoxy, of sect and schism and dogma; one which showed that Christ's real purpose was to unite human hearts with the power of Divine love; such a Christ as none had really conceived, eager, vigorous, bringing together people of all sorts and kinds and races and nations and overwhelming the prejudices and traditions which separated them. The natural force of His own warm, buoyant, loving nature gave power and reality to His presentation so that He was able to reveal a new Christ such as the people had never realized.
>
> His American addresses open on a note of joy, of spontaneous abounding happiness and gratification at His meeting so many radiant hearts ready to listen to the Message which, in spite of His old age and imperfect health, He had come so far to give them. Only love from God

and them would have brought Him. Heart and soul 'Abdu'l-Bahá radiated a triumphant confidence, clear and strong as can be, as He extolled the glory of Christ and Bahá'u'lláh, showing their closeness, the unity of their effort and their purpose.

His appeal was not to authority as was that of Bahá'u'lláh addressing the kings. He did not command. His appeal rather was to reason, to logic, to faith and to facts. He exposed the false hopes of the arrogant white race, not by disproof but by drawing in a quite natural manner a picture of the true antecedents of the Kingdom, showing it to be involved in the original creation of man.

He drew, in many aspects, a picture of the whole universe as governed by one unchanging law, as being created, ruled over and directed by one universal, independent, living Will. This great, out-working Spirit actuated the affairs and movements of all creatures in the world; it was the one Power which animated and dominated all existence. 'Abdu'l-Bahá spoke on this subject in an attitude of soul as logical as it was religious, as much in the mood of science as of faith. He treated the subject not only in a broad and general manner but in close detail. He traced, for example, the coursing of the atom through the kingdoms of nature – mineral, vegetable and animal – showing the changes that it assumes in its progress, through an activity not originating by itself. He showed that the one, living, independent Will of God which directed the transition of the atom directed likewise the movements which led mankind from one stage to another on its journey to the Kingdom. Thus He brought all nature into the same plane as man and showed, not only the oneness of mankind but of the whole universe – everything contributing, each in its own way – even if it be a preparatory way – towards the one great spiritual goal shown at its highest in the Kingdom of God.

During the course of His eight-months' tour of ceaseless lecturing in North America, 'Abdu'l-Bahá laid the foundation stone of the first Bahá'í House of Worship in the West. It was sited at Wilmette, on the shore of Lake Michigan, north of Chicago.

As he left the American continent to return, via Europe, to Haifa, the Master with sadness of heart announced the approaching outbreak of the First World War. During that war He issued, from His home in the Holy Land, a series of fourteen letters to various geographical sections of North America,

a stirring summons to all Bahá'ís to arouse themselves and go forth through the length and breadth of the world to call all nations to the Kingdom of God. Once more He quoted the wonderful examples of the Apostles of Christ as a challenge to self-sacrifice. Fourteen of these letters constitute 'Abdu'l-Bahá's Divine Plan in which He detailed a vigorous and forthright programme for the carrying of the message of the New Day throughout the continents and the islands of the sea, – a plan fully worked out and likely to be in use for many generations to come. No great response was aroused among the Bahá'ís by this appeal, a fact which caused 'Abdu'l-Bahá poignant sorrow, compelling Him to realize how deep the suffering of the world would be which all His efforts had not been able to mitigate. Broken in heart He passed to His end three years after the War, foretelling that another war, fiercer than the last, would follow before long.

These letters became known as the *Tablets of the Divine Plan* and were taken up by the Guardian as the charter for teaching the Faith of Bahá'u'lláh throughout the world. Having guided a few Bahá'í communities in various nations and regions to autonomous administration within the framework of the world-wide Bahá'í community, Shoghi Effendi launched, in 1953, the first global plan for the implementation of this master plan of 'Abdu'l-Bahá's.[1] Many world-wide Plans have followed the Guardian's, the current one being a Seven Year Plan to terminate in 1986, and there are others to come. They are all phases of 'Abdu'l-Bahá's Divine Plan, which, as George remarked, is 'likely to be in use for many generations to come'.

'Abdu'l-Bahá passed away in 1921.

On His death the most deeply conceived and constructive of His works was published, known as *The Will and Testament of 'Abdu'l-Bahá*. It completed the great masterpiece of Bahá'u'lláh – His book of laws – the two works together composing one complete and harmonious whole.

George devotes a chapter to it, elucidating his preamble:

> Jesus Christ said, *'My kingdom is not of this world,'* and Christian people have been inclined to think that pure religion is subjective and mystical only and has little or no connection with the organization of institutions or the making of laws or ordinances. This idea is quite alien to the New and the Old Testaments. The Kingdom of God is indeed a Kingdom, the ruler of which is not a philosopher or a teacher, but a King with laws and subjects. The New Jerusalem which comes down from heaven and becomes the centre of the Kingdom represents the Law of God, while the distinctive function of the Lord of Hosts on earth is that 'the government shall be upon his shoulder' and that He will administer 'judgment and justice from henceforth, even forever'.
>
> *The Will and Testament of 'Abdu'l-Bahá* sets forth the administrative order by which this is to be accomplished, and, fathered by Bahá'u'lláh, provides the Bahá'í Faith with its historically unique feature – an administrative system based on the inviolable written Scripture, establishing the succession, defining the institutions, conferring authority, preventing schism, guarding the Revealed Word from adulteration, providing for its authoritative interpretation, and perpetuating the Divine guidance of the Lord of Hosts Himself.

[1] See page 286.

The subject is a study in itself, possible only to a humanity at last coming of age and able to understand the three great unities: God, man, and the relationship between them, called Religion.

George's final chapter again shows how far were Western ideas of progress, at the end of the nineteenth century, from the vision of the Kingdom of God which had inspired the Prophets of the Old Testament and concluded the canon of the New. Rather, he says, was it the Kingdom of man than of God and

> not of all men but of one race only and of certain members of that race who had achieved for themselves supremacy over the others. It would mean a world-wide Church, the domination of the white man, of white man's civilization, and it contemplated the perpetuation of an ever-increasing trade.

There was no widespread appreciation of the appalling crisis facing the human race. The Promised One had indeed come like a thief in the night and the leaders of the world had refused to be informed of it. 'The principle of the Oneness of Mankind – the pivot round which all the teachings of Bahá'u'lláh revolve . . .'[1] found no echo in their philosophy and aspirations.

The great calamities of the first half of the twentieth century wrecked for ever the old order, dispelled the last vestiges of that moral authority once exercised by the Churches of Christendom, and the western world, swiftly followed by the rest of humanity, relapsed into the permissive age, the dangerous age of super-power skirmishing. Mankind became adrift on the uncharted sea of godlessness, unprincipled and aimless, polluting its home, victimized by its own terrorism, unable to control its animal propensities, and approaching ever more swiftly the final débâcle.

Yet God had done His part and kept His promise. 'Bahá'u'lláh was endowed with the creative power to regenerate the whole of humanity and unify it in a single spiritual organism' and in the midst of the turmoil and confusion attendant upon the rolling up of man's disorderly world, the foundations of the very Kingdom of God were being laid in the hearts and aspirations of an ever-growing number of people of all races, nations, religious backgrounds, temperaments and stages of civilized life. As George completed his book, he was able to state that they had, through a reawakened love of God and all humanity, been able, under the inspired leadership of the Guardian of the Faith, to weld themselves into a world community, organic, united, severely tested, joyfully confident that the path it is pursuing is the ancient one laid out by God, leading to the grand fulfilment of the

[1] Shoghi Effendi, *The Goal of a New World Order,* 1931

evolutionary process, the realization here and now of the age-old vision of God's Kingdom on earth in all its splendour and majesty, conferring upon every member of the human race the ineffable treasures stored up for them:

> It is the ancient vision coming true at last, the glorious Kingdom of hope and faith descending from heaven to encompass all the earth.

> > 'And I saw a new heaven and a new earth: for the first heaven and the first earth were passed away; and there was no more sea. And I John saw the holy city, new Jerusalem, coming down from God out of heaven, prepared as a bride adorned for her husband. And I heard a great voice out of heaven, saying, Behold, the tabernacle of God is with men, and he will dwell with them, and they shall be his people, and God himself shall be with them, and be their God. And God shall wipe away all tears from their eyes; and there shall be no more death, neither sorrow, nor crying, neither shall there be any more pain: for the former things are passed away.'[1]

George's Epilogue, his last expression in this world, is taken from the latter part of the manifesto which he had penned, shortly after his relinquishment of his ecclesiastical Orders. It is printed as Appendix 3. For his present purpose he changed the ending, using only the first of the three passages from Bahá'u'lláh's *Súriy-i-Mulúk,* which he had quoted in the original, and concluding with a final appeal to Christians to recognize the New Age of mankind inaugurated by Christ, Who had indeed come again in the glory of the Father. This was the call he had voiced and the objective he had pursued, with all the strength of his spirit, since the day he had received his second Tablet from 'Abdu'l-Bahá. George's last appeal was:

> O, Christian believers! for your own sakes and for the sake of the Churches, for the sake of all mankind, for the sake of the Kingdom, cast away your conflicting dogmas and interpretations which have caused such disunity and led us to the verge of wholesale self-destruction. Recognize the age of Truth. Recognize Christ in the glory and power of the Father, and heart and soul, throw yourselves into His Cause.

A World-wide Campaign

The Guardian sent letters to National Spiritual Assemblies of the English-speaking countries, urging them to use *Christ and Bahá'u'lláh* as the basis of a very active campaign of teaching and publicity. In Canada and the United States more than a thousand copies were sent to religious leaders, often in association with a well-advertised public meeting to which all local clergy were specifically invited (in many

[1] Rev. 21:1-4

cases personally) to discuss the book's message. In Australia, of which more anon,[1] a Bahá'í published, in the *Northern Argus*, the entire book over a series of sixteen weeks, one chapter per week.

In Britain a truly 'active campaign' was launched. The two archbishops of the established Church, and its forty-two bishops, were all sent copies. Canterbury and nineteen bishops acknowledged receipt, only the Bishop of St Albans saying he didn't think it right to keep it as he felt sure he would have no time to read it. Many other community leaders were sent copies, and there is in the files a charming letter from the Town Clerk of Cardiff who expressed the hope that 'it will be made known very widely'.

But the main thrust of the British effort (which included Ireland) was through displays in bookshops coordinated with public meetings. Thousands of leaflets were printed announcing the book as 'The Most Challenging and Controversial Book of the Century'; these were overprinted with the details of the public meeting, delivered to the co-operating bookseller who stamped them (many hundreds in each case) with his name and address and sent them out to his usual mailing list. A large display of copies (sometimes three dozen) was made in the main window for a week and other copies were displayed inside the shop around a large coloured showcard. In several cities a bookstall was organized at the public meeting by the bookseller. During May and June 1957 George's book was the basis for such an effort in twenty main cities, and the pattern was followed in many others in succeeding months.

The press ignored the book, although it was advertised and sent for review. Local papers reported the public meetings, two (Brighton and Cambridge) noting that discussion was lively and some of the audience walked out. An incident occurred in Belfast which would have delighted George. A large group of the fiercely Protestant residents filled the back rows of the Farmer's Union and the local Bahá'ís were congratulating themselves on the good attendance, with accessory bookstall arranged by Erskine Mayne's Bookshop. The chairman of the meeting was Lady Hornell, a diminutive but very dignified 'little old lady', of sweet and gentle nature, who was at that time 'pioneering' in Belfast. After the address she invited questions and immediately the leader of the back row delegation jumped to his feet and proclaimed in forceful tones that they had had enough of this blasphemy and he was calling upon all those who had been washed in the blood of the Lamb to stand and declare 'Hallelujah', which they all promptly did, upright and resoundingly. The speaker was about to rise to his feet to give battle when Kathleen Hornell stood up and with

[1] See Appendix 4, '*The Anglican, Australia*'.

the sweetest voice and most radiant smile said, 'Thank you. Next question, please.' The subsequent laughter dissolved all tensions and the evening went smoothly, even the back-benchers joining in the final informal discussion.

The Bahá'í community profited from its efforts to bring the message of George's book to their fellow countrymen, a small number of whom became sufficiently interested to pursue their investigation. But the leaders of religion were conspicuously absent, responding neither to general proclamations nor personal invitations.

By any literary or scholarly standards *Christ and Bahá'u'lláh* is a great work, an epic no less. It contains some of its author's finest writing and its logical development is compelling and unfaltering. As a summation of a view of the vast kaleidoscope of history, tracing the thread of Divine purpose from the beginning 'that has no beginning to the end that has no end', following always the gradual evolution to the grand climax – which is itself but another beginning to an infinite period of unimaginable splendour and felicity – it is a masterpiece. The brevity with which some of its themes are presented, while others are only indicated, makes it a 'mother book' from which many more will be born in future as the knowledge of God becomes restored to human consciousness. It is indeed a work of genius.

One of the great enigmas of human life is man's freedom, alone among all created beings, to say 'No' to God, to refuse His guidance and persecute His Messengers, actions which have led him through misery and disaster to his present desperate plight. Yet it is the same freewill which enables him to say 'Yes', to return, like the prodigal son, to his Father's house and enter the kingdom destined for him on earth.

And whatever mankind may have done, or may do now, the unfoldment, stage by stage, of God's plan and its fulfilment, as George declared in the beginning of his trilogy, 'at the date ordained by the Author no human misunderstanding or opposition [can] prevent or postpone'.

Chapter 17

THE MYSTIC

GEORGE Townshend's mysticism was, like himself, unspectacular but highly developed. Through it he attained to peaks of spiritual awareness only given to those whose inner beings have been burnished by the fire of suffering and self-immolation.

In view of the general widespread misapprehension about mysticism, it seems advisable to define our terms. The ground is cleared at once by declaring that it is not occultism, spiritualism, palmistry, astrology or any of those arcane arts which flourish as religion declines. Mysticism is an essential and personal aspect of revealed religion and is taught by the Revealers.

Like other teachings of those Manifestations of God it has been traduced, ignored, doubted, misapprehended. Yet in spite of this, great schools of mysticism have flourished; in the far east within Buddhism and Hinduism; Islám has produced Ṣúfism, while the annals of Christianity are illumined by the lives of a host of great mystics, both men and women.

All have agreed that the ultimate purpose is the attainment of union with God, whether it be, as with the Psalmist, the perpetual awareness of His Presence, or the ecstasies experienced by St Catherine of Siena. Mysticism is the essence of true religion, and in that sense orthodox, and it has been expounded, purified and its bounds set by Bahá'u'lláh.

George would have been the first to point out that Bahá'u'lláh's exposition of the subject confirms at all points the statement by Jesus, *I am the way, and the truth, and the life: no man cometh unto the Father, but by me*.[1] This is the voice of the Eternal Christ, that Way or Gate which is perpetually opened by Him, under whatever name He appears, and

[1] John 14:6

perpetually closed up in the centuries after His appearance, by the creeds and philosophies and rituals and barnacles with which the portal of religion is encrusted by men, only to be reopened again by the Manifestation of God. The utter transcendence of God is a continuous theme throughout Bahá'u'lláh's Revelation, but in *Kitáb-i-Íqán*, written in reply to a relation of the Báb who had submitted several questions to Him in writing, He reveals in great detail, using the terminology of the mystics themselves, that all such concepts as 'reunion', 'The Divine Presence', the 'Day of Resurrection', the 'Return', the 'Path to God', the 'ocean of understanding', refer to the Manifestations of God on earth. As Jesus so emphatically stated, He is not God incarnate but God's appearance in a Son of man, revealing Him in accordance with man's capacity and need. He, the eternal Christ, the Manifestation of God, is the nearest that man can ever attain to the Divine Essence. *He that hath seen me hath seen the Father.* Yet, *My Father is greater than I.*[1]

For Bahá'ís, the true mysticism is to strive to draw nearer and ever nearer to the Manifestation of God, to follow His commandments, to immerse oneself in the 'ocean of His utterance'. There is no attainment through asceticism and withdrawing from the world; Bahá'u'lláh requires everyone to lead an active social life; he calls on the monks and nuns whose *'pious practices are remembered before God'* to come out of their seclusion, to engage in the work of the world, as must everyone. God cannot be served by abandoning obligations to family and society. But knowledge of Him and of His truth may be acquired and an ever-nearer approach may be made to Him by prayer and meditation and by following the precepts enjoined by His Manifestation in every age. This was the mystical path which George pursued, as we have seen.

The enlightenment or second birth which visited him in the Rocky Mountains was not the result of arduous striving but the unsolicited and, we can only believe, pre-ordained Divine gift which set him on the path of his destiny. Thereafter he was driven by irresistible compulsion to seek the Truth of God. Fifteen years later and in another continent he attained to 'the Fountain of Truth' and his cup was overflowing. But the passionate yearning of his heart, far from being stilled, burst forth in fiercer flame. To attain the bounty for which 'Abdu'l-Bahá had offered His prayer *that thou . . . mayest sacrifice thy soul to the Beloved of the World and consecrate thy life to the diffusion of the Divine Fragrances* became the sole and directing purpose of his existence. His supplication to Bahá'u'lláh, written in the highest form of expression he knew, mystical poetry, was ever after followed with

[1] John 14:9, 28

ceaseless striving to attain that station of spiritual insight and power which 'Abdu'l-Bahá had unveiled to him.

> Only Beloved! With a heart on fire
> And all my longings set in one desire
> To make my soul a many-stringed lyre
>   For Thy dear hand to play,
> I bend beneath Thy mercy-seat and pray
> That in the strength of perfect love I may
> Tread with firm feet the red and mystic way
>   Whereto my hopes aspire.
>
> I have forgotten all for love of Thee
> And ask no other joy from destiny
> Than to be rapt within Thy unity
>   And – whatso'er befall –
> To hear no voice on earth but Thy sweet call,
> To walk among Thy people as Thy thrall
> And see Thy beauty breathing throughout all
>   Eternal ecstasy.
>
> Lead me forth, Lord, amid the wide world's ways,
> To bear to Thee my witness and to raise
> The dawn song of the breaking day of days.
>   Make my whole life one flame
> Of sacrificial deeds that shall proclaim
> The new-born glory of Thy ancient name;
> And let my death lift higher yet the same
>   Triumphal chant of praise!

His prayer was answered in full measure. 'The red and mystic way' became one of constant striving to renounce the self in order to obtain divine gifts.

> I do not shun pain in Thy path. Whatever it cost me, do not permit me to delay on my journey to Thee, nor to turn aside from Thy way. Send me whatever difficulties or suffering my soul shall need to cleanse and purify it utterly of all that is false and wicked. Help me to grow in self-knowledge and wisdom, and to put into practice what I learn, till each weakness is turned into strength, and I pass into the realm of Thy might through the gates of victory.[1]

In February 1955, with but two years left of mortal life, he was still pursuing this knowledge. On the 17th of that month, unable to write legibly himself, he dictated to Una a letter to the Guardian which he was able to sign shakily:

About fifty years ago, after reading the Gita, I earnestly took the

---

[1] *The Altar on the Hearth*, p. 120

attainment of the Knowledge of God, there described, as the one objective of my life. I never have given it up and have never won it. Progress lately, however, has been very interesting through the use of Bahá'í prayers, of *The Seven Valleys* and of a book of Abu'l-Faḍl's.[1] But without great help from outside me I shall never gain the goal . . . Any hint or strength or clarification you may be prepared to give me will be a priceless boon and I hope will enable me to do much better work in the Faith.

The Guardian's reply to this particular question, written by Ruḥíyyih Khánum on March 3, 1955, was:

As we almost never attain any spiritual goal without seeing the next goal we must attain still beyond our reach, he urges you, who have come so far already on the path of spirituality, not to fret about the distance you still have to cover! It is an infinite journey, and, no doubt in the next world the soul is privileged to draw closer to God than is possible when bound on this physical plane.

And Shoghi Effendi's personal note reads:

May the Almighty, Whose Cause you promote with such love, zeal and distinction, reward you a thousandfold for your historic labours, fulfil every desire you cherish, and aid you to enrich continually the record of your unforgettable achievements.

In addition to Bahá'u'lláh's exposition of mysticism in *Kitáb-i-Íqán*, much of His revelation is specifically mystical in character. Two short works, well known and loved in the West, are *Hidden Words* and *The Seven Valleys*. We have already seen that one of George's earliest Bahá'í essays was his 'Reflection' on *Hidden Words*, which so delighted the Guardian.[2] The particular verse which always seems to characterize George's life is number seven from the Arabic:

O Son of Man!
If thou lovest Me, turn away from thyself; and if
thou seekest My pleasure, regard not thine own;
that thou mayest die in Me and I may eternally
live in thee.

His meditation on *The Seven Valleys* was published in *The Bahá'í World*, vol. VII (pages 623–5) and must therefore have been written before 1938. Among his published writings it is the only one at all self-revealing or autobiographical of the years before his enlightenment, and clearly indicates that in that time he was not utterly unconscious

[1] Mírzá Abu'l-Faḍl, 1844–1914, generally regarded as the greatest Bahá'í scholar, author of many books including *The Bahá'í Proofs* and *The Brilliant Proof*. He received a Tablet from Bahá'u'lláh.
[2] See p. 78.

spiritually; some vision of truth, whose reality he tried to discover in the beauty of nature, held him, until he read the Bhagavadgita and determined to find the 'knowledge of God' spoken of there. The first part of his essay is a thanksgiving for 'those holy melodies which Thou hast chanted to the wayward heart of man' and for the disclosing of the Hidden Way to 'that dear Paradise which is to be the traveller's goal' and which is 'never wholly hidden but pours its fragrance far down all Thy Seven Valleys to sweeten the toils of the seeker's way.'

> He cannot accomplish the journey nor travel forth upon it without pain; nor can he so much as find the beginning of the path without patience.
>
> Thou art veiled from Thy servant, O my companion, and the entrance to the true path is hidden likewise. Though he knows it not, Thy servant's own self-love has woven this veil; and much is to be done, much to be suffered, ere he can see the door Thou hast opened before him.
>
> Urged by an inborn need, Thy servant seeks blindly self- satisfaction in this activity and that. He follows in the train of the world, grasping at what he sees others grasp at. He becomes lost among wayward inclinations, among diverse examples and a multitude of counsellors. There is no realization of desire in this; only disappointment and disillusion. The vision – the truth – of Something out of the plane of this activity abides with him – holds him. Its influence grows more distinct. This is of Thy Mercy, O Lord, which reaches through every veil! Thy servant knows of a surety there exists a Hidden Reality, and that with which he busies himself is a shadow-life. The stars, the seas, the lonely mountains, the quiet of the countryside, with one voice of ecstasy tell him of that Beauty which eludes him in human life. For lack of knowledge of Thee, my Lord, in ignorant love he makes the wilderness his home. But lo! he is rebuked by the sense of a greater beauty – the beauty of holiness. In the Sacred Writ of ancient days he reads of Beings who walked this earth of ours, full of love for all mankind, and spread about them a glory that outlasts the centuries and even at this distance of time makes all the splendour of dawn and day and night seem temporal and poor. These are the Prophets of Beauty, the Guardians of Perfect Truth, the Messengers to man of deathless Reality.
>
> What, O Mighty Ones, is this earth whereon you walked, this mortality you shared? What is the wisdom of sorrow and wrong and mutability? Where is our deliverance – and why is there a Prison-house from which to be delivered? What is this 'Knowledge of God' of which you speak as the great attainment of spiritual man, as the opening of mysteries, the end of illusion and ignorance?
>
> Thy servant seeks for one who has this knowledge and would, if heaven permit it, impart it to him.
>
> Years pass; and he finds none.
>
> Thy servant seeks for one who desires this knowledge and who will not rest till he find it. How precious would be a mortal companion in this search!

He tries many openings. Disappointment follows disappointment. He is baffled; and again baffled. He seems to be more completely at a loss, more near to desolation than ever, when lo! in a moment, almost unawares he finds Thee.

A moment of all moments!

At first it was but an echo that came from far away. There is no voice like the voice of the True One; nor is there any intonation of any voice like that of His!

In rapture, transported with delight, Thy servant answered that remote call.

Here George quoted three verses from his poem *Recognition*, which may be read on page 49.

Happiness wrapped Thy servant about, and his mind passed through opening doors of truth from wonder to wonder.

It is as though the few stray filaments of light which had pierced the gloom and saved it from utter darkness now strengthened one by one and slowly spread seeking perchance to join the edges of their rays and to combine at last to make one ocean of all-encompassing light.

By slow degrees there were revealed the outline and the perspective of the land wherein Thy servant dwelled and wandered. He watched and thought and measured and marvelled. Change after change came upon him. The old loveliness and sanctitude that had seemed the utmost and the highest lost its supremacy; lost its sufficiency. A great Beauty dawned. A sovereign Glory outshone lesser Thrones. Thy servant's restless heart no longer wandered in uncertainty; it turned from reflected lights to the one source of light.

How little had he within that hall of blackness known of the realities that lay about him all his life! How unimaginably rich and vast this earth and heaven which the Dawn brings out of the Unseen! And this Thy servant, what is he in the midst of it, O Lord!

How little (as he bathed his thoughts in that increasing glory) how little did he grasp the meanings that were unfolded before him! How blind was he to opportunities Thou offeredst him! How deaf to Thy answer to his prayers!

Is he wiser now? What ancient darkness reigns yet in Thy servant's heart steeping his thoughts in error? What illusions still dim and distort his vision? What false affections numb his soul?

Far off the scene grows clear, but not the path at hand. He presses forward and misses the way and stumbles; and recovering presses on. Well has it been said, O Lord, that the path to Thee is narrow as a hair and sharp as a sword . . . Has light, too, its rhythms and its waves?

Now again it seems to brighten. Ah, it is one thing to greet a dawn that rises on the distant horizon; it is another to welcome it when it stands in fire on your own threshold. It is one thing to dream and to admire; it is one thing to applaud those who challenged terror and with unblenched cheek walked through the horrors of the Pit; it is another to recognize that Truth's sanctuary is guarded eternally by walls of flame through which no doubt or fear can ever pass alive.

Thy servant must go on. He cannot do otherwise. Sooner or later everyone who worships Truth and Thee must face the searing fire. But from him whose heart loves only Thee, the flames will bend back.

And when the Seven Valleys are traversed to the end; and the Goal is won and Thy Paradise attained, what will remain for any servant of Thine but to begin his journey again and travel on and on for ever through infinitudes of wisdom and love, passing from light to fuller light, from Truth to further Truth, from Beauty to a more perfect Beauty?

This portrait of the adventurous seeker, '*transferred from one condition to another*', challenging in ignorant love the Rocky Mountain wilderness, seeking 'in stars, the seas, the lonely mountains', in the quiet of the remote Irish countryside, 'that Beauty which eludes him' until 'more near to desolation than ever . . . in a moment, almost unawares he finds Thee,' rings true and the heart's cry, 'How precious would be a mortal companion in this search!' will not have been unnoticed.

George developed the thought expressed in the final paragraph of his Meditation in a letter to Walter Wilkins[1] on December 22, 1937 but at greater length to Nellie in 1942:

> What is your idea about Seven Valleys? It is terribly hard; but I've a notion we move in a spiral going through the valleys again and again on different levels as we progress: when we are in one valley we also are in all the earlier valleys too: when we are at our best, in our higher moments, we see far ahead of where we are, whole valleys ahead, and though we may take a long time to travel over the ground we saw across, we are forever different once we have seen.

His comments on prayer are interesting not only for their content but for their indication of his simple, realistic view of the many worlds of existence. When a young Bahá'í, Bridget Hill, was killed in an air crash early in 1942 he wrote:

> From the other side, she will help us all in a very special way, I have no doubt. When we are more highly evolved, I am sure the thought or truth in 'the communion of saints' will become a conscious reality, and we will be more clearly aware how great souls from beyond leaven and inspire and direct our lives and efforts here in the valleys . . .

[1] A veteran London Bahá'í who had found Bahá'u'lláh by reading Dr Esslemont's book, *Bahá'u'lláh and the New Era,* borrowed from a public library. When the Six Year Plan was launched in Britain (see p. 185) he bought, for the first time in his life, a one way ticket out of London. He pioneered Birmingham, Blackburn, Norwich and Canterbury, helping to form the Bahá'í communities in each place. He died in Canterbury, at the age of ninety, loved, trusted and honoured.

To Nellie, a month later, he wrote:

Yes, I'm sure Bahá'u'lláh answers all prayers but there is surely much more to it than that. *Gleanings*[1] shows that the departed faithful conduct the progress of the world and produce the arts and wonders of civilisation: though beyond the veil they are still the leaven of the life of men on earth. Therefore we can pray to and get answers from them (prayer of course is not worship, not adoration) about the matters that are in their province . . . I take it Bahá'u'lláh uses mediators, trustees, giving them certain permission and responsibilities. But always it is His power that is employed and He is conscious of all that is done.

And on contemplation:

It is marvellous how if you dig and keep on digging into these Truths, meanings and more meanings continually open up . . . These past two years I've had the most wonderful experiences and am getting back to that lyrical happiness which was mine when the first vision broke on me. Then it passed and for ten or twelve years there was just darkness and witch-faces; now the vision has cleared again and it will never weaken but expand forever. The movement is like long distance running – you may lose your first wind but if you get your second it is permanent though you run all day long!

Of suffering:

What you say about suffering for every one who wishes to make progress (however slight) spiritually is assuredly true. He has to suffer constantly, even to the limit of his physical endurance: a little more would kill him. This is no fairy story. And when he looks back on it, the climax is he perceives it was all his own fault, there is no one to blame except himself. He'll be wiser next time!

Suffering was no stranger to him; in fact he had made a friend of it, together with frustration and disappointment, and nourished his soul upon them. Triumph and disaster he recognized as twin impostors to be treated just the same. The world could neither afflict nor exalt him; its sole hold on him was in the opportunities it provided of service to his Lord. He could truly proclaim, 'I have forgotten all for love of Thee.'

He was always firmly convinced that spiritual development was the firm basis of progress and success in human undertakings. Material means and the use of brains, imagination, knowledge, persistence he never discounted, but spiritual health was the essential foundation. We have seen how he was always ready to meet difficulties by striving to purify his own spiritual condition, and his whole life bore witness to

Gleanings from the Writings of Bahá'u'lláh, LXXXI

the growing intensity of this self-discipline. This was the practicality of his mysticism, and the truth of it was gloriously vindicated by the victory of his final years, when, his physical powers declining, the radiance of his spirit illumined the world around him. He had conquered the self and the world and lived only to serve his Lord.

Chapter 18

BAHÁ'Í PIONEER IN DUBLIN

THE contrast between the spacious, three-storeyed country house, standing in its own grounds with ample gardens and lawns, trees and paddock, which was the Rectory at Ahascragh, and the 'newly decorated bungalow in excellent repair, on ¼ acre of land, convenient to Churches, schools and on No. 62 bus service', which was 'Ripley' in the Dublin suburb of Dundrum, was more than matched by the contrast between the style of life at Ahascragh and that which ensued for the Townshends at 'Ripley'. The change of circumstance wrought more disturbingly on Nancy than on George. At Ripley there was no housemaid or gardener, no willing villagers to come and work for a few hours when needed. In Ahascragh Nancy had been the Archdeacon's lady and her friends were the surrounding gentry; in Dundrum they were unknown, although Brian managed to interest the girl next door in the Bahá'í Faith, to which she rendered, and still renders, sterling service.

Mrs Samandarí (née Ursula Newman), whom we have already met in connection with George's resignation,[1] wrote of those days:

> When the Townshends first came to Dublin, Nancy had not yet become a Bahá'í. She felt the difference of living in a small suburban house in Dublin from the rambling old home they had left; and from being a very important person to become an unknown. She was very afraid that the Bahá'ís would treat their small home as a Bahá'í Centre, so we never held meetings there until the great day when the first Local Spiritual Assembly was elected.

Orpen's copy of his portrait of George's father,[2] which had been

---

[1] See pp. 190-97

[2] See Plate 1, it was given by Brian, who inherited it, to Mr Stephen Powell of Co. Offaly, 'the grandson most interested in family heirlooms' and who very kindly supplied the family photograph reproduced on Plate 2.

amply accommodated in the library at Ahascragh, now occupied an entire wall of the best front room at Ripley. The house proved to be inadequately protected from heavy rains flooding down the hillside and before the 'confusion of settling in', which George wrote about, was over, they had to deal with water in the back rooms. A drainage ditch and ramp were made and then a new bungalow was built within feet of Nancy's bedroom. A protecting wall was built. Then the roof leaked. And so it went.

George met these and all such difficulties with well-practised patience in adversity, and did his best to shield Nancy from the worst discomforts. He swept the entrances to the bungalow and the garage, did a very large proportion of the housework, tried to keep the garden and dealt with contractors, civil authorities and neighbours. His real hardship was being dependent on the Bahá'í Fund, to which he had been a constant contributor for a quarter of a century.[1] His own small patrimony had been exhausted long ago and the royalties which he earned from his books gave him the only private income which he would use for this purpose. Now he had no income whatever beyond the royalties of his Bahá'í books.[2] With the warm approval of the Guardian the National Spiritual Assembly had agreed with George a very modest figure below which they would not allow his income to fall, and they assured him that should he die before Nancy, they would maintain her income to the same standard. After a few months it became clear that the agreed figure was inadequate and it was increased. The extra expenses involved in the house repair obviously had had to be met by the Assembly. All these negotiations were painful to George. After years of striving he had achieved the freedom he wanted, with a united family, but for Nancy, whom he never ceased trying to conciliate and win to recognition of Bahá'u'lláh, there was none of the joy and blessedness of making a sacrifice for God; she stayed with George out of a sense of loyalty.

The Guardian had written on July 7, 1948:

> I am thrilled by the news of your resignation – a truly remarkable and historic step. Your past and notable services in connexion with the exposition of the essentials of the Faith to the public in the West, your bold and challenging act at present in dissociating yourself from the Church and its creed, and your subsequent resolve to pioneer in Dublin and help in establishing the administrative basis of the Bahá'í new world order in Ireland are deeds that history will record and for which future generations will feel deeply grateful and will extol and admire. May the blessings of

[1] See p. 193.

[2] He had previously earned good sums from *The Altar on the Hearth* and *The Genius of Ireland*, both of which were now out of print.

29. George as a pioneer in Dublin; taken in front of Ripley

30. *George with Dr Mihdí Samandarí and Ursula Newman (later Mrs Samandarí), Dublin 1950*

31. *July 9, 1950: Dublin Bahá'ís gathered to commemorate the martyrdom of the Báb*

32. *George at his first Bahá'í Convention, London 1951*

33. George, Nancy and Una with Manúchir Zabíḥ, Dublin, 1947

34. George in Edinburgh, with James Robertson, one of the first Scottish Bahá'ís, Isobel Locke, pioneer from California and now Counsellor Isobel Sabri of Kenya, and Luṭfu'lláh Ḥakím, who translated 'Abdu'l-Bahá's second Tablet to George

Bahá'u'lláh be abundantly vouchsafed to you, guide every step you take, remove all obstacles from your path, and aid you to win still greater victories for His Cause in the days to come.

The part of the letter written by the Guardian's secretary on his behalf commented:

No doubt this is a great step for dear Mrs Townshend to have to make at her age. But he feels sure she too will come to rejoice in this new freedom and the constructive activity it will bring in its wake.

George replied three weeks before he was due to leave Ahascragh:

My resignation becomes effective on September 30th and we expect to move to our new home, 'Ripley', Mount Annville Road, Dundrum, County Dublin, Eire, in a couple of weeks. Letters addressed here will be forwarded, if necessary.

The British National Spiritual Assembly with a faith, enterprise, generosity, sympathy and kindness for which I never can thank them enough, and in a way which was totally unlooked for, have provided me with a way of living and writing and serving the Cause of Bahá'u'lláh.

The chance has been – and is – far greater, deeper, more continuous, more embracing and more progressive than I had imagined.

I am glad beyond words to be a full Bahá'í. With my whole family I attended the Summer School at Hornsea and learned much there. It was a great privilege to meet so many Persians and to come into communication with their devotional and heroic tradition.

There is urgent need of every kind of work for the Faith in these islands.

Brian, Una and I kept the 19 Day Feast of 'Izzat on September 8th here in the rectory.

My days and years of struggle and suffering here are over. I write now particularly to thank you for all you have done for me these many years and to ask for your blessing on our new home, 'Ripley', as it is now called, that there we may all be united in serving the Great Beloved; and that I may be transformed and invigorated spiritually, mentally and physically, and may live long yet giving to men this supreme Glad Tidings with ever growing ardour and chanting the Song of the Dawn of God's victory, to the end.

Faithfully, humbly, lovingly . . .

George's resignation reverberated throughout the Bahá'í world and it became a source of happiness to him that all nine National Spiritual Assemblies[1] of that time contributed to his support, considering it an honour to do so. What a remarkable evidence of the influence of Bahá'u'lláh in transforming religious prejudice and hostility into close

[1] This was the figure in 1948. By 1953 when the Guardian launched the Ten Year Crusade there were twelve, and the crusade concluded with fifty-six. At the time of writing there are 136.

association and friendship! The Bahá'í community of India, Pakistan and Burma was drawn from Zoroastrian, Muslim, Buddhist and Hindu traditions, while those of Egypt and Sudan, and 'Iráq were Sunní Muslims in background; the Persians were of Shí'ih Muslim heritage. All these people of non-Christian extraction were proud of this Bahá'í brother, this distinguished Christian priest, who had given up his high position and comfort to join them in promoting the Cause of Bahá'u'lláh, Whom they all recognized as fulfilling the greatest hope of all the sacred Scriptures of the past. They joined their Western brothers of Australia and New Zealand, the British Isles, Canada, Germany, the United States, in expressing, through their elected representatives, their love for George and happiness at his action. He himself wrote to the British National Assembly on being informed of the world-wide use being made of his 'manifesto' and the Indian National Spiritual Assembly's contribution, that the news 'brought me much happiness: I am glad you are relieved of that much of the financial burden and much moved by the generous spirit of the Indian Bahá'ís; and also am glad *Old Churches* is really thought to be useful.'

The last decade of George's life, upon which he was now embarked, became the period most outwardly revealing of his inner reality. It was as though the tree of his spirit had reached high summer and was putting forth its blossoms in full sunlight. His spiritual station, his influence, his achievements unfolded even as his worldly circumstances plummeted. No stranger to disappointment, having exploited it all his life to his soul's benefit, he now took it in his stride and built victories upon it. The joyful, constant association with large numbers of Bahá'ís which he had so eagerly anticipated did not materialize. The handful of Dublin Bahá'ís, generally, had had little training in Bahá'í aims and purposes compared with George's thirty years of deep study and service to the Guardian, and were neither so aflame with love of the Faith nor so eager to continually discuss its every aspect, as was this new 'full Bahá'í', bursting with the euphoria of his anticipations of service.

Una found a job in Dublin and, to her father's delight, stayed at home for more than a year, when she went to Liverpool to help establish the Spiritual Assembly there – one of the goals of the British Six Year Plan. Brian was also at home, having suffered a relapse in health and was looking for employment. So the little house in Dundrum was full. It became crowded when a Persian Bahá'í, Manúchir Zabíh, a student at Tübingen University, whom the Townshends put up for a week, fell ill and stayed on for several more while trying to obtain the required visa to return to Germany. This apparent calamity, however, was a providence, for Zabíh charmed everyone, and particularly Nancy. She became much better disposed to all things Bahá'í, and made the effort to probe deeper into its claims and teachings. She eventually enrolled and became a member of the first Spiritual Assembly of the Bahá'ís of Dublin, the first in Ireland and as the Guardian wrote 'the foundation stone for the work in Eire'.

These two victories were invigorating to George's spirit. He wrote glowingly to the Guardian about Zabíḥ, 'whose charm and earnestness and wisdom have done almost all that has been done of late and have carried the knowledge of the Cause to scores and probably hundreds of people'. George revelled in the opportunity to discuss the Faith at all times and on all occasions and to hear about the community in Persia. The far more important achievement of founding the Bahá'í Administrative Order in Ireland's capital city is comparable only to the introduction of Christianity to that island of saints and scholars. The historic occasion took place on April 21st, 1948, at Ripley, which, in spite of its inadequacies, was thereby ensured eternal fame. The document was signed on George's desk.

George did his best with the Assembly of which he soon became chairman. He organized a study class, which he was careful to conduct only when asked, and bicycled the five miles into Dublin's centre many times a week to meet as many of the friends as could gather at some café. We turn again to Ursula Samandarí who describes the Assembly as

> . . . a very curious combination of individuals – ex-Church of Ireland, ex-rationalist, ex-Roman Catholic, ex-Jews and ex-Church of England! He was extremely gentle and forbearing as chairman. A good deal of time was taken up with personal chats amongst groups of the members. Sometimes I said to Mr Townshend, 'Mr Chairman, don't you think you ought to call us to order?' Later, when I had left Dublin and had married Mehdi, he said to Mehdi at Summer School, 'We miss our Secretary. There is no one to keep the Chairman in order!'
>
> Mr Townshend had a most sympathetic nature and could always converse with people of all ages or levels of intelligence. He used to discuss football with Dora Coleman's son, Piers. Mrs Townshend was a very valuable member of the Local Spiritual Assembly. She had such a beautiful, soft voice and so could say quite tough things without hurting the feelings of people. Also, she gave the community a sort of stability and respectability – we were such a curious mixture!

George's inability to complete his manifesto during the first year after his resignation has already been dealt with, but there were more intractable circumstances preventing him from carrying out the Guardian's desire that he should write for the Cause. He moved into Ripley on October 6, 1947. On March 7, 1948 the following exchange of correspondence with the National Spiritual Assembly was initiated by him:

> I have to put before you a serious obstacle to my writing efforts that has shown itself here. I have had so far to spend the best working hours of every day in housework; and the rest of the day my time is broken.
>
> This is nobody's fault, as Nancy is doing her utmost and working beyond her strength.
>
> In a small house there is no seclusion.
>
> I have never had so little time to give to concentrated literary work as these months here. All the winter, I have got up at four a.m. in order to have time to myself; and in this way I have got through a good deal.
>
> My essay on leaving the Church to be called 'Calling all Christians' has proved the most difficult assignment I have ever had, being a personal spiritual problem rather than a literary one. It is virtually done now and I can go ahead with other things and shall never have anything so difficult again.
>
> I do not yet know *what* I can do about all the housework. Help is hard to get and hard to pay. But unless the problem is solved my output will be reduced and my life will be unsatisfying.

On March 12 he wrote:

> About administrative work – certainly I will act on the Local Assembly and do anything like that which is a plain duty as well as privilege. What I feel strongly is that I must concentrate on writing (and teaching) which is the Guardian's instruction, especially while I have many household duties, and ought to keep out of any committee or similar work altogether; administrative work takes a lot of time and thought and labour.
>
> The fact is, I am worried at having so little writing to show for my winter here . . .

The National Spiritual Assembly replied on April 5:

> Your comments concerning the way your day is spent were read to the Assembly at its last meeting and we deplore that your working time should be occupied with housework. We are anxious to remove this obstacle to your writing and, if you feel that domestic help would solve the problem, will you please let us know what would be required and how much it would cost.
>
> Your comments on administrative work were also noted and the National Assembly will not itself ask you to undertake any administrative duties. Should you find the Local Assembly giving you work to detract from your major effort, will you please advise us.
>
> The Persian National Assembly has asked us to convey to you their greetings and appreciation on the occasion of your leaving the Church. They add – 'We trust he will receive every confirmation in his services'.

George's reply on April 8 is revealing:

The psychological change involved in my removal from our old home of 30 years and from the Church has been rather more searching than I looked for. My conclusion now is that my inability to write is due to something in myself and not to lack of time or of leisure or of anything of that sort. If I had the strong concentrated impulse and resolution no such obstacles would stop me at all. We all here have lots to do. We are not so young as we were. But the remedy is not to gain leisure for writing by withdrawing from teaching and administrative activity; but instead, on the contrary, to seek out every Bahá'í activity I can and by throwing myself into it to gain the power I have found lacking of late.

Therefore after talking it over with Nancy who is always anxious to help me in every way and whom I can never now thank enough, I write to offer myself for any service of the Cause you can put me at, especially teaching, in England or northern Ireland or anywhere, from next month till the winter sets in. I am ready to leave my home for any length of time in this service.

I am always happy among Bahá'ís and want to associate with them. Even if people are utterly different from me in temperament and so on, if they are Bahá'ís they are my own and I love to be with them. I want to be in the current of activity, so far as one of my years can be. And I shall then create time to write and find the enthusiasm needed to do so.

Once again we meet George's belief that difficulties are to be solved by inner spiritual growth. This guiding principle of his life is commented on in Chapter 17 but we may note now that nothing in his experience of the past thirty years had caused him to abandon or modify it.

His offer to go out and teach resulted in his visiting Belfast on two occasions, where he spent a week each time, and gave public addresses and spoke and answered questions at 'fireside' meetings in private homes. He made a teaching trip involving visits to Edinburgh, Liverpool, Birmingham, where there were struggling Bahá'í communities and commented in a letter written from Hunts Hotel, Liverpool: 'It has been a very interesting trip indeed and a wonderful experience to be among Bahá'ís in this way. What I missed all these years!'

Having sent off the manuscript of *The Old Churches and the New World-Faith* he attended Summer School in Derbyshire where he took part in a workshop organized to produce a manual for Bahá'í teachers. His contribution to the discussion on the Will and Testament of 'Abdu'l-Bahá was deemed so cogent that he was asked to put his remarks in writing for inclusion in the final script. They were not only valuable to the manual but are highly pertinent to our appreciation of his deep understanding of the spiritual basis of the Bahá'í Administrative Order, which, as we have seen, he viewed at first with

The Baháʼís of Edinburgh

present

GEORGE TOWNSHEND, M.A.

(Sometime Canon of St. Patrick's Cathedral, Dublin, and Archdeacon of Clonfert)

Author of

THE PROMISE OF ALL AGES

in a series of meetings
to discuss

THE BAHÁʼÍ
WORLD-FAITH

All Welcome

PUBLIC MEETINGS

April 5th

A FAITH FOR A MODERN MAN TO LIVE BY

Chairman: Miss Isobel Locke

Speaker: George Townshend

April 12th

BAHÁʼÍ: THE NEW WORLD-FAITH

Chairman: Richard Backwell

Speaker: George Townshend

26 Frederick Street
8.oo p.m.

Questions Invited

GROUP DISCUSSIONS

Four evenings of informal discussion on some aspects of the Baháʼí Teaching, led by George Townshend, who has just resigned his offices in the Church in order to proclaim this New Message.

April 6th. Its Animating Spirit

,,   7th. Its Fulfilment of the Ancient Covenant

,,   8th. Its Idea of God

,,   11th. Its Supreme Purpose

26 Frederick Street
8.oo p.m.

An invitation card, from the Baháʼís of Edinburgh, presenting 'George Townshend, M.A. ...' in a series of meetings to discuss The Baháʼí World-Faith'.

some trepidation and eventually with utter fascination.[1] He wrote:

> The distinctive feature of this Dispensation is The Victory of God, 'God Himself shall rule His people' . . . the Will sets forth the divine method by which this victory shall be established, perpetuated and applied down the centuries . . . The Will creates a perfect earthly form through which this general Spirit of Regeneration can operate among mankind. This form or body is what we know as the Administrative Order.
>
> Man of himself could never have devised this perfect form or attained the spirit of regeneration.
>
> The Will therefore may be regarded as a climax and a summary of the Teachings of the Faith and should be gradually and carefully led up to throughout the instruction of every student.

By the end of his first year as a layman, he wrote cheerfully to the Guardian (November 29, 1948):

> God has been wonderfully good to us. My wife and I are here together in the Faith; her wisdom in human relationships is being appreciated, and I feel a new man and people know I am. (I hope to be still newer soon!) [A typical Townshendism.]
>
> I am writing to you now to ask if you will kindly give me instructions and counsels about my service to Bahá'u'lláh and the Cause that I may make the best use of my opportunities and do what I can to meet my great responsibilities.
>
> My pamphlet *The Old Churches and the New World-Faith* is at last in the printer's hands and ought to be out very soon: 24 pages. The Archbishop of Dublin promised to get me a chance to speak before some clerical union and I hope to read it to them. Nancy, Una and I are now making useful contacts. The Bishops think (so far) I have 'a bee in my bonnet': so do the Roman Catholic authorities who sent for some months agents to our public meetings . . .
>
> Except in Belfast, I have had no active hostility to meet yet . . .
>
> I am re-writing *The Heart of the Gospel* using about one-third of the old book and making it in effect the first of two volumes on 'Christ and Bahá'u'lláh'. I am writing the second volume too, and it is the best beloved of all my efforts . . .
>
> You would be cheered if you knew the publicity and the kindly reception beginning to be given to the Message and to *The Promise of All Ages* in Ireland. The *Church of Ireland Gazette* has promised me a sympathetic notice featuring the cause of my retirement. The Dean of St Patrick's writes with delight of the book – 'an amazing message from a great and rare witness' – and he is putting it in the Cathedral Library. I gave that Message myself years ago from the Cathedral pulpit! *The Belfast News Letter* (an important paper) has drawn favourable attention to the Cause and to my book, and wonders if this can really be the means of revitalising Christianity . . .

[1] See chapter 9.

I should greatly appreciate any instructions you will give me and I have no desire except to serve you.

Shoghi Effendi's reply read:

I strongly feel that you should concentrate in the years to come, on writing for the Cause, whose literature you can, more than anyone else throughout the Bahá'í world, enrich. You should also, I feel, lend your valuable assistance in both the teaching and administrative fields, but only as subsidiary activities. I will pray for the success of your historic pamphlet, and fervently hope it will arouse the public and achieve a brilliant victory for the Faith, which you serve so well and love so dearly.

That same letter, in the part written by his secretary, suggested a form of writing which he had not yet used: 'Have you ever thought of working on what they call in America a "study outline"? There is a need for the friends everywhere to become more deeply *spiritual* in their way of thinking, of seeing life, and of acting. He feels with your long background of spiritual education and study, as a Christian and as a Bahá'í, that you can help the friends to deepen their knowledge and their inner life.'

George took this up and filled the margins of his books of Scripture with paraphrasing, précis and comment, which, alas, he found no opportunity to get into typescript; they will doubtless be rescued and published. *Kitáb-i-Íqán, Prayers and Meditations by Bahá'u'lláh, Epistle to the Son of the Wolf, Tablets of 'Abdu'l-Bahá* (three volumes) and *Some Answered Questions* are the main items so treated, while his notes on the items in *Gleanings from the Writings of Bahá'u'lláh* are closely written on both sides of thirty-one loose pages from an exercise book. On July 15, 1949 he informed the Guardian, 'I am working on those outlines you kindly suggested . . . *very* useful work, I believe, particularly to *me*, in the first place!'

The *Dublin Evening Mail* for April 6, 1950 reported an address to the Spectrum Friendly Circle by 'Mr George Townshend, MA introducing the Bahá'í Faith and the precepts laid down by the Persian prophet, Bahá'u'lláh.' The speaker 'made evident the clear cut simplicity of a religion which embraces in its search for truth all sects, nations, classes and races. Love of humanity forms the basis of the Bahá'í creed, he said, and offers a solution to the many complex problems of the world today.'

There were meetings in the rooms of the Theosophical Society, at the Shelbourne Hotel, other places,[1] at all of which George was present and taking a leading part.

[1] Sometime in 1950 George notified Adib Taherzadeh that the second floor at 5 Leinster Street had been booked for three Thursdays a month, beginning October 12. He hoped they would have 'more contacts and less tea'.

The difficulties of the first eighteen months at Ripley were only slightly ameliorated by all the circumstances attending a new situation. Nancy tried to adjust but soon became embittered and life in the bungalow was far from peaceful. We have already seen the hardship imposed on George. No more early tea in bed, reading or meditating till seven and an hour's writing; now it was up at four in order to have a little privacy and time to write, and a large part of the day filled with household chores. He bore all this with cheerful patience. Una, whose notes are revealing, left home and only returned when George really needed her help. She records of that time that George's resignation and move to Dublin to give all his time and effort to Bahá'í work

was just like a dream come true but it turned out to be more like an anti-climax. He felt like a horse put out to pasture; whereas he had always been used and wanted, now nobody seemed to want him; nobody knew him there and nobody wanted to know him. In terms of Bahá'í activity he was only a little less isolated than in Ahascragh; there were very few Bahá'ís in Dublin and my mother was not co-operative about using Ripley as a Bahá'í home. There was so much he could have done; he had so many talents. But he was – well, just stuck in that little house on the outskirts of Dublin, quite a distance from a bus for an old man. When he went up there he was able to ride his bicycle, but by degrees his health went to pieces. The situation at home wasn't happy, so that to write was very hard. He used to get up about four or five so that he could have some peace to try and work, but he wasn't able to produce as much as he had done when he was in Ahascragh. After the Geneva project fell through, my mother seemed to lose interest in the Faith, but she didn't turn against it until after she had actually enrolled. Then she became disgusted with the life there and blamed the National Spiritual Assembly and the Faith and my father and got very upset with everything. On one very bad occasion when Brian and I both asked him why he put up with it, he turned to us and said, 'If they poison your lives, sweeten their souls.'[1]

Counsellor Adib Taherzadeh's account of his relationship with George Townshend was recorded for this biography. It has already been invoked in connection with George's developing understanding of the independent nature of Bahá'u'lláh's Revelation (see p. 150). The following edited passages are from Mr Taherzadeh's cassettes, one of the chief sources of our knowledge of George's daily life as a pioneer in Dublin.

I had heard about George Townshend but never met him until the Teaching Conference in Manchester in 1950. Frankly I wasn't really

[1] From a letter written by 'Abdu'l-Bahá to a group of Bahá'ís. See *Selections from the Writings of 'Abdu'l-Bahá*, page 24.

impressed at that stage. He was speaking at the Centre and I thought I was going to hear a great and forceful personality; but because of his wonderful meekness and humility, such as I had never seen in anybody, I could not believe this was the famous George Townshend I had heard about.

Later on I came to realize that this was really the source of his greatness – his humility and modesty. I realized on looking back, that he never spoke of himself, of the things he had done for the Faith. He never said anything for instance about his work for Shoghi Effendi, about the fact that he received those portions of *God Passes By* in instalments from Haifa. It was Nancy who used to tell me all these things, and George would just listen and say very little.

At my first meeting with him, I remember I spoke to him for a little while and then we began to correspond; I have these letters, mostly concerning some work he was doing for the Americans – writing an article or something, and he used to write and ask me to give him some explanations about various aspects of the *Seven Valleys*, the *Kitáb-i-Íqán*, or *Epistle to the Son of the Wolf*. I am sure he knew most of the answers – perhaps not some of the Persian references. In this way we developed a very wonderful relationship, and then when he heard that we were going to Ireland he was delighted and there are some letters expressing this joy, and I came to realize that he really was lonely in Ireland.

George's letters of the time fully support Adib Taherzadeh's memory. He wrote on June 25, 1950: 'I am very fortunate indeed to have got into touch with you who know so much about these abstruse things and are so ready to take so much trouble to pass your knowledge on.'

George had plied him with queries on 'Persian references', Qur'ánic subjects, names of early believers addressed by Bahá'u'lláh, and a dozen oriental conventions unfamiliar even to a scholar of George's wide ranging knowledge. Adib, born in the heart of the cradle of the Faith (Yazd – famous for its three contingents of seven martyrs, in 1891, 1955 and 1980) and steeped in its traditions and background, was a mine of information to George and, more important, offered him that true Bahá'í fellowship for which he so hungered.

Immediately George heard of the possibility of Adib and his wife moving to Dublin, as Bahá'í pioneers, he overwhelmed them with loving encouragement. 'Daily I am praying and hoping the road to Dublin will be opened to you . . .' He asked about their visas. 'Is there anything any of us can do at this end?' 'We are lonely, and it would be great company to have you. I think, too, you would be specially equipped to understand and deal with the Irish mind and point of view.' ' . . . we will do all we can to help you at this end'. He continued to ask for 'facts about our Scriptures I need to know', and about more esoteric matters, while maintaining his encouragement to them to come. '. . . you and your wife will be invaluable to our difficult work here. You will surely get a job at once as one of our members is an electrical engineer[1] of long standing and well known and will be able to introduce you to the right people.' This promise was fulfilled.

Adib continues:

I remember the day we arrived and the boat docked in Dublin very early in the morning. The tall figure of George Townshend, distinguished in his black suit and a very nice hat and one could see a man of great character, standing there ready with his car, to drive us to our boarding house which he had himself booked for us, and he was so delighted I can see his face now, the great joy to see somebody coming with whom he could have some Bahá'í companionship. This was the whole essence of that meeting because he really was radiant with joy. I have seen him sometimes radiant – this was one of the occasions, and he assured me in fact that everything would work out here for me . . . George really gave me so much encouragement at that time. It was one of great unemployment; there were parades in this city, about employment – and I came here as a Persian. He took me to see his wife and family and from then on he took a very special interest in our affairs. He used to come every day to see whether we were all right at the guest house, and we quickly formed a very wonderful Bahá'í companionship.

I think it is important to know the background of the Dublin Bahá'í community at that time because until we know that we cannot appreciate his work and his services to the Cause. I must say that when I first met the community here I felt that there were many people in it who were not touched by the light of Bahá'u'lláh's Revelation at all and later events proved this. There was only his family, plus one or two others, who had really recognized the Faith.

There was a Welshman, a great friend of George's – he actually came into the Faith because George was a Bahá'í. He didn't understand anything about the Faith; he was a very good man and he helped me to get a job. But he never understood the Faith; he told me so himself; and he actually left the Faith, during George Townshend's life. There were others who had no conception of what the Faith was. They came in because they liked the teachings or something like that.

When George left Ahascragh for Ripley, of course the circumstances were very very different, and I think we must appreciate the difficulties that Nancy faced in this new sort of life. George really showed his nobility there by taking on a great burden of domestic work in the house to relieve his wife, and he did everything that was possible to make her happy and to compensate for what they had lost. We can appreciate how difficult it must have been for her to sever all those connections and to resign from such a position, and especially so in those days when the Faith was so small and in

---

[1] Adib was, and is, an electrical engineer and deviser of electronic systems.

her sight perhaps very insignificant, and the people who were associated
with it were very insignificant in her view maybe, so I think we must
appreciate that the great difficulty George had in resigning from the
Church was opposition from Nancy. He told me the story of the
clergyman who sent his book *The Promise of All Ages* to the Archbishop of
Canterbury and what happened.[1]

Well, Nancy threw in her lot with George and she supported him then –
she knew of course that her husband could not recant or refute what he had
already published, and in this way Nancy really gave great support for
George to resign, and agreed to it. I think that was the time also that Nancy
joined the Faith, possibly because she wanted to support George. I am sure
she had a loyalty to him, and she understood that this was his life – he had
written these books – he could not refute them – and therefore she stood by
him. The same thing happened when George died. She made a stand and
insisted on giving him a Bahá'í funeral because she respected his views.

We used to have community meetings of course, Nineteen Day Feasts,
and once or twice we had them in the Townshends' home and I could see
that there were difficulties there although I didn't know what they were.
George of course did everything to keep unity in the family – marvellous,
marvellous man in that way. And therefore, although he longed for me to
go and meet him at Ripley, in the first year it wasn't really practical because
if you wanted to go and see him you had to talk to Nancy and make
arrangements and it wasn't very easy, and I knew that it would be an
intrusion really and so I very seldom used to go there. But gradually I used
to go up to the house and work for them sometimes. I offered to help, for
instance, with their electrical fittings or things like that, so gradually,
gradually I was accepted by Nancy. And then I used to go more often. I
would go after work, in the evenings – maybe about once a week in the
beginning, and then more often later on.

George used to bring out all sorts of papers and letters, and his writings,
and we would discuss them. For instance, I remember the time that he was
writing *Christ and Bahá'u'lláh*, he used to speak a great deal about Islám and
we talked about this. So when at the end of the evening I was going to
catch the bus to go home, he would insist, whether it was raining or
whether it was not, and whether it was cold or warm, on accompanying
me all the way to the bus stop, which was quite a distance away. And quite
often his wife did not want him to go out, but he insisted that he wanted to
accompany me and he would then quietly say 'I love this Bahá'í
companionship. Let me come with you'. He even made me sometimes ask
him to come with me because he wanted to get out and come to the bus
stop. And sometimes I would miss the bus and he would stand there for
maybe half an hour till the next one came. He wouldn't go home and we
would talk 'Bahá'í'. He was filled with such love for the Faith.

When he became handicapped and couldn't come to town to meet me so
often, he would ask me to drop in in the evenings, and if I didn't turn up
one night, the next day he would pick up the telephone, quietly when there

[1] See page 186

was nobody around, and ring me up in the office, and all I could hear from the other side was this: 'Come tonight', and he would put the telephone down! And of course I would go there and he would say 'Don't say that I have telephoned you'.

One of his great ambitions was to teach the Faith, and when he saw that many of us were moving around, speaking here and there, you could see how very much in his heart he wished to do the same. I remember on one occasion a meeting of the National Teaching Committee of Ireland, we thought now this is the time that George should be encouraged to travel and go to various parts, especially the North (in those days there was a great deal of activity in the North). I wrote to him and asked would he undertake a teaching trip to Ulster. Immediately he got the letter, he rang me up and said 'I will, I will,' and then the next day he said there are difficulties, will you come and discuss it with me? So I went there and found that Nancy felt he shouldn't go. There was a lot of discussion and George became very forceful. It is very difficult to visualize George confronting anyone forcefully but there, in his own way, he said very definitely, 'But I want to go to teach'. Eventually it was decided that the best thing would be if Nancy and George would go together and spend a few days in the North, and in fact they spent some time with the Villiers-Stuarts.[1] George was very happy and they arranged a very good programme for him.

We used to go together from time to time, to meetings of other Faiths. He wanted to find an opportunity to talk about the Faith, so we would stand up in the audience and ask questions. I would ask a question and then he would get up and ask some more, or sometimes he would enlighten the audience by his remarks. He loved this because to him, it constituted teaching the Cause, and he loved to do this. Several friends came to the Faith through him in the early days, although he believed that he hadn't taught anybody. This was one of the things that he was sad about; he said that he had not been successful in teaching the Faith, and I often told him that his books were great teachers, not only for now but for generations to come.

I remember the last day of his life when I was at the hospital in Baggot Street – he had received *Christ and Bahá'u'lláh* in his hands, and he couldn't express anything because he was so ill. He just barely conveyed to me that he was happy that this was printed and he asked me what I thought about it, and I told him that this book would be used for generations and generations into the future, it would be a historic book through which many thousands and in fact millions of people will come into the Faith, and you could see the smile on his face, really a fantastic smile. I told him that I didn't think the present generation was worthy of understanding these things; they are not at this stage, but in the future millions in fact will come

[1] The original Bahá'í family in Ulster; the three daughters and a son, now grown up, are serving the Faith in Africa, Asia, England and Ireland itself, while the family home outside Belfast has become known to visiting Bahá'í teachers from all parts of the world.

to the Faith, not only through this book but through all his books.

Among his friends was a Mr Pat Turner. He used to come quite a lot. He was of the same age, I think, as George, and had travelled around the world. He had come in contact with the Faith and became so enamoured of the Writings that he constantly used to propagate the message of Bahá'u'lláh to everybody. He carried Bahá'í books with him everywhere he went – the *Íqán*, the *Gleanings, Epistle to the Son of the Wolf, Seven Valleys* – and he knew them by heart and in fact he had written out many of them by hand. He never became a Bahá'í but George always said 'He's a Bahá'í carrier'. He greatly admired George and wherever he went he spoke very highly of him to the people.

George used often to make an excuse to come into the city; for instance he used to come on a bicycle to Ranelagh which was about five miles, to buy a cake and go back home, when he could have got it somewhere nearer, but he would leave his bicycle in our place and then we would both go out to a park, or to his church once or twice, and we would sit down and talk about the Faith. (St Patrick's Cathedral I meant when I said 'church'.) This is how we began our relationship.

We went once or twice to the gardens of the church. I told him I was not very keen, I would become depressed if I went every day to the church and sat inside it and so we used to go to the gardens. And he told me all about the cathedral and showed me where he once actually stood and mentioned the Name of Bahá'u'lláh and that nobody took any notice; they thought it was something he was interested in and they all thought it was very nice. In this way we got together at least once a week, in fact in the early days maybe twice a week, and spent perhaps half a day talking about Bahá'í things. These talks ranged from weighty matters to trivial things but he told me a great deal about how he became a Bahá'í.

It would be very natural to suppose some sense of poignancy in these episodes of an elderly man revisiting the scene where he had once held high position, walked in those very gardens, perhaps in his gaiters and shovel hat, now seeking the spiritual companionship of a young man from a distant land to whom he was more closely related than to his erstwhile colleagues or even to most of his own flesh and blood. But we may be confident that no such sentiment arose in George's heart. We recall with what delight he announced his first day as Mr, not the Reverend, and we may be sure there were no regrets or nostalgia for what he had given up. He revelled in the opportunities to talk of his 'Only Beloved', to associate with another soul glowing with the same fire that burned within himself. In one of his early letters to Adib, George had written, 'It is lonely in a pioneer job and there is little talk on Bahá'í subjects in general as none of us know enough to keep a conversation going. It would be great to hear from you about the East and the Cause as it stands now and as it used to be. The whole atmosphere would change.'

Adib's notes continue:

His life in Ahascragh was so much based on helping people and loving people. A few years back I was in Ahascragh and I stopped a few people to ask if they knew George Townshend and if so to tell me what they knew about him, and everybody was unanimous about his great qualities. I was told that when the Catholic people could not get satisfaction from their own clergymen they turned to George and this is really unheard of; he had that quality of universal love which 'Abdu'l-Bahá portrayed, and people could see that. In Dublin it seemed to me that – how shall I put it – as a flower which opens up, he unfolded into a greater and greater being, I think from the time that he resigned from the Church. All the qualities were there, but this very act of resignation, this great sacrifice, endowed him with such capacity that he developed to the full all the powers and attributes which God had given him, and I saw this development really and clearly.

His love for the Faith was so much that he was always longing for the night when we had a 'fireside'. Now these meetings were quite a distance from his home; he was living about five miles out of the city centre and during the time that he was mobile, I can never remember him once missing a Bahá'í meeting. He was always the first one there; only when he became ill and his physical faculties were failing him, did he insist that people bring him to the meetings. I used myself to go and bring him and of course Una and Brian did too. Towards the end his coming to the firesides became more infrequent. But in the early days, he never missed one meeting.

He would become depressed about anything which, in his view, would damage the Faith, such as disunity among the friends. And at that time in Ireland we had quite a lot of this. George displayed this sadness very clearly, and you could see he was longing to do something to help bring unity to them.

During the final years before his passing, he went to one or two nursing homes for short periods and every time he immediately let me know, rang me up and said 'Now come and bring the friends here, all the time'. That is what he said 'all the time'. It meant that there were no problems there and he knew that he would not impose on the family and that people were free to come to the nursing home; so I used to go there quite often, and was able to spend hours with him.

I have no doubt, I have no shadow of doubt, that George Townshend was one of those gems that Bahá'u'lláh had prepared for His Revelation in the West and I believe that because of this the influence that he will exert on the hearts of men in the western world in the future will be very very great and very very significant; these things do not happen haphazardly – he was prepared. Look at the material he got for example. I believe one or two little pamphlets, because of course in those days there was very little literature, and through those things he recognized the Faith.

This is not ordinary – he must have been prepared by Bahá'u'lláh for the mission of his life, and therefore I believe that whatever happens in Ireland and whatever happens in the world (Shoghi Effendi has referred to him as the greatest writer – at least some say in the West and some say for the whole world), he certainly plays a very significant role in the destiny of the Western people, and nobody knows about it yet, and perhaps [they] don't appreciate these things.

I am sure that through his works and through his spirit people *will* appreciate him. No doubt. Shoghi Effendi said in his cable: '. . . one of three luminaries shedding brilliant lustre annals Irish, English, Scottish Bahá'í communities'.

George was the ideal pioneer. He was self-starting in spreading the message of Bahá'u'lláh and used every opportunity and incident of daily life to give the 'glad tidings'. For instance, after visiting, in company with a tax expert, the offices of the Income Tax Commissioners, he reported that 'the Commissioners and others at the examination looked through the pamphlet entitled *The Bahá'í Faith* and *Glad Tidings* [John Murray]; and also heard some dissertation on the Faith from me. So it's all propaganda!' He won his case.

A further incident illustrates both his eagerness to spread the great message and his constant concern with bridge-building. The third edition of *The Promise of All Ages* was reviewed in an Irish newspaper and quoted the author as admitting that so far the Bahá'í Faith had touched only a small, though important, section of the human race. George immediately seized the opportunity to send a letter to the editor, noting the 'kindly review' and informing him of the wide expansion of the Faith since the book was written and of interest aroused in United Nations

' . . . circles on the Continent on account of the originality and appropriateness of its social programme. But to the Christian its special interest is that the Bahá'í patterns and principles of World Order are based fair and square on spiritual foundations and that the spiritual teachings of Christ are accepted in their entirety.

Thus the Bahá'í Faith presents the most cogent answer to the common charge being made today that the Christian Gospel is irrelevant to our world problems. It provides a clear scheme of world order in which the Christian ethic is fundamental and all-penetrating and which is so statesmanlike that it is winning more and more the attention of those well qualified to judge of these matters. It is not only its spiritual quality, but also its combination of the spiritual and the material that constitutes the claim of the Bahá'í Teaching to investigation.

George gave a great deal of thought to the problem of bringing the 'glad tidings' of the new Revelation to the masses. He discussed it often in his letters. For instance:

As day by day passes I realise more clearly that Church people are going now to get a large part of their first impression of the Cause from the author of *The Promise*.

It is an appalling responsibility. Also a life-long opportunity. A hundred thoughts come to me. A new phase of propaganda ought to be opened: none of our books, Esslemont's,[1] Lady B's,[2] and certainly not my little two meet the coming need. An appeal to the many. The élite have known and rejected the truth. Now declare it to the multitudes. Something more practical and more emotional. I have an idea for a practical essay: but oh! if I could write a *play*. Or even a novel or novelette!

He never confused proclamation of the great news with spiritual teaching, which was a much deeper and more delicate problem. He commented on this latter to Nellie, in his letter of August 5, 1941:

I have been thinking a lot about the art of religious teaching, and about the reasons for the slowness of the progress of the Cause. Some of my notions are that the personal, human, and devotional side of the Faith is not emphasized enough, and that there are no simple, human and spiritual introductions with a heart-appeal to erring struggling human beings. The literature is too highbrow. There is not the popular appeal in it that, say, 'Abdu'l-Bahá used to make. There is nothing to take the place of those charming accounts by pilgrims of their visits to 'Abdu'l-Bahá in His prison or the stories and speeches of Him when He visited Paris and London and your country. This lack, when a great popular extension is desired and expected, is regrettable and a serious hindrance. I myself, so far as my little books count at all, am an offender in this respect. That is one reason why I am now so much concerned about this matter. I hope to do better in future, heaven helping me! What do you think about all this? And what ideas or information of Bahá'í experience have you yourself or your friends on the subject of teaching, especially religious teaching? The modern art of teaching arose in a secularised age, and probably we have not been qualified to understand how spiritual truth can best be presented. Surely it is a most delicate matter, and the way to know the right method is probably best found by penetrating the method of the Master. There seems to me to be nothing now in the presentation of the Faith that would win over people's hearts and sympathies as mine were won over by the personal message and life of the Prisoners of 'Akká.

A personal item is of interest. In June 1948 he was advised that the new edition (third) of *The Promise of All Ages* had earned him £25 (worth possibly £650 in today's values). He expressed delight and surprise. 'I can't tell you how your news pleases me! . . . The thought of really earning some money of my own and of being to that extent independent stimulates and cheers me and fills me with the hope of

---

[1] Dr J.E. Esslemont, *Bahá'u'lláh and the New Era*.
[2] Lady Blomfield, *The Chosen Highway;* see p. 171.

doing more in the same way to a much larger extent soon.'

George attended his first Bahá'í Convention in 1951, in London at the Bonnington Hotel. He reported afterwards to the Guardian:

> I was at Convention for the first time this year (being a delegate from Dublin) and suggested everyone should watch out for broad-minded clergymen and church members and put me in touch with any such at an opportune moment. (I have corresponded in this way with American clergymen). We all find Irish Christians difficult to assess. The clergy won't let me approach. I wish I knew better how to get at them. If other Bahá'ís ferret out the open-minded clergy these might suffer me to write to them.
>
> I am going to Summer School this year through the kindness of the Committee, my first visit since 1948, and giving a study course and a lecture. I am hoping, praying and expecting to bring my wife along. Our Assembly here is much stronger than it was and we all look forward to our happy and harmonious meetings.

He was active as chairman of the Local Assembly. He found meeting places and encouraged the friends to attend and bring *their* friends. He planned the addresses and briefed and encouraged the speakers; he was always present to back them up with his knowledge and authority. He composed a small introductory booklet for translation into Irish which was published by the National Spiritual Assembly, and is still in use. Its first words are a quotation from 'Abdu'l-Bahá, which George knew only too well were greatly needed: *Beware of prejudice; light is good in whatsoever lamp it is burning. A rose is beautiful in whatsoever garden it may bloom. A star has the same radiance whether it shines from the East or from the West.*

He shepherded and cared for his immature community. One of the most endearing records of that time is the letter he wrote to Adib's daughter, Vida, on the second day of her life. It is reproduced on the opposite page.

The constricted life at Ripley, the primitive condition of the newly formed Bahá'í community in Dublin, and the lack of any spectacular results from his resignation all combined with more frequent and painful bouts of neuritis to bring about a fit of depression, totally alien to his natural cheerfulness. His letter to the Guardian of May 7, 1951, full, as we have seen of plans, hopefulness and confidence, was followed by another on November 5, in which he poured out his heart 'aching with contrition and grief' over what he considered, in his lowered condition of physical and spiritual vitality, to be his failure to achieve 'anything substantial' since he left the Church. He was really in the abyss, appreciating

To

Miss Malmiri
(two day old)

Dear Little baby Persian,
Here is a little gift to your

own wee self
with lots of love and good
wishes to you and to your mother
and your father
from your great-uncle
George and your great-aunt
Nancy

Sept. 1953

A note accompanying George's gift to his 'great-niece', Vida Malmiri

. . . more warmly than before your selfless patience and kindness and forgiveness in dealing with me all these years. To you I owe everything. I long to serve you and make amends of any possible kind, living and dying, for that which has escaped me. It is an awful thought that I should fail again to do my part for you and 'Abdu'l-Bahá.

I have prayed for pardon but it does not reach me in the form I feel the need of – sustained enthusiasm and vigour in writing and becoming witness to the Faith.

My main book is in its argument after great labour ready but I have not that impassioned flow of eagerness and determination that will put it on paper, complete.

My health and strength are failing. 'Abdu'l-Bahá wrote *Christ says thy body is weak and grieved but thy spirit is in the greatest joy. Know thou by this spirit thy body shall be strengthened.*[1] I need that joy now in my extremity that it should come through and help my body and my soul. And I turn to you, the sign of God for us all and the Heart of the Bahá'í community, begging you to intercede for me and to help me so that my penitence may be fixed and deepened, and my heart filled with an over-mastering enthusiasm of consecration to your service and the service of the Cause of Bahá'u'lláh.

George had no reply from the Guardian until December 24 when a personal cable informed him that he had been appointed a Hand of the Cause of God.

---

[1] He was obviously quoting from memory. See p. 50 for text of letter.

Chapter 19

THE HAND OF THE CAUSE

The obligations of the Hands of the Cause of God are to diffuse the Divine Fragrances, to edify the souls of men, to promote learning, to improve the character of all men and to be, at all times and under all conditions, sanctified and detached from earthly things. They must manifest the fear of God by their conduct, their manners, their deeds and their words.

Thus the Will and Testament of 'Abdu'l-Bahá, a document described by the Guardian of the Faith as the Charter of Bahá'u'lláh's world order. While this is no place for a dissertation on the Bahá'í Administrative Order, some comment on the institution of the Hands of the Cause is necessary if we are to appreciate the exalted rank to which George Townshend was elevated. The institution is unique. Bahá'u'lláh, Who created it, has described its members as 'the learned in Bahá' in contradistinction to the members of the legislative bodies whom He named 'the rulers'. The latter have no individual authority and are elected by the mass of the faithful. The Hands are appointed by the Head of the Faith and function individually with the spiritual authority conferred by him. As their name indicates they are hands to him, occupied in the important services of his office, responsible to him and operating under his direction. They are the highest officers of the Faith and act on their own initiative as counsellors, advisers, guides to the governing bodies. Their specific functions are the protection and propagation of the Faith. In his last statement about them the Guardian designated them 'Chief Stewards of Bahá'u'lláh's embryonic World Commonwealth'.

Bahá'u'lláh appointed a very few Hands of the Cause. 'Abdu'l-Bahá in His Will and Testament, delineated their responsibilities and method of appointment, and referred to some prominent believers, after their deaths, as Hands. The Guardian of the Faith, after thirty years of developing the Administrative Order, appointed, in 1951, the 'first contingent' of twelve Hands of the Cause, three each for the World Centre, Asia, America and Europe. George was the first named for Europe. Later the Guardian raised the number of living Hands to twenty-seven and indicated there would be more in future. But he died in 1957, leaving the institution of the Hands of the Cause as one of his most precious legacies. It played a vital and heroic part in the security of the new Faith at one of the greatest crises in its history. But that is another story.[1]

George received the news of his appointment by telephone on December 24, 1951, from the Secretary of the National Spiritual Assembly in London, who read to him the text of the Guardian's cable: MOVED CONVEY GLADTIDINGS YOUR ELEVATION RANK HAND CAUSE STOP APPOINTMENT OFFICIALLY ANNOUNCED PUBLIC MESSAGE ADDRESSED ALL NATIONAL ASSEMBLIES STOP MAY SACRED FUNCTION ENABLE YOU ENRICH RECORD SERVICES ALREADY RENDERED FAITH BAHAULLAH

SHOGHI

He replied to the secretary on December 25:

> This is to thank you very warmly for your thoughtfulness in phoning me at once the Guardian's Glad Tidings cablegram, and for the kind words which you yourself spoke.
>
> It is all a little overwhelming and overawing at first, coming as it did out of the blue; and a great cheer.
>
> Many thanks.
>
> How much, how very much I have to be grateful to the enterprise, sympathy and courage of the British National Spiritual Assembly and their unfailing kindness.
>
> I hope you will be good enough to keep me informed about the public message the Guardian is sending and anything else about this matter.
>
> Ever, with love and greetings to you and to all the members of the National Spiritual Assembly.
>
> P.S. Please feel yourself free to mention the contents of the cable to any one if you wish to.

George was no stranger to spiritual authority and we may note his immediate exercise of it in his request to be kept informed and in the permission given in his postscript. He received, during his thirty-six years of service to the Guardian, a number of cables from him; twenty-four of these he kept on file, flat and in chronological order, but this one was kept in an envelope with a simple notation, 'Shoghi Effendi's cablegram'.

[1] See *The Bahá'í World*, vol. XIII, pp. 333–94.

George's response to the Guardian was expressed in his letter of January 14, 1952:

Dear Shoghi Effendi,

From my inmost heart with deep humility I thank you for the bounty you have bestowed on me in appointing me a Hand of the Cause of God.

In response I wish now to offer my entire submission to you as Guardian of the Cause and state my ardent desire to give all I am and all I have to the service of the Faith of Bahá'u'lláh. May He grant me an ever warmer love, and ever deeper wisdom, in following His will and bearing witness to His truth.

Permit me to pay you a humble tribute of the utmost admiration and gratitude for the nearing vision of the Victory of God which you, almost by your sole might, now have spread before the astonished Bahá'í world.

Now, may strength of soul and body be vouchsafed me to serve you faithfully to the end in whatever duty you may assign me.

Yours in the servitude of Bahá'u'lláh,

P.S. I am working hard and steadily at the difficult but enthralling and illuminating work of completing my book on Christ and Bahá'u'lláh. It will be finished before long. G.T.

Shoghi Effendi, pressed by the ever-growing demands of the Cause found time to send George a letter which answered his every need. Ruhíyyih Khánum, the Guardian's wife and secretary wrote that he

is very happy to take this opportunity to assure you that he considers that your devotion and steadfastness, and the services that you have rendered the Faith through your pen, fully merit the honour recently conferred upon you . . .

The Guardian feels sure that your services to the Faith are far from over; and he urges you to go forward with a joyful and confident heart. He sends his loving greetings to you and all the members of your family.

A postscript is of interest to the Irish Bahá'í community: 'He was very happy to hear the Assembly work there is progressing, as the Dublin Assembly is certainly the foundation stone for the work in Eire.'

The Guardian's own personal note, in large, vigorous letters, reads:

May the Almighty protect and sustain you, bless continually your high endeavours, and aid you to enrich the notable record of your unforgettable and meritorious services to the Cause of Bahá'u'lláh. Your true and grateful brother, Shoghi.

George replied to a letter of loving congratulation from the National Spiritual Assembly:

Thank you a thousand times for yours of January 25th about my being made one of the Hands of the Cause, and for the very kind and precious message from the British community which concludes it.

This appointment is the most thrilling, uplifting and invigorating thing that has happened to me since I received the two letters from 'Abdu'l-Bahá in 1919 and 1920. There are special individual reasons which bring me from it comfort, reassurances, hope and joy and strength.

I trust, pray and believe life will become a new thing for me at last, and I shall be endued through Bahá'u'lláh's infinite patience and mercy with power to achieve the results 'Abdu'l-Bahá writes of in His letters.

I trust you will help me with your prayers – I need them.

Gratefully yours, in deep full servitude to the Guardian.

The importance which the Guardian attached to George's work on *Christ and Bahá'u'lláh* is nowhere better evidenced than in a proposal now made by a Persian believer who visited George and suggested they should collaborate to produce translations of some of Bahá'u'lláh's Tablets, the Persian to translate, George to polish up the English. George, of course, referred this to the Guardian, saying that '. . . has mentioned Tablets to his father, for one item'. He received a reply to the effect that it was neither necessary nor advisable to embark on the suggested translations; 'There is too much more essential work ahead, not the least of which is your own creative writing. He hopes your book will soon be perfected, and assures you he will pray for this important work, and for your dear self . . . '

In February 1952 the Hand of the Cause Leroy Ioas, an American believer who had been one of the twelve Hands of the Cause appointed at the same time as George, was invited to Haifa to become Secretary-General of the International Bahá'í Council, the forerunner of the Universal House of Justice, which today is the head of the Faith. His aeroplane put down in Shannon for a brief stop and he used the opportunity to telephone to his fellow Hand in Dublin. George was delighted and wrote on May 13, 1952:

Dear Friend and brother in the Cause,

It was good of you to ring me up from Shannon Airport and I was so glad to get into personal touch with you in that way. And your letter written in flight is before me now, and at last I write to thank you for it and for all the kind messages and encouragement it has brought me. Indeed like you I was overawed and overwhelmed by the news of being made a Hand of the Cause; and as things develop and wonder is added to wonder and the vision of the Guardian's achievements and hopes opens up, I am sure the sense of awe and humility and gratitude will not lessen for any of us. We had in London a very impressive Convention, permeated with a great spirit. You are indeed called to a great service and a glorious privilege and your heart must be filled with joy and happiness. I should think the experience of so much bestowed at once – the Guardian and the Holy Shrines and the Holy Places and the Holy Scenes one has read and heard so much about, and the Divine Atmosphere surrounding it all – must be bewildering and overcoming: one could not absorb it. But God tempers these things to us, and strengthens us to measure up to what is required of us. You must be so busy with all your work that your very activity will protect you and prevent your meditating too much on the Celestial Forces that press all about you.

Let me wish you the fulness of joy and of success in your high endeavours.

He asked that his love be given to the Guardian and to all he knew at Haifa, 'And I live in hope of meeting you somewhere at the Conferences next year.'

During 1952 his book *The Mission of Bahá'u'lláh* was published. It is a compilation of many of his devotional pieces reprinted from *The Altar on the Hearth*, eight of his essays, including the title piece which was his Introduction to the Guardian's *God Passes By*, and *The Genius of Ireland*; his poems to Bahá'u'lláh and 'Abdu'l-Bahá are given special prominence. Six copies were bound in leather and sent to him with the request that he sign them and return three and accept the others. He wrote, 'I feel so proud of having a book of mine bound in leather.'

His elevation to the rank of Hand of the Cause apparently brought no amelioration of the constant pattern of frustration of the most ardent and natural longings of his heart – to meet the Guardian, to make pilgrimage to the Holy Land, to rouse the Church of Ireland, to revisit America. He had already refused an invitation to remove permanently to the United States (see page 193) in order to comply with the Guardian's clearly expressed preference for him to remain in Ireland. But now an opportunity arose which would have amply realized his thirty-year-old dream of seeing the Faith in action in the heart of the vigorous American Bahá'í community. He received a 'cordial invitation' from the National Spiritual Assembly there, to attend, as its guest, the great celebrations which were to take place at the Bahá'í House of Worship in Wilmette, whose foundation stone had been laid by 'Abdu'l-Bahá Himself (see page 310). The conjunction of three historic occasions during the days from April 20 to May 6, 1953 made that brief period one of enduring significance and historical importance. It was the centenary of the birth, in the loathsome Síyáh-Chál of Tihrán, of the Mission of Bahá'u'lláh; it witnessed the dedication to public worship of 'the holiest Mashriqu'l-Adhkár of the Bahá'í world', and the convocation in Chicago of the All-American Intercontinental Teaching Conference at which was launched the first global Teaching Crusade of the entire Bahá'í world. These were the Jubilee celebrations to which George was invited and the National Assembly did not fail to enquire whether he could 'undertake some teaching work in the United States before or after the programs'.

This invitation was dated December 24, 1952 and George's letter of February 24, 1953, clearly indicates some interim correspondence to do with time for him to make his final reply. His letter was addressed to Horace Holley, a Hand of the Cause and Secretary of the National Spiritual Assembly:

My dear Friend and Brother in the Cause,

Though under special treatment, my health during the last few weeks has greatly improved and I have started on a road which is likely, I hope, to lead to a complete restoration to normal efficiency and well being; nevertheless the doctor does not consider me able to undertake the strain of going to Wilmette and partaking in the glorious celebrations there; and I am therefore obliged with a very sad heart to tell you I definitely cannot accept the invitation the American National Spiritual Assembly left open to me in such a largehearted and generous way and in such cordial terms.

I have a lot of priority work for the Cause to do over here in the way of writing and in other ways; and this work will absorb for the present all my strength and time.

I have been very much touched by the extremely generous attitude of the National Spiritual Assembly and feel utterly unworthy of such kindness and I want to offer to the members again my heartfelt and deep gratitude and appreciation.

It is hard to abandon the joy of meeting you all personally and of teaching the dear Faith among you. How eagerly I have looked forward to it!

But so it must be.

The hope of meeting you all at some other date is not given up, however; and perhaps I shall have the privilege and blessings of going to Stockholm and of seeing some of you there.

With my warmest thanks for the wonderful opportunity offered to me by your National Spiritual Assembly and my deep regrets that I cannot accept it.

The substance of the missing correspondence is not hard to guess. George had been urged by the Guardian to concentrate on his own creative writing and he would not put in jeopardy completion of *Christ and Bahá'u'lláh* which Shoghi Effendi was so eagerly anticipating. Not even for this most seductive of all enticements. He therefore consulted his doctor and accepted the verdict. His obedience to the Guardian was *'instant, exact and complete'.*[1]

About this time he took Nancy to the churchyard in Enniskerry where his mother lay, a mile from the home which had welcomed him

[1] From a prayer revealed by Bahá'u'lláh. See *Bahá'í Prayers*, Bahá'í Publishing Trust, London, revised 1951.

when he returned from America, and selected a spot a few yards from Anna Maria's grave for his own. He arranged with the vicar for his body to lie in the church overnight and for his Bahá'í friends to read prayers and passages from Scripture and to conduct the burial without any service of the Church.

He was careful to secure the future benefits of his royalties to Nancy by signing a contract for publication of all his written works and appointing a literary executor.[1] The ever-present note of irony in his life was not absent from this arrangement. The largest cheque he ever received for royalties was less than a fourth of the amount sent to Nancy within twelve months of his passing.

When the Guardian called for the four Intercontinental Teaching Conferences[2] to be held during 1953 he summoned the nine Hands of the Cause outside the Holy Land to attend them as his representatives. George asked for instructions, as to whether he should make a continuous tour or return home in the intervals. He was advised to work out with the British National Spiritual Assembly the best plan, and the Guardian added, 'May the Almighty bless you in your high endeavours and enable you to attend all the four Intercontinental Conferences, where your presence and collaboration will, I am sure, be greatly appreciated and valued, and will contribute decisively to their success . . .'

In the event George was able to attend only the Stockholm Conference, the effect of which upon *Christ and Bahá'u'lláh* we have already noted.[3]

Those present were able to observe the loving care with which his thirteen fellow Hands of the Cause surrounded him. His address, carefully prepared and read by him was entitled *The Sufferings of Bahá'u'lláh and Their Significance*. In it he reached a peak of his presentation of the profound perception and understanding of spiritual processes, particularly those emanating from the earthly life of a Manifestation of God, which his long years of study and meditation had revealed to him. Its literary merit is beyond praise but is shadowed by the depth and passion of his exposition of suffering and its power to open the floodgates of God's love upon His chosen Messenger and all who will brave the fire with which heaven is walled about.

Wrongs done to the founder of a religion have two inevitable effects: one is that of retribution against the wrong done – the severity of which we may

---

[1] He conferred this honour on me and my firm, George Ronald, Publisher.
[2] See *The Bahá'í World*, vol. XII, p.115.
[3] See page 90.

judge from the two thousand year exile of the Jewish people. The other is that of reward to the High Prophet whom they enable to release fresh powers of life that would have otherwise lain latent, to pour forth Divine energies which in their boundlessness will utterly overwhelm the forces of evil and empower Him to say: 'Be of good cheer. I have overcome the world.'

The sufferings of Bahá'u'lláh enable us in some degree to measure the immensity of His love for mankind, to appreciate the sacrifice He made for love of us. The story of them enables us to keep in remembrance the heinous blackness and cruelty of the world of man from which He saved us; it enables us to realize the meaning and the need of Divine redemption, it proves to us the invincibility of God and the lone majesty of God's victory over evil.

Bahá'u'lláh's 'great poem known as the Fire Tablet' runs as a theme through the whole essay and its soaring, dramatic passages are quoted to great effect:

In that battle which we – all of us – wage with pain and suffering and sorrow, those are God's last words to us:

Where the swords flash, go forward;
Where the shafts fly, press onward.

He concludes with a verse from an ancient hymn of India 'which proclaims a truth as real now as it was in distant times':

Love is a priceless thing only to be won at the cost of death.
Those who live to die, those attain; for they have shed all thoughts of self.
Those heroic souls who are rapt in the love of the Lord, they are the true lovers.

Three years later the British National Spiritual Assembly published this essay in its Bahá'í Journal at George's special request. The Guardian included it in The Bahá'í World, vol. XII and it appeared again, twenty-two years later in vol. XVI. It is a brilliant and moving testimony to George's discharge of his duty as a Hand of the Cause to edify the souls of men.

Stockholm was his last foray into the world. From then on he directed his Board members from Ripley or whatever nursing home he might be in, and concentrated upon completing Christ and Bahá'u'lláh.

As early as 1952 the Guardian had informed the Hands of the Cause that they were to establish in each continent, during Riḍván 1954, an Auxiliary Board, whose members were to be appointed by the Hands and to serve as their deputies, advisers and assistants. For the first few years those deputies worked under the personal direction of the Hand

35. *Hands of the Cause attending the Intercontinental Teaching Conference, Stockholm, 1953. George Townshend, old and frail, is fourth from the left in the front row.*

36. *Stockholm 1953: Una, George, Nancy and the Hand of the Cause Amelia Collins*

37. *Family group at Stockholm, 1953: Una, George and Nancy*

39. *A sketch by Vivian Isenthal, 1952*

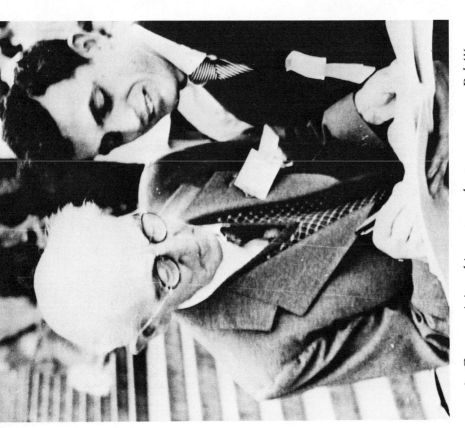

38. *George giving his autograph to a young Bahá'í, Stockholm, 1953*

40. *A Bahá'í sculptor, G.H. Ḥakím, putting the finishing touches to a bust of George. Bahá'í Summer School, Bangor, North Wales, 1952.*

who had appointed them. Thus George, as his health began to fail, acquired two vigorous, experienced, wholly dedicated helpers,[1] who understood the source and nature of the spiritual authority which flowed through him, and were able to assist him effectively in the discharge of his weighty responsibilities. He was charged with fostering the spiritual welfare of the Bahá'ís in the entire area of the British Isles, including its islands, Norway, the Faroe islands and Iceland, and of continually encouraging the propagation of Bahá'u'lláh's message by Spiritual Assemblies and individual believers. His message to the British National Convention of 1956, not only reveals his deep inner perception of those functions but equally the realization that only the power of God could accomplish the superhuman task of regenerating the human race. It reads:

> In the Bahá'í Administrative Order there are two outstanding universal institutions – the Guardianship and the Universal House of Justice. The Guardian is surrounded by the Hands of the Cause who, like planets, wheel around him . . . never will they be more needed than they are today for they stand for something which civilisation lacks and dies for want of – true belief in God and especially the fear of God.
>
> This Bahá'í teaching came into a world more full of human pride than ever had been known. Bahá'u'lláh said the kings were so full of pride they could not see their own material interest, much less such a great and perspicuous Revelation. The Western world had put God out of practical politics and invented secular history . . . their civilisation would go from strength to strength, would endow man with increasing wealth and power and would never end.
>
> Such was the view of life in which I, personally, was brought up. I never heard it questioned. It has been questioned now but nothing has been put in its place. Our minds are poisoned with pride, we are steeped in it.
>
> The first task of the Hands of the Cause is to try to drive out pride and instil humble belief and love and adoration. If we can achieve this our other tasks will come easier. But who can do it and how? All we can do is to deepen and strengthen our belief in God, and by everything in our power to spread it through this dark, unhappy generation. Let us praise God that He has chosen us to recognise the Light and let us remember the awful responsibility our knowledge imposes on us.

Now the long years of self-discipline and spiritual aspiration came to harvest. The tree of his life put forth abundantly its leaves and blossoms and even before his passing the fruits of that tree began to be gathered. There was a power and a radiance about him which vibrated throughout the world-wide Bahá'í community. The friends in the British Isles – individuals, local Spiritual Assemblies, the National Assembly alike – felt this new force of love which poured forth from

[1] Dorothy Ferraby and Marion Hofman

him; and from their gatherings such as summer schools, conventions, teaching or youth conferences and the like, his blessing, advice and encouragement were sought.

Individual believers wrote to him for explanation of passages in the Scriptures which they found difficult to understand; many of Christian background asked him about Biblical prophecies and other subjects, and some, after seeing him or meeting him at some Bahá'í occasion, just wrote to thank him for his presence among them and for the sense of upliftment and happiness which he had brought them. For instance, after the Convention in 1952, Miss Jean Campbell,[1] secretary of the Spiritual Assembly of Oxford, wrote on behalf of the Assembly to enquire about prophecies referring to the present day and the Dispensation of Bahá'u'lláh. She had spoken to him at Convention and his reply to her letter began, 'It was good to see your calligraphy and to know your address!' He referred her to his article in the March issue of *Bahá'í Journal*, the news-letter of the National Spiritual Assembly of the British Isles, and added a list of twenty-one references in the Old and New Testaments, many of them cross-documented to passages in Bahá'í writings. He added, 'The subject is a big and intriguing one. I have perhaps given enough references. If you want more information, ask me for it.' And he added an additional, '*Jeremiah* 31:31–4 is too a remarkable prophecy of Israel today.' The pleasure evoked by so generous a response became a deeper feeling by his closing paragraph: 'I am so pleased the Oxford Community wrote to me, and to hear my Convention remarks interested some people in this tremendous and astonishing subject. With love and best wishes to you all.' When the Oxford community acquired a Bahá'í Centre of their own and planned its dedication for December 12, 1954, they wrote to their beloved Hand, asking a message for the occasion. The reply is an historic document.

> I am happy and greatly honoured to be asked to send a message to the Spiritual Assembly of the Bahá'ís of Oxford on the occasion of the opening and dedication of their Centre. Only one greater happiness could be mine – to be with them myself to read the message.
>
> For centuries in English history Oxford has shown conspicuously devotion and self-sacrifice in support of great causes which she loved; but she has shown of late years a ready sympathy too with progressive movements in scholarship, moral betterment and the like.
>
> May she prove herself responsive to this Summons, which we Bahá'ís revere as the most comprehensive of all great causes and prove that – as her

---

[1] The first Oxford resident to become a Bahá'í after pioneers settled there. She was a foundation member of the Assembly and served as its secretary for many years. She later pioneered to Aberdeen and, at an advanced age, to Malta.

motto claims – God is indeed her light.[1]

Let me mention to you some outstanding points of contact the University has made with Bahá'u'lláh. It may have struck you as remarkable that there are in English literature no author prophets – there is no Isaiah, no Amos. There is, however, one poet whose work, once at least, rises near the prophetic level, Shelley, who in 'Prometheus Unbound' (counted by some as the most sublime English poem) writes of the Regeneration of the Universe, giving mention in his text to the crucified Christ and to the three thousand years prophesied by Zoroaster before the coming of the Kingdom. The hero of the poem, Prometheus, is a god man who invites long ages of suffering for himself that he may thereby redeem mankind from its misery, helplessness and degradation and be enabled to destroy the tyrant god who subjected man to his cruel will. The imagery of the poem is Greek and the action shows the end of Prometheus' suffering, his joyous liberation, the salvation of the human race, Prometheus' marriage with the Spirit of Nature and the destruction of the Tyrant of Evil, who is hurled from his throne. Later, Shelley wrote a final act in which all the powers and elements of the universe joined in a hymeneal chant on the rapture of their liberation. The poem, so far as is known, springs from nowhere but the poet's intuitive response to the birth of that holy Being, known in the Bible as the Lord of Hosts, Who had come to earth at that time to fulfil the long-promised redemption of humanity.

The only poet of the West to greet the coming of Bahá'u'lláh and to show an appreciation of its meaning for mankind was an Oxford man (Shelley), and the first divine of the West to recognise Bahá'u'lláh and to enroll himself among His followers was likewise an Oxford man (Canon Cheyne). The Canon wrote a letter to John Craven, stating that he was a Bahá'í but without resigning his membership of his mother church.[2]

When 'Abdu'l-Bahá came to England He made a point of visiting Oxford. While in this city He spoke to the students of Manchester College.

To this signal honour paid to Oxford a further honour was to be added: 'Abdu'l-Bahá chose to send the future Guardian of the Cause, Shoghi Effendi, to enter as a student at Balliol College.

What a proud heritage for Oxford! May God speed you!

George's fascination with the subject of the fulfilment, in our own times, of ancient Scriptural prophecies was again confirmed in his message to the Manchester Bahá'í community, sent to them on his own initiative as a Hand of the Cause in November 1954.

My dear Bahá'í friends of the Manchester Community,

I am asking my dear and trusty deputy to read to you this special message from me, to give you a direct personal greeting and also to say

[1] Dominus illuminatio mea.
[2] See p. 123.

how very glad I am Marion is speaking to you on the great Bahá'í subject of the hour, the dispersal of pioneers to weak key points. How I wish I could myself get over and join Marion and talk with you over a subject that enthralls me, the fulfilment of all the Bible prophecies and promises of these days. This fulfilment is surely one of the most urgently important matters for every Bahá'í to keep in the fore-front of his mind and heart in these terrific and momentous days. We are living, you and I, whether we know it or not, in the middle of events that have been foreseen and foretold for hundreds, even thousands of years. We are living at the highest point of human history and things which the generations have spoken of with bated breath are happening around us on every side. One of the prophecies (it is given in Daniel 12, for instance) was that when these things occurred most people would not recognise them! The fearful conflict in the midst of which our lot is cast is told of in Ezekiel and other prophets and in Revelations; . . .

All through Jewish and Western history the awe and the terror and the majesty of the times we are living in have gripped and held the imagination of mankind. Now it is all happening mankind refuses to believe a word of it. I urge you as Bahá'ís to do all your thinking in the light of these ancient prophecies.

With warm and loving greetings to you all, and to all whom Marion will have the privilege of addressing, and in particular to my many personal friends among you.

Yours ever in the service of the Beloved Guardian

Some time earlier Bernard Leach had written from his pottery in St. Ives, suggesting, as George's reply indicates, an exchange of thought on the teachings of Bahá'u'lláh. George welcomed the proposal and continued: 'It is most interesting you have some people studying the Cause in St. Ives, and there's no harm their entering slowly, for if their thought is progressive they will surely get right in and they may be more steadfast for having started quietly.

'But for my part, I fell head over heels in love with 'Abdu'l-Bahá's words when first I read them in print and I have been getting deeper and deeper in all these years. And I shall never get out!'[1]

Not in the British Isles only, but from far distant parts of the world, Bahá'ís who had never met him and of whom he had never heard sent letters of gratitude to him for his books and the great example he had set. Bahá'í travellers from the United States, from Persia, Egypt, Canada, Australia and New Zealand came to see him and were thankful for the privilege. Brian's beautiful memoir of him[2] relates

[1] Efforts are being made to trace this correspondence which could be of very great interest in showing the exchange of thought between two such highly developed minds.

[2] See *The Bahá'í World*, vol. XIII, pp. 844-5.

that 'Fresh signs of the believers' regard for him were continually appearing,' and cites a letter from Bermuda: 'There radiated from him such a penetrating love, that one was immediately at ease . . . His love seemed to see into one's inmost spirit . . . His name mentioned at a convention immediately caused a cathedral stillness.'

Ronald Taherzadeh, Counsellor Adib's son, now grown up with a family of his own, writes from Malawi where he is a pioneer, 'I fondly cherish a number of childhood memories of dear Mr Townshend, particularly during the last months of his life. So revered was he in our home that the mere mention of his name or the reference by either of my parents to 'Ayádí 'Amru'lláh'[1] would bring a calm air of stillness into our home.'

The Africa Campaign[2] had met with remarkable success, particularly in Uganda, where large communities of Bahá'ís rapidly emerged. Their members had mostly been to Christian mission schools where they had learned with gratitude to read and write and had become puzzled by the literalism of doctrines such as hell fire,[3] heaven, the sun being darkened, stars falling on the earth, resurrection of the body and the like. George received from the 'Bahá'ís of Kampala' a list of eleven questions to which they wanted his answers. His replies were so cogent, so well documented from the Bible itself that the British National Spiritual Assembly shared the file with the National Assembly of the United States, which body published it in a cyclostyled edition with a foreword explaining its provenance, and commenting:

'The statements and quotations are of particular interest to individuals of Jewish and Christian background, and will be very helpful in answering questions raised in public meetings, firesides and discussion groups.'

Its cover reads, 'Questions about the Second Coming – answers by George Townshend.' However, not all the questions are about the second coming. The very first one, 'Is there anything in the Bible to prove that religion must be in agreement with our reason?' refers both to the Bahá'í principle of the harmony of religion and science, and to the medieval picture of the earth as a green platform between heaven above and hell below, which is still offered by the Churches, (e.g. Christ's body went up to heaven after He descended into hell). George's brochure is widely used as is his Summary of *Some Christian*

---

[1] Persian for The Hand of the Cause of God.
[2] See p. 96, n. 5.
[3] Jomo Kenyatta, who attended in 1939 the first British Summer School, related how he experimented to see how long he could endure one finger in the flame of a brand from his camp fire. He decided at once that that religion was not for him.

Subjects, twenty chapters comprising Part II of 'Abdu'l-Bahá's famous *Some Answered Questions*.

Constantly he encouraged the friends in their service and stressed the spiritual aspects of life, always seeking to strengthen their relationship to Bahá'u'lláh and His revelation. Unable to attend the summer school in North Wales in 1956 he sent the following message from his nursing home:

> Alláh-u-Abhá.[1]
> My deepest love to each and all of you! Summer School is very important. In America, Australia and all over the world its importance is being realised more and more.
> In every other Dispensation the Teachings of the Founder have become corrupted within 50 years of the Prophet's death. But the Teachings of Bahá'u'lláh are the same now as when they were revealed. Bahá'u'lláh and 'Abdu'l-Bahá are our Teachers – therefore Summer School is very important.
> Praise be to God for this great bounty.

A letter of June 17, 1954 from the Guardian to the British National Spiritual Assembly contained, in the section written by his secretary, the following passage: 'His devotion is so single-hearted and touching, and his determination to carry on at all costs is exemplary, and should inspire the young people to follow in his footsteps.'

George's Board member, Dorothy Ferraby, sent a little memoir of him reminiscent of the happy anecdote related on page 154. 'During the three years before his death he was always encouraging when one was doing anything special, but I think it was mostly by telegram; or sometimes, when he could write, it would be a postscript on a letter to John:[2] 'Please tell herself . . .'

George had long recognized the dynamic effect of the power which flowed through the Guardian. He had seen it galvanize and transform the Bahá'í world community. In his own life he strove to tap this power by complete and exact obedience to every guidance or intimation which came from the Guardian. Advised to husband his strength for completion of *Christ and Bahá'u'lláh* he refused tasks which his natural inclination urged him to accept but which might have overtaxed him. As a Hand of the Cause, he endeavoured to guide the believers to the same vision of the Guardian's divine authority which he himself had and at the same time show them how to attain the spiritual strength needed to follow the paths delineated by the Guardian. These two objectives are wonderfully apparent in his

[1] A universal greeting among Bahá'ís; it means 'God is the Most Glorious'.

[2] John Ferraby, Secretary of the National Spiritual Assembly, appointed a Hand of the Cause in October 1957.

immediate decision about a matter referred to him by his Auxiliary Board member Marion Hofman in August 1955.

In July of that year the National Spiritual Assembly had received a directive from the Guardian to the effect that the British Bahá'í community must henceforth adhere to the general rule that the areas of jurisdiction of local Spiritual Assemblies should conform to the civil limits of their respective towns. This was a shattering blow to the struggling community in Britain, many of whose twenty-four hard-won Assemblies comprised members living outside the civil boundaries. Thirteen Assemblies were so affected as to fall below the requisite number to form or maintain that institution, and the question was raised as to the possibility of preserving those Assemblies while at the same time forming the new ones scheduled for April 1956. The reply from the Hand of the Cause was the following:

> . . . The Guardian has put the matter before the community as a definite injunction, not leaving any express option. He would not do this unless he knew that success was possible and you may be sure he will help all he can with all his resources. Therefore, I would not hesitate but let the community go ahead as hard as they can, feeling full of confidence and determined to do their utmost without permitting themselves to doubt or fear. To succeed in this way, their first and greatest effort will have to be spent on strengthening their faith and doubling their assurance by every possible means. This will call for an intense and continuous endeavour on devotional and moral level, something deeper and certainly not less trying than the endeavour to win contacts. But it all depends on the personal effort of each individual. For instance, one will have to be very dutiful in saying one's prayers with intensity and regularity; on reading scripture daily with a real wish to discover its meaning (as Bahá'u'lláh enjoined in the Íqán). This regular reading is most strengthening. Bahá'u'lláh says every believer should check his conduct *twice* every day, morning and evening. To do such things as these is one main way of toughening faith which won't grow of itself. 'An effort is needed', said Bahá'u'lláh. By such methods and increasing obedience and an effort to enrich one's love for God faith can become stronger, otherwise it may grow weaker.
>
> If the community would resolve on doing such things as these then they will be able to meet the Guardian's challenge and win a victory...
>
> The Guardian says in some pilgrim's notes that the English are too cautious (if they have any fault at all). Well, the English accept the challenge and go through with it, he won't say again they're too cautious! It's a dangerous undertaking except for those who are ready to dare to the limit.

He authorized his Board member, who had been asked to present the subject to the friends at the forthcoming Summer School, to 'Use it as you please', and added 'How I wish I were with you all instead of being tied up in a sack here.'

He constantly requested his Board members to emphasize the spiritual side of things. 'I know this is the Guardian's thought. Also it was 'Abdu'l-Bahá's before him.' And he himself set the example, not only in all his messages and talks to the friends, but in his own self-striving. On April 1, 1953, a year and three months after he had become a Hand of the Cause, in his seventy-seventh year he confided to the Guardian,

> A great impulse to a better moral and spiritual condition has come upon me and I have been drawn to make direct contact with the spirituality that I reached in 1928 – since which year real happiness vanished. Now I recite many times daily the Prayer I wrote then beginning, 'Only Beloved, with a heart on fire/And all my longings set in one desire/To make my life a many-stringed lyre/For Thy dear hand to play' and every day I learn some new truth . . .

In that same letter he gave some indication of his day to day work for the Faith:

> I am rewriting *Christ and Bahá'u'lláh* with a new vigour, and have published at least one article in every Bahá'í Journal for ten months, and have more articles ready; am preparing a pamphlet on Christ and the Gospel for the National Spiritual Assembly (they like the work done very much); and I hope and pray I will work soon more quickly. Also I make frequent talks to the British community. The National Spiritual Assembly gives their British Hand of the Cause good opportunities.

Counsellor Taherzadeh had noted that when George became a Hand of the Cause the British Bahá'ís turned to him. He recalled his first attendance at a Convention as a Hand of the Cause, in 1953: 'George spoke to the Bahá'ís and this was a tremendous occasion for him. When he came back you could see the difference, the joy in his face, the radiance, because he had been able to see the friends, to talk with them and to associate with them and to join in their activities.'

During the last years of his life he spent varying periods in nursing homes in different parts of Dublin. They were Brighton House, at Rathgar; Hatley, his old home where he was born – the Burlington Clinic; Portobello; Mount Carmel, in Braemor Park on the southern edge of the city. Irony pursued him even now for this nominal attainment was the closest he ever came to the land of his heart's desire, in spite of invitations from the Guardian and his own longing. Una thinks it was the one where he was happiest. It was operated by an Order of nuns called Blue Sisters who 'gave him excellent care; they

41. *Mr and Mrs Townshend, after the resignation*

42. George, Nancy and Brian outside Ripley, circa 1950

43. George at Summer School, Bangor, North Wales, 1952

44. *Two of the nursing homes where George spent time under care.*
Portobello above and Kilbarron below. The latter was the scene of the
visit of two Hands of the Cause to George (see page 363).

45. *The cemetery at Enniskerry Church*

were dedicated and had no staffing problems'. Kilbarron Nursing Home, Sandy Cove, just south of Dun Laoghaire, was a pleasant, neat-looking house facing the sea. As he entered there in February 1955, he was informed that two Hands of the Cause, Dr Grossmann from Germany and Mr Leroy Ioas, whom we have already met, were in London. Eager to meet his fellow Hands, George requested Adib Taherzadeh to send telegrams to them both asking them to come and see him. Dr Grossmann arrived first and stayed overnight in a nearby Guest House, leaving next day, much to George's regret, just before Mr Ioas arrived by plane. George and Leroy spent a wonderful day together, going over and over Leroy's accounts of their beloved Guardian and all the work in Haifa. It was a splendid and memorable occasion for George and undoubtedly one of the happiest moments in his life. Ireland is fortunate to have the episode preserved for it has already entered the annals of Irish Bahá'í history and will undoubtedly, in centuries to come, be one of the interesting events of the early days of the Bahá'í Faith in that land, days when their own beloved Hand lived and worked among the first believers and poured out upon them and future generations the love and guidance which flowed through him from the Guardian of the Faith.

George died in the Baggot Street Hospital at 11 p.m. on March 25, 1957. His worn-out old body was interred with gentle and befitting ceremony in the beautiful churchyard of Enniskerry, close to the graves of his mother and sister. Sheep were grazing in the adjacent field and the sun lit the peak of Sugar Loaf to the south and brightened all the surrounding hills. He lay in the church overnight and next day they carried his coffin to the southern edge of the churchyard where, beneath the splendid pines the flowers awaited him and a special place had been prepared for the service. It was a glorious shining day and the birds sang all through our prayers. We were a small company of Bahá'ís for a while, including the secretary of the National Spiritual Assembly and Kathleen Hornell for Northern Ireland. Bahá'u'lláh's prescribed prayer for the dead was read. Then at 5 p.m. two of George's sisters, a brother-in-law and daughter and Luke Mahon from Ahascragh joined us for prayers and readings, chosen by his family from his own favourites, not omitting the vision of St John of the descent of 'the holy city, New Jerusalem' which played so great a part in George's life. 'For us it seemed all a miracle – this truly Bahá'í service in the heart of a much-loved Christian churchyard. "Christ and Bahá'u'lláh" – for George of all men such a fitting close, and for this we honour and applaud dear Nancy.'[1]

[1] For this and all the detail of the funeral we are indebted to George's Board member, Marion Hofman. The particular mention of Nancy refers to the incident, already

Memorial meetings were held in the Bahá'í national headquarters in London, in Belfast and in Dublin. The National Spiritual Assembly published a four-page centre piece in its *Bahá'í Journal* entitled 'George Townshend Supplement'. It began with the Guardian's cable (see below), and contained George's photograph and a snapshot of his grave with the wreaths and flowers covering it, excerpts from 'Abdu'l-Bahá's second Tablet to him, from his own message to Convention 1956 (see page 355), four meditations from *The Altar on the Hearth,* his poem to Bahá'u'lláh, a long tribute by a member of the Assembly, and a brief *curriculum vitae.* It concluded, 'His memory is one of the most precious possessions of the British Bahá'í Community.'

The clergy in George's old diocese of Clonfert arranged a memorial service for him in the little Ahascragh church, burned down in 1922 and rebuilt under George's rectorship. Miss Dillon invited Nancy, Brian and Una to stay at Clonbrock for the occasion. The service and the tributes paid are described in Chapter 12, but Una wrote to his two Board members:

> Letters of sympathy have been pouring in . . . from old non-Bahá'í friends . . . Everyone in Ahascragh paid the highest tributes . . . One of the people we called on (a Roman Catholic) told us how she and many others went to him for advice when in trouble; they knew he would never breathe a word to anyone. She spoke of his absolute goodness and said the local people all said he was a saint. It was lovely to hear all these tributes and to know how everybody loved him but it was heartbreakingly lonely to be back there again without him . . . But in his sorrows, frustrations and heartbreaks he was following in the footsteps of his Beloved, Bahá'u'lláh, and now, seeing everything in perspective, I am sure he would not have wished it otherwise.

She concluded: 'Finally, I want to thank you both very much for all your help and support to my dear father. Indeed you did all the work latterly. My father had a great admiration for you both and was very fond of you, and I know he will continue to do so and he will help you in the days ahead.'

---

intimated in Adib Taherzadeh's notes and previously, when she stood firm for the carrying out of George's own plans for his burial made a few years before (see page 353). By 1957 there was a new vicar at Enniskerry who had not known of these plans and who, not unreasonably, wanted to know what was intended in his church without his participation. He telephoned Nancy and the conversation lasted an hour and a half as attested by Nancy herself, Brian and Una. The vicar was opposed to the whole scheme, but Nancy stood firm, explained that the plans had been approved at the time they were made and offered to refer to higher authority. Eventually she demanded a clear statement that he would not give George harbourage in his church if that were his intention. 'Will you say that, for then we must quickly make other plans?' The vicar capitulated with a curt 'No'. We must have some sympathy for him as well as honour for Nancy.

Brian wrote a beautiful memorial article for *The Bahá'í World.*[1] He opened with George's poem 'Only Beloved . . .' and continued:

No other words are worthy to describe, or indeed can convey an image of the all-consuming, ever-burning fire of devotion that dominated, governed and so remarkably sustained my father's life. Driven always by a restless urge to seek, to study and later to proclaim the Day of God, he seems not to have known real contentment nor, despite the tributes paid to him, to have realised what he had done or been aware that his prayer was granted. His great humility blinded him to his achievements. He saw only unattainable goals ahead.

The cable from the Guardian of the Faith gloriously sealed the record of this heroic, dedicated life:

March 27, 1957

DEEPLY MOURN PASSING DEARLY LOVED MUCH ADMIRED GREATLY GIFTED OUTSTANDING HAND CAUSE GEORGE TOWNSHEND. HIS DEATH MORROW PUBLICATION HIS CROWNING ACHIEVEMENT ROBS BRITISH FOLLOWERS BAHÁ'U'LLÁH THEIR MOST DISTINGUISHED COLLABORATOR AND FAITH ITSELF ONE ITS STOUTEST DEFENDERS. HIS STERLING QUALITIES HIS SCHOLARSHIP HIS CHALLENGING WRITINGS HIS HIGH ECCLESIASTICAL POSITION UNRIVALLED ANY BAHÁ'Í WESTERN WORLD ENTITLE HIM RANK WITH THOMAS BREAKWELL DR. ESSLEMONT ONE OF THREE LUMINARIES SHEDDING BRILLIANT LUSTRE ANNALS IRISH ENGLISH SCOTTISH BAHÁ'Í COMMUNITIES. HIS FEARLESS CHAMPIONSHIP CAUSE HE LOVED SO DEARLY SERVED SO VALIANTLY CONSTITUTES SIGNIFICANT LANDMARK BRITISH BAHÁ'Í HISTORY. SO ENVIABLE POSITION CALLS FOR NATIONAL TRIBUTE HIS MEMORY BY ASSEMBLED DELEGATES VISITORS FORTHCOMING BRITISH BAHÁ'Í CONVENTION. ASSURE RELATIVES DEEPEST LOVING SYMPATHY GRIEVOUS LOSS. CONFIDENT HIS REWARD INESTIMABLE ABHÁ KINGDOM.

[1] *The Bahá'í World*, vol. XIII, pp. 841–6

ENVOI

NANCY survived George by nearly four years. She remained a nominal member of the Bahá'í community but withdrew from activity in it and arranged for her funeral to be conducted by the Church of Ireland. Una went to the United States where she married Richard Dean and later moved to Canada where they are now both active Bahá'ís. Brian inherited Ripley, where he lived for a time before selling it, and retiring to private life in his beloved Ireland.

The lack of any correspondence between George and Nellie after 1953 is a serious one, which is not likely to be repaired. We can only surmise her rejoicing when George was made a Hand of the Cause and her perception of his high spiritual destiny was confirmed. She survived him by sixteen months and died honoured by the American Bahá'ís and the city of Nashville.

George was an undistinguished member of a distinguished family until God seized hold of him and thrust His banner into his hands. Even then he became no knight in shining armour, but a modest standard bearer attempting to point the way to his colleagues. When the frustrated longings of his heart were answered by a call to battle, then he did assault, with all his powers of mind and persuasion, the Establishment and its hierarchy, having first renounced all it had conferred on him of honours, emoluments, status and security. His father, his sisters and brothers dealt successfully with the great world. George was a wanderer and a seeker until the age of thirty when he suddenly knew that the rest of his life would be spent in the search for Truth, and even then a further thirteen years were to elapse before a definite path was opened to him and he received a clear, firm mandate from his Lord. From that time on he followed the guidance of the

Centre of the Covenant, and served with fervent dedication and growing distinction the Cause of Bahá'u'lláh, Whom he recognized, with awe and a throbbing heart, as the Lord of Hosts, Christ returned in the glory of the Father.

By long years of patient effort in face of frustration, by unwearying cheerfulness and heroic sacrifice, he attained, in the final years of pain and poverty, a spiritual elevation by which he surpassed not only the extraverted coterie of his family, but all his countrymen and became a star in the triple constellation of the New Heaven from which he shines forever, a luminary shedding brilliant lustre on the annals of Irish, English and Scottish Bahá'í history.

and I saw a new heaven and a new earth

REV. XXI

Appendix 1

THE IRISH QUESTION

Extracted from *Europe Since* 1815, by C.D. Hazen

To understand the question, a brief survey of Irish history in the nineteenth century is necessary. Ireland was all through the century the most discontented and wretched part of the British Empire. While England constantly grew in numbers and wealth, Ireland decreased in population, and her misery increased. In 1815 Ireland was inhabited by two peoples, the native Irish, who were Catholics, and settlers from England and Scotland, who were for the most part Anglicans or Presbyterians. The latter were a small but powerful minority.

The fundamental cause of the Irish question lay in the fact that Ireland was a conquered country, that the Irish were a subject race. As early as the twelfth century the English began to invade the island. Attempts made by the Irish at various times during six hundred years to repel and drive out the invaders only resulted in rendering their subjection more complete and more galling. Irish insurrections have been pitilessly punished, and race hatred has been the consuming emotion in Ireland for centuries. The contest was unequal, owing to the far greater resources of England during all this time. The result of this turbulent history was that in 1815 the Irish were a subject people in their own land, as they had been for centuries, and that there were several evidences of this so conspicuous and so burdensome that most Irishmen could not pass a day without feeling the bitterness of their situation. It was a hate-laden atmosphere which they breathed.

The marks of subjection were various. The Irish did not own the land of Ireland, which had once belonged to their ancestors. The various conquests by English rulers had been followed by extensive confiscations of the land. Particularly extensive was that of Cromwell. These lands were given in large estates to Englishmen. The Irish were mere tenants, and most of them tenants-at-will, on lands that now belonged to others. The Irish have always regarded themselves as the rightful owners of the soil of Ireland, have regarded the English landlords as usurpers, and have desired to recover possession for themselves. Hence there arose the agrarian question, a part of the general Irish problem.

Again, in 1815 the Irish were the victims of religious intolerance. At the time of the Reformation they remained Catholic, while the English separated from Rome. Attempts to force the Anglican Church upon them only stiffened their opposition. Nevertheless, in 1815 they were paying tithes to the Anglican Church in Ireland, though they were themselves ardent Catholics, never entered a Protestant church, and were supporting their own churches by voluntary gifts. Thus they contributed to two churches, one alien, which they hated, and one to which they were devoted. Thus a part of the Irish problem was the religious question.

Again, in 1815 the Irish did not make the laws which governed them. In 1800 their separate Parliament in Dublin was abolished, and from 1801 there was only one Parliament in Great Britain, that in London. While Ireland henceforth had its quota of representatives in the House of Commons, it was always a hopeless minority. Moreover, the Irish members did not really represent the large majority of the Irish, as no Catholic could sit in the House of Commons. There was this strange anomaly that, while the majority of the Irish could vote for members of Parliament, they must vote for Protestants – a bitter mockery.

The Irish demanded the right to govern themselves. Thus another aspect of the problem was purely political.

The abuse just mentioned was removed in 1829,[1] when Catholic Emancipation was carried, which henceforth permitted Catholics to sit in the House of Commons. The English statesmen granted this concession only when forced to do so by the imminent danger of civil war. The Irish consequently felt no gratitude. Moreover, at the moment when Catholics were being admitted to Parliament, most of them lost their vote by the much higher franchise qualification enacted at the same time, for the qualification was raised in Ireland from forty shillings to ten pounds, though for England it remained at forty shillings. Shortly after Catholic Emancipation had been achieved, the Irish, under the matchless leadership of O'Connell, endeavored by much the same methods to obtain the repeal of the Union between England and Ireland, effected in 1801, and to win back a separate legislature and a large measure of independence. This movement, for some time very formidable, failed completely, owing to the iron determination of the English that the union should not be broken, and to the fact that the leader, O'Connell, was not willing in last resort to risk civil war to accomplish the result, recognizing the hopelessness of such a contest. This movement came to an end in 1843. However, a number of the younger followers of O'Connell, chagrined at his peaceful methods, formed a society called 'Young Ireland,' the aim of which was Irish independence and a republic. They rose in revolt in the troubled year, 1848. The revolt, however, was easily put down.

As if Ireland did not suffer enough from political and social evils, an appalling catastrophe of nature was added. The Irish famine of 1845–7, to

[1] Catholics were permitted to hold offices after 1828 by the abolition of the Test Acts.

which reference has already been made, was a tragic calamity, far-reaching in its effects. The repeal of the Corn Laws did not check it. The distress continued for several years, though gradually growing less. The potato crop of 1846 was inferior to that of 1845, and the harvests of 1848 and 1849 were far from normal. Charity sought to aid, but was insufficient. The government gave money, and later gave rations. In March 1847 over 700,000 people were receiving government support. In March and April of that year the deaths in the workhouses alone were more than ten thousand a month. Peasants ate roots and lichens, or flocked to the cities in the agony of despair, hoping for relief. Multitudes fled to England or crowded the emigrant ships to America, dying by the thousands of fever or exhaustion. It was a long drawn out horror, and when it was over it was found that the population had decreased from about 8,300,000 in 1845 to less than 6,600,000 in 1851. Since then the decrease occasioned by emigration has continued. By 1881 the population had fallen to 5,100,000; by 1891 to 4,700,000, by 1901 to about 4,450,000. Since 1851 perhaps 4,000,000 Irish have emigrated. Ireland, indeed, is probably the only country whose population decreased in the nineteenth century.

For many years after the famine, and the failure of 'Young Ireland' in 1848, Irish politics were quiescent. Year after year the ceaseless emigration to the United States continued. Finally, there was organized among the Irish in America a secret society, called the Fenians, whose purpose was to achieve the independence of the republic of Ireland. The Irish in the two countries co-operated and in 1865 and 1866 were active. James Stephens, the leader in Ireland, announced that the flag of the Irish republic would be raised in 1865. The Government, alarmed, took stringent measures, arresting many of the leaders, and even securing from Parliament the suspension of the Habeas Corpus Act in Ireland. In May 1866 the Fenians in the United States attempted an invasion of Canada. About 1,200 of them crossed the Niagara River, but were soon driven back, though only after blood had been shed. Several, taken prisoners, were tried by courts-martial and shot. In 1867 various Fenian outrages occurred in Ireland and in England. There were many arrests, trials, and some executions. The chief significance of the Fenian movement was the alarm it aroused in England, and the vivid evidence it gave of the unrest and deep-rooted discontent of Ireland. The Irish question thus became again an exciting topic for discussion, a problem pressing upon Parliament for solution.

When Gladstone came into power in 1868 he was resolved to pacify the Irish by removing some of their more pronounced grievances, the three branches of the Irish Upas tree, as he called them – the Irish Church, the Irish land laws, and Irish education.

The question of the Irish Church was the first one attacked. This was the Anglican Church established and endowed in Ireland at the time of the Reformation. It was a branch of the Church of England. Its position was anomalous. It was a state church, yet it was the church not of the people, but of a small minority. Established to win over the Catholics to Protestantism, it had signally failed of its purpose. Its members numbered less than an eighth of the population. There were many parishes, about 150, in which there was not a single member. There were nearly 900 in which there were less than fifty members. Yet these places were provided with an Anglican clergyman and a place of worship, generally the former Catholic church building. The Church was maintained by its endowment and by the tithes which the Catholics, as well as the Protestants, paid. Sidney Smith said of this institution: 'On an Irish Sabbath the bell of the neat parish church often summons to service only the parson and an occasional conforming clerk; while two hundred yards off, a thousand Catholics are huddled together in a miserable hovel, and pelted by all the storms of heaven,' and he added, 'There is no abuse like it in all Europe, in all Asia, in all the discovered parts of Africa, and in all that we have heard of Timbuctoo.' This favored corporation did not even discharge its religious functions with zeal. Many a clergyman used his position simply for the salary attached, employed a curate to perform his duties, and himself lived in England. The Irish resisted the payment of tithes, and the result was the so-called tithe war, in which the peasant's property, his cow or goat, his chickens or kettles, were seized and sold for payment. Even such methods were not successful. In 1833 out of £104,000 due only £12,000 could be collected. At length, in 1838 the system was abandoned. The tithes were made a tax upon the land, which simply meant that the peasants no longer paid them directly, but paid them indirectly in the form of the increased rent demanded by the landlord. The Catholics were still supporters of a wealthy and alien corporation. Meanwhile, their own priests were exceedingly poor, and their own services had to be held in the open air or in wretched buildings. The existence of this alien church was regarded as humiliating and oppressive.

Gladstone in 1869 procured the passage of a law abolishing tithes, even in this roundabout form, and disestablishing and partly disendowing the Church. The Church henceforth ceased to be connected with the State. Its bishops lost their seats in the House of Lords. It became a voluntary organization and was permitted to retain a large part of its property as an endowment. The rest was to be appropriated as Parliament should direct. It was to have all the church buildings which it had formerly possessed. It was still very rich, but the connection with the Church of England was to cease January 1, 1871. The bill, though very favorable to the Church, was denounced as sheer robbery, as 'highly offensive to Almighty God,' as the 'greatest national sin ever committed.' Nevertheless, it passed and became law. One branch of the famous Upas tree had been lopped off.

Gladstone now approached a far more serious and perplexing problem – the system of land tenure. Ireland was almost exclusively an agricultural country, yet the land was chiefly owned, not by those who lived on it and tilled it, but by a comparatively small number of landlords, who held large estates. Many of these were Englishmen, absentees, who rarely or never came to Ireland, and who regarded their estates simply as so many sources of revenue. The business relations with their tenants were carried on by agents or bailiffs, whose treatment of the tenants was frequently harsh and exasperating. In the minds of the Irish their landlords were foreigners, who had acquired by robbery land which they regarded as rightly belonging to themselves. This initial injustice they never forgot. There had been from the beginning a wide gulf between the two. As, however, there were almost no industries in Ireland, the inhabitants were obliged to have land. They were, therefore, in an economic sense, at the mercy of the landlord. There was, properly speaking, no competition among landowners to rent their land, forcing them, therefore, to treat their tenants with some liberality and consideration. There was competition only among the applicants for land, applicants so numerous that they would offer to pay much more for a little plot on which to raise their potatoes, which furnished the chief food, than the value of the land justified. The result was that in many cases they could not pay the stipulated rent and were evicted. Their position only became still more deplorable, for land they must have or starve; consequently, they would promise a higher rent to some other landlord, with, in the end, another eviction as a result. Now, eviction was easy, because these petty farmers were tenants-at-will, that is, tenants who must leave their holdings at the will and pleasure of the landlord, or on short notice, generally six months, obviously a most insecure form of tenure. Lands were not rented for a year or five years or ten, but only as long as the owner should see fit. Occupation could be terminated abruptly by the landlord, starvation faced the peasant. Moreover, Irish landlords rented, as was correctly stated at the time, not farms, that is, land and the necessary buildings and improvements, but simply land. The tenant put up at his own expense such buildings and made such improvements in the way of fences, draining, clearing, fertilizing, as he could, or wished; in very many cases the land would have had no value whatever, but for these improvements. Yet, as the law then stood, when a landlord evicted his tenant he was not obliged to pay for any buildings or improvements made during the tenant's occupation. He simply appropriated so much property created by the tenant.

It would be hard to conceive a more unwise or unjust system. It encouraged indolence and slothfulness. The land was wretchedly cultivated, because good cultivation of it was penalized. Why should a tenant work hard to improve the quality of his holding, to erect desirable farm buildings, when he knew that this would merely mean a higher rent or his eviction in favor of someone who would offer a higher rent, in which case all his improvements would benefit others and not himself? In other words, it was a positive disadvantage to a tenant to be prosperous. If prosperous, he made efforts to conceal the fact, as did the peasants in pre-revolutionary France. Now, the social effects of this system were disastrous in the extreme. Chronic and shocking misery was the lot of the Irish peasantry. 'The Irish peasant,' says an official English document of the time, 'is the most poorly nourished, most poorly housed, most poorly clothed of any in Europe; he has no reserve, no capital. He lives from day to day.' His house was generally a rude stone hut, with a dirt floor. The census of 1841 established the fact that in the case of forty-six per cent of the population, the entire family lived in a house, or more properly, hut of a single room. Frequently the room served also as a barn for the livestock.

Stung by the misery of their position, and by the injustice of the laws that protected the landlord, and that gave them only two hard alternatives, surrender to the landlord, or starvation, and believing that when evicted they were also robbed, and goaded by the hopeless outlook for the future, the Irish, in wild rage, committed many atrocious agrarian crimes, murders, arson, the killing or maiming of cattle. This in turn brought a new coercion law from the English Parliament, which only aggravated the evil.

Such was the situation. Mr. Gladstone, desiring to govern Ireland, not according to English, but according to Irish ideas, faced it resolutely. He had an important argument at hand. While the system just described was the one prevailing throughout most of Ireland, a different one had grown up in a single province, Ulster, the so-called system of 'tenant right.' The tenant's right was undisturbed possession of his holding as long as he paid his rent, and fair payment for all permanent improvements, in case he should relinquish his holding, whether voluntarily or because of inability to pay the rent. This was mere custom, not law. But the result was that the peasants of Ulster were hard-working and prosperous, whereas in the rest of Ireland the contrary was the case. The outgoing peasant received, as a matter of fact, for his improvements from five to twenty times the amount of his annual rent. It paid him, therefore, to make them. Mr. Gladstone took this local custom and made it a law for all Ireland. In the Land Act of 1870 it was provided that if evicted for any other reason than for the non-payment of rent, the tenant could claim compensation for disturbance from the landlord, and also that he was to receive compensation for all improvements of a permanent character on giving up his holding. It was hoped that thus the peasants would have a sense of security in their occupation, and that with security would come prosperity and peace.

There were certain other clauses in the bill, not greatly approved by Gladstone, but strongly urged by Mr. Bright, whose influence with the people Gladstone did not wish to alienate. Bright desired that the Irish peasants should gradually cease to be tenants of other people's land, and should become landowners themselves. This could only be done by purchasing the estates of the landlords, and this obviously the peasants were unable to do. The Bright clauses, therefore, provided that the State should help the peasant up to a certain amount, he in turn repaying the State for the money loaned by easy instalments, covering a long period of years. Accordingly, carefully guarded land purchase clauses were put into this bill.

The bill thus proposed went through Parliament with comparative ease [1870].

Appendix 2

NELLIE ROCHE

Mary Watkins's contribution to the story of Nellie Roche and George Townshend is beyond all evaluation. Without her knowledge and the documents which she provided almost nothing would have been known of this vital thread running through two lives, and affecting them so profoundly. In the course of research into George's first knowledge of the Bahá'í Faith I was directed to Mrs Evelyn Hardin, a Bahá'í of Meridian, Mississippi, who knew that Nellie had met George in Sewanee, had become engaged to him but 'broke it off shortly before he returned to Ireland. He wrote her about the Faith, as I recall, and carried on quite a correspondence through the years. He would tell about his books and send her first copies.' And that would have been the extent of our knowledge of this remarkable story had not Mrs Hardin referred me to Mary Watkins. Her contribution comprises:

> 39 letters from George to Nellie, ranging from April 25, 1939 to October 15, 1947.
> Typewritten copies of 10 letters from Nellie to George (21 pages all told).
> 13 typewritten pages of Nellie's own notes on her "Life experiences".
> Telegram from George to Nellie, August 5, 1947 (see p. 198).
> Nellie's notes, written in firm, pencilled, staccato phrases fourteen months before her death in 1958, summarizing the main events in her relationship with George.
> George's essay, *The Angel of the Valley*, inscribed in his hand, 'To Nellie from the author G.T.'
> George's poem *War and Peace*.
> Letter from Marion Little to Nellie, dated May 16, 1939, about Nellie's assistance to George.
> Photograph of George at Sewanee (see plate 11).
> Photograph of Nellie, aged about thirty, signed on the back (see plate 13)
> Photograph of 'Ripley', George's home in Dublin after resignation from the Church (see plate 29).

Christmas greeting card from 'The Townshends', 1941, using picture of
   Ripley.

Mary Watkins's own knowledge of the circumstances surrounding the
   relationship, recorded on cassette, together with answers to
   innumerable questions, when on pilgrimage to the Bahá'í World
   Centre in 1977.

An obituary notice from *The Nashville Banner* (see below).

NASHVILLE BANNER July 31, 1958
MISS NELLIE JENNINGS ROCHE DIES: RITES TO BE FRIDAY

Miss Nellie Jennings Roche, 78, recognized as one of the South's outstanding
women in the insurance profession, died at 3 a.m. today at Vanderbilt Hospital
after a brief illness.

Known as the dean of the life insurance women of Nashville, 'Miss Nell' was
consulted by men and women from all walks of life for personal as well as financial
advice.

For 35 years Miss Roche had been with the Nashville agency of the
Massachusetts Mutual Life Insurance Co., where she was a life underwriter.

Even after her official retirement in January, she continued as a field assistant to
the company's general agent for Middle Tennessee, Martin Nunelley.

The great-great-granddaughter of Gen. James Robertson, founder of Nashville,
she had lived in Nashville all her life and been active in its civic and religious affairs.
She was the daughter of Samuel S. and Lydia Robertson Roche.

Miss Roche attended public schools in East Nashville and the Peabody School.

For a number of years she taught in Ross, Elliott and Hume-Fogg schools, and
many outstanding Nashville businessmen received a vital part of their education
from Miss Roche.

A member of the Altrusa Club for 38 years, she was in 1922–23 the club's fourth
president. She was also a member of the Daughters of the American Revolution.

Miss Roche was an active member of the Nashville Association of Life
Underwriters and was believed to be the only woman in the state to hold the title of
Chartered Life Underwriter.

A pioneer leader in women's politics, she served as comptroller for the City in
1921 under Mayor Felix Wilson.

Originally a member of St Ann's Episcopal Church, Miss Roche became a
member of the Bahá'í Faith about 30 years ago.[1] She served as chairman of the
Bahá'í community here several years ago.

She resided at the Reeves Apts, 2325 Elliston Place.

The body is at Finley–Dorris and Charlton Funeral Home where services will be
held at 10:30 a.m. Friday. Members of the Bahá'í comunity will conduct the
services, the burial will be in Woodlawn Cemetery.

[1] Should have been 'about 20 years ago'.

Appendix 3

THE OLD CHURCHES AND
THE NEW WORLD-FAITH

The text of this Appendix has been photographed from the original
edition of the pamphlet, published in 1949. (See Chap. 11)

HAVING identified myself with the Faith of
Bahá'u'lláh and sacrificed my position as a canon
and a dignitary of the Church of Ireland that I
might do so, I now make this statement on the
relation of this Faith to Christianity and to the
Churches of Christ.

It is submitted to all Christian people in general
but more especially to the bishops and clergy and
members of my own communion, with the humble
but earnest and urgent request that they will give
it their attention as a matter of vital concern to
the Church. Only through an impartial investigation of the Cause of Bahá'u'lláh will they find,
I fully believe, a means of reviving the fortunes of
the Church, of restoring the purity and the power
of the Gospel and of helping to build a better and
more truly Christian world.

Bahá'u'lláh (Whose approaching advent had been
announced in Persia nineteen years before by
His prophetic Herald, the Báb, Himself a world-
famous figure) made His public declaration as a
Messenger of God in Baghdad in the year 1863.

He affirmed that His appearance fulfilled the promised Return of Christ in the glory of the Father. He brought a Teaching which though ampler and fitted to a more advanced Age was in spirit and purpose the same as that of Christ. He revealed those *"other things"* which Jesus told His disciples He had to give them but which they could *"not bear"* at that time. His mission was to bring the work of Christ to its completion and realisation, to reconstruct the social order of the world and build the long promised Kingdom of God in very fact.

He addressed individual letters or specific messages to the monarchs of the West and to the members of the various ecclesiastical orders of the Christian Churches, and directed numerous and repeated exhortations and warnings to the entire Christian world. These without exception were ignored by Christendom when they were made, and they have now been set aside and disregarded for some eighty years. During that period the long established influence of Christ in Christendom has suffered a decline so unprecedented, so precipitous that the Bishops gathering for the Lambeth Conference were greeted in the London press with the challenge that "Christianity is fighting for its life"; while the Bahá'í Faith proclaimed at that time by one lone Prophet shut in a Turkish prison has spread through the whole globe, has led the constructive thought of our time, has created a spiritual world-community joining the East and the West, and is fast making good its right to a place in the age-long succession of world-faiths.

" *Followers of the Gospel,*" exclaimed Bahá'u'-lláh addressing the whole of Christendom, " *behold*

*the gates of heaven are flung open, He that had
ascended unto it is now come. Give ear to His
voice calling aloud over land and sea, announcing
to all mankind the advent of this Revelation—a
Revelation through the agency of which the Tongue
of Grandeur is now proclaiming: ' Lo, the sacred
Pledge has been fulfilled, for He, the Promised One
is come.' " . . . " The voice of the Son of Man
is calling aloud from the sacred vale, ' Here am I,
here am I, O God, my God ' " . . . whilst from the
Burning Bush breaketh forth the cry, " Lo, the
Desire of the world is made manifest in His transcendent glory." The Father hath come. That
which ye were promised in the Kingdom of God
is fulfilled. This is the Word which the Son
veiled when He said to those around Him that at
that time they could not bear it. . . . Verily the
spirit of Truth is come to guide you unto all truth. . . .
He is the one who glorified the Son and exalted
His Cause." . . . " The Comforter whose advent
all the Scriptures have promised is now come
that He may reveal unto you all knowledge and
wisdom. Seek Him over the entire surface of the
earth, haply ye may find Him."*

Through a period of some twenty-five years from
about 1865 to 1890, Bahá'u'lláh sent letters and
messages to the monarchs and leaders of mankind
proclaiming to them that—however little they
recognised it—a world-crisis had already taken
shape and profound changes on a world-scale were
at hand; the old civilisation would pass away and
another take its place; a new race of men would
arise, and reverence, unity, peace, justice would
become watch-words in a new and happier order.
He challenged them in burning words of power to
acknowledge the spiritual cause of world-events.

already coming into view and to fill the lofty and noble part for which God and Christ had prepared them. He warned them not to let prejudice or dogma or superstition or self-interest or desire for leadership and glory from men deter them from accepting this summons. Again and again He urged on their notice that the true cause of this New Age and its happenings was spiritual and that they would find the key to it in the Gospel which they so continually perused.

In a Tablet to Napoleon III, the most outstanding monarch of the moment, He informed his Majesty that in the providence of God a new age of unprecedented changes in human history was opening. He outlined certain features of its ordained pattern, which would vitally concern a King-statesman, and called on him to arise, humble himself before God, follow the guidance of God's Prophet and take a bold initiative in unifying mankind. This, he wrote, was the Wondrous Age Christ had come to announce. Christ's dominion had spread westward that the West and its rulers might now give a lead in His holy service. Would Napoleon now play the man in the precious Cause of God, he would make himself an emperor of the wide world.

Bahá'u'lláh had already been in communication with Napoleon and had discovered his hypocrisy and insincerity. He makes mention of this, and warns the Emperor (then in the plenitude of his pride and power) to give immediate heed to the Prophet's word, else, He writes, " *thy kingdom shall be thrown into confusion and thine empire shall pass from thy hands. . . . commotions shall seize all the people in that land. . . . We see abasement hastening after thee, whilst thou art of the heedless."*

The contemptuous rejection of this warning was followed not many months after by the sudden outbreak of the Franco-Prussian war, the utter defeat and capture of Napoleon at Sedan, and the collapse of his empire.

To Queen Victoria Bahá'u'lláh sent a letter in the course of which He declared His identity : " *O Queen in London! Incline thine ear unto the voice of thy Lord, the Lord of all mankind. . . . He in truth hath come into the world in His most great glory and all that is mentioned in the Gospel hath been fulfilled. . . . Lay aside thy desire and set thine heart towards thy Lord, the Ancient of Days. We make mention of thee for the sake of God and desire that thy name may be exalted through thy remembrance of God, the Creator of earth and heaven. . . . Turn thou unto God and say : O my Sovereign Lord, I am but a vassal of Thine, and Thou art, in truth, the King of Kings. . . . Assist me then, O my God, to remember Thee amongst Thy hand-maidens and to aid Thy Cause in Thy lands. . . . "*

To Alexander II He wrote, "*O Czar of Russia! Incline thine ear unto the Voice of God, the King, the Holy. Beware lest thy desire deter thee from turning unto the face of thy Lord, the Compassionate, the Most Merciful. . . . He verily is come with His Kingdom, and all the atoms cry aloud, ' Lo, the Lord is come in His great majesty.' He who is the Father is come, and the Son in the holy vale crieth out, ' Here am I, here am I, O Lord, My God.' . . . Arise thou amongst men in the name of*

this all-compelling Cause and summon, then, the
nations unto God. . . . Could'st thou but know the
things sent down by My Pen and discover the
treasures of My Cause and the pearls of My
mysteries. . . . thou would'st in thy love for My
Name and in thy longing for My glorious and
sublime Kingdom lay down thy life in my path. . . ."

He wrote to Pope Pius IX announcing that " *He*
who is the Lord of Lords hath come " and that he
who is the Rock (meaning Peter), crieth out saying
" *Lo, the Father is come, and that which ye were*
promised in the Kingdom is fulfilled."   Bahá'u'lláh
bade him—" *Arise in the name of the Lord, the*
God of Mercy, amidst the peoples of the earth and
seize thou the cup of life with the hands of confidence
and first drink thou therefrom and proffer it then to
such as turn towards it amongst the peoples of all
faiths."   He warned him not to repeat the error of
the Pharisees and of the men of learning who on His
first coming opposed Jesus Christ and pronounced
judgment against Him, whilst he who was a fisherman believed on Him.   He called on him to " *sell*
all the embellished ornaments thou dost possess
and expend them in the path of God " to " *abandon*
thy kingdom unto the kings, and emerge from thy
habitation," and should anyone offer him all the
treasures of the earth " *refuse to even glance upon*
them " : then, detached from the world, let him,
" *speak forth the praises of thy Lord betwixt earth*
and heaven " and warn the kings of the earth
against injustice in their dealings with men.

In the concluding pages of His communication to
the Pope which contain some of the most tender,
moving and impassioned passages in these writings
He expresses the warmth of His desire, the earnest-

ness of His effort to bring the followers of the Gospel into the Most Holy Kingdom of God and to enable the true-hearted to discern its opened Gates. He urges them to rend the spiritual veils that blind their eyes, to cast away everything, everything that prevents them accepting this divine deliverance. He calls them to come out of the darkness into the light poured forth by the sun of the Grace of God. He tells them of the sovereignty that awaits them in the Kingdom on High if they will but heed and obey, of the friendship of God and His companionship in His everlasting realm of Beauty and of Power that He longs to bestow on them according to His ancient promise. The Kingdom is theirs of right. He has bidden them welcome to it, and His heart is sad to see that others enter but they, alas! tarry before its gates in the darkness. How blessed are those who will keep the covenant Christ made with His people, who will watch for their Lord's return as He bade them, and know His voice when He calls them. Blessed are they who will walk forward in the path Christ laid out for them so straight and true and will take their rightful place in the van of the Legions of Light.

Elsewhere in these letters to the kings, and also in other writings, Bahá'u'lláh speaks to the entire Christian world and addresses directly officers of the various ecclesiastical orders in Christendom. For instance : " *O concourse of archbishops ! He who is the Lord of all men hath appeared. In the plain of guidance He calleth mankind whilst ye are yet numbered with the dead. Great is the blessedness of him who is stirred by the Breeze of God and hath arisen from amongst the dead in this perspicuous Name.*"

" O concourse of bishops! . . . He who is the Everlasting Father calleth aloud between earth and heaven. Blessed the ear that hath heard and the eye that hath seen and the heart that hath turned unto Him. . . . " And, *" the stars of the heaven of knowledge have fallen, they that adduce the proofs they possess in order to demonstrate the truth of my Cause and who make mention of God in My Name; when however I came unto them in My majesty, they turned aside from Me. They, verily, are of the fallen. This is what the Spirit [Jesus] prophesied when He came with the truth and the Jewish Doctors cavilled at Him. . . . "*

He addressed the priests, telling them it was their duty to proclaim aloud the Most Great Name among the nations—they chose to keep silence when every stone and every tree shouted aloud *" The Lord is come in His great glory! " " The Day of Reckoning,"* He wrote, *" hath appeared, the Day whereon He who was in heaven hath come. He verily is the One whom ye were promised in the Books of God. . . . How long will ye wander in the wilderness of heedlessness and superstition ? "* . . .

He warned the monks that they little understood the real greatness of Jesus Christ which had been *" exalted above the imagination of all that dwell on the earth. Blessed are they who perceive it." " If ye choose to follow Me,"* He wrote, *" I will make you heirs of My Kingdom; and if ye transgress against Me I will in My long suffering endure it patiently."* He expressed His wonder at their men of learning who read the Gospel and yet refused to acknowledge its All-Glorious Lord on His appearance.

Again and again, in general statements and in particular prophecies, Bahá'u'lláh warned the rulers of the world and their peoples that if these clear, solemn and public pronouncements went unheeded and the reforms enjoined were not made, then divine chastisement would descend from all sides upon mankind: irreligion would spread and deepen; from it would flow anarchy; authority and power would pass from the priesthood; the social order would break up and dissolve to make place for another which God would guide men to build in its stead.

Whatever "Lesser Peace" the war-weary nations might at last arrange among themselves, it would not bring them a final solution of their problems. This would come only with "The Most Great Peace" of which He wrote in His Tablet (or letter) to Queen Victoria, with the creation of a world-commonwealth and with the ultimate emergence of a divine world-civilisation.   These objectives could be attained only through acceptance of the Prophet of the Age and through the adoption of the principles, plans and patterns for the new World Order which were transmitted by Him from God.

When no heed was given to Bahá'u'lláh's Declaration that His prophethood was the return of Christ, when His appeal for the examination of His Cause and the redress of cruel wrongs inflicted on Him was ignored; when no one regarded His forecast, so forcefully and so fully presented, that a new Dawn had broken, a New Age had come (new in a spiritual sense, in a moral sense, in an intellectual sense), an Age which would bring a new outlook and new concepts, an Age of Divine Judgment, in which tyranny would be thrown down, the rights of the people asserted, and in which the social structure of the human race would be changed; when no attention was paid to the vision He opened, to the opportunities He offered, to the bold challenge which He had from prison flung before the mighty ones of the world; then alas! the Churches as the years went by found themselves caught into a current which bore them irresistibly downward at an ever increasing speed and which at the end of eight decades was still to be bearing them down to lower and yet lower levels in their political standing, in their moral influence, in their intellectual prestige, in their social authority, in their numbers and their financial resources, in the popular estimate of the relevancy and the reality of the religion which they taught and even in the vigour and unanimity of their own witness to the basic truth upon which the Church itself had been founded.

No comparable period of deterioration is to be found in the long records of the Christian Faith. In all the vicissitudes of fifteen eventful centuries (and they were many); in all the misfortunes, the mistakes, the failures and the humiliations in which from time to time the Church was involved, no such catastrophic decline is to be traced. The sovereignty which the church had wielded in the Middle Ages had indeed by the nineteenth century become in Western Europe a thing of the past; but the diminution had been gradual and moderate. The loss suffered during the previous eight hundred years can hardly be compared with the vital damage inflicted during the last eighty.

In past crises the foundations of faith and of western society were not shaken; hope remained dominant, and from tradition and memory men drew inspiration. Society remained Christian and to that extent unified. But now the very foundations have gone. Reverence and restraint are no more. The heights of human nature are closed: its depths opened. Substitute systems of ethics, man-made and man-regarding, are invented, dethroning conscience. The dignity of reason and of knowledge is denied: truth itself is impugned.

The story of this calamitous decline is well known to all, and its outstanding features can be briefly summarised.

In the year 1870, not long after the despatch of Bahá'u'lláh's Tablet to his Holiness, the Pope was through King Victor Emmanuel's seizure of Rome deprived by force of virtually the whole of that temporal power which Bahá'u'lláh had advised him to renounce voluntarily. His formal acknowledgment of the Kingdom of Italy by the recent Lateran Treaty sealed this resignation of sovereignty.

The fall of the Napoleonic Empire was followed in France by a wave of anti-clericalism which led to a complete separation of the Roman Catholic Church from the State, the secularisation of education, and the suppression and dispersal of the religious orders.

In Spain, the monarchy which for so long had been in Christendom the great champion of the Roman Church was overthrown and the State secularised.

The dismemberment of the Austro-Hungarian monarchy caused the disappearance both of the last remnant of the Holy Roman Empire and of the most powerful political unit that gave to the Roman Church its spiritual and financial support.

In Soviet Russia an organised assault directed against the Greek Orthodox Church, against Christianity, and against religion, disestablished that church, massacred vast numbers of its hundred million members, stripped it of its six and a half million acres of property, pulled down, closed or perverted to secular uses countless thousands of places of worship and by "a five year plan of god-lessness" sought to eradicate all religion from the hearts of the people.

In every land and in all branches of the Christian Church, even where there was no system of Establishment, the rising power of nationalism continually made churches more and more subservient to the interests and the opinions of the State— a tendency brought into strong relief and notoriety in the first world-war.

The gradual decay of the intellectual prestige of religion in Europe had extended over many generations, but it was brought prominently before the public mind in the seventies of the last century, largely through the controversies which followed Tyndale's Belfast address in 1874. The character of this decay has been epitomised by Professor Whitehead, writing in 1926, thus:

"Religion is tending to degenerate into a decent formula wherewith to embellish a comfortable life. . . . For over two centuries, religion has been on

the defensive, and on a weak defensive. The period
has been one of unprecedented intellectual progress.
In this way a series of novel situations has been
produced for thought.   Each such occasion has
found the religious thinkers unprepared. Something
which has been proclaimed to be vital has, finally,
after struggle, distress and anathema been modified
and otherwise interpreted. The next generation of
religious apologists then congratulates the religious
world on the deeper insight which has been gained.
The result of the continued repetition of this
undignified retreat during many generations has at
last almost entirely destroyed the intellectual
authority of religious thinkers. Consider this contrast; when Darwin or Einstein proclaim theories
which modify our ideas, it is a triumph for science.
We do not go about saying there is another defeat
for science, because its old ideas have been
abandoned. We know that another step of scientific
insight has been gained.''

The loss in the moral and spiritual field has been
even more vital and conspicuous, especially of
recent years. There is no need to enlarge upon the
matter. The sickness at the heart of Christian life
and thought which made these humiliations possible
has been the decay of spirituality. Love for God,
fear of God, trust in God's overruling providence
and ceaseless care have been no longer active forces
in the world. The religious thinkers find themselves baffled by the portents of the time: when men
in disillusionment, in anguish and despair come to
them for counsel, seek from them comfort, hope,
some intelligible idea as to what this cataclysm
means and whence it came and how it should be met,

they are completely at a loss. Though the Church for nineteen centuries has proclaimed, and has enshrined in its creeds, the emphatic and repeated promise of Christ that He would come again in power and great glory to judge the earth, would exalt the righteous and inaugurate the Kingdom of God among mankind, yet they believe and teach that through all these years of deepening tribulation no Hand has been outstretched from heaven, no light of Guidance has been shed upon the earth; that God has withheld from His children in their deepest need His succour, His comfort and His love; that Christ has utterly forgotten His promise or is impotent to redeem it and has permitted His universal Church to sink in ruin without evincing the least small sign of His interest or His concern.

Meantime the Bahá'í Message has kindled once more on earth the ancient fire of faith that Jesus kindled long ago, the fire of spontaneous love for God and man, a love that changes all life and longs to show itself in deeds of devotion and of self-sacrifice even to death and martyrdom. To them who have recognised Christ's voice again in this Age has been given in renewed freshness and beauty the vision of the Kingdom of God as Jesus and the Book of Revelation gave it—the same vision, but clearer now and on a larger scale and in more detail. A new enthusiasm has been theirs, a power that nothing could gainsay or resist. Their words reached the hearts of men. With a courage, a determination that only divine love could quicken or support they rose in the face of ruthless persecution to bear witness to their faith. Fearless, though comparatively few, weak in themselves but invincible in God's Cause, they have now at the close

of these eighty years carried that Faith far and wide
through the globe, entered well nigh a hundred
countries, translated their literature into more than
fifty languages, gathered adherents from East and
West, from many races, many nations, many creeds,
many traditions, and have established themselves as
a world-community, worshipping one God under
one Name.

The Bahá'í Faith today presents the Christian
Churches with the most tremendous challenge ever
offered them in their long history: a challenge, and
an opportunity. It is the plain duty of every earnest
Christian in this illumined Age to investigate for
himself with an open and fearless mind the purpose
and the teachings of this Faith and to determine
whether the collective centre for all the constructive
forces of this time be not the Messenger from God,
Bahá'u'lláh, He and no other; and whether the way
to a better, kinder, happier world will not lie open
as soon as we accept the Announcement our rulers
rejected.

" *O Kings of the earth; He Who is the Sovereign
Lord of all is come. The Kingdom is God's, the
Omnipotent Protector, the Self-Subsisting. Worship none but God and with radiant hearts lift up
your faces unto your Lord, the Lord of all names.
This is a Revelation to which whatever ye possess
can never be compared could ye but know it.*

" *Ye are but vassals, O Kings of the earth! He
Who is the King of Kings hath appeared, arrayed in
His most wondrous glory, and is summoning you
unto Himself, the Help in Peril, the Self-Subsisting.
Take heed lest pride deter you from recognising*

the Source of Revelation, lest the things of this world shut you out as by a veil from Him Who is the Creator of Heaven. Arise and serve Him Who is the Desire of all nations, Who hath created you through a word from Him and ordained you to be for all time emblems of His sovereignty. . . .

" O Kings of Christendom! Heard ye not the saying of Jesus, the spirit of God. ' I go away and come again unto you ' ? Wherefore, then, did ye fail, when He did come again unto you in the clouds of heaven, to draw nigh unto Him, that ye might behold His face and be of them that attained His Presence. In another passage He saith : ' When He the Spirit of Truth, is come, He will guide you into all truth.' And yet behold how when He did bring the truth ye refused to turn your faces towards Him and persisted in disporting yourselves with your pastimes and your fancies. . . . "

GEORGE TOWNSHEND.

Appendix 4

THE ANGLICAN, AUSTRALIA

The Anglican, a newspaper published in Sydney, proclaiming itself on its letterhead 'The Newspaper for the Church of England in Australia', printed in its issue of April 4, 1958, on page 5, an utterly irresponsible, factually incorrect and ignorant article on the Bahá'í Faith, which concluded with the following paragraphs:

> The propaganda being put about by this interesting sect includes an article by 'George Townshend, MA, sometime Canon of St Patrick's Cathedral, Dublin, Archdeacon of Clonfert.'
>
> The truth is that Archdeacon Townshend died a few years ago, and that the form of the advertisements, and the way his name is used, is misleading.
>
> He actually retired in 1947, drifted away from the Church, and wrote several books on comparative religion, from which he drifted into adherence to Bahá'ísm.
>
> No action was taken against him by the Church authorities, for the heresies which had attracted him in the twilight of his life drew little attention. He spent some time in the United States with members of the Bahá'í sect.
>
> Shortly before his death, however, he renounced the heresies of Bahá'ísm, and was received back into the fold of the Church.
>
> This makes the continued use of his name all the more reprehensible.

I took legal advice, both in England and Australia, and acting on it wrote to the editor, pointing out that 'In these five [last] paragraphs . . . there is not one true statement about George Townshend . . .' and requesting him to publish, in the same feature column, an attached article giving the true facts. Seven weeks later, no acknowledgement having been received, I sent a telegram requesting a reply to my letter. When this was also ignored I requested a firm of solicitors in Sydney to act for me. They were able to extract a Memorandum from the managing director in reply to their two questions, had my communications been received and 'what steps you intend to take', which stated baldly '1. Yes. 2. Appropriate steps as soon as sufficient further information has reached us and as soon as we have time to consider them.' Two weeks later my solicitors wrote again asking 'what further information you require as our client has instructed us to take proceedings under the Defamation Act.' The reply to this was, 'It is entirely up to your client what instructions he gives you concerning proceedings under the Defamation Act or the Registration of Dogs Act for that matter.' And this courteous reply was signed by F. James, the managing director of the newspaper for the Church of England in Australia.

Appendix 5

LIST OF
GEORGE TOWNSHEND'S
KNOWN WORKS

Published Books and Booklets

The Altar on the Hearth. Dublin and Cork, Talbot Press, 1926.
Christ and Bahá'u'lláh. London, George Ronald, 1957; rev. 1966; 1976.
   French: Berne, 1959; Brussels, 1968; 1978.
   Dutch: The Hague, 1973.
   German: Bahá'í Verlag, 1970.
   Portuguese: Rio de Janeiro, 1959; 1976.
   Spanish: Buenos Aires, E.B.I.L.A. 1960; 1972; 1977.
The Covenant, An Analysis. Manchester, Bahá'í Publishing Trust, 1950.
The Conversion of Mormonism. Hartford, Conn., 1911.
The Genius of Ireland (and other essays). Dublin and Cork, Talbot Press, 1930.
The Glad Tidings of Bahá'u'lláh. London, John Murray, 1949; Oxford, George Ronald, rev. 1975.
The Heart of the Gospel. London, Lindsay Drummond, 1939; New York, Bahá'í Publishing Committee, 1940; Oxford, George Ronald, rev. 1951; 1972.
The Mission of Bahá'u'lláh (and other literary pieces). Oxford, George Ronald, 1952; 1965; 1976.
The Old Churches and the New World-Faith. London, National Spiritual Assembly of the Bahá'ís of the British Isles, 1949.
   German: 1951(ms).
   Spanish: Madrid, 1967.
The Promise of All Ages. (Christophil). London, Simpkin Marshall, 1934; New York, Bahá'í Publishing Committee, 1935; London, George Ronald, rev. (George Townshend) 1948; 1961; 1972.
   Arabic: Cairo, 1945.
   French: Brussels, 1971.
Why I am not a Mormon. Denver, 1907.

Published Essays, Pamplets and Poems

' 'Abdu'l-Bahá, A Study of a Christlike Character', *Church of Ireland Gazette*, 1935; *World Order*, Oct. 1936; pamphlet with *Hidden Words* (see below); included in *The Mission of Bahá'u'lláh*, 1952 .

'The Approach to Religion', (by A.G.B.), *World Order*, June 1938.

'Bahá'u'lláh and World Unity (from *The Heart of the Gospel*)', *Herald of the South*, April 1946.

'Bahá'u'lláh in the Síyáh-<u>Ch</u>ál', *Bahá'í Journal* (London), Jan. 1953.

'Bahá'u'lláh's Ground Plan of World Fellowship', *World Order*, Nov. 1936; *The Bahá'í World*, vol. VI, 1934–1936; *Faiths and Fellowship*, Watkins, London, 1936.

'Be of Good Cheer', *The Mission of Bahá'u'lláh*, 1952.

'The Beauty of Ireland' (included in *The Genius of Ireland*).

'The Call to God: A Meditation', *The Bahá'í World*, vol. X, 1944–1946; *The Mission of Bahá'u'lláh*, 1952.

'The Call of the Martyrs', *Bahá'í Journal* (London), Oct. 1944; *Bahá'í News* (U.S.A.), July, 1950; *The Bahá'í World*, vol. XII, 1950–1954.

'Constructive Religion', (by A.G.B.), *World Order*, March 1939; *The Bahá'í World*, vol. VIII, 1938–1940.

'The Day of God', *The Bahá'í World*, vol. VII, 1936–1938; pamphlet.

'The Descent of the New Jerusalem', *The Bahá'í World*, vol. V, 1932–1934; see footnote p. 240.

'The Epic of Humanity', (from *The Promise of All Ages*) by Christophil, *The Bahá'í World*, vol. VI, 1934–1936; *World Order*, Nov. 1940.

'European Auxiliary Board', *Bahá'í Journal* (London), Sept. 1954.

'For Christian Contacts', *Bahá'í Journal* (London), Sept./Oct./Nov. 1954; *Bahá'í News* (U.S.A.), Aug. 1956.

Glossary [of Persian terms used in Bahá'í literature], with the help of Bahá'í scholars in Persia. Incorporated in *Epistle to the Son of the Wolf*, Bahá'í Publishing Trust, Wilmette, 1976.

'The Hidden Words of Bahá'u'lláh: A Reflection', pamphlet, Haifa, 1930; *The Bahá'í World*, vol. III, 1928–1930; *World Order*, Sept. 1937; *Herald of the South*, Oct. 1943.

Introduction to *The Dawn-Breakers*, New York, Bahá'í Publishing Committee, 1932.

'Introduction to *The Hidden Words* of Bahá'u'lláh', U.S.A., 1954.

'Introduction to *God Passes By*', *Herald of the South*, July 1952.

'An Introduction to *The Promised Day is Come*', *Bahá'í Journal* (London), Oct. 1955.

'Irish Humour', (included in *The Genius of Ireland*).

'Joined by God', *The Bahá'í World*, vol. IX, 1940–1944; *World Order*, July 1945.

'A Kinship in Genius: The English Poet-Prophets', (included in *The Genius of Ireland*).

'The Language of the Commonwealth', (included in *The Genius of Ireland*).

'Letter to the Bishop of Utah', *Bahá'í News Bulletin* (Australia and New

Zealand), July 1949; *Bahá'í News* (U.S.A.), March 1950.

'The Letters of 'Abdu'l-Bahá', *The Mission of Bahá'u'lláh*, 1952.

'A Little Child Shall Lead Them', (poem), *The Mission of Bahá'u'lláh*, 1952.

'The Mission of Bahá'u'lláh', (from the Introduction to *God Passes By*, by Shoghi Effendi), *World Order*, Jan. 1945.

'The Mission of the Lord Christ', (a chapter in *The Promise of All Ages*), *World Order*, Aug. 1945; *Herald of the South*, Oct. 1940.

'Nabíl's History of the Báb', *World Order*, Jan./Feb./March/April 1940; *The Mission of Bahá'u'lláh*, 1952.

'The Old Churches and the New World-Faith', *The Bahá'í World*, vol. XI, 1946–1950; vol. XIII, 1954–1963.

'Our Task in Europe', *Bahá'í Journal* (London), Dec. 1953.

'Prelude', (poem), *The Altar on the Hearth*, 1926; *World Unity* (New York), April 1933.

'Queen Marie of Rumania and the Bahá'í Faith', *The Bahá'í World*, vol. VIII, 1938–1940; Arabic: Baghdád, 1946; *The Mission of Bahá'u'lláh*, 1952.

'Questions and Answers' (on Christian subjects), Bahá'í Publishing Committee, U.S.A., 1953.

'Recognition', (poem), 'To 'Abdu'l-Bahá', *The Bahá'í World*, vol. IV, 1930–1932; *The Mission of Bahá'u'lláh*, 1952.

'Religion and the New Age', (by A.G.B.), *World Order*, Aug. 1938; *Herald of the South*, April 1947.

'The Seven Valleys by Bahá'u'lláh: A Meditation', *World Order*, Dec. 1937; *The Bahá'í World*, vol. VII, 1936–1938.

'The Significance of the Holy Year', *Bahá'í Journal* (London), April 1953.

'Some Answers', *Bahá'í Journal* (London), Dec. 1952/Jan./April/May–June 1953.

'A Song of the Dawn', (poem), *The Bahá'í World*, vol. IX, 1940–1944.

'Station of Bahá'u'lláh', *Bahá'í Journal* (London), March/April–May/June–Aug./Sept.–Oct./Nov. 1952.

'The Sufferings of Bahá'u'lláh and Their Significance', *The Bahá'í World*, vol. XII, 1950–1954; vol. XVI, 1973–1976; *Bahá'í Journal* (London), Oct. 1956; *Bahá'í News Letter* (India), Dec. 1956.

'To Bahá'u'lláh', (poem), 'Consecration' in *The Altar on the Hearth*, 1926. *The Bahá'í World*, vol. XIII, 1954–1963; *The Mission of Bahá'u'lláh*, 1952.

'Two articles: Prayer and study (and) God's Zero Hour', *Bahá'í Journal* (London), Jan.–March 1955.

'The Way of the Master', *The Bahá'í World*, vol. IV, 1930–1932.

'The Wellspring of Happiness', (by A.G.B.), *World Order*, Nov./Dec. 1938; *The Bahá'í World*, vol. VIII, 1938–1940; *The Mission of Bahá'u'lláh*, 1952.

'The Wonder of It', (by C.P.L.), *World Order*, July 1936.

'The Year "9"', *Bahá'í News* (U.S.A.), July 1953.

Unpublished Works

The Angel of the Valley; mystical fantasy.
The Divine Art of Fiction; note books.

Synopses: *Kitáb-i-Íqán*
           The Dawn-Breakers
           Gleanings from the Writings of Bahá'u'lláh
The Seven Valleys by Bahá'u'lláh: A Commentary.
A Rejoinder; written to repudiate an attack on the Bahá'í Faith by a Church of England clergyman.
Irish Mythology: contributed to *The Sewanee Review*, Oct. 1915.
England's Atonement for Old Wrongs: contributed to *The Sewanee Review*, April 1912.

INDEX